6

# Love&Lies

LOVE and LIES by MUSAWO

# CONTENTS

# Chapter 23: The One Beloved

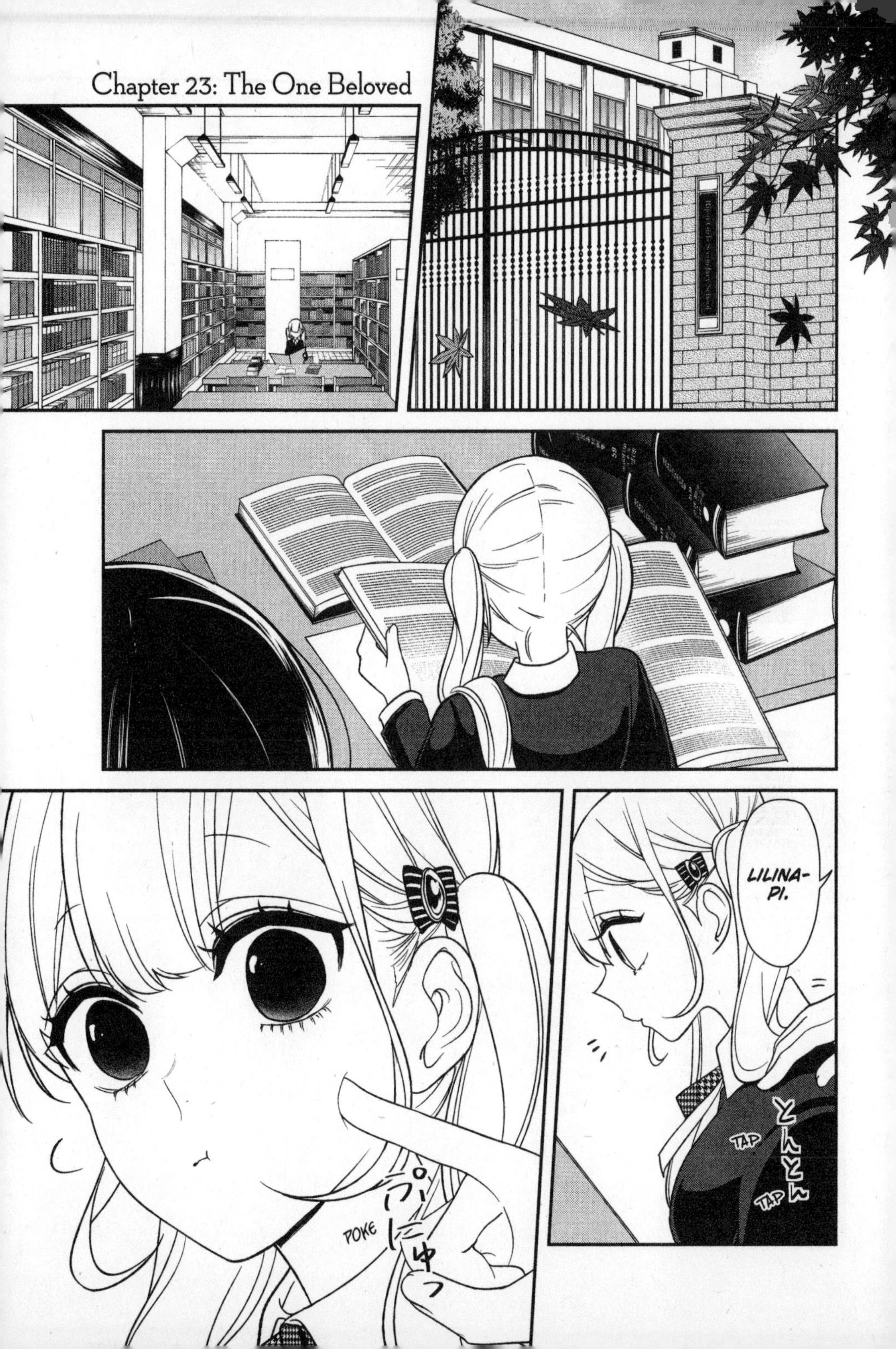

LILINA-PI.
TAP
TAP
とんとん
POKE
ぷにゅっ

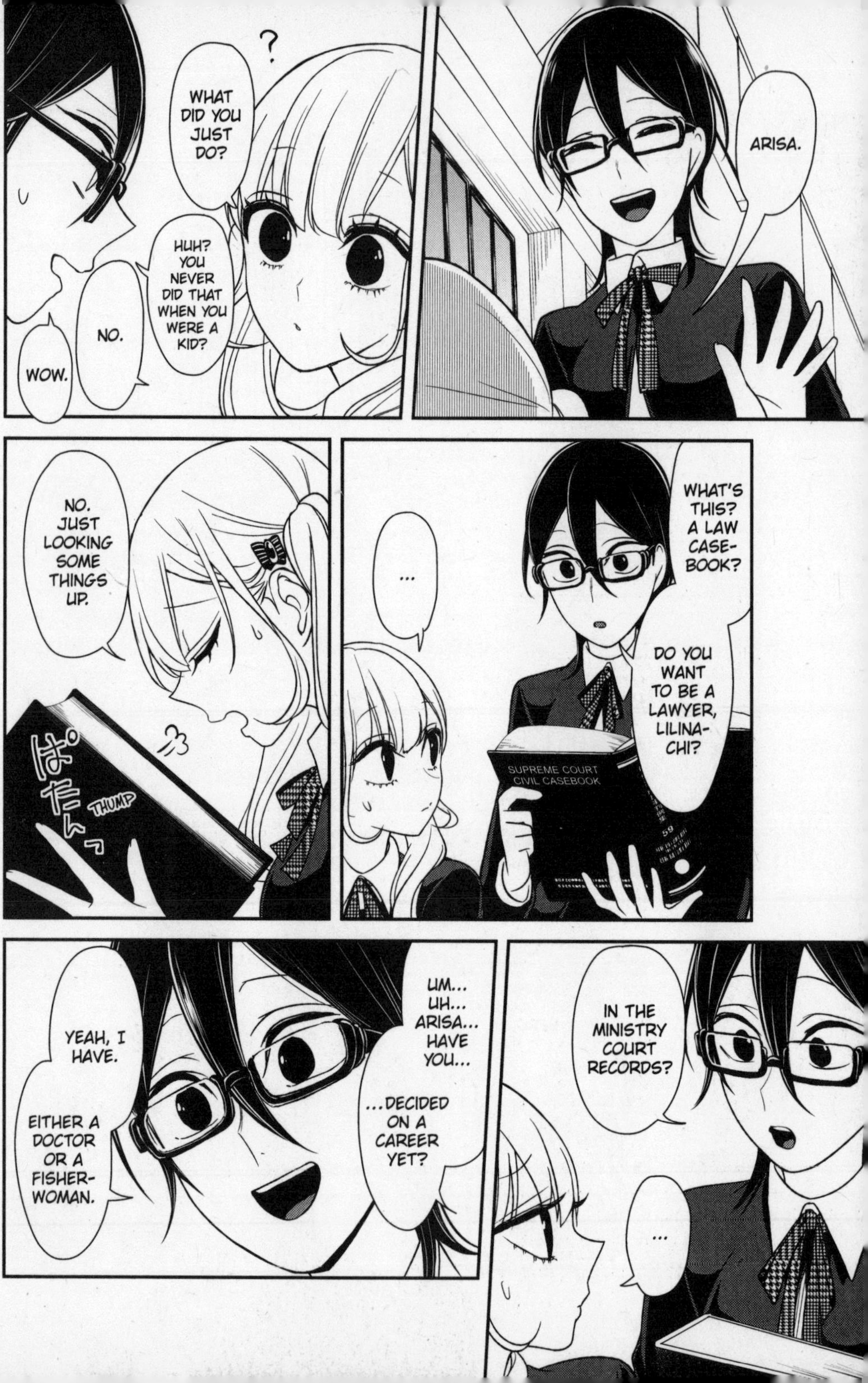
ARISA.
WHAT DID YOU JUST DO?
?
HUH? YOU NEVER DID THAT WHEN YOU WERE A KID?
NO.
WOW.
WHAT'S THIS? A LAW CASE-BOOK?
DO YOU WANT TO BE A LAWYER, LILINA-CHI?
SUPREME COURT CIVIL CASEBOOK
...
NO. JUST LOOKING SOME THINGS UP.
ぱたんっ
THUMP
IN THE MINISTRY COURT RECORDS?
...
UM... UH... ARISA... HAVE YOU...
...DECIDED ON A CAREER YET?
YEAH, I HAVE.
EITHER A DOCTOR OR A FISHER-WOMAN.

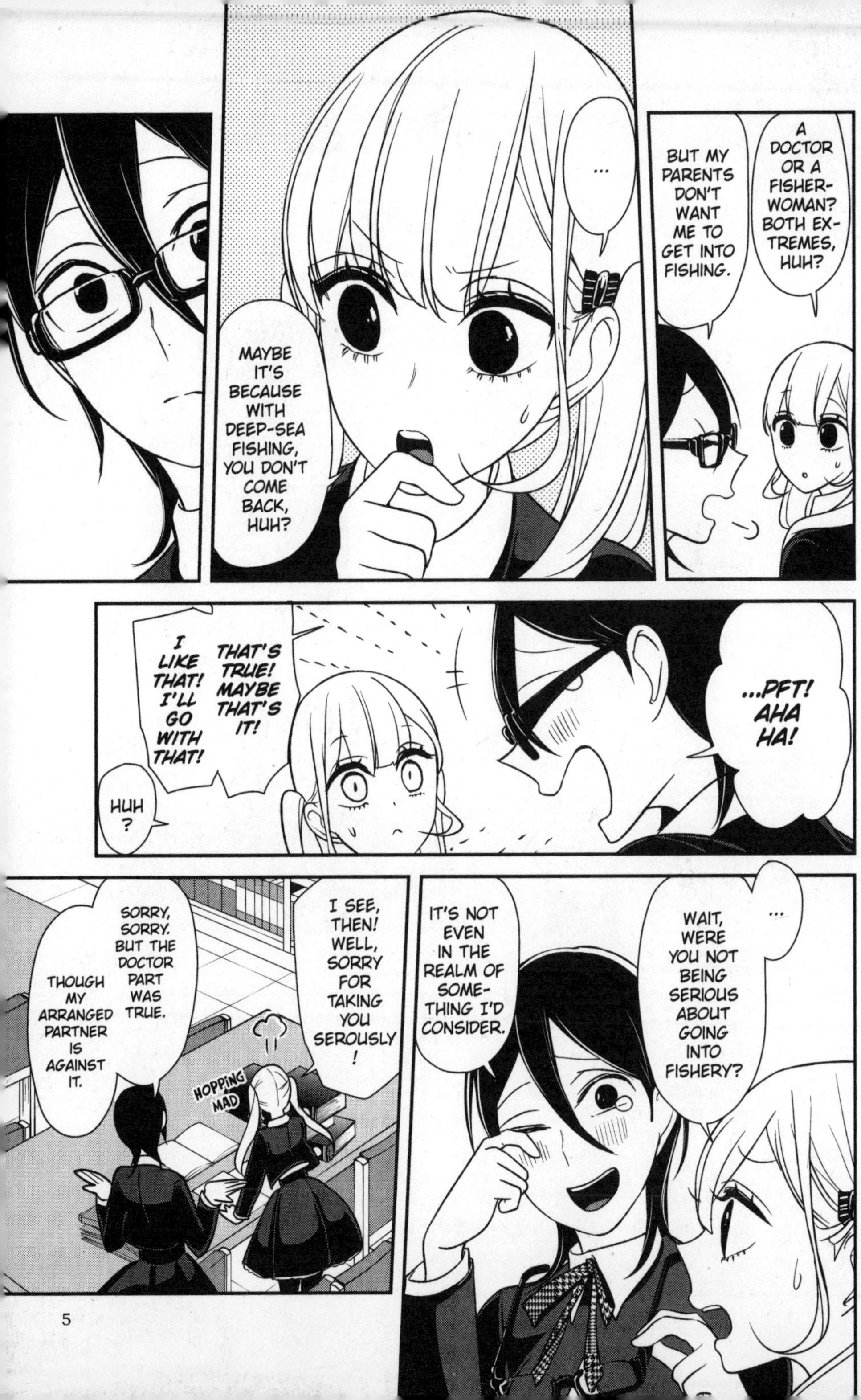
A DOCTOR OR A FISHER-WOMAN? BOTH EXTREMES, HUH?
BUT MY PARENTS DON'T WANT ME TO GET INTO FISHING.
...
MAYBE IT'S BECAUSE WITH DEEP-SEA FISHING, YOU DON'T COME BACK, HUH?
...PFT! AHA HA!
THAT'S TRUE! MAYBE THAT'S IT!
I LIKE THAT! I'LL GO WITH THAT!
HUH?
...
WAIT, WERE YOU NOT BEING SERIOUS ABOUT GOING INTO FISHERY?
IT'S NOT EVEN IN THE REALM OF SOME-THING I'D CONSIDER.
I SEE, THEN! WELL, SORRY FOR TAKING YOU SEROUSLY!
HOPPING MAD
SORRY, SORRY. BUT THE DOCTOR PART WAS TRUE.
THOUGH MY ARRANGED PARTNER IS AGAINST IT.

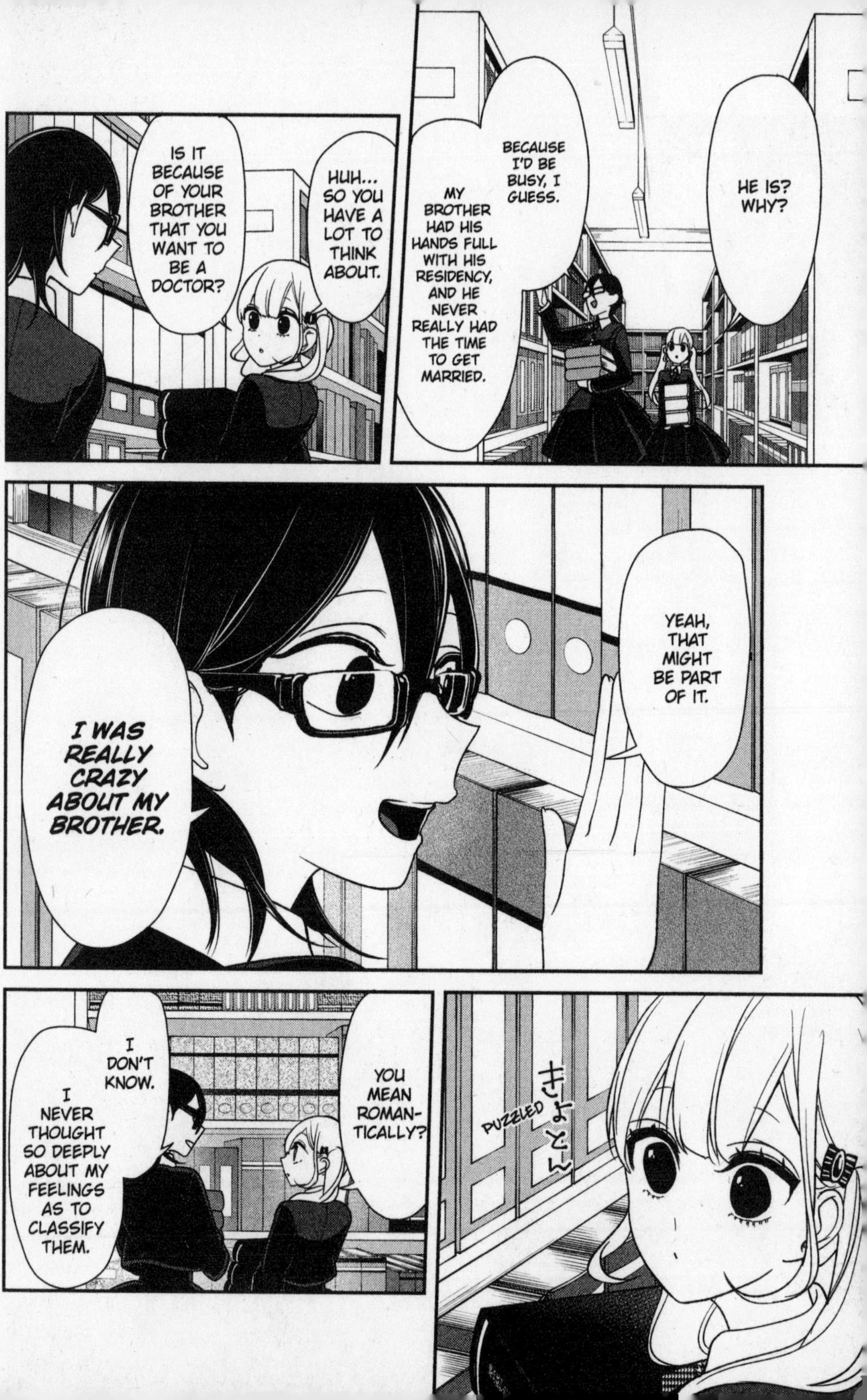
HE IS? WHY?
BECAUSE I'D BE BUSY, I GUESS.
MY BROTHER HAD HIS HANDS FULL WITH HIS RESIDENCY, AND HE NEVER REALLY HAD THE TIME TO GET MARRIED.
HUH... SO YOU HAVE A LOT TO THINK ABOUT.
IS IT BECAUSE OF YOUR BROTHER THAT YOU WANT TO BE A DOCTOR?
YEAH, THAT MIGHT BE PART OF IT.
I WAS REALLY CRAZY ABOUT MY BROTHER.
PUZZLED
きょとん
YOU MEAN ROMANTICALLY?
I DON'T KNOW.
I NEVER THOUGHT SO DEEPLY ABOUT MY FEELINGS AS TO CLASSIFY THEM.

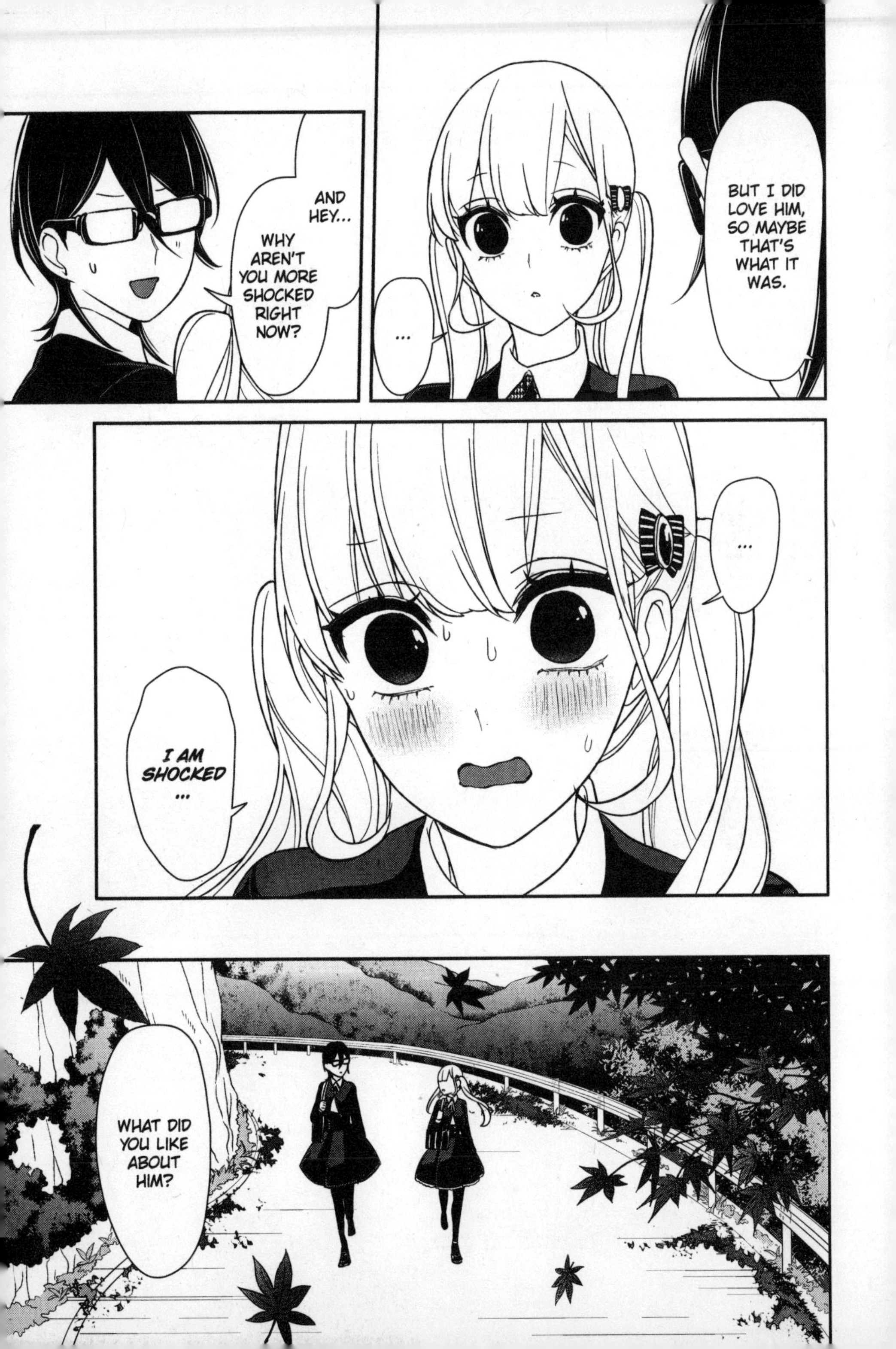
BUT I DID LOVE HIM, SO MAYBE THAT'S WHAT IT WAS.
...
AND HEY...
WHY AREN'T YOU MORE SHOCKED RIGHT NOW?
...
I AM SHOCKED ...
WHAT DID YOU LIKE ABOUT HIM?

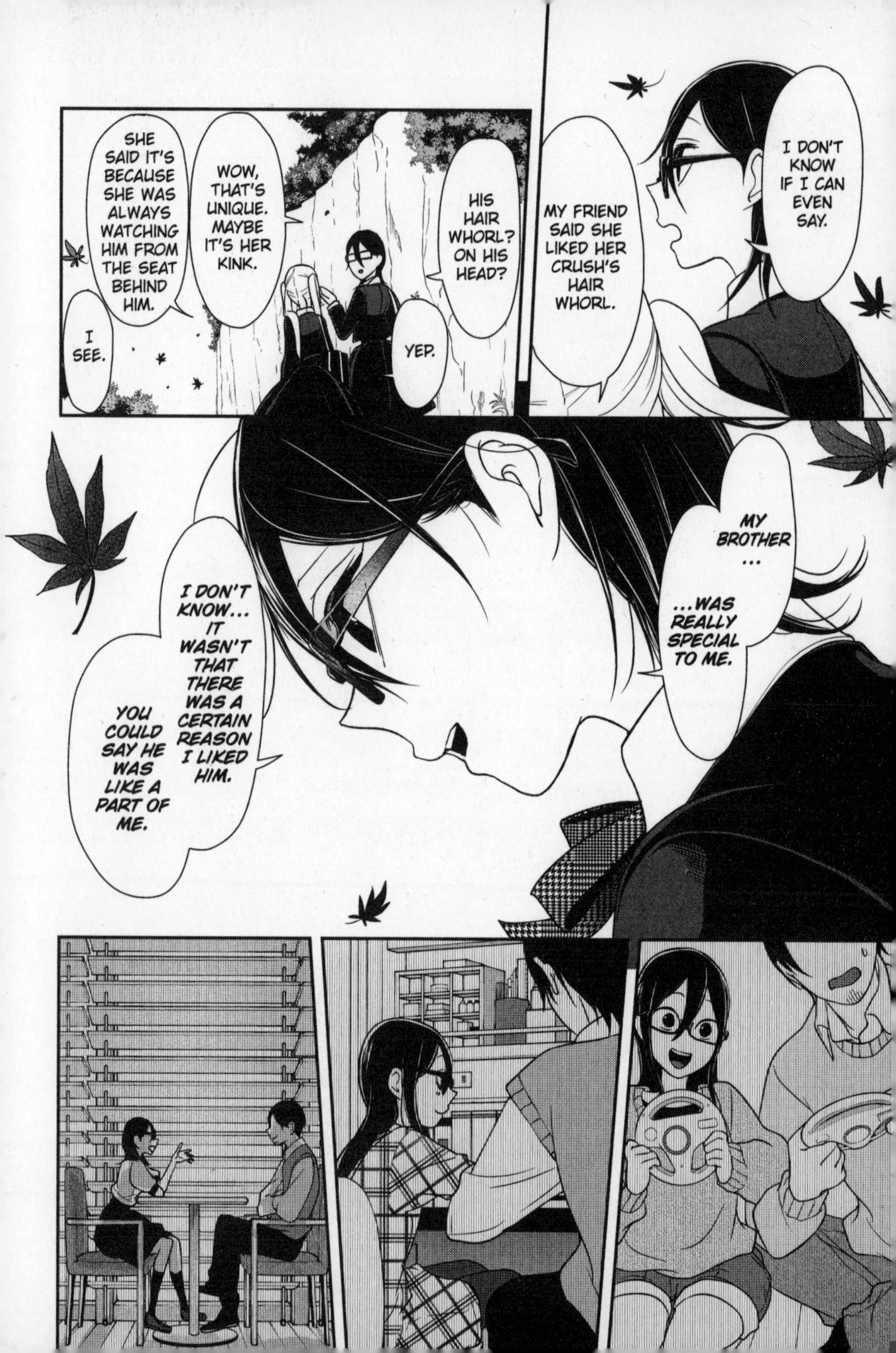
I DON'T KNOW IF I CAN EVEN SAY.
MY FRIEND SAID SHE LIKED HER CRUSH'S HAIR WHORL.
HIS HAIR WHORL? ON HIS HEAD?
YEP.
WOW, THAT'S UNIQUE. MAYBE IT'S HER KINK.
SHE SAID IT'S BECAUSE SHE WAS ALWAYS WATCHING HIM FROM THE SEAT BEHIND HIM.
I SEE.
MY BROTHER...
...WAS REALLY SPECIAL TO ME.
I DON'T KNOW... IT WASN'T THAT THERE WAS A CERTAIN REASON I LIKED HIM.
YOU COULD SAY HE WAS LIKE A PART OF ME.

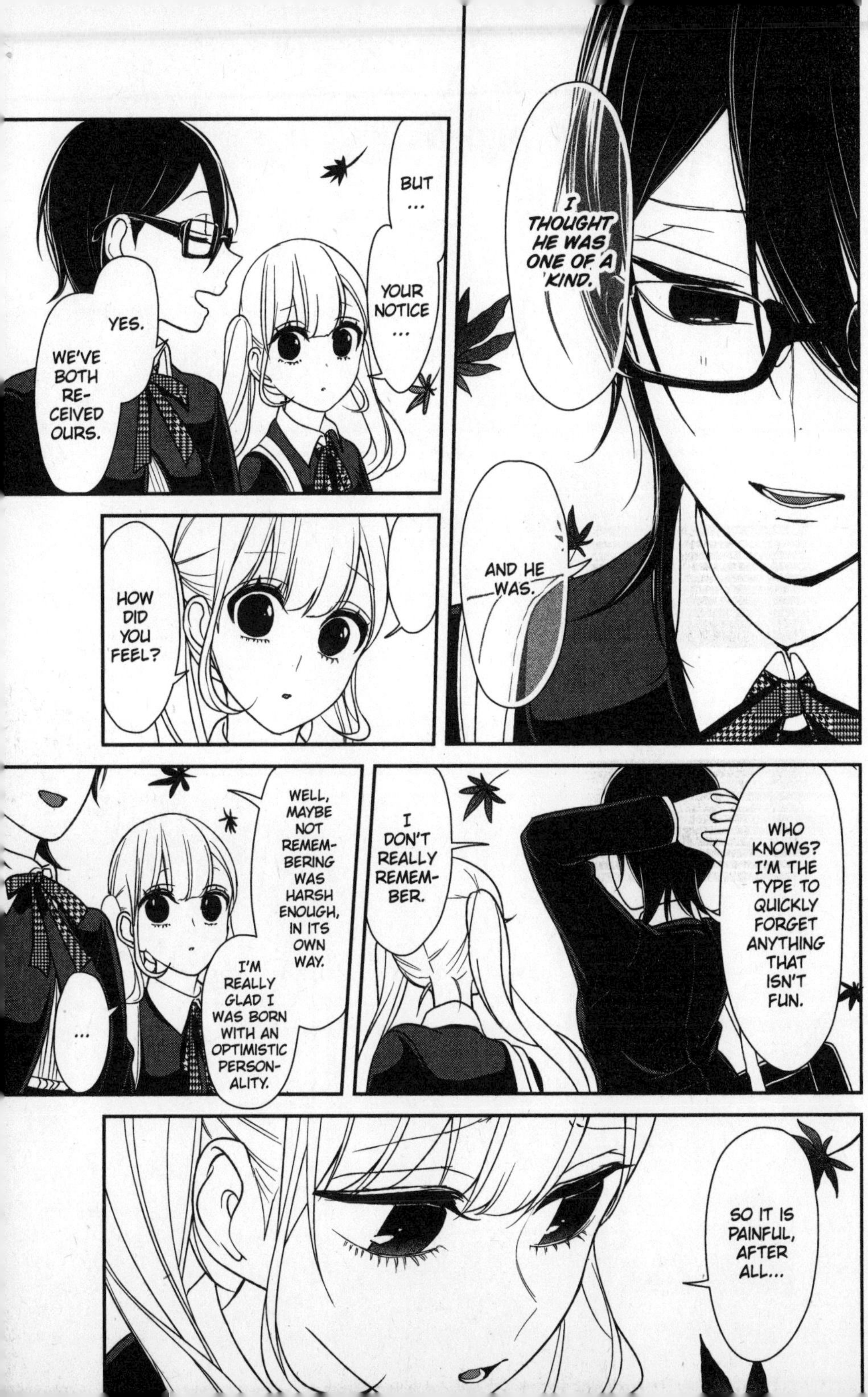

I THOUGHT HE WAS ONE OF A KIND.
AND HE WAS.
BUT... YOUR NOTICE...
YES. WE'VE BOTH RE-CEIVED OURS.
HOW DID YOU FEEL?
WHO KNOWS? I'M THE TYPE TO QUICKLY FORGET ANYTHING THAT ISN'T FUN.
I DON'T REALLY REMEM-BER.
WELL, MAYBE NOT REMEM-BERING WAS HARSH ENOUGH, IN ITS OWN WAY.
I'M REALLY GLAD I WAS BORN WITH AN OPTIMISTIC PERSON-ALITY.
...
SO IT IS PAINFUL, AFTER ALL...

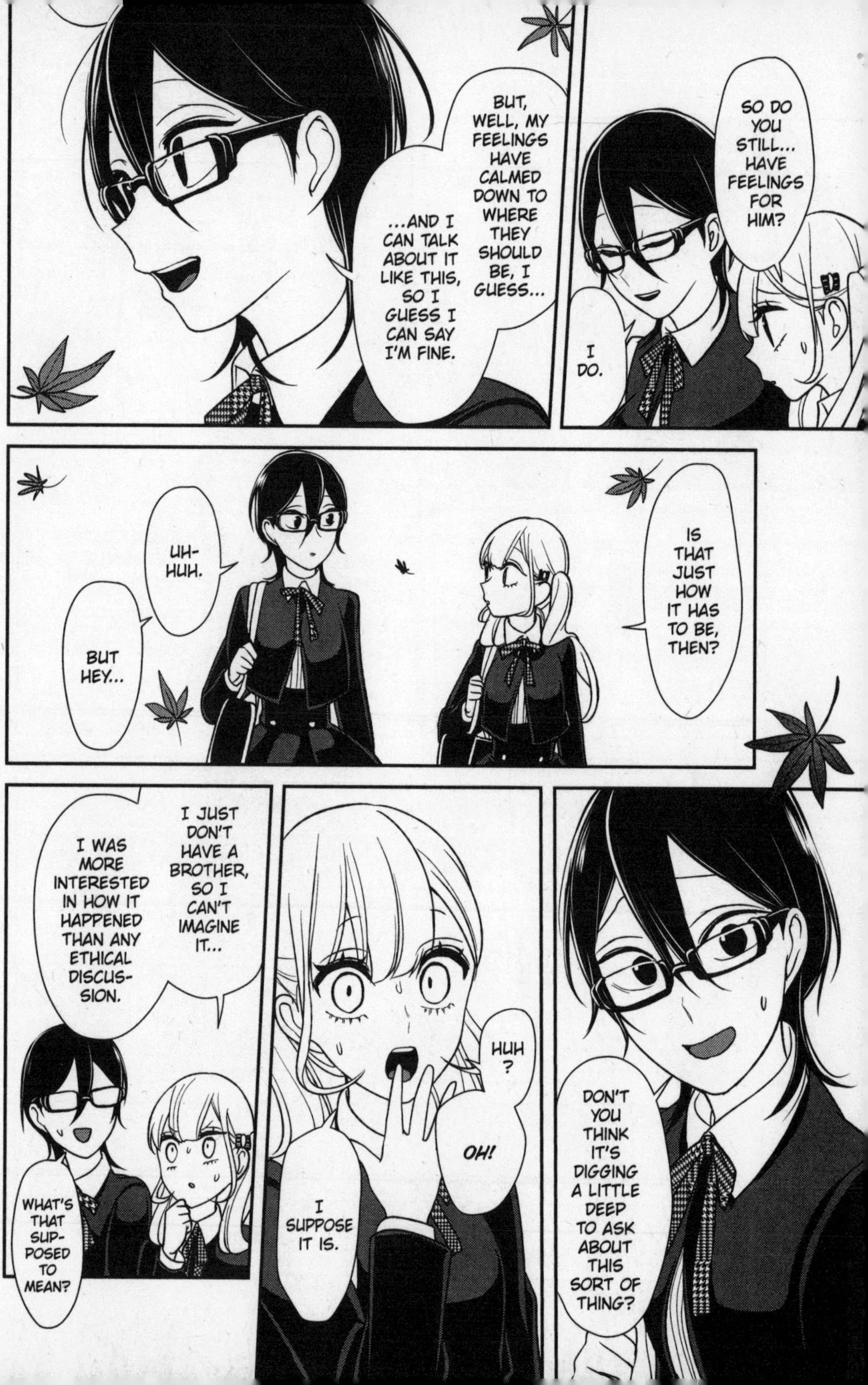
SO DO YOU STILL... HAVE FEELINGS FOR HIM?
I DO.
BUT, WELL, MY FEELINGS HAVE CALMED DOWN TO WHERE THEY SHOULD BE, I GUESS...
...AND I CAN TALK ABOUT IT LIKE THIS, SO I GUESS I CAN SAY I'M FINE.
IS THAT JUST HOW IT HAS TO BE, THEN?
UH-HUH.
BUT HEY...
DON'T YOU THINK IT'S DIGGING A LITTLE DEEP TO ASK ABOUT THIS SORT OF THING?
HUH?
OH!
I SUPPOSE IT IS.
I JUST DON'T HAVE A BROTHER, SO I CAN'T IMAGINE IT...
I WAS MORE INTERESTED IN HOW IT HAPPENED THAN ANY ETHICAL DISCUSSION.
WHAT'S THAT SUPPOSED TO MEAN?

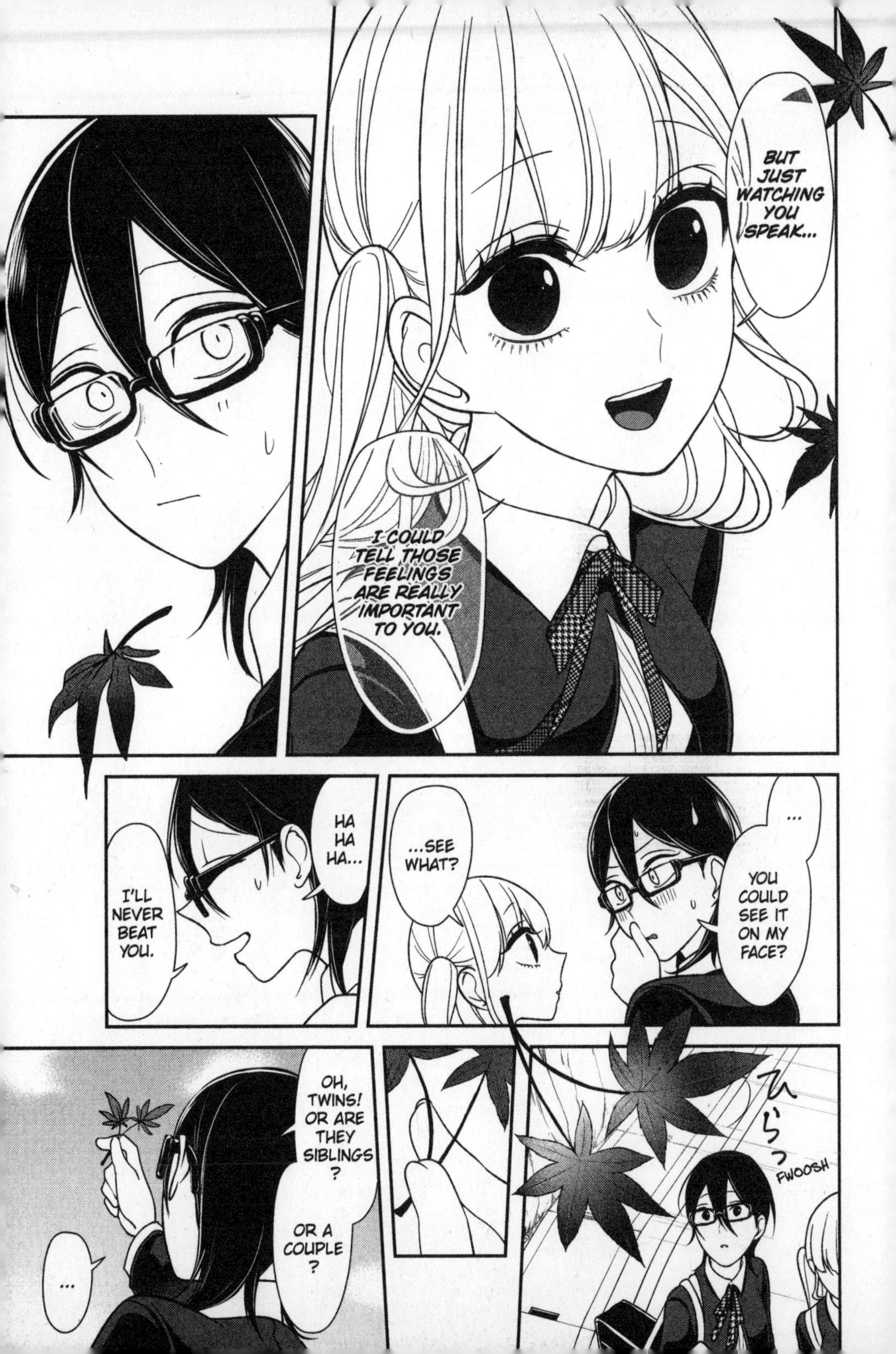
BUT JUST WATCHING YOU SPEAK...
I COULD TELL THOSE FEELINGS ARE REALLY IMPORTANT TO YOU.
...
YOU COULD SEE IT ON MY FACE?
...SEE WHAT?
HA HA HA...
I'LL NEVER BEAT YOU.
ひらっ
FWOOSH
OH, TWINS! OR ARE THEY SIBLINGS?
OR A COUPLE?
...

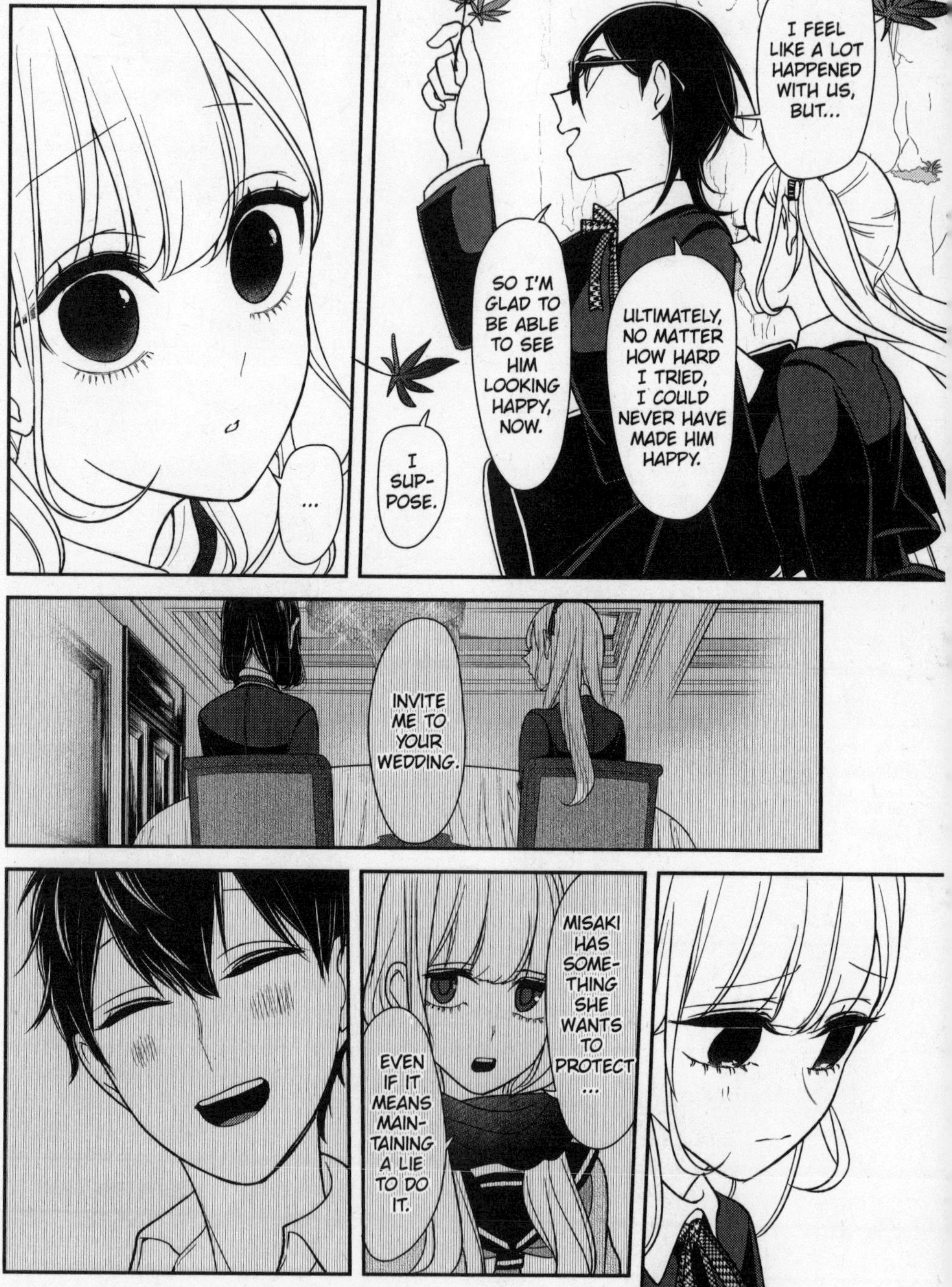
I FEEL LIKE A LOT HAPPENED WITH US, BUT...
ULTIMATELY, NO MATTER HOW HARD I TRIED, I COULD NEVER HAVE MADE HIM HAPPY.
SO I'M GLAD TO BE ABLE TO SEE HIM LOOKING HAPPY, NOW.
I SUP-POSE.
...
INVITE ME TO YOUR WEDDING.
MISAKI HAS SOME-THING SHE WANTS TO PROTECT ...
EVEN IF IT MEANS MAIN-TAINING A LIE TO DO IT.

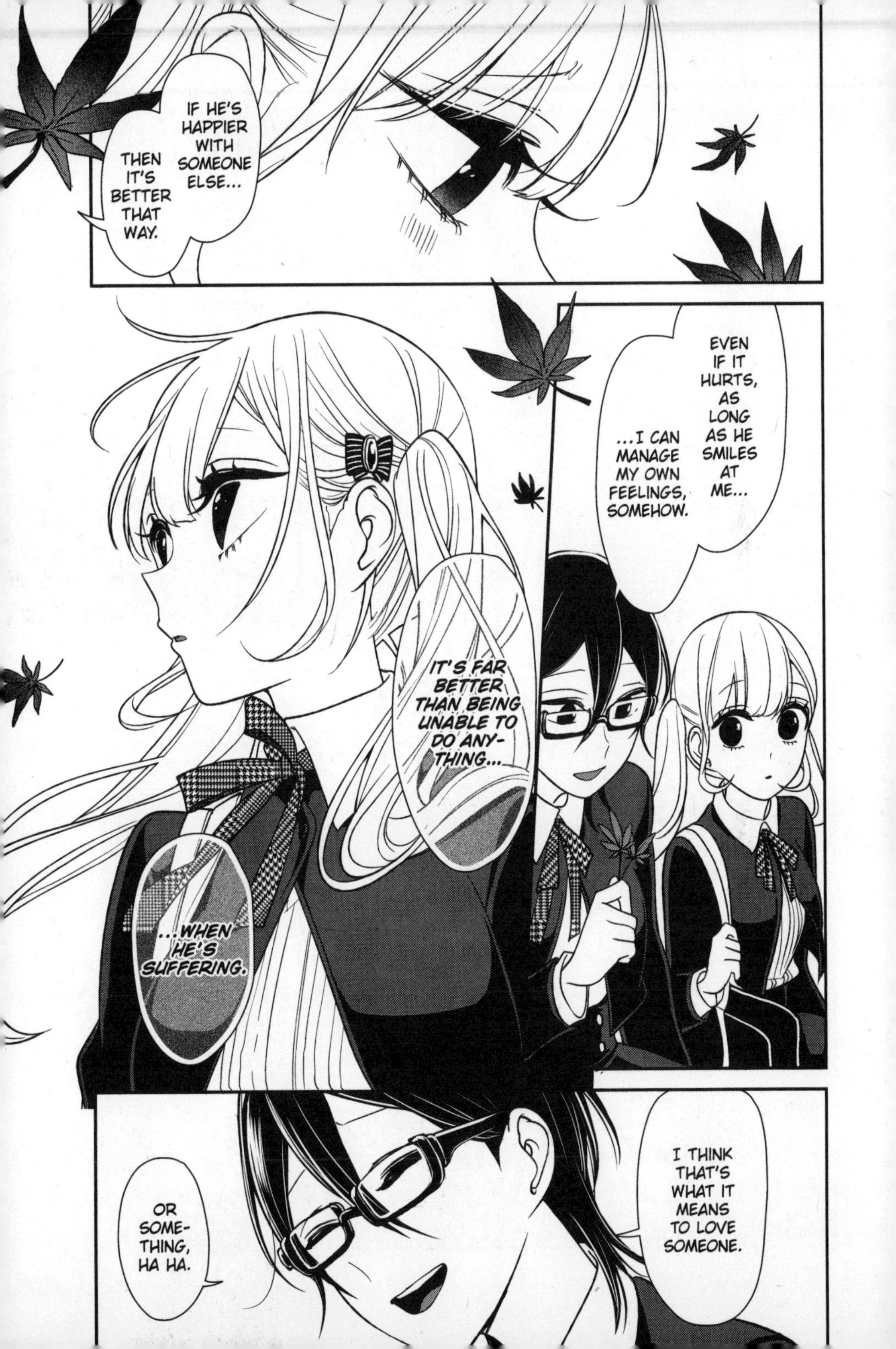
IF HE'S HAPPIER WITH SOMEONE ELSE...
THEN IT'S BETTER THAT WAY.
EVEN IF IT HURTS, AS LONG AS HE SMILES AT ME...
...I CAN MANAGE MY OWN FEELINGS, SOMEHOW.
IT'S FAR BETTER THAN BEING UNABLE TO DO ANYTHING...
...WHEN HE'S SUFFERING.
I THINK THAT'S WHAT IT MEANS TO LOVE SOMEONE.
OR SOMETHING, HA HA.

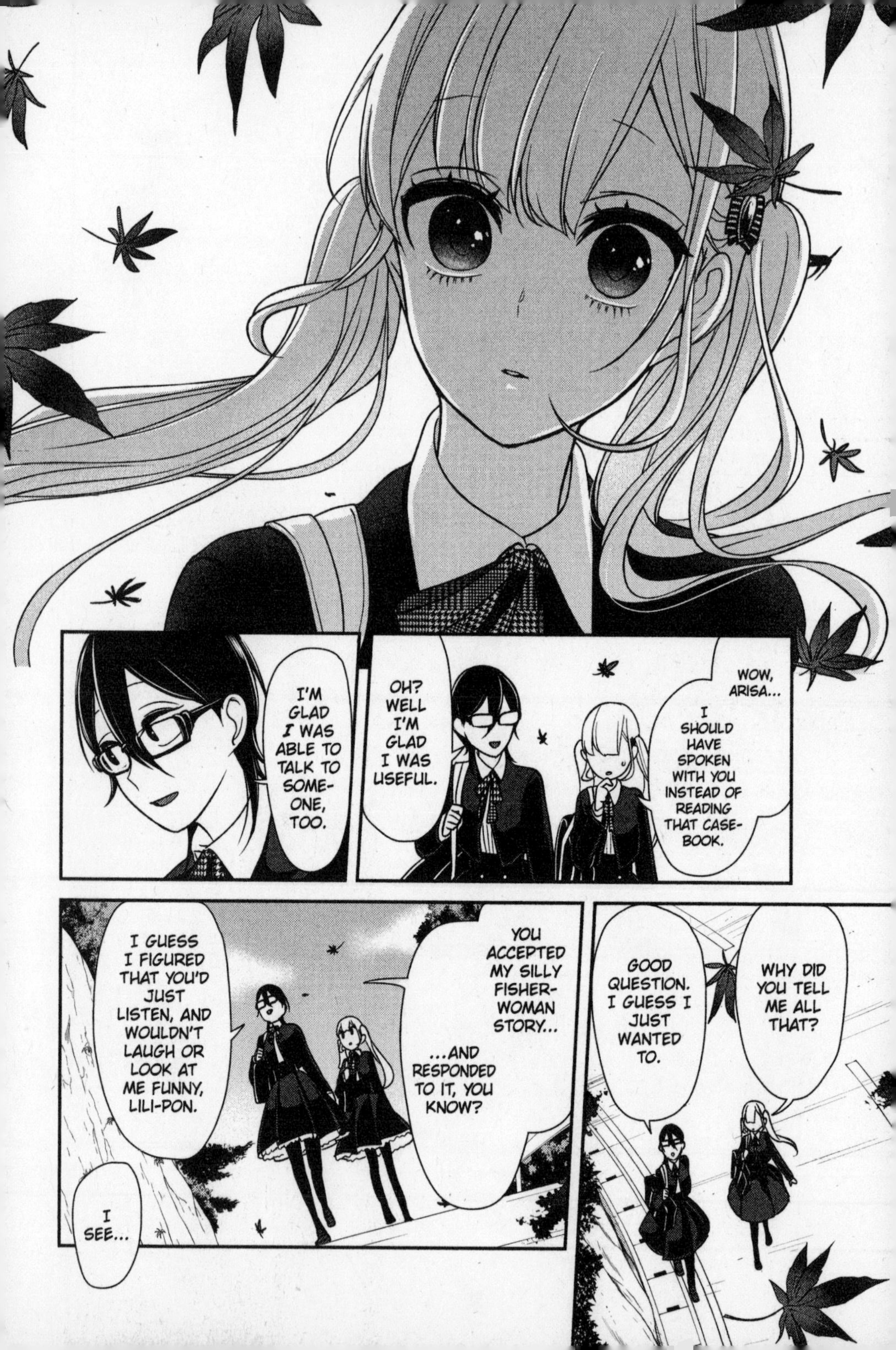
WOW, ARISA... I SHOULD HAVE SPOKEN WITH YOU INSTEAD OF READING THAT CASEBOOK.
OH? WELL I'M GLAD I WAS USEFUL.
I'M GLAD *I* WAS ABLE TO TALK TO SOMEONE, TOO.
WHY DID YOU TELL ME ALL THAT?
GOOD QUESTION. I GUESS I JUST WANTED TO.
YOU ACCEPTED MY SILLY FISHERWOMAN STORY...
...AND RESPONDED TO IT, YOU KNOW?
I GUESS I FIGURED THAT YOU'D JUST LISTEN, AND WOULDN'T LAUGH OR LOOK AT ME FUNNY, LILI-PON.
I SEE...

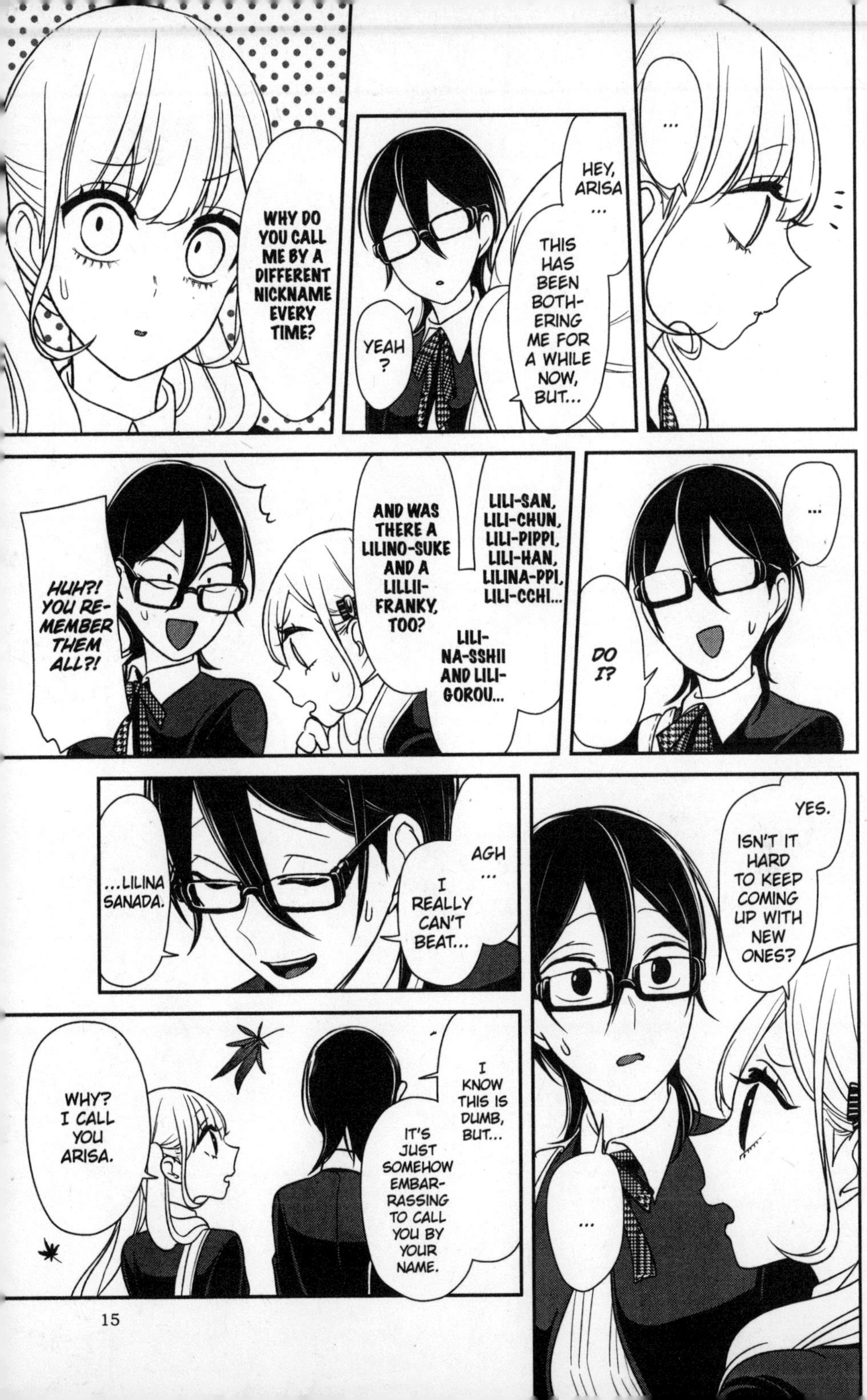
...
HEY, ARISA...
THIS HAS BEEN BOTHERING ME FOR A WHILE NOW, BUT...
YEAH?
WHY DO YOU CALL ME BY A DIFFERENT NICKNAME EVERY TIME?
...
DO I?
LILI-SAN, LILI-CHUN, LILI-PIPPI, LILI-HAN, LILINA-PPI, LILI-CCHI...
AND WAS THERE A LILINO-SUKE AND A LILLII-FRANKY, TOO?
LILI-NA-SSHII AND LILI-GOROU...
HUH?! YOU RE-MEMBER THEM ALL?!
YES.
ISN'T IT HARD TO KEEP COMING UP WITH NEW ONES?
...
AGH...
I REALLY CAN'T BEAT...
...LILINA SANADA.
I KNOW THIS IS DUMB, BUT...
IT'S JUST SOMEHOW EMBAR-RASSING TO CALL YOU BY YOUR NAME.
WHY? I CALL YOU ARISA.

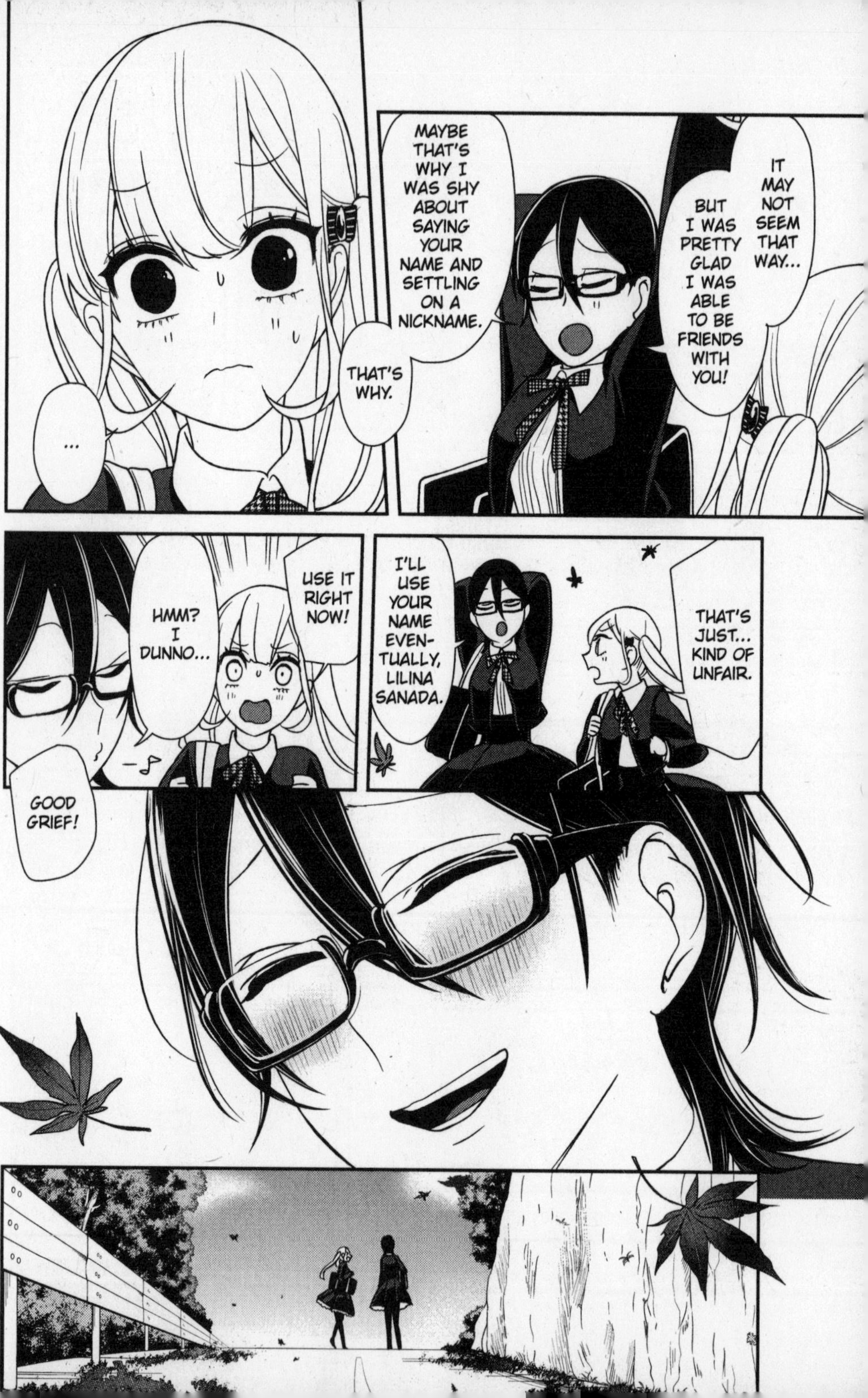
IT MAY NOT SEEM THAT WAY...
BUT I WAS PRETTY GLAD I WAS ABLE TO BE FRIENDS WITH YOU!
MAYBE THAT'S WHY I WAS SHY ABOUT SAYING YOUR NAME AND SETTLING ON A NICKNAME.
THAT'S WHY.
...
THAT'S JUST... KIND OF UNFAIR.
I'LL USE YOUR NAME EVENTUALLY, LILINA SANADA.
USE IT RIGHT NOW!
HMM? I DUNNO...
GOOD GRIEF!

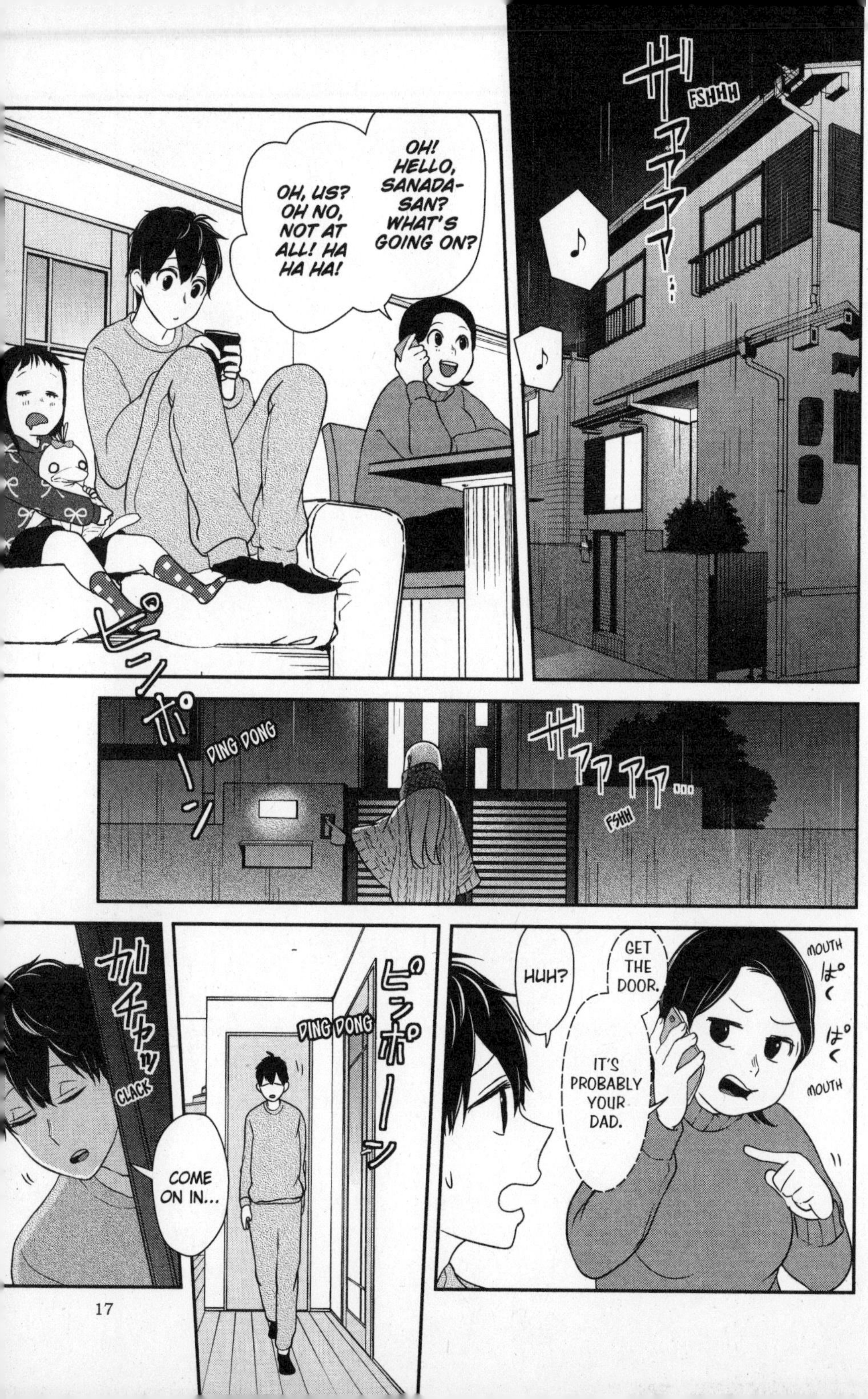
FSHHH
♪
♪
OH! HELLO, SANADA-SAN? WHAT'S GOING ON?
OH, US? OH NO, NOT AT ALL! HA HA HA!
DING DONG
FSHH
MOUTH
MOUTH
GET THE DOOR.
IT'S PROBABLY YOUR DAD.
HUH?
DING DONG
CLACK
COME ON IN...

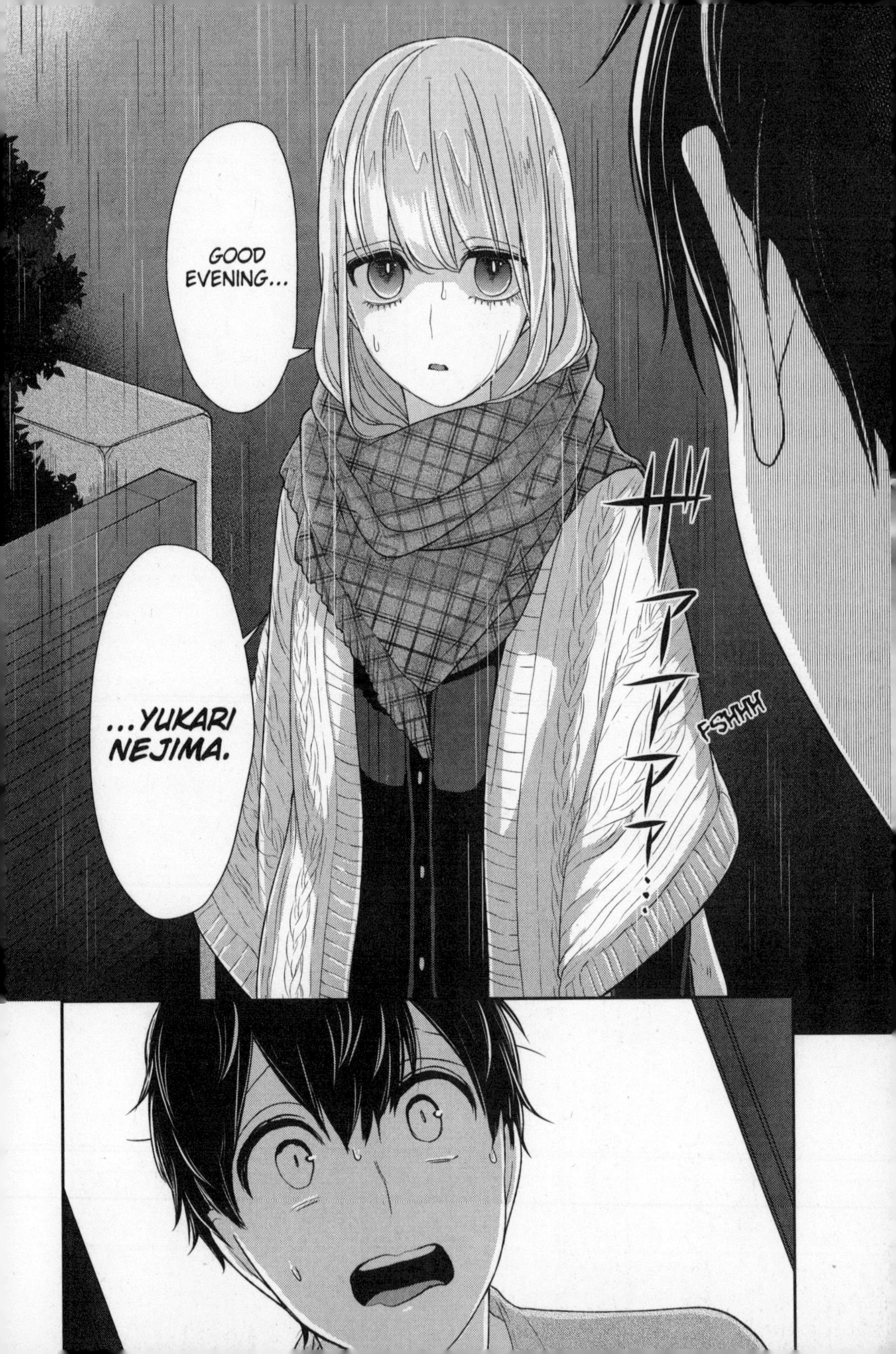
GOOD EVENING...
...YUKARI NEJIMA.
FSHHH

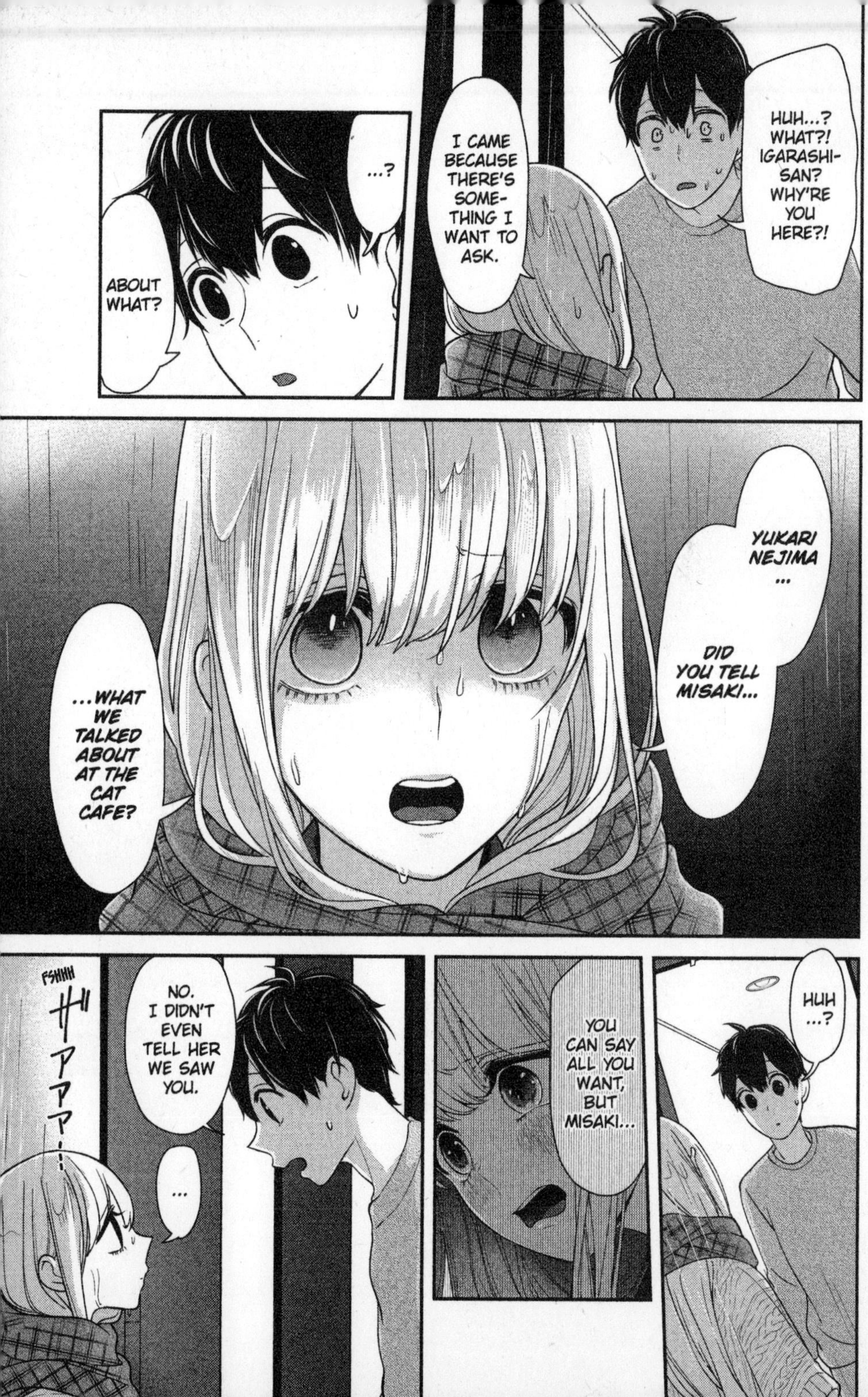
HUH...? WHAT?! IGARASHI-SAN? WHY'RE YOU HERE?!
I CAME BECAUSE THERE'S SOME-THING I WANT TO ASK.
...?
ABOUT WHAT?
YUKARI NEJIMA...
DID YOU TELL MISAKI...
...WHAT WE TALKED ABOUT AT THE CAT CAFE?
HUH...?
YOU CAN SAY ALL YOU WANT, BUT MISAKI...
NO. I DIDN'T EVEN TELL HER WE SAW YOU.
...
FSHHH

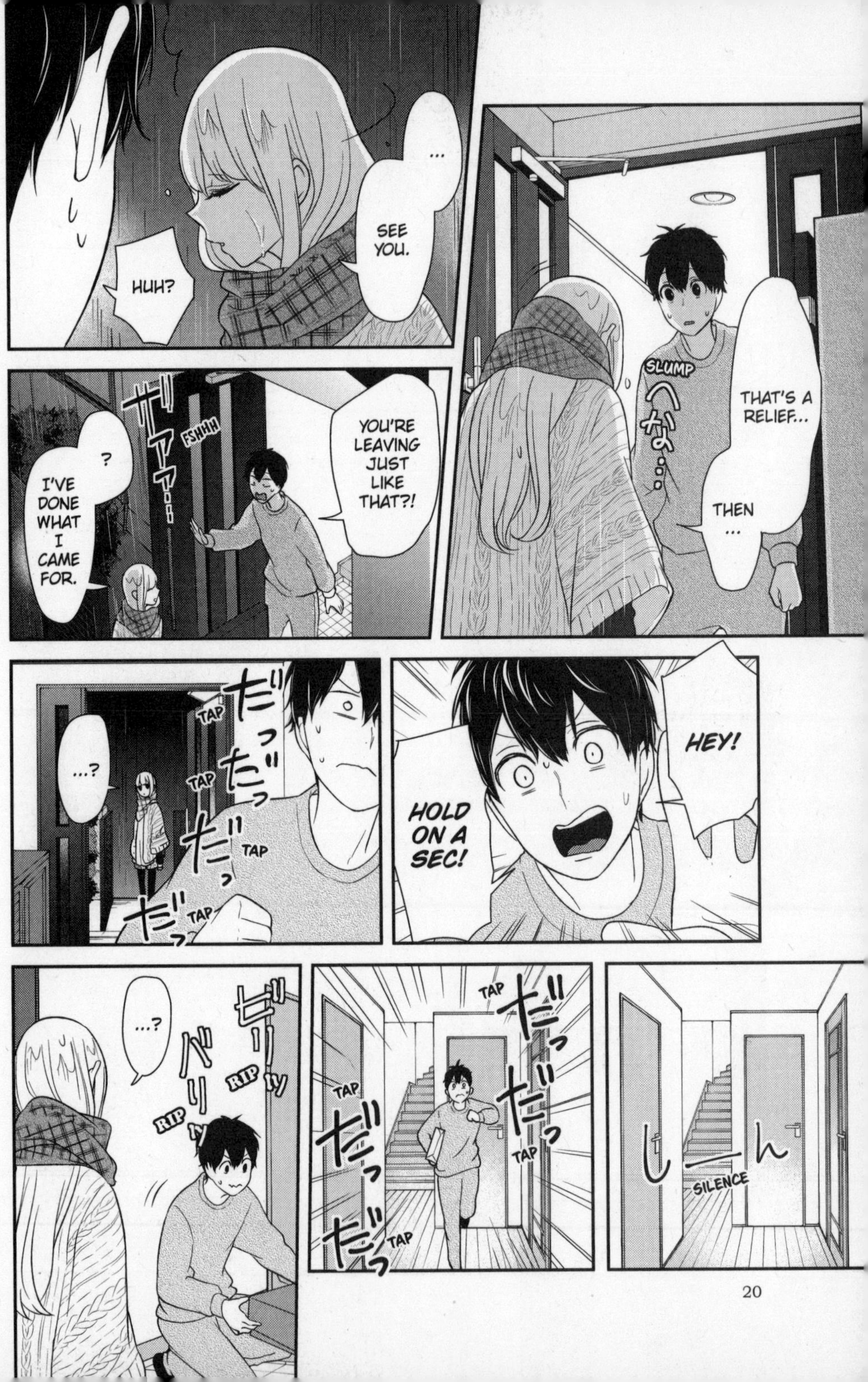
THAT'S A RELIEF...
SLUMP
へな…
THEN ...
...
SEE YOU.
HUH?
YOU'RE LEAVING JUST LIKE THAT?!
ザアァ…
FSHHH
?
I'VE DONE WHAT I CAME FOR.
HEY!
HOLD ON A SEC!
だっだっだっだっ
TAP
TAP
TAP
TAP
...?
しーん
SILENCE
だっだっだっだっ
TAP
TAP
TAP
TAP
ビリバリ
RIP
RIP
...?

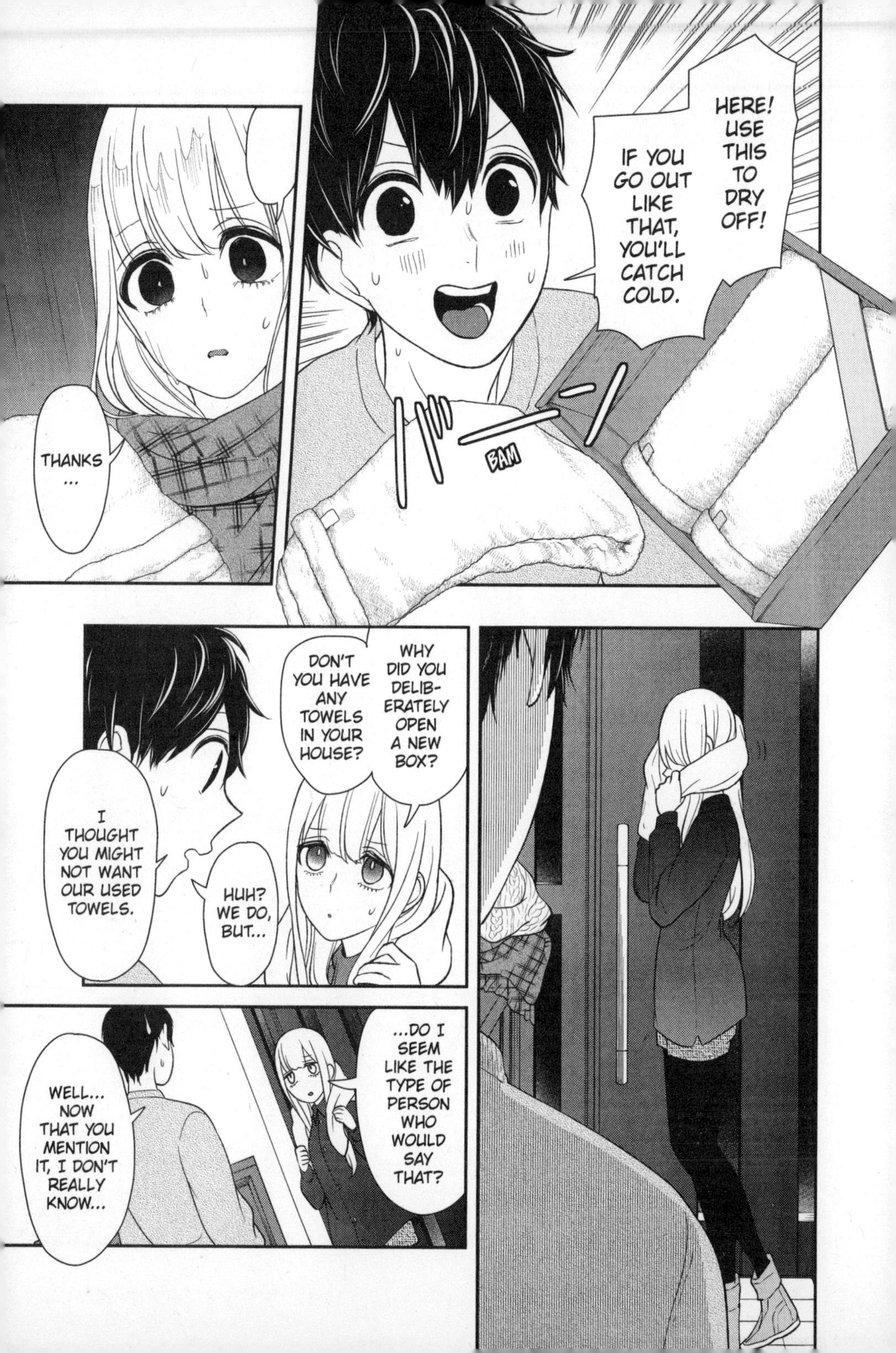
HERE! USE THIS TO DRY OFF!
IF YOU GO OUT LIKE THAT, YOU'LL CATCH COLD.
BAM
THANKS ...
WHY DID YOU DELIB-ERATELY OPEN A NEW BOX?
DON'T YOU HAVE ANY TOWELS IN YOUR HOUSE?
HUH? WE DO, BUT...
I THOUGHT YOU MIGHT NOT WANT OUR USED TOWELS.
...DO I SEEM LIKE THE TYPE OF PERSON WHO WOULD SAY THAT?
WELL... NOW THAT YOU MENTION IT, I DON'T REALLY KNOW...

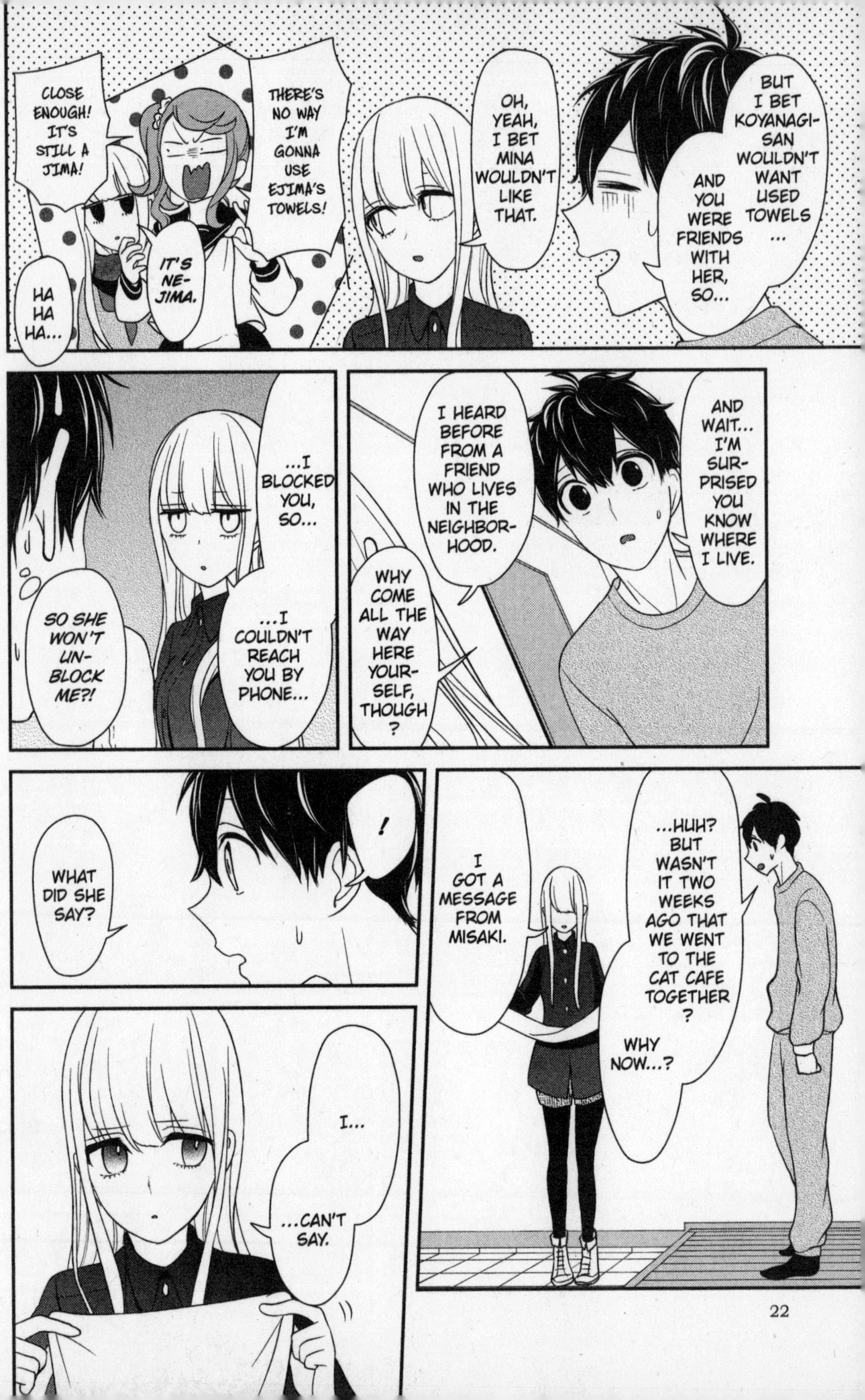
BUT I BET KOYANAGI-SAN WOULDN'T WANT USED TOWELS...
AND YOU WERE FRIENDS WITH HER, SO...
OH, YEAH, I BET MINA WOULDN'T LIKE THAT.
THERE'S NO WAY I'M GONNA USE EJIMA'S TOWELS!
IT'S NE-JIMA.
CLOSE ENOUGH! IT'S STILL A JIMA!
HA HA HA...
AND WAIT... I'M SUR-PRISED YOU KNOW WHERE I LIVE.
I HEARD BEFORE FROM A FRIEND WHO LIVES IN THE NEIGHBOR-HOOD.
WHY COME ALL THE WAY HERE YOUR-SELF, THOUGH?
...I BLOCKED YOU, SO...
...I COULDN'T REACH YOU BY PHONE...
SO SHE WON'T UN-BLOCK ME?!
...HUH? BUT WASN'T IT TWO WEEKS AGO THAT WE WENT TO THE CAT CAFE TOGETHER?
WHY NOW...?
I GOT A MESSAGE FROM MISAKI.
!
WHAT DID SHE SAY?
I...
...CAN'T SAY.

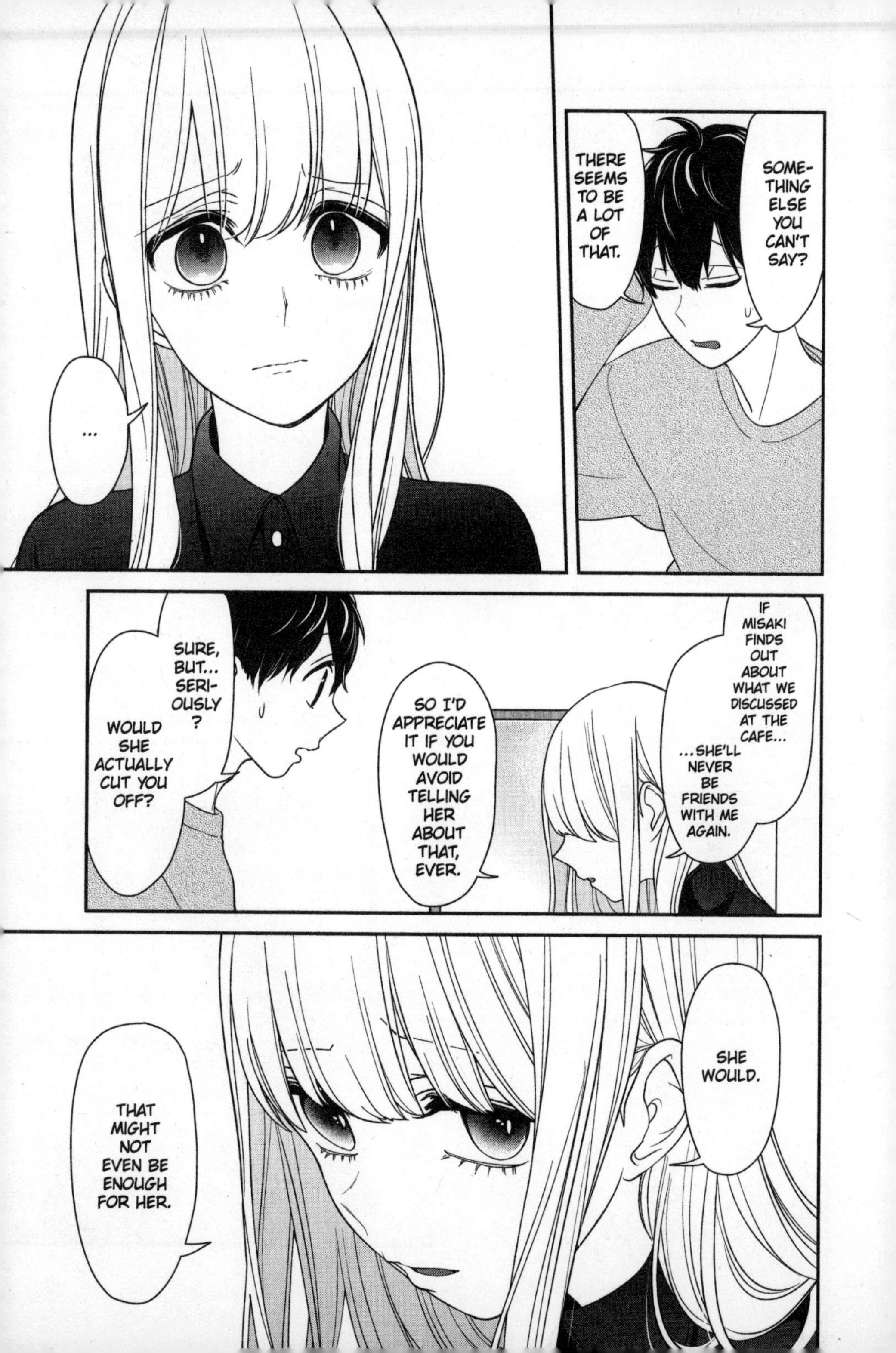
SOME-THING ELSE YOU CAN'T SAY?
THERE SEEMS TO BE A LOT OF THAT.
...
IF MISAKI FINDS OUT ABOUT WHAT WE DISCUSSED AT THE CAFE...
...SHE'LL NEVER BE FRIENDS WITH ME AGAIN.
SO I'D APPRECIATE IT IF YOU WOULD AVOID TELLING HER ABOUT THAT, EVER.
SURE, BUT... SERIOUSLY?
WOULD SHE ACTUALLY CUT YOU OFF?
SHE WOULD.
THAT MIGHT NOT EVEN BE ENOUGH FOR HER.

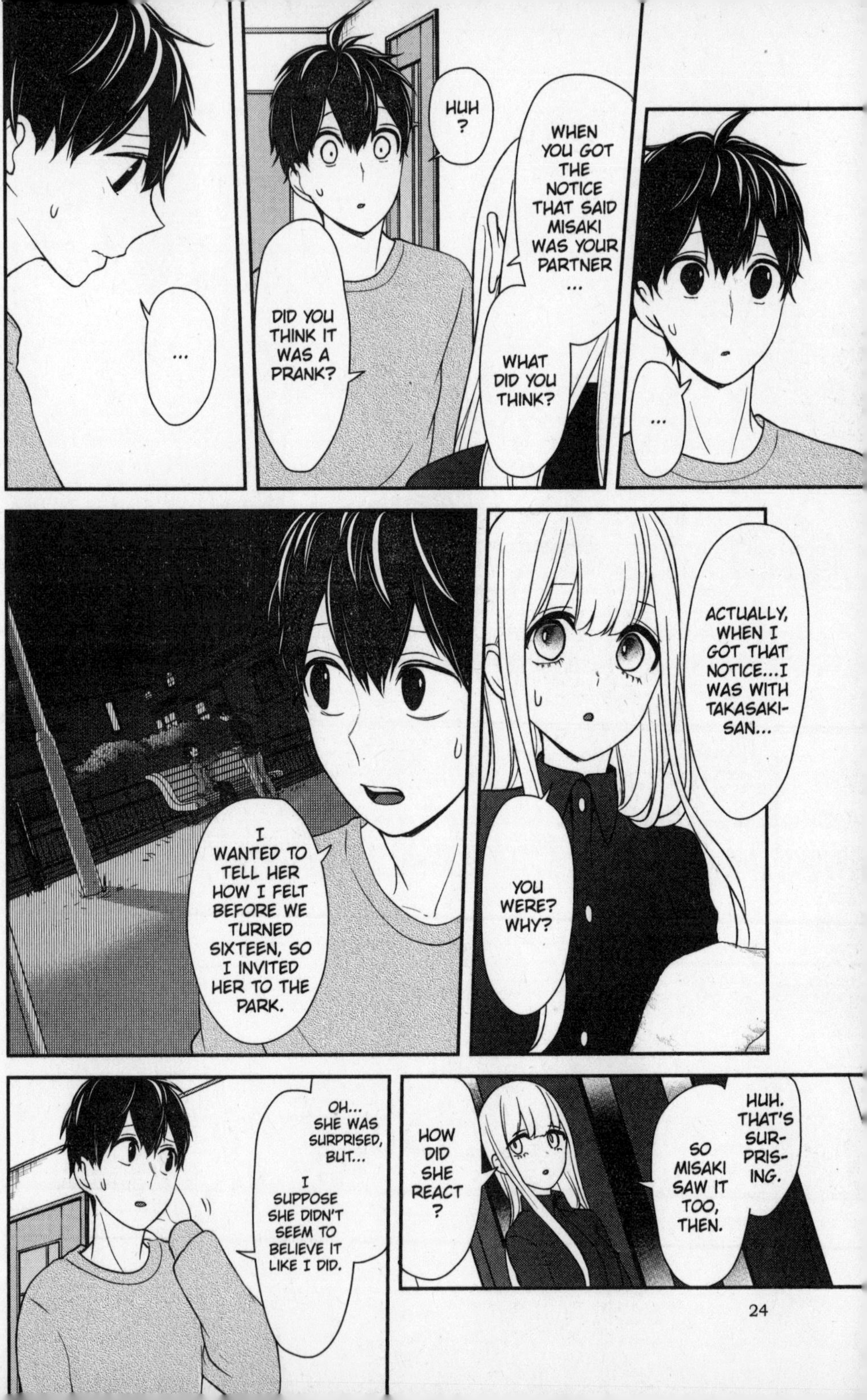
WHEN YOU GOT THE NOTICE THAT SAID MISAKI WAS YOUR PARTNER...
WHAT DID YOU THINK?
...
HUH?
DID YOU THINK IT WAS A PRANK?
...
ACTUALLY, WHEN I GOT THAT NOTICE...I WAS WITH TAKASAKI-SAN...
YOU WERE? WHY?
I WANTED TO TELL HER HOW I FELT BEFORE WE TURNED SIXTEEN, SO I INVITED HER TO THE PARK.
HUH. THAT'S SURPRISING.
SO MISAKI SAW IT TOO, THEN.
HOW DID SHE REACT?
OH... SHE WAS SURPRISED, BUT...
I SUPPOSE SHE DIDN'T SEEM TO BELIEVE IT LIKE I DID.

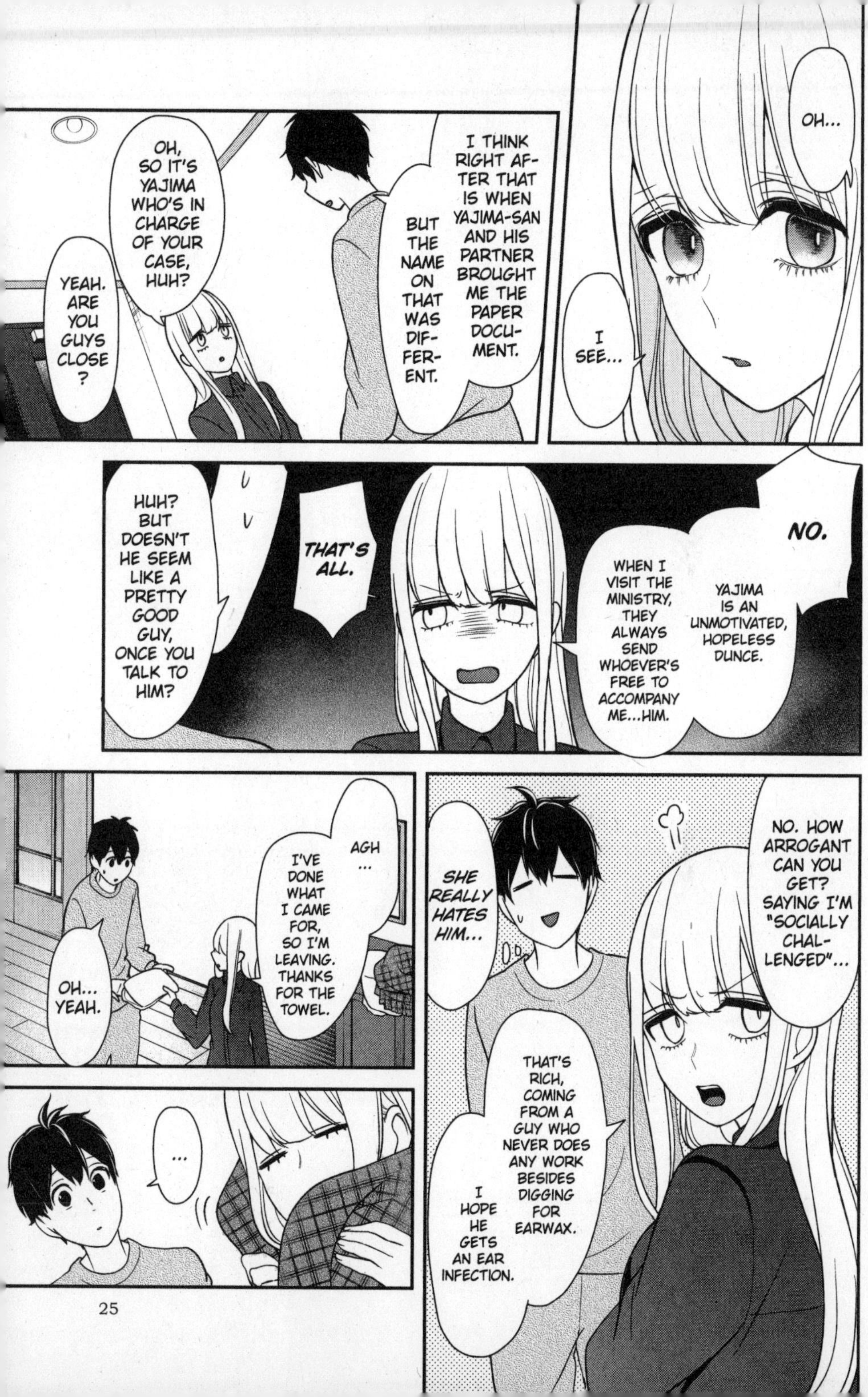

OH...
I SEE...
I THINK RIGHT AFTER THAT IS WHEN YAJIMA-SAN AND HIS PARTNER BROUGHT ME THE PAPER DOCUMENT.
BUT THE NAME ON THAT WAS DIFFERENT.
OH, SO IT'S YAJIMA WHO'S IN CHARGE OF YOUR CASE, HUH?
YEAH. ARE YOU GUYS CLOSE?
NO.
YAJIMA IS AN UNMOTIVATED, HOPELESS DUNCE.
WHEN I VISIT THE MINISTRY, THEY ALWAYS SEND WHOEVER'S FREE TO ACCOMPANY ME...HIM.
THAT'S ALL.
HUH? BUT DOESN'T HE SEEM LIKE A PRETTY GOOD GUY, ONCE YOU TALK TO HIM?
NO. HOW ARROGANT CAN YOU GET? SAYING I'M "SOCIALLY CHALLENGED"...
SHE REALLY HATES HIM...
THAT'S RICH, COMING FROM A GUY WHO NEVER DOES ANY WORK BESIDES DIGGING FOR EARWAX.
I HOPE HE GETS AN EAR INFECTION.
AGH...
I'VE DONE WHAT I CAME FOR, SO I'M LEAVING. THANKS FOR THE TOWEL.
OH... YEAH.
...

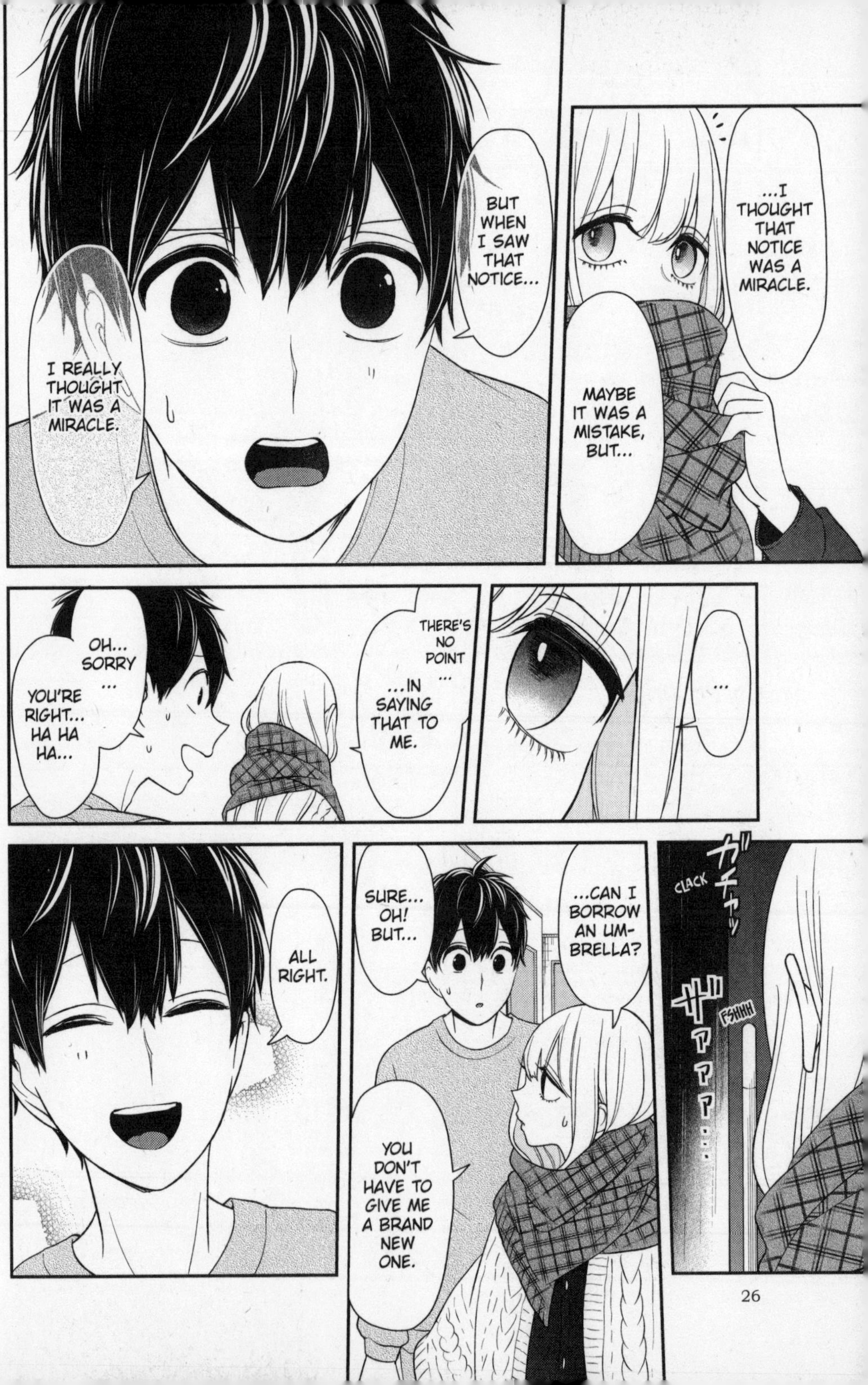
...I THOUGHT THAT NOTICE WAS A MIRACLE.
MAYBE IT WAS A MISTAKE, BUT...
BUT WHEN I SAW THAT NOTICE...
I REALLY THOUGHT IT WAS A MIRACLE.
...
THERE'S NO POINT ...
...IN SAYING THAT TO ME.
OH... SORRY ...
YOU'RE RIGHT... HA HA HA...
ガチャッ
CLACK
ザァァァ...
FSHHH
...CAN I BORROW AN UM-BRELLA?
SURE... OH! BUT...
YOU DON'T HAVE TO GIVE ME A BRAND NEW ONE.
ALL RIGHT.

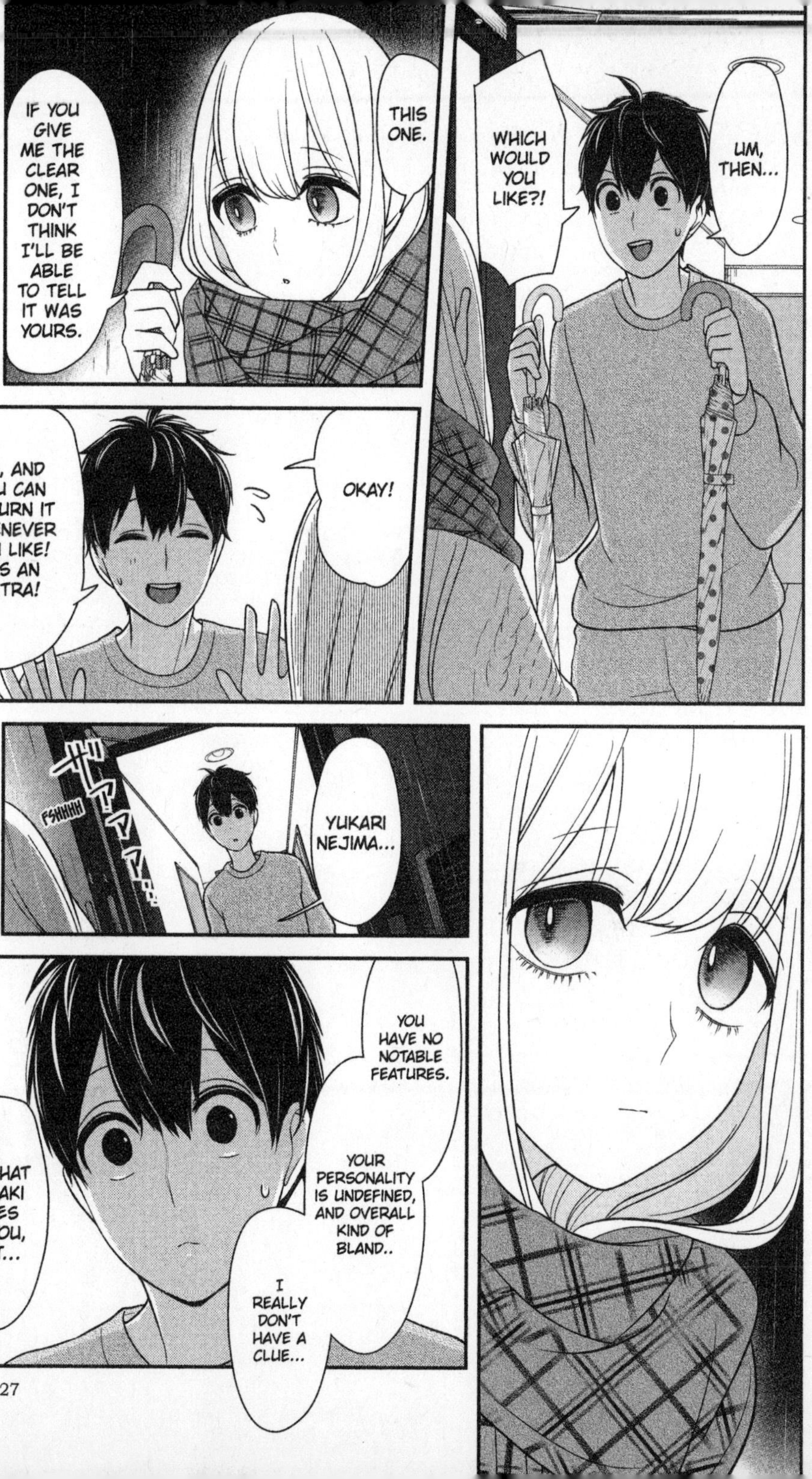
UM, THEN...
WHICH WOULD YOU LIKE?!
THIS ONE.
IF YOU GIVE ME THE CLEAR ONE, I DON'T THINK I'LL BE ABLE TO TELL IT WAS YOURS.
OKAY!
OH, AND YOU CAN RETURN IT WHENEVER YOU LIKE! IT'S AN EXTRA!
YUKARI NEJIMA...
FSHHHH
YOU HAVE NO NOTABLE FEATURES.
YOUR PERSONALITY IS UNDEFINED, AND OVERALL KIND OF BLAND..
I REALLY DON'T HAVE A CLUE...
...WHAT MISAKI SEES IN YOU, BUT...

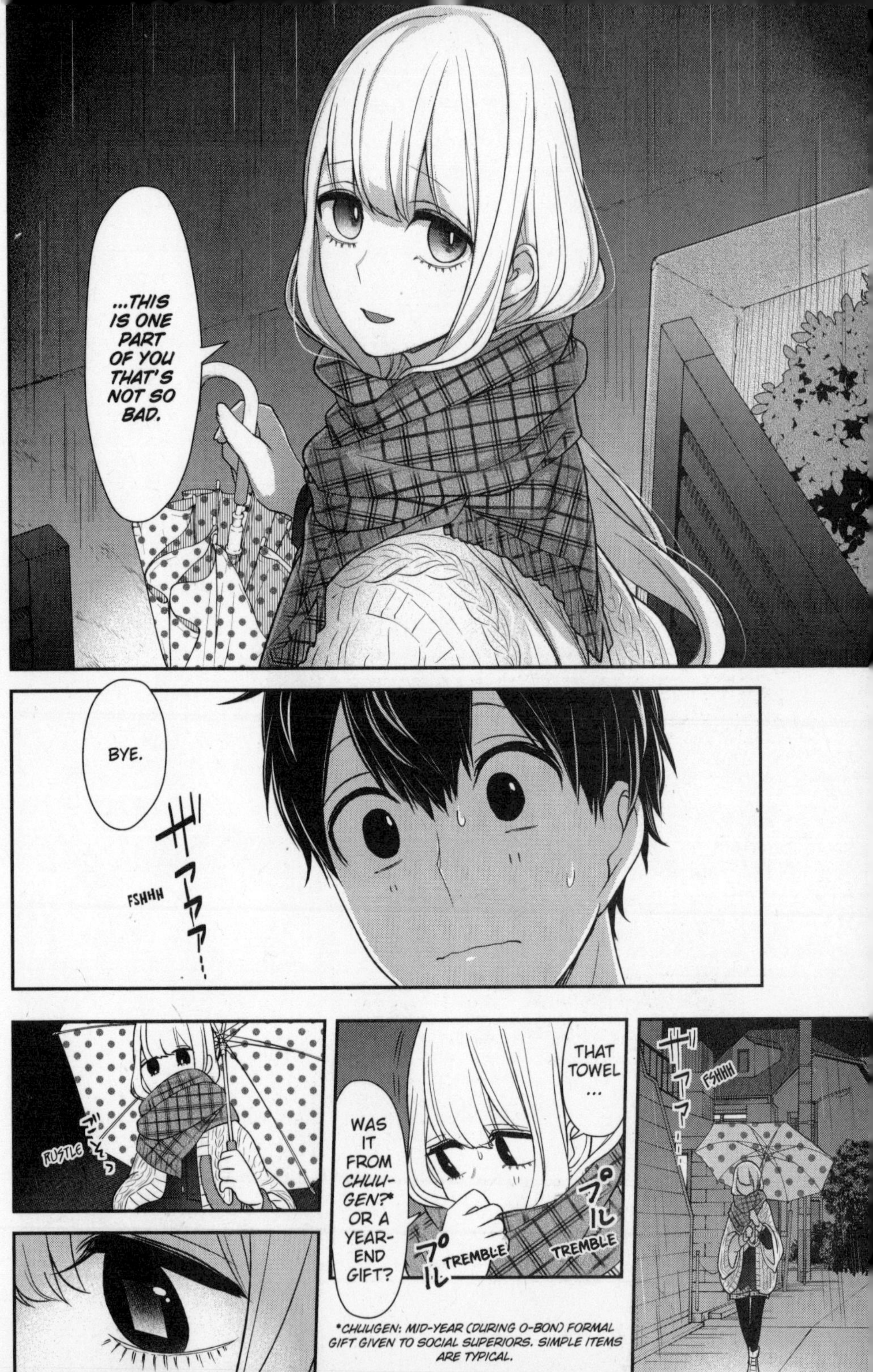
...THIS IS ONE PART OF YOU THAT'S NOT SO BAD.
BYE.
ザァァァ...
FSHHH
ザァァァ...
FSHHH
THAT TOWEL...
WAS IT FROM CHUUGEN?* OR A YEAR-END GIFT?
プル
TREMBLE
プル
TREMBLE
RUSTLE

*CHUUGEN: MID-YEAR (DURING O-BON) FORMAL GIFT GIVEN TO SOCIAL SUPERIORS. SIMPLE ITEMS ARE TYPICAL.

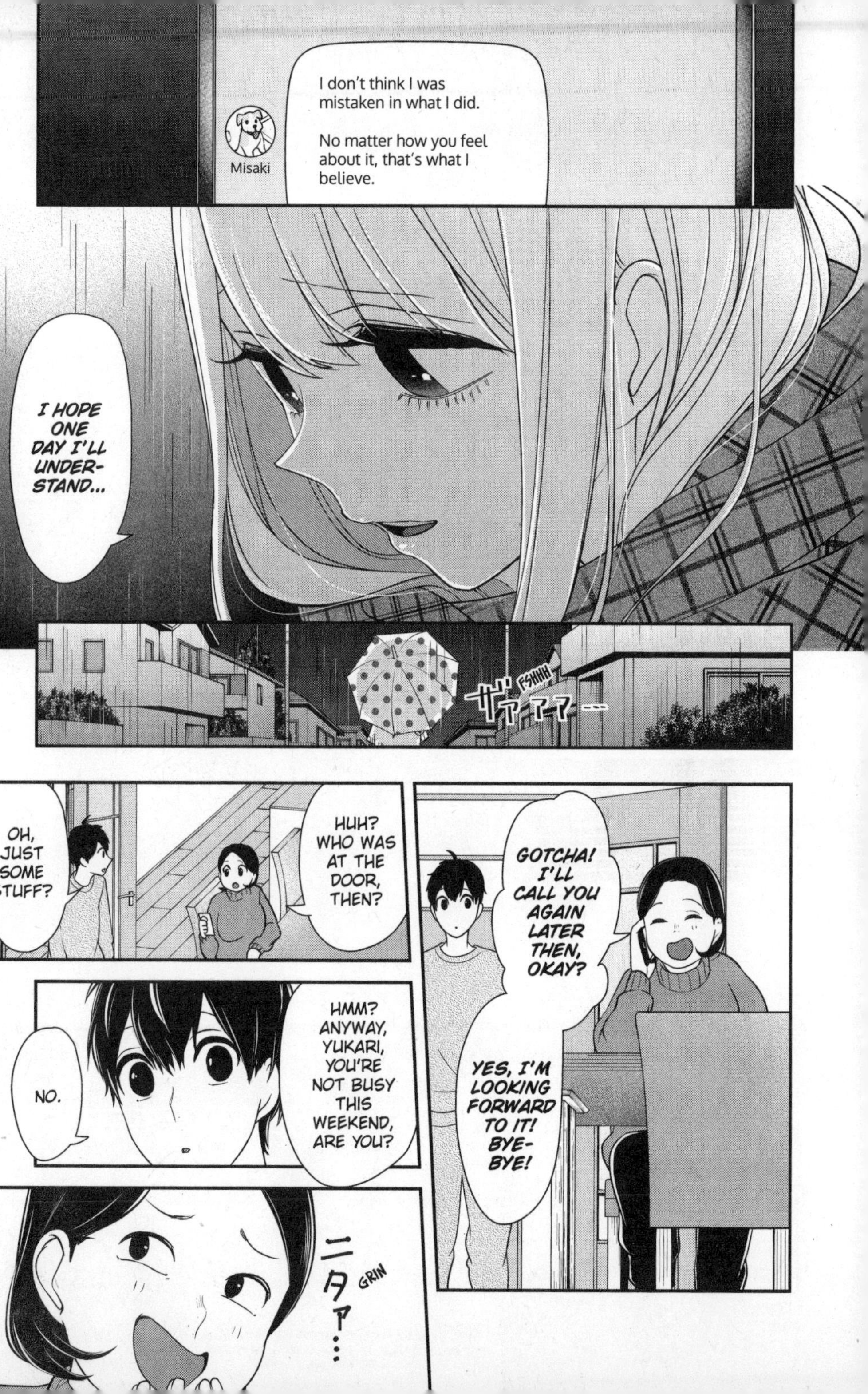
Misaki
I don't think I was mistaken in what I did.
No matter how you feel about it, that's what I believe.
I HOPE ONE DAY I'LL UNDER-STAND...
ザァアア… FSHHH
GOTCHA! I'LL CALL YOU AGAIN LATER THEN, OKAY?
YES, I'M LOOKING FORWARD TO IT! BYE-BYE!
HUH? WHO WAS AT THE DOOR, THEN?
OH, JUST SOME STUFF?
HMM? ANYWAY, YUKARI, YOU'RE NOT BUSY THIS WEEKEND, ARE YOU?
NO.
ニタァ… GRIN

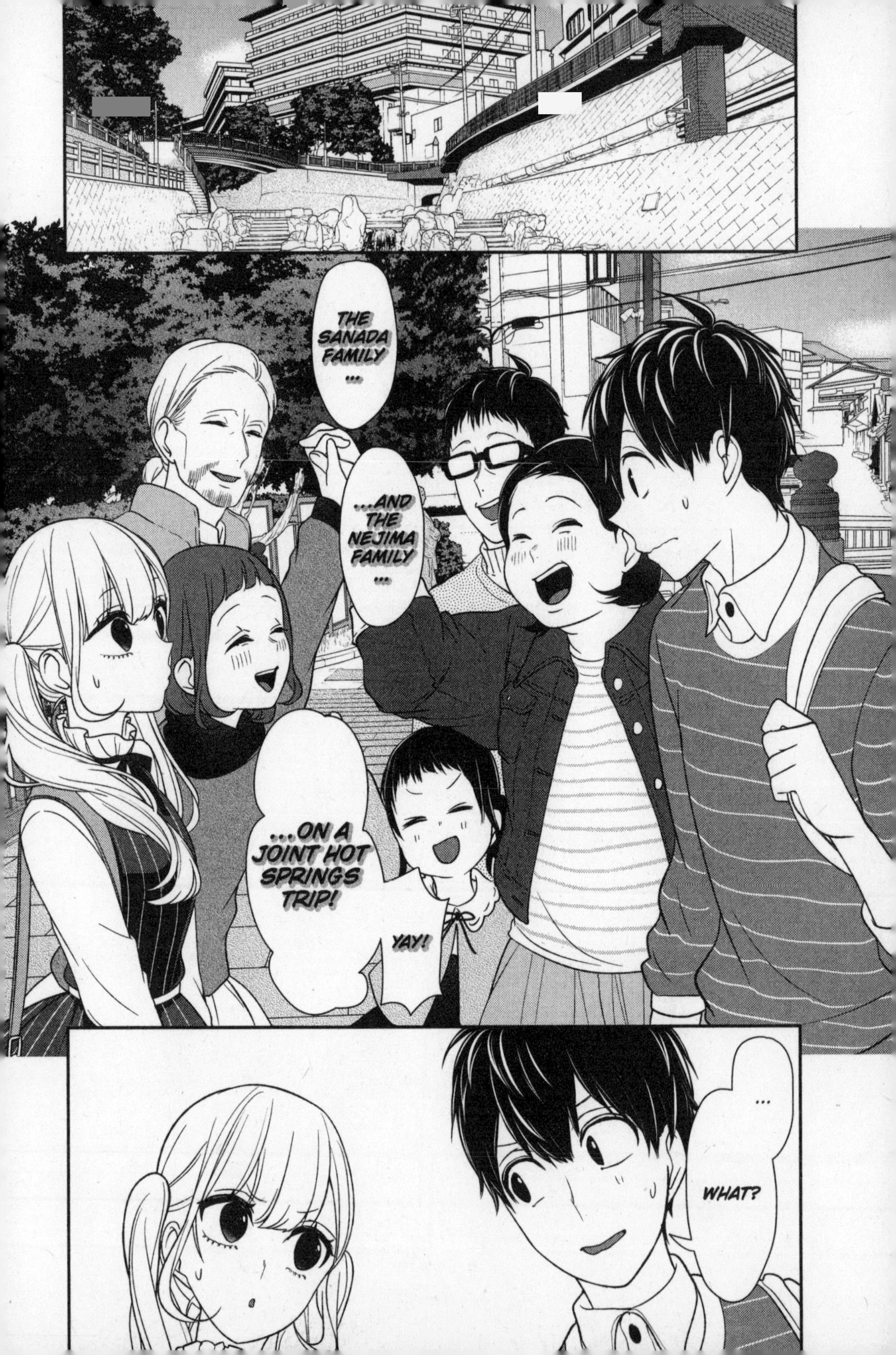
THE SANADA FAMILY ...
...AND THE NEJIMA FAMILY ...
...ON A JOINT HOT SPRINGS TRIP!
YAY!
...
WHAT?

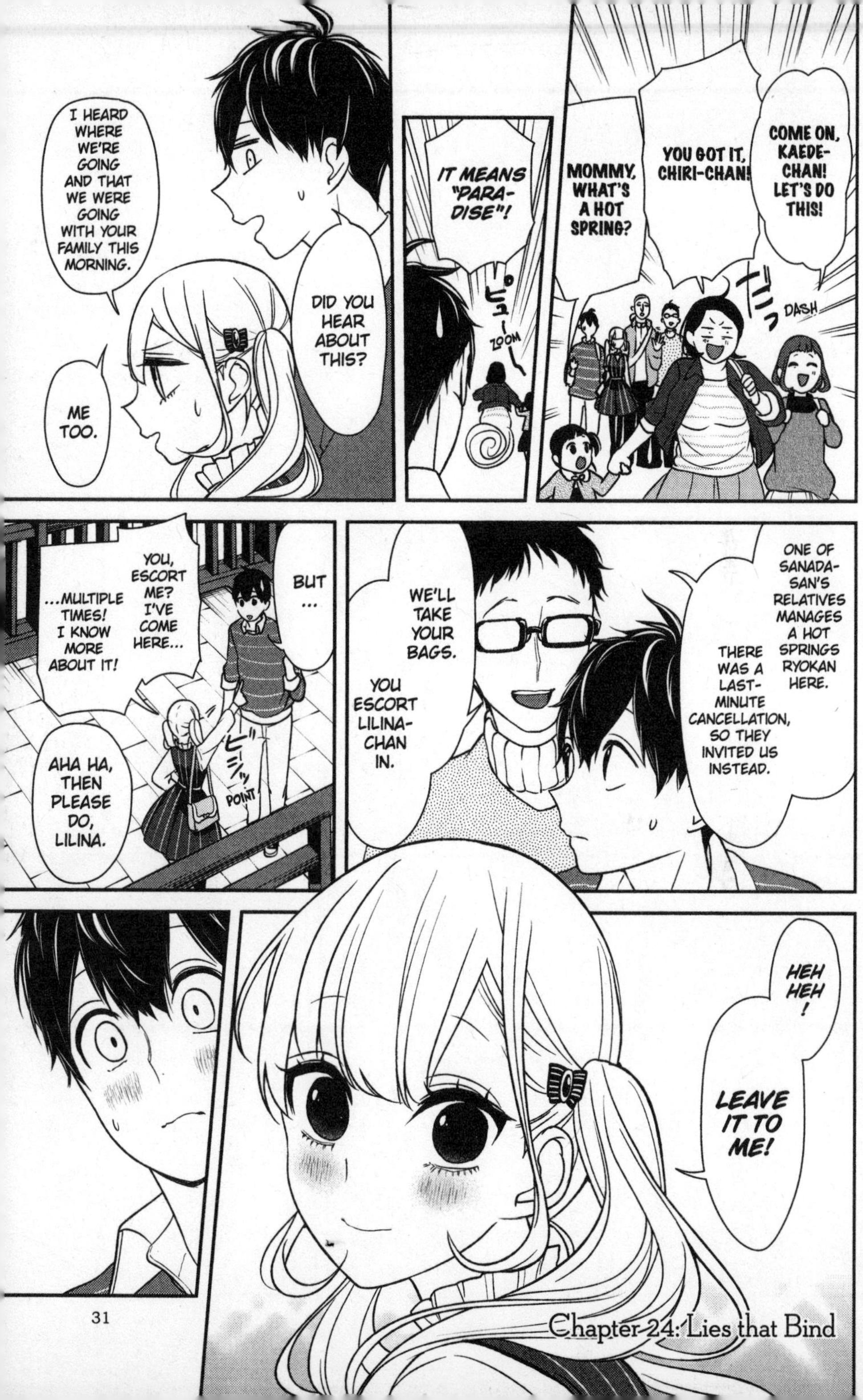
COME ON, KAEDE-CHAN! LET'S DO THIS!
YOU GOT IT, CHIRI-CHAN!
DASH
MOMMY, WHAT'S A HOT SPRING?
IT MEANS "PARA-DISE"!
ZOOM
I HEARD WHERE WE'RE GOING AND THAT WE WERE GOING WITH YOUR FAMILY THIS MORNING.
DID YOU HEAR ABOUT THIS?
ME TOO.
ONE OF SANADA-SAN'S RELATIVES MANAGES A HOT SPRINGS RYOKAN HERE.
THERE WAS A LAST-MINUTE CANCELLATION, SO THEY INVITED US INSTEAD.
WE'LL TAKE YOUR BAGS.
YOU ESCORT LILINA-CHAN IN.
BUT ...
YOU, ESCORT ME? I'VE COME HERE...
...MULTIPLE TIMES! I KNOW MORE ABOUT IT!
POINT
AHA HA, THEN PLEASE DO, LILINA.
HEH HEH!
LEAVE IT TO ME!

# Chapter 24: Lies that Bind

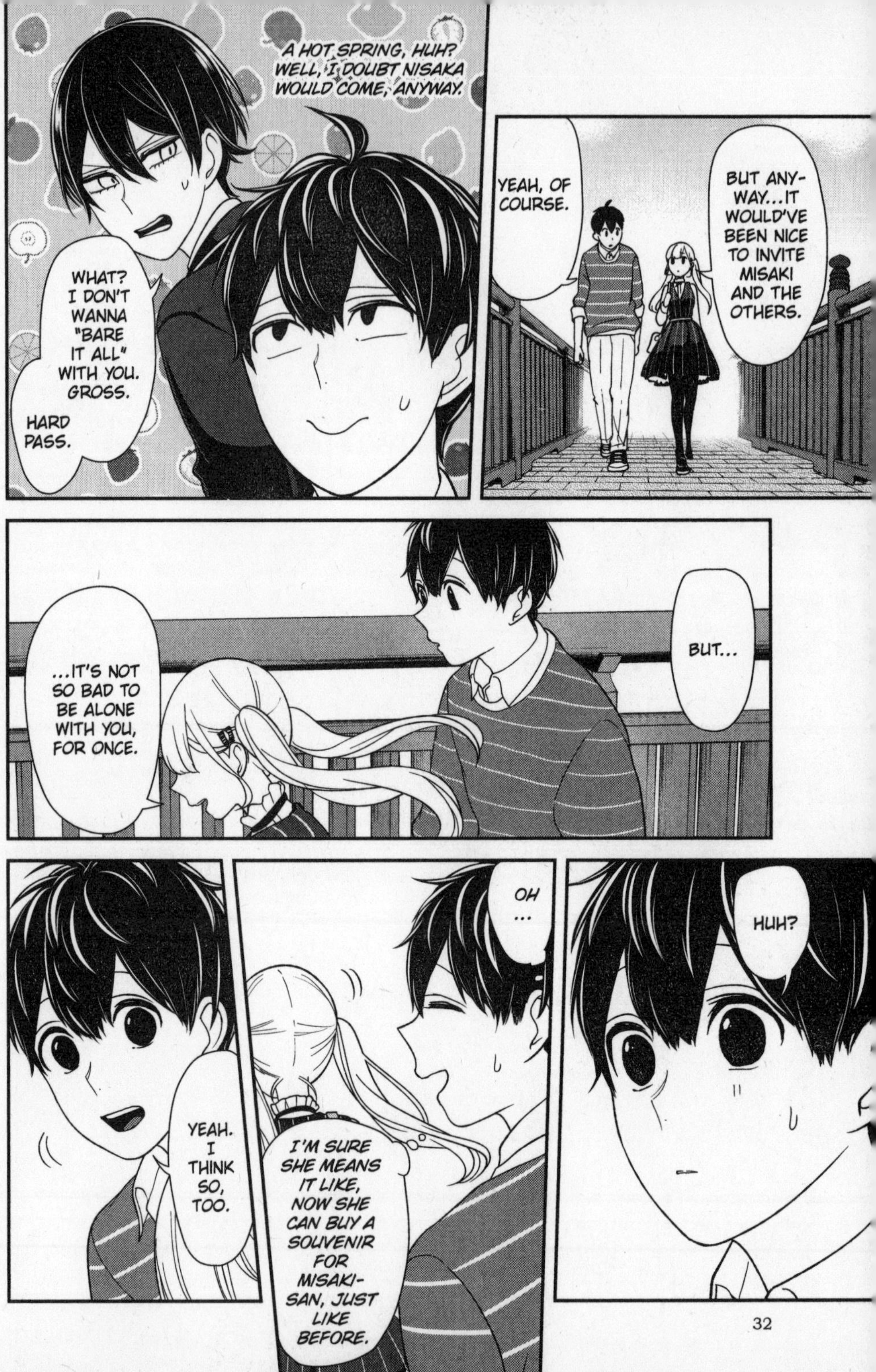
BUT ANYWAY...IT WOULD'VE BEEN NICE TO INVITE MISAKI AND THE OTHERS.
YEAH, OF COURSE.
A HOT SPRING, HUH? WELL, I DOUBT NISAKA WOULD COME, ANYWAY.
WHAT? I DON'T WANNA "BARE IT ALL" WITH YOU. GROSS.
HARD PASS.
BUT...
...IT'S NOT SO BAD TO BE ALONE WITH YOU, FOR ONCE.
HUH?
OH ...
I'M SURE SHE MEANS IT LIKE, NOW SHE CAN BUY A SOUVENIR FOR MISAKI-SAN, JUST LIKE BEFORE.
YEAH. I THINK SO, TOO.

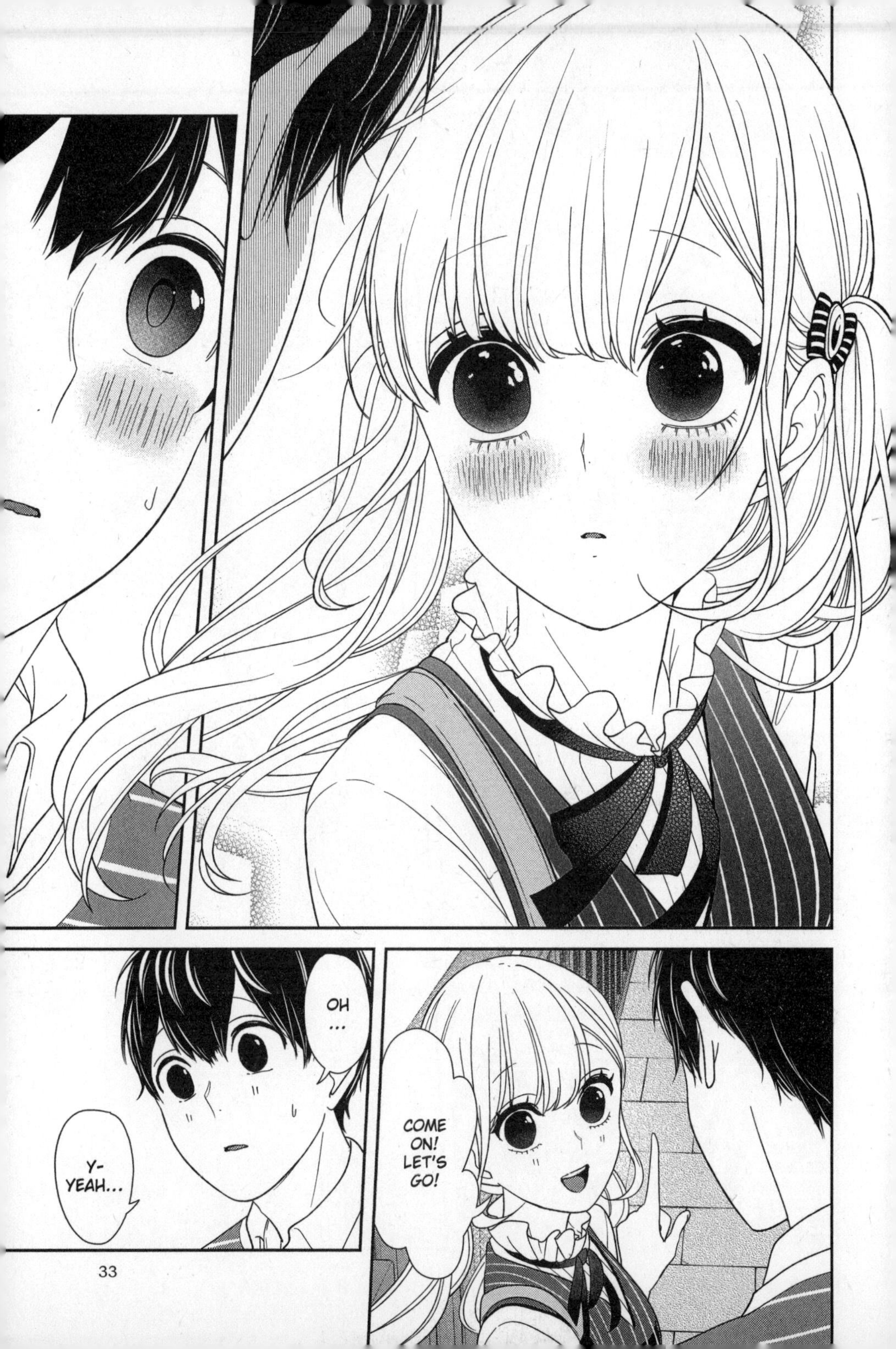
COME ON! LET'S GO!
OH ...
Y- YEAH...

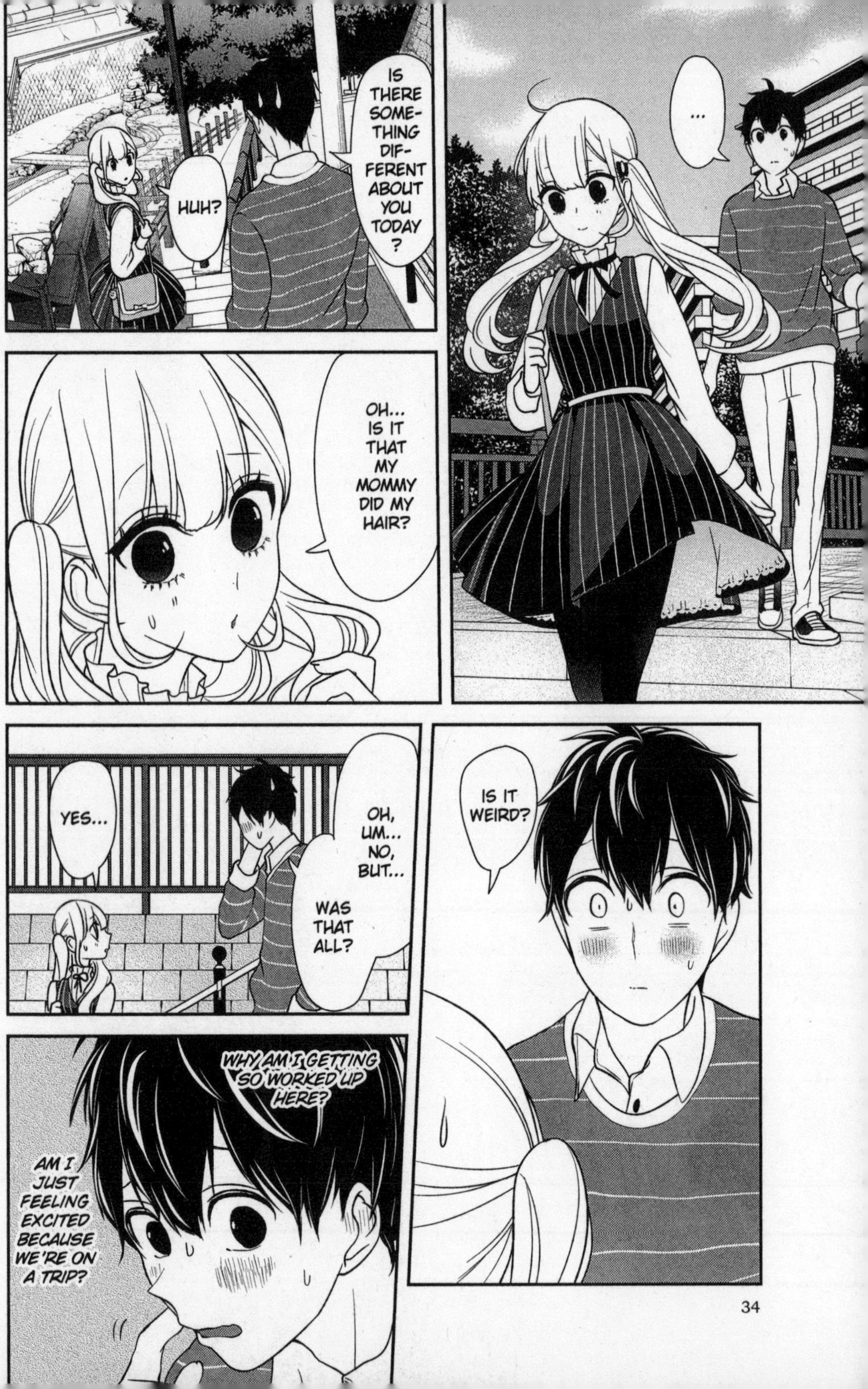
...
IS THERE SOMETHING DIFFERENT ABOUT YOU TODAY?
HUH?
OH... IS IT THAT MY MOMMY DID MY HAIR?
IS IT WEIRD?
OH, UM... NO, BUT...
WAS THAT ALL?
YES...
WHY AM I GETTING SO WORKED UP HERE?
AM I JUST FEELING EXCITED BECAUSE WE'RE ON A TRIP?

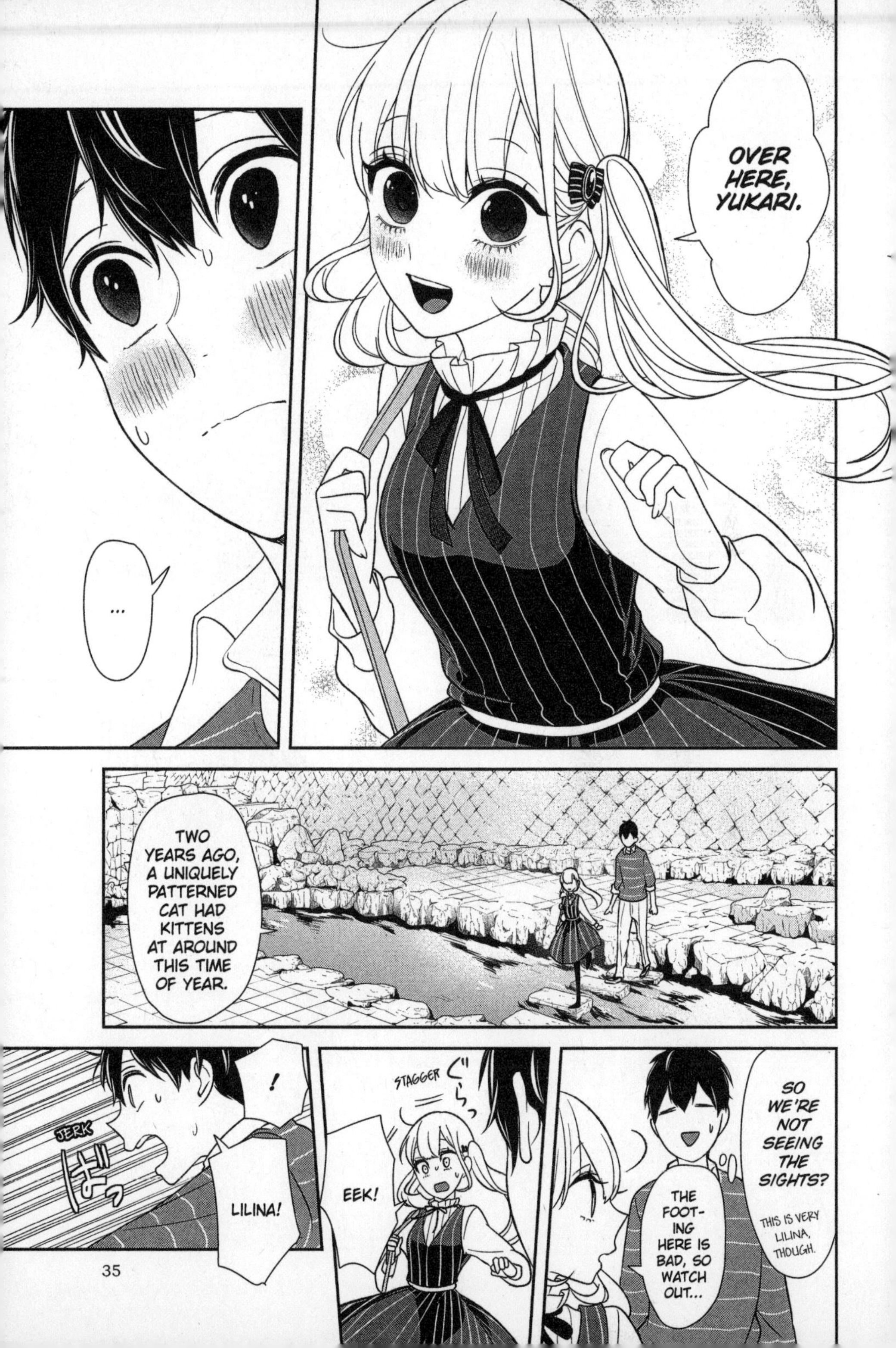
OVER HERE, YUKARI.
...
TWO YEARS AGO, A UNIQUELY PATTERNED CAT HAD KITTENS AT AROUND THIS TIME OF YEAR.
SO WE'RE NOT SEEING THE SIGHTS?
THIS IS VERY LILINA, THOUGH.
THE FOOT-ING HERE IS BAD, SO WATCH OUT...
STAGGER
EEK!
!
JERK
LILINA!

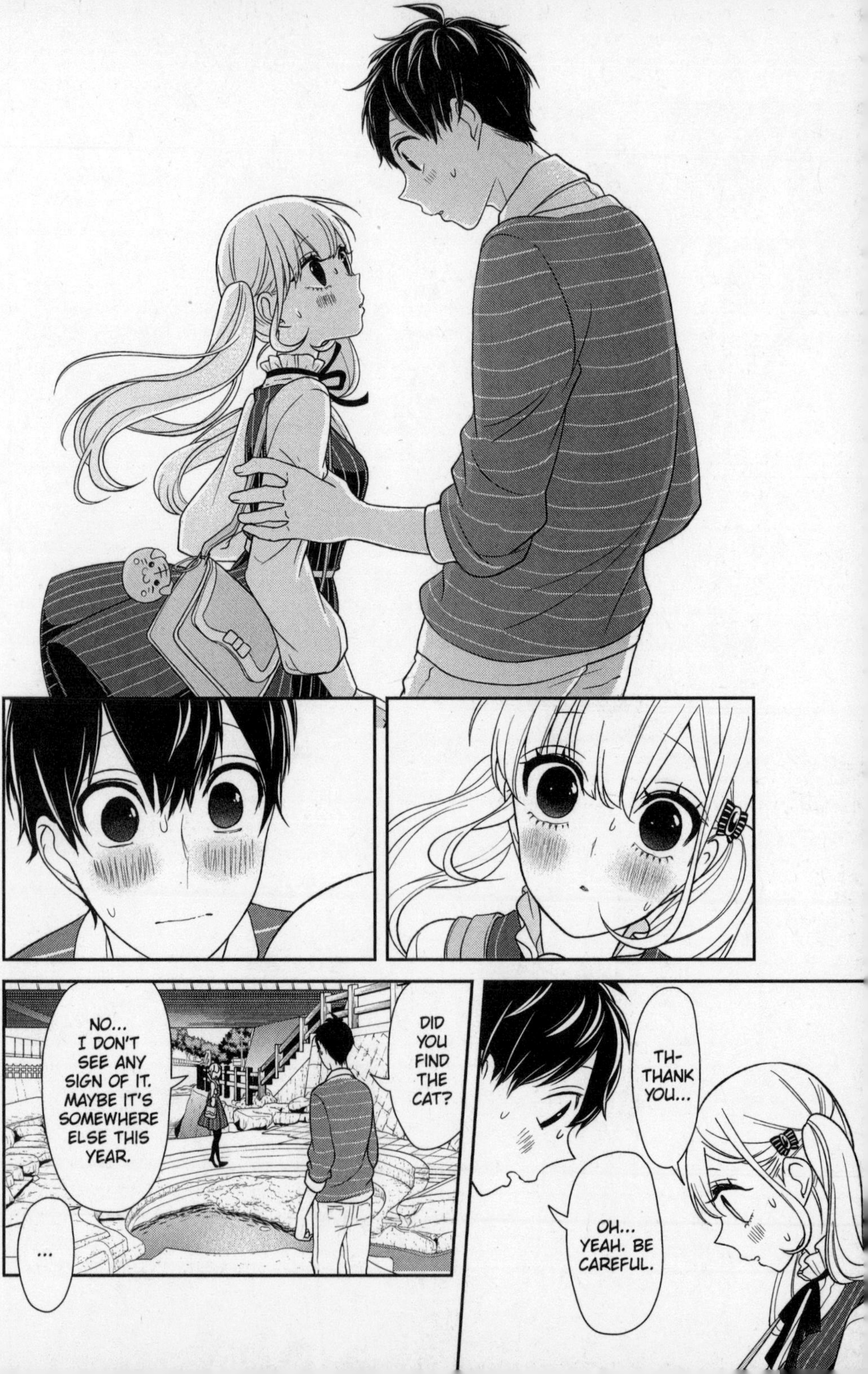
TH-THANK YOU...
OH... YEAH. BE CAREFUL.
DID YOU FIND THE CAT?
NO... I DON'T SEE ANY SIGN OF IT. MAYBE IT'S SOMEWHERE ELSE THIS YEAR.
...

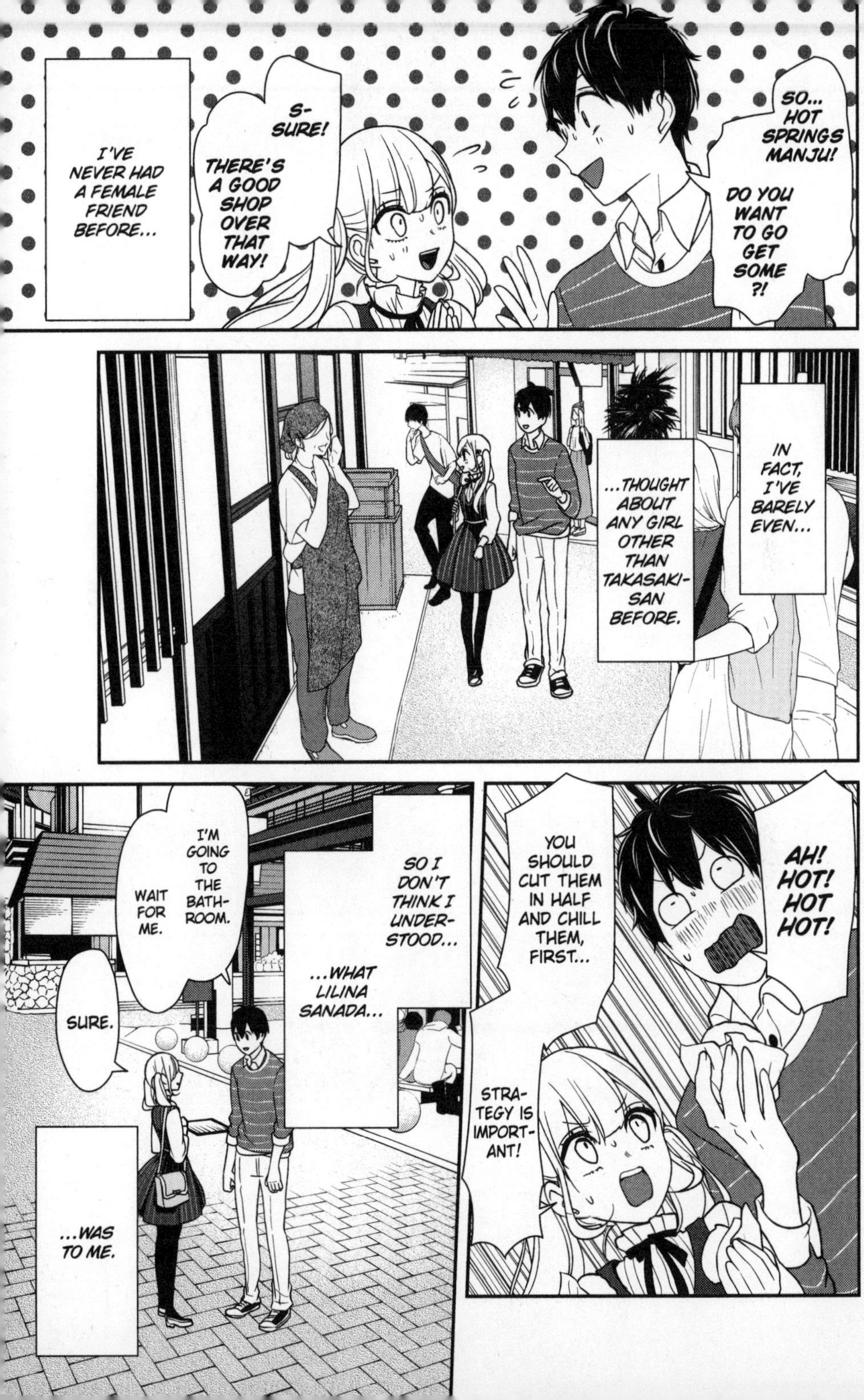
SO... HOT SPRINGS MANJU!
DO YOU WANT TO GO GET SOME?!
S-SURE!
THERE'S A GOOD SHOP OVER THAT WAY!
I'VE NEVER HAD A FEMALE FRIEND BEFORE...
IN FACT, I'VE BARELY EVEN...
...THOUGHT ABOUT ANY GIRL OTHER THAN TAKASAKI-SAN BEFORE.
AH! HOT! HOT HOT!
YOU SHOULD CUT THEM IN HALF AND CHILL THEM, FIRST...
STRATEGY IS IMPORTANT!
SO I DON'T THINK I UNDERSTOOD...
I'M GOING TO THE BATHROOM.
WAIT FOR ME.
...WHAT LILINA SANADA...
SURE.
...WAS TO ME.

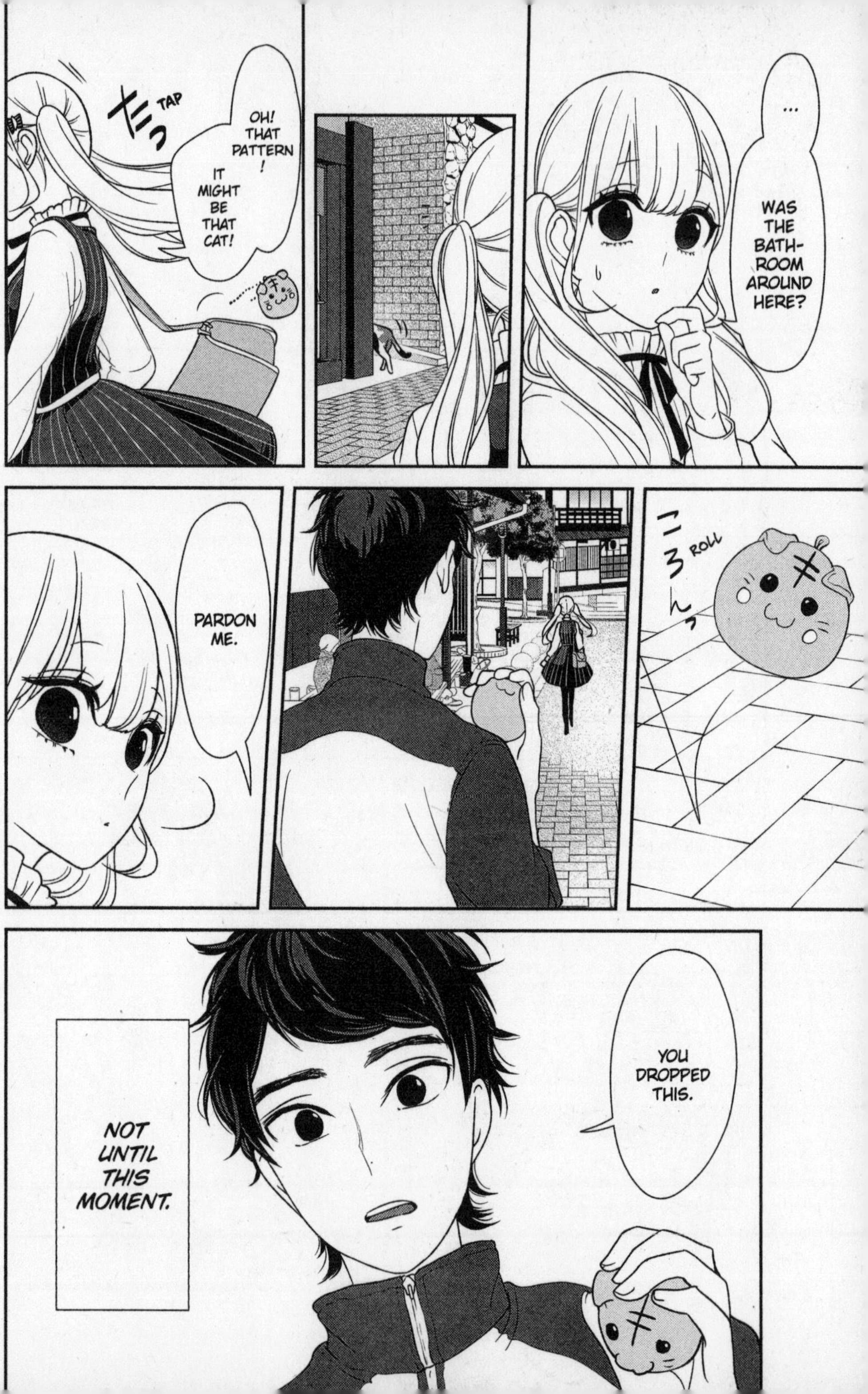
...
WAS THE BATH-ROOM AROUND HERE?
TAP
OH! THAT PATTERN!
IT MIGHT BE THAT CAT!
ころんっ ROLL
PARDON ME.
YOU DROPPED THIS.
NOT UNTIL THIS MOMENT.

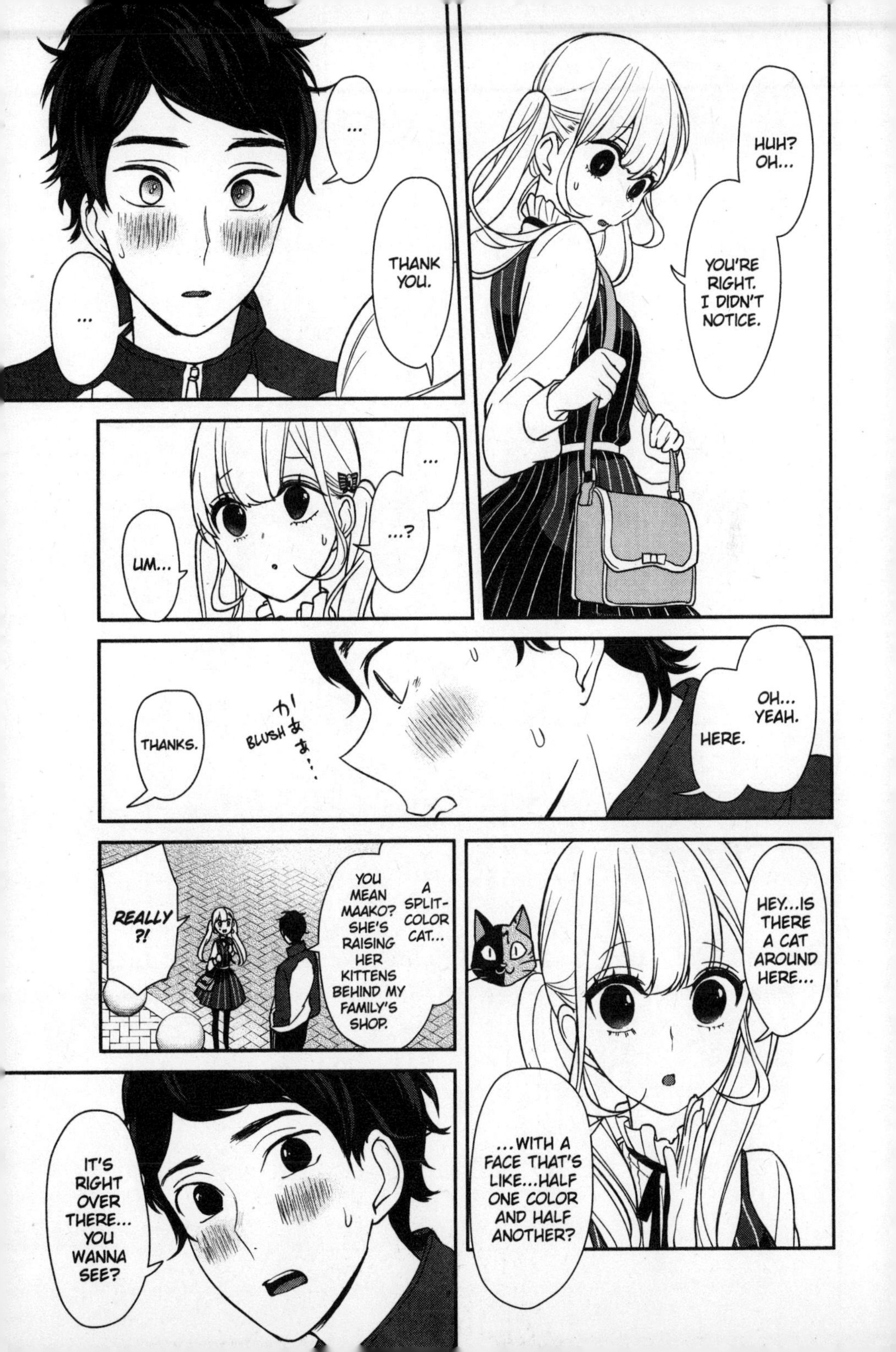
HUH? OH...
YOU'RE RIGHT. I DIDN'T NOTICE.
...
THANK YOU.
...
...
...?
UM...
OH... YEAH.
HERE.
BLUSH
THANKS.
HEY...IS THERE A CAT AROUND HERE...
...WITH A FACE THAT'S LIKE...HALF ONE COLOR AND HALF ANOTHER?
A SPLIT-COLOR CAT...
YOU MEAN MAAKO? SHE'S RAISING HER KITTENS BEHIND MY FAMILY'S SHOP.
REALLY?!
IT'S RIGHT OVER THERE... YOU WANNA SEE?

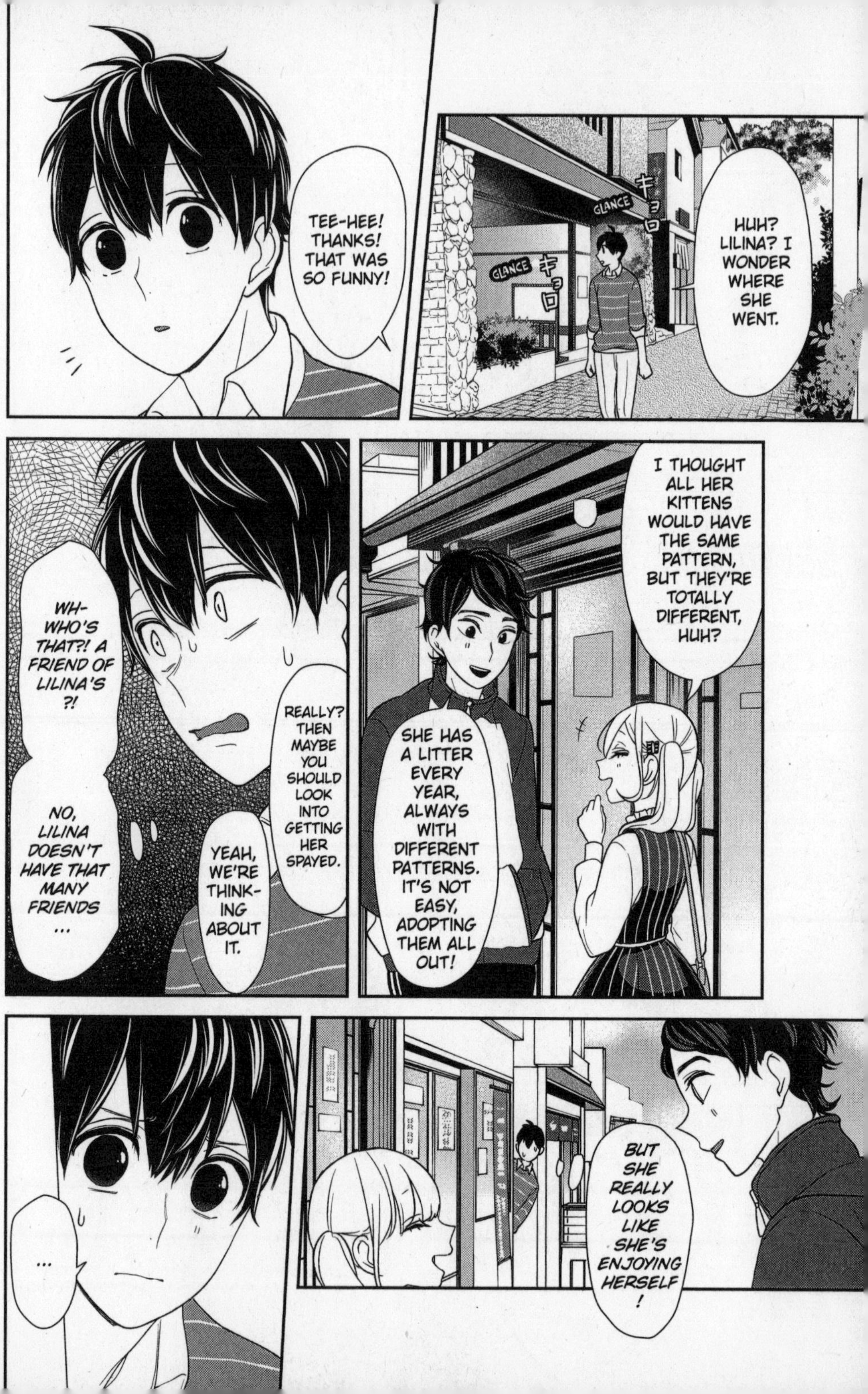
HUH? LILINA? I WONDER WHERE SHE WENT.
GLANCE キョロ
GLANCE キョロ
TEE-HEE! THANKS! THAT WAS SO FUNNY!
I THOUGHT ALL HER KITTENS WOULD HAVE THE SAME PATTERN, BUT THEY'RE TOTALLY DIFFERENT, HUH?
SHE HAS A LITTER EVERY YEAR, ALWAYS WITH DIFFERENT PATTERNS. IT'S NOT EASY, ADOPTING THEM ALL OUT!
REALLY? THEN MAYBE YOU SHOULD LOOK INTO GETTING HER SPAYED.
WH-WHO'S THAT?! A FRIEND OF LILINA'S?!
YEAH, WE'RE THINKING ABOUT IT.
NO, LILINA DOESN'T HAVE THAT MANY FRIENDS...
BUT SHE REALLY LOOKS LIKE SHE'S ENJOYING HERSELF!
...

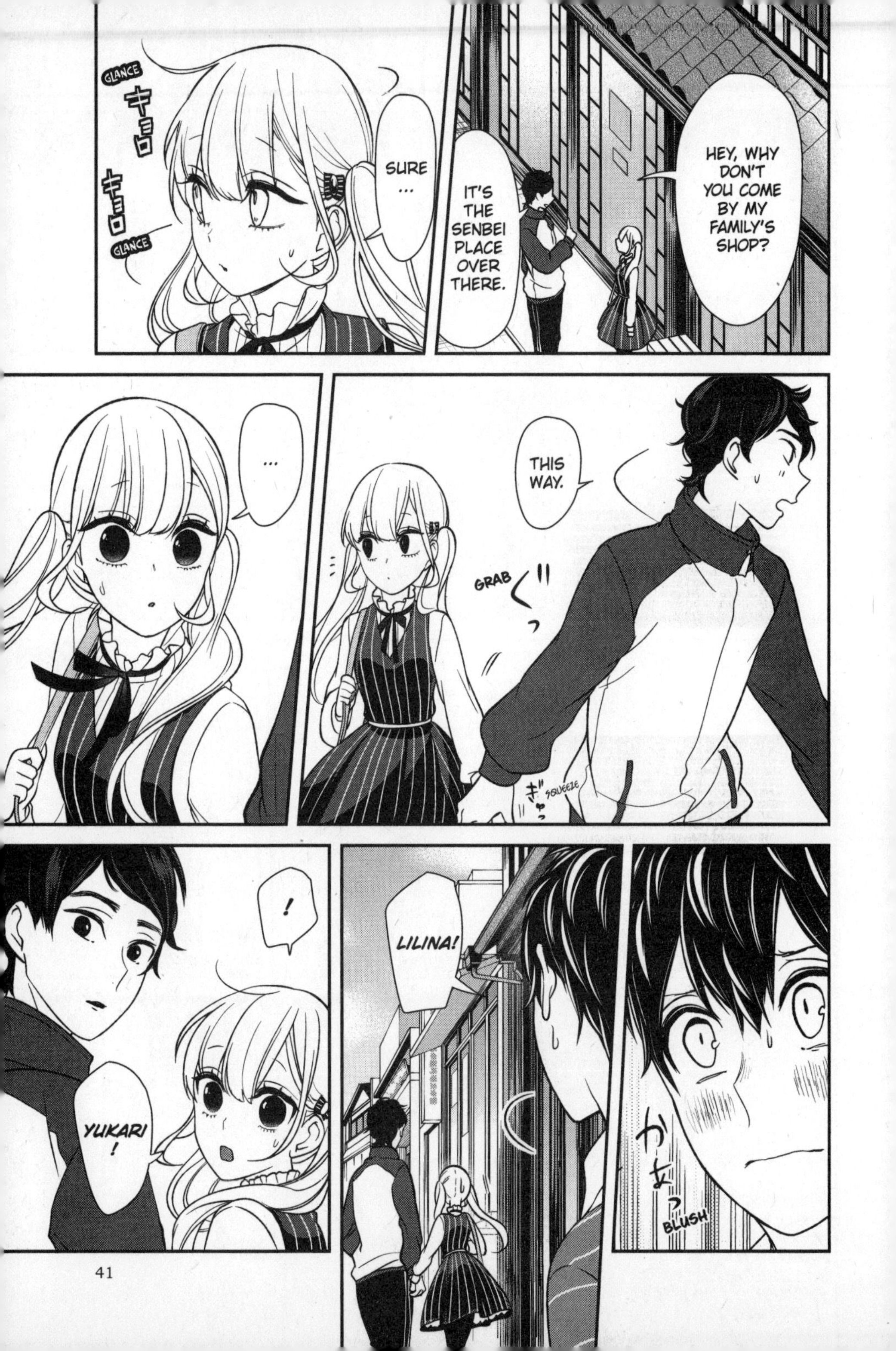
HEY, WHY DON'T YOU COME BY MY FAMILY'S SHOP?
IT'S THE SENBEI PLACE OVER THERE.
SURE ...
GLANCE キョロ
キョロ GLANCE
THIS WAY.
GRAB ぐっ
ぎゅっ SQUEEZE
...
かぁっ BLUSH
LILINA!
!
YUKARI!

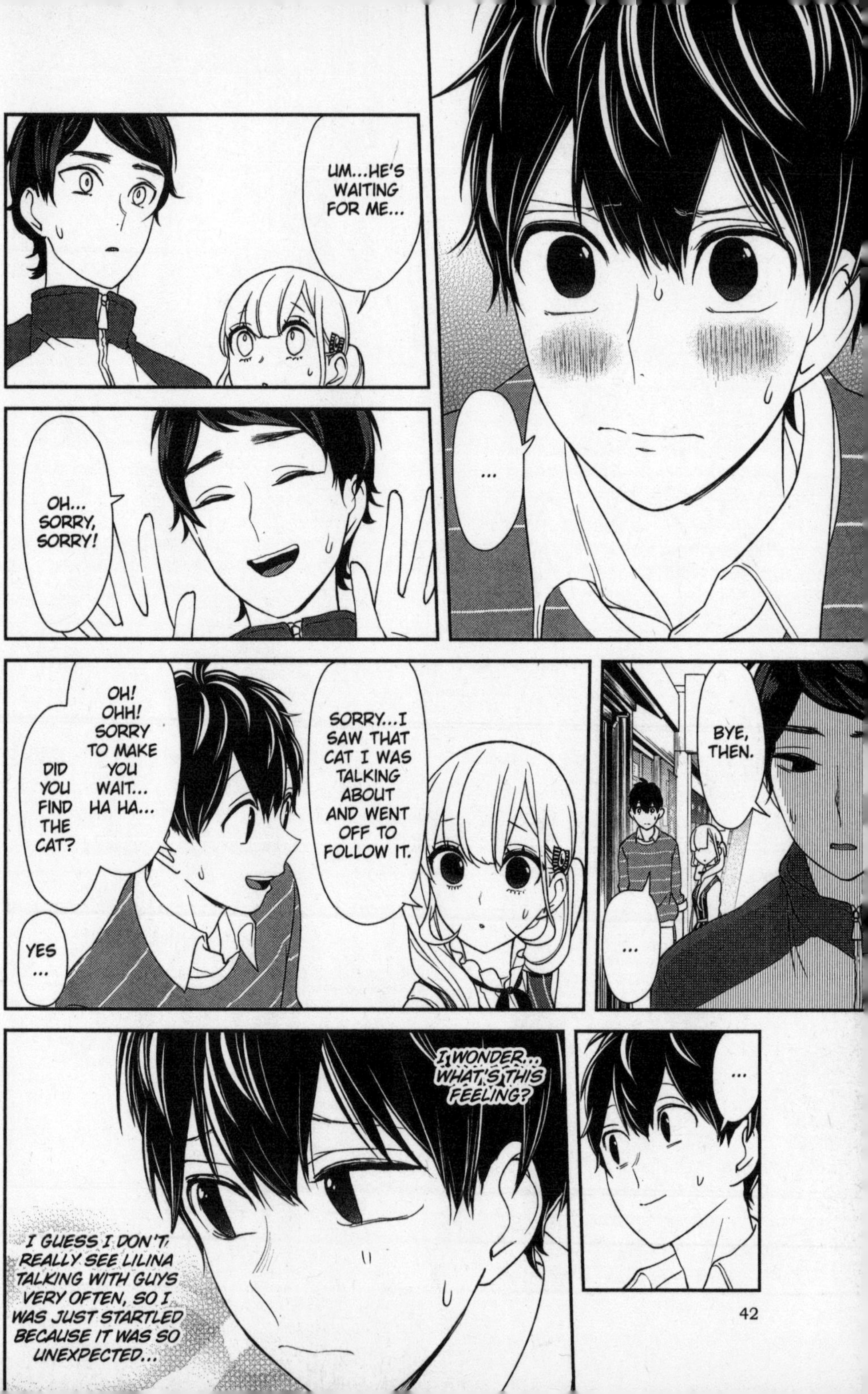
...
UM...HE'S WAITING FOR ME...
OH... SORRY, SORRY!
BYE, THEN.
...
SORRY...I SAW THAT CAT I WAS TALKING ABOUT AND WENT OFF TO FOLLOW IT.
OH! OHH! SORRY TO MAKE YOU WAIT... HA HA...
DID YOU FIND THE CAT?
YES ...
...
I WONDER... WHAT'S THIS FEELING?
I GUESS I DON'T REALLY SEE LILINA TALKING WITH GUYS VERY OFTEN, SO I WAS JUST STARTLED BECAUSE IT WAS SO UNEXPECTED...

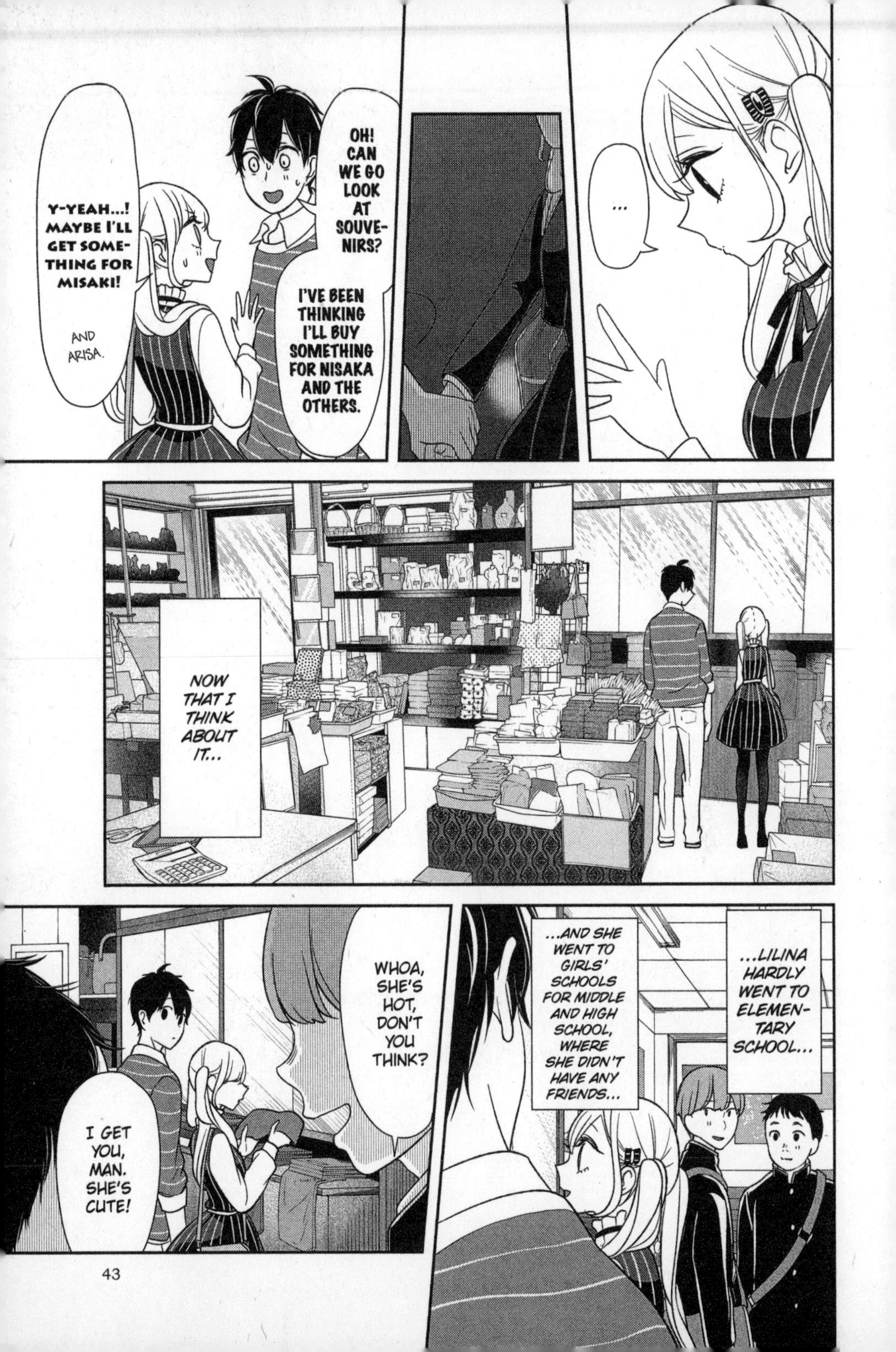
...
OH! CAN WE GO LOOK AT SOUVENIRS?
I'VE BEEN THINKING I'LL BUY SOMETHING FOR NISAKA AND THE OTHERS.
Y-YEAH...! MAYBE I'LL GET SOMETHING FOR MISAKI!
AND ARISA.
NOW THAT I THINK ABOUT IT...
...LILINA HARDLY WENT TO ELEMENTARY SCHOOL...
...AND SHE WENT TO GIRLS' SCHOOLS FOR MIDDLE AND HIGH SCHOOL, WHERE SHE DIDN'T HAVE ANY FRIENDS...
WHOA, SHE'S HOT, DON'T YOU THINK?
I GET YOU, MAN. SHE'S CUTE!

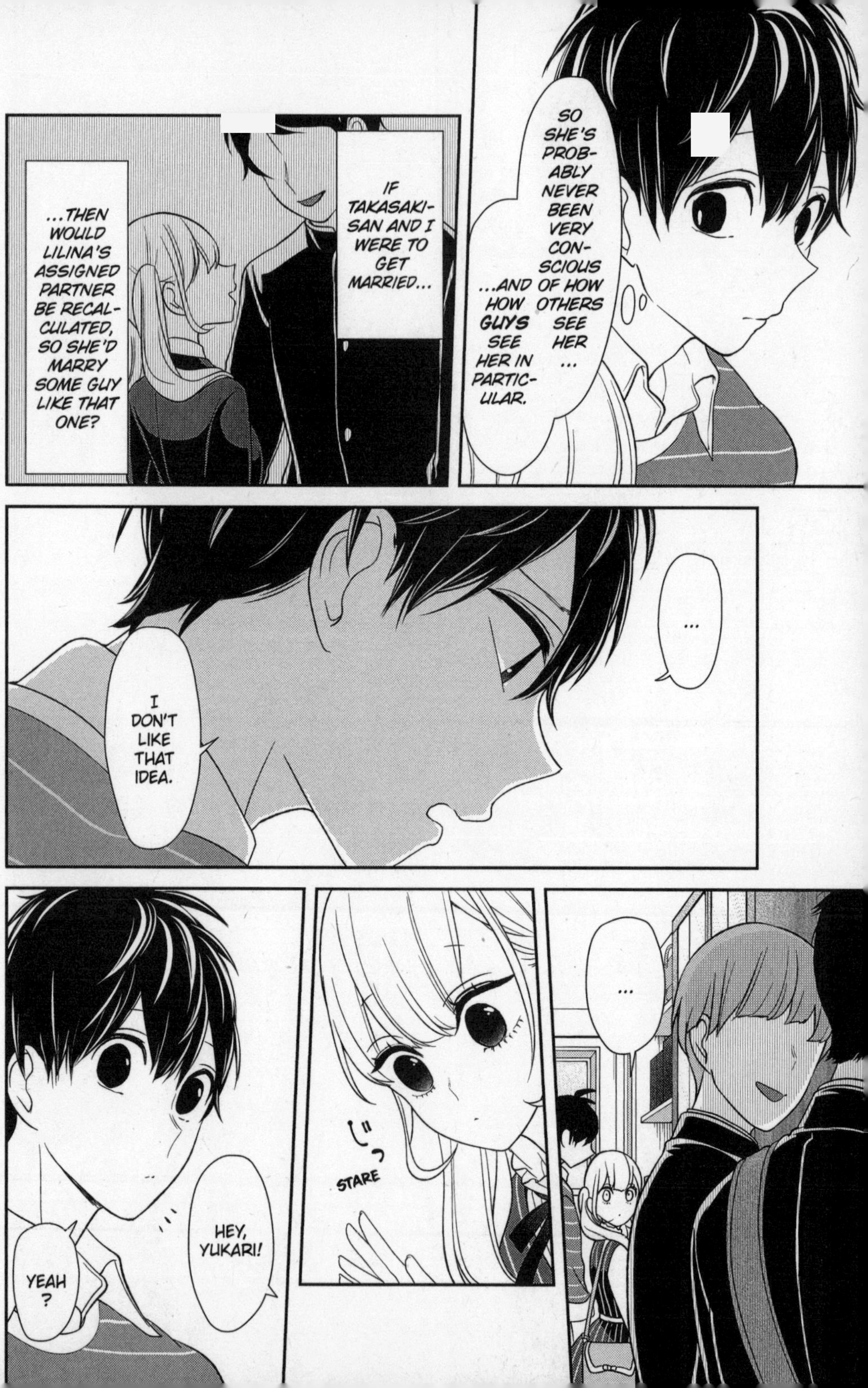
SO SHE'S PROBABLY NEVER BEEN VERY CONSCIOUS OF HOW OTHERS SEE HER...
...AND HOW GUYS SEE HER IN PARTICULAR.
IF TAKASAKI-SAN AND I WERE TO GET MARRIED...
...THEN WOULD LILINA'S ASSIGNED PARTNER BE RECALCULATED, SO SHE'D MARRY SOME GUY LIKE THAT ONE?
...
I DON'T LIKE THAT IDEA.
...
STARE
HEY, YUKARI!
YEAH?

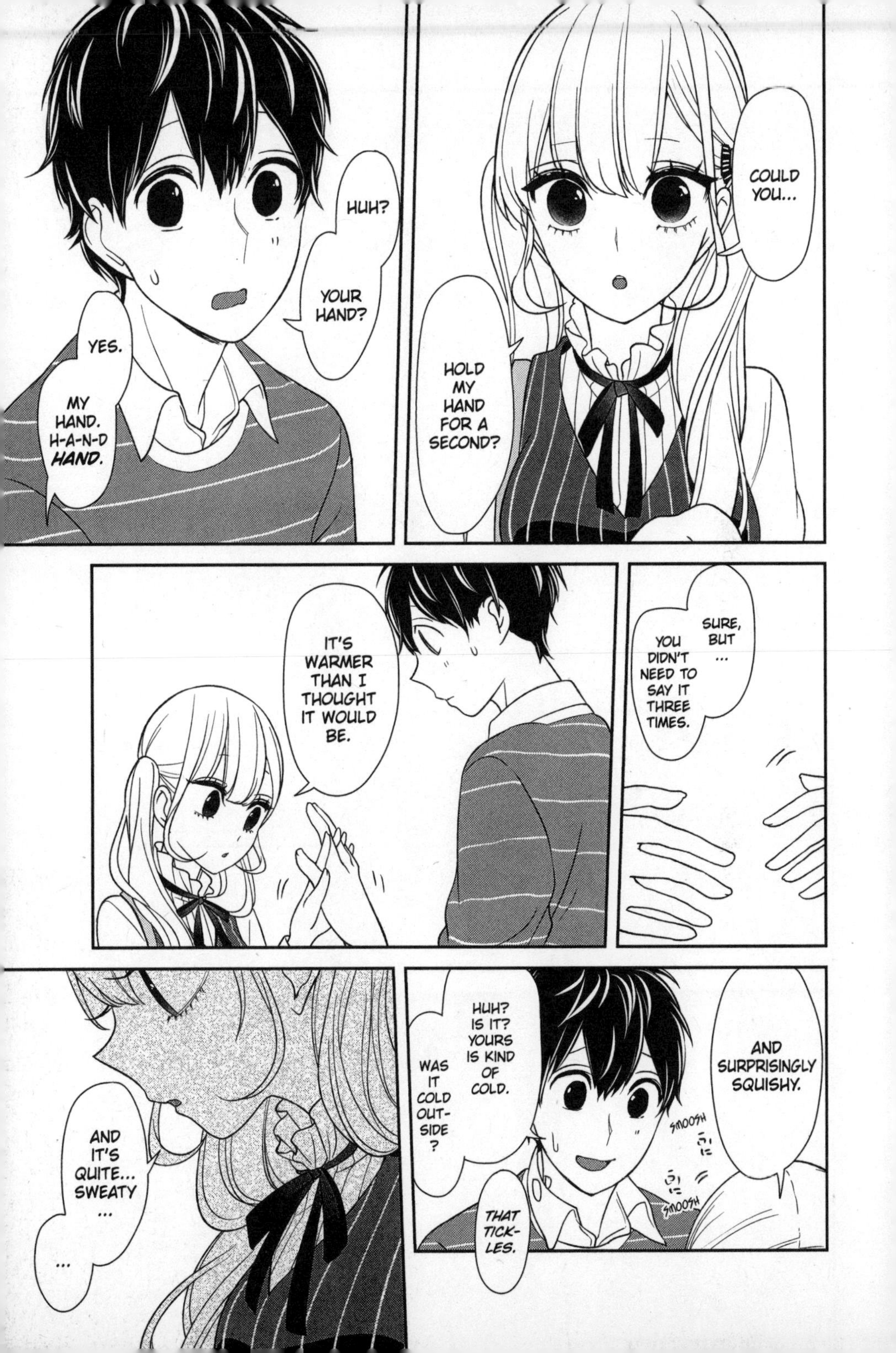
COULD YOU...
HOLD MY HAND FOR A SECOND?
HUH?
YOUR HAND?
YES.
MY HAND. H-A-N-D *HAND*.
SURE, BUT ...
YOU DIDN'T NEED TO SAY IT THREE TIMES.
IT'S WARMER THAN I THOUGHT IT WOULD BE.
AND SURPRISINGLY SQUISHY.
HUH? IS IT? YOURS IS KIND OF COLD.
WAS IT COLD OUT-SIDE?
SMOOSH
SMOOSH
THAT TICK-LES.
AND IT'S QUITE... SWEATY ...
...

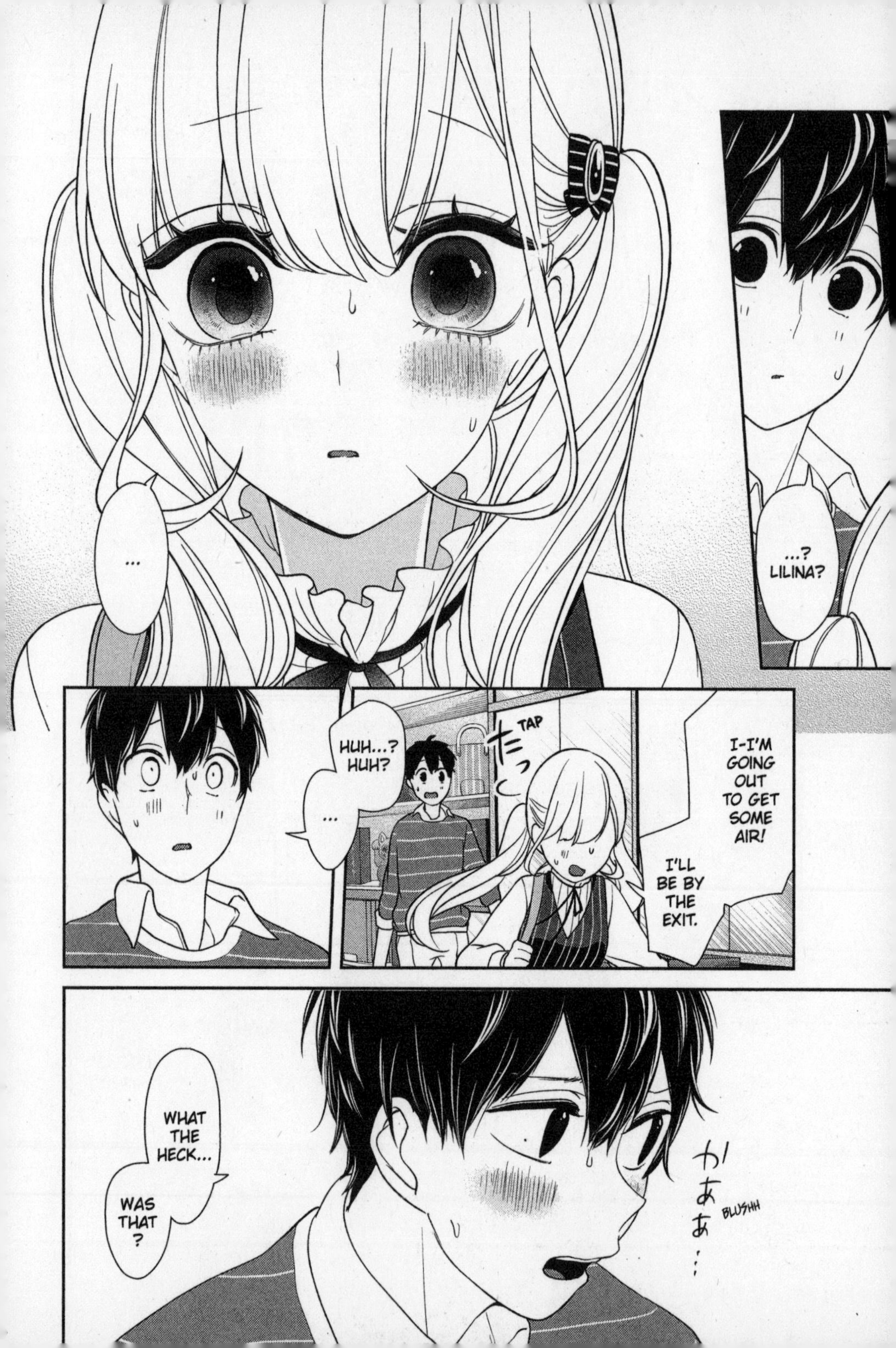
...? LILINA?
...
I-I'M GOING OUT TO GET SOME AIR!
I'LL BE BY THE EXIT.
TAP
HUH...? HUH?
...
WHAT THE HECK...
WAS THAT?
BLUSHH

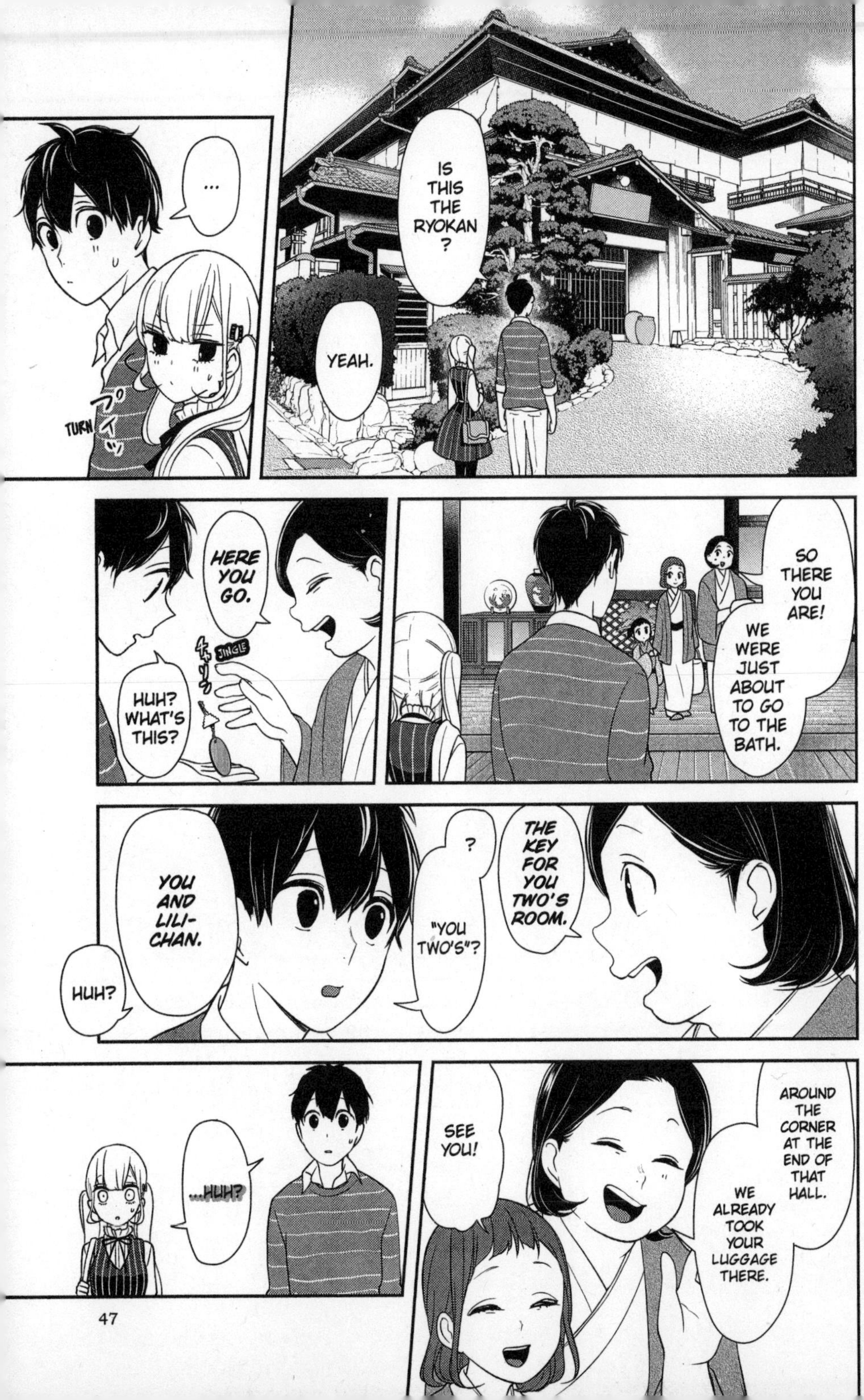
IS THIS THE RYOKAN?
YEAH.
...
TURN
SO THERE YOU ARE! WE WERE JUST ABOUT TO GO TO THE BATH.
HERE YOU GO.
JINGLE
HUH? WHAT'S THIS?
THE KEY FOR YOU TWO'S ROOM.
?
"YOU TWO'S"?
YOU AND LILI-CHAN.
HUH?
AROUND THE CORNER AT THE END OF THAT HALL.
WE ALREADY TOOK YOUR LUGGAGE THERE.
SEE YOU!
...HUH?

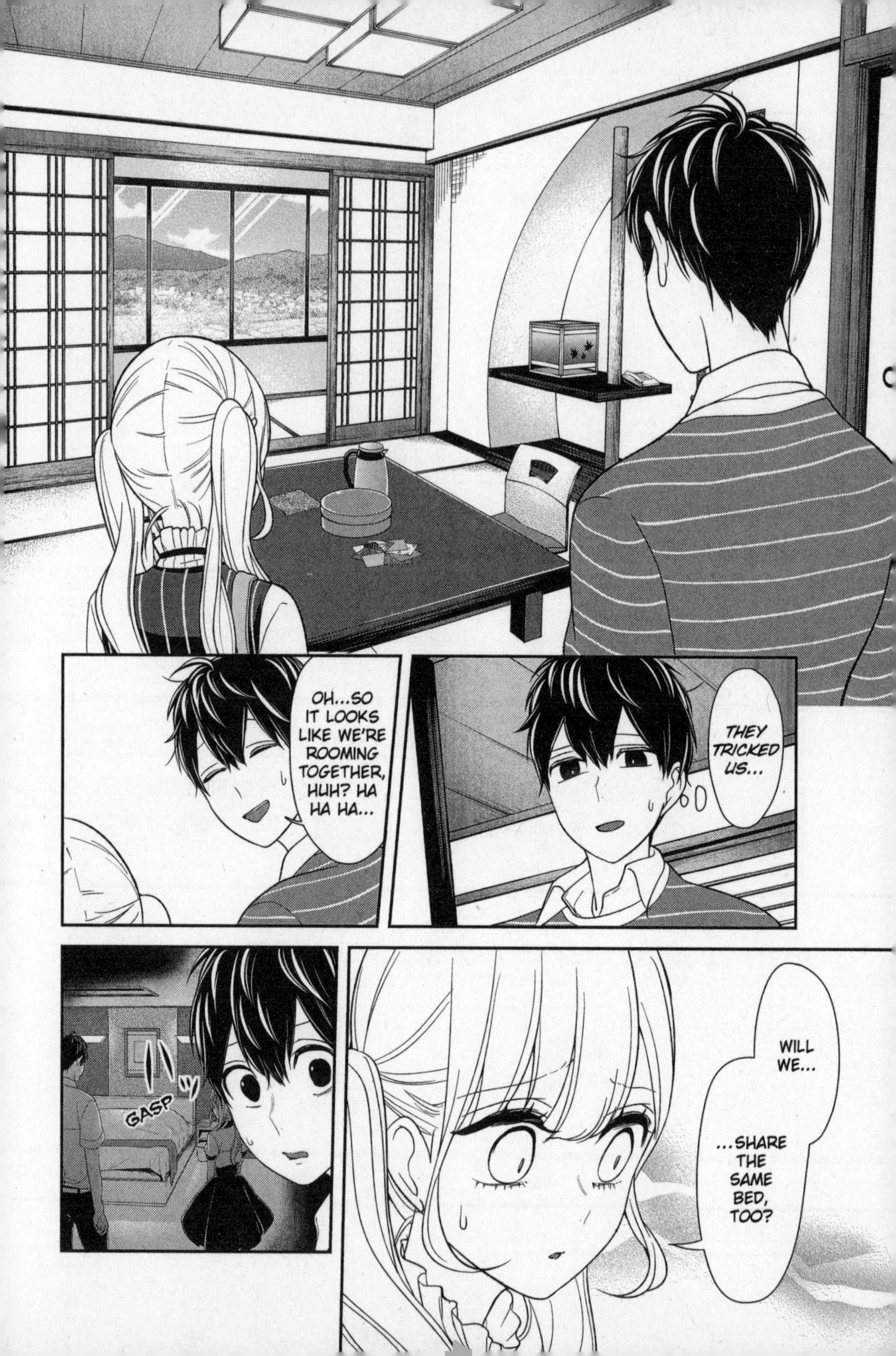
THEY TRICKED US...
OH...SO IT LOOKS LIKE WE'RE ROOMING TOGETHER, HUH? HA HA HA...
WILL WE...
...SHARE THE SAME BED, TOO?
GASP

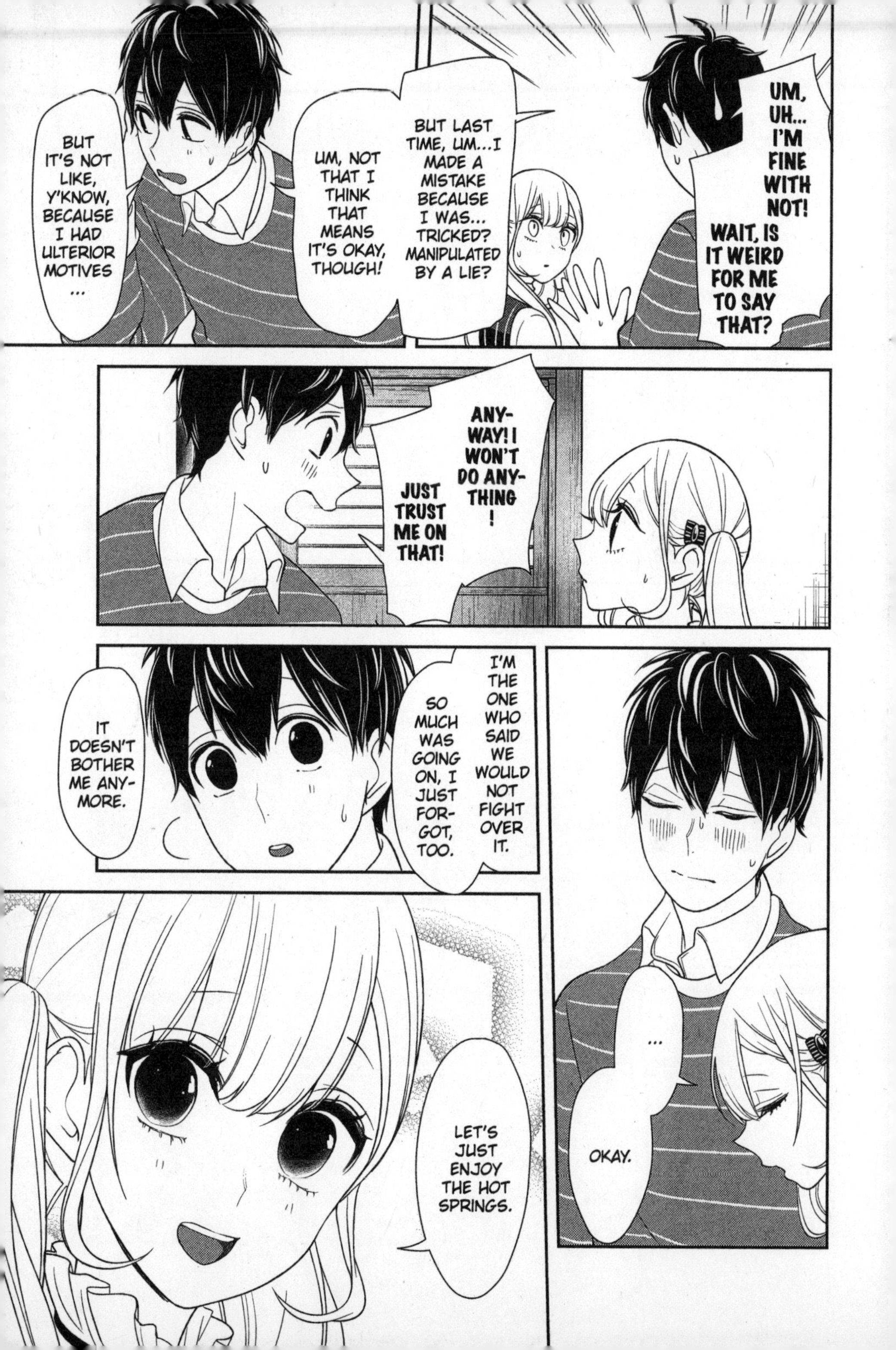
UM, UH... I'M FINE WITH NOT!
WAIT, IS IT WEIRD FOR ME TO SAY THAT?
BUT LAST TIME, UM...I MADE A MISTAKE BECAUSE I WAS... TRICKED? MANIPULATED BY A LIE?
UM, NOT THAT I THINK THAT MEANS IT'S OKAY, THOUGH!
BUT IT'S NOT LIKE, Y'KNOW, BECAUSE I HAD ULTERIOR MOTIVES ...
ANY-WAY! I WON'T DO ANY-THING!
JUST TRUST ME ON THAT!
...
OKAY.
I'M THE ONE WHO SAID WE WOULD NOT FIGHT OVER IT.
SO MUCH WAS GOING ON, I JUST FOR-GOT, TOO.
IT DOESN'T BOTHER ME ANY-MORE.
LET'S JUST ENJOY THE HOT SPRINGS.

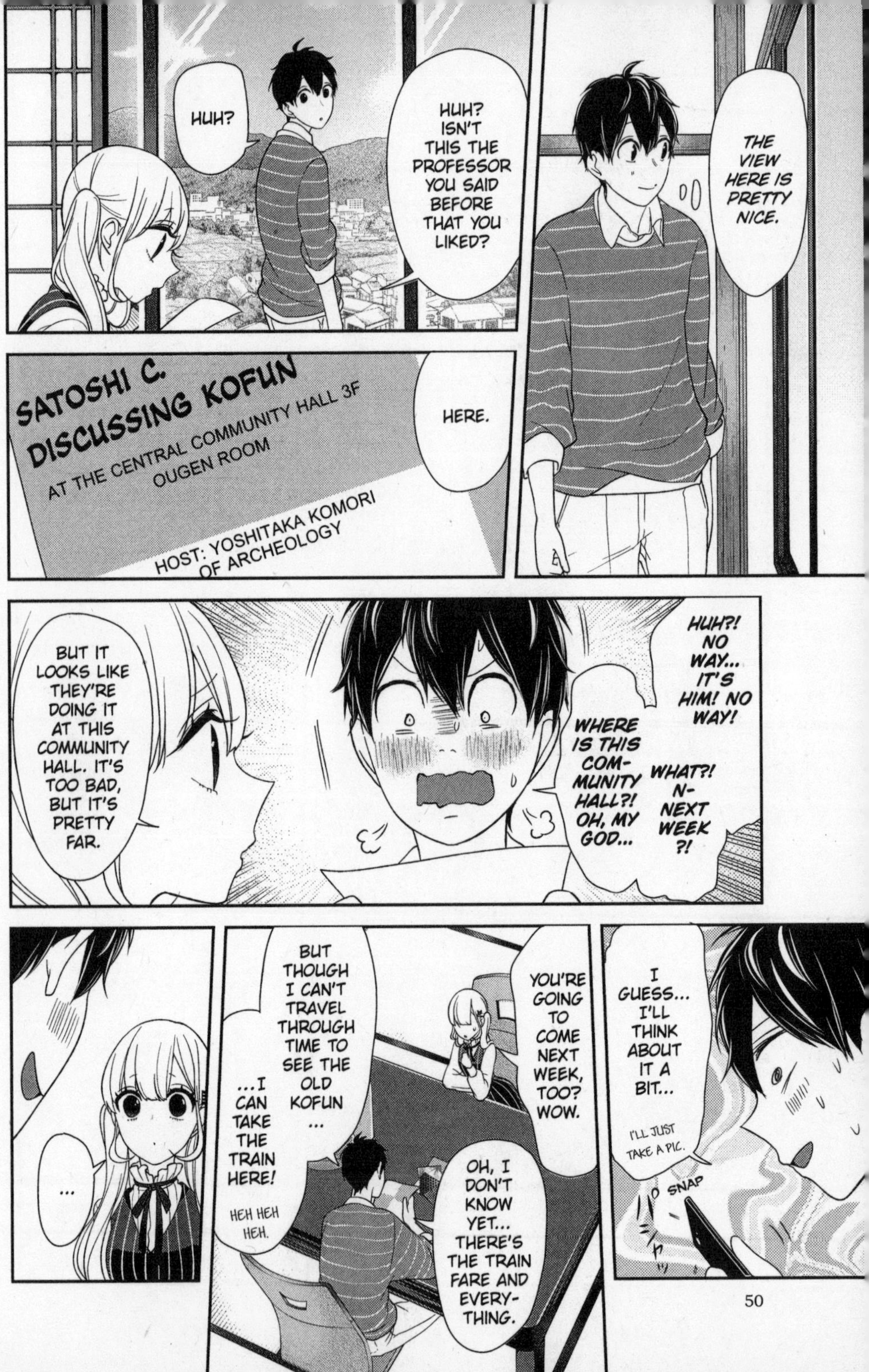
THE VIEW HERE IS PRETTY NICE.
HUH? ISN'T THIS THE PROFESSOR YOU SAID BEFORE THAT YOU LIKED?
HUH?
HERE.
SATOSHI C. DISCUSSING KOFUN
AT THE CENTRAL COMMUNITY HALL 3F OUGEN ROOM
HOST: YOSHITAKA KOMORI OF ARCHEOLOGY
HUH?! NO WAY... IT'S HIM! NO WAY!
WHAT?! N-NEXT WEEK ?!
WHERE IS THIS COM-MUNITY HALL?! OH, MY GOD...
BUT IT LOOKS LIKE THEY'RE DOING IT AT THIS COMMUNITY HALL. IT'S TOO BAD, BUT IT'S PRETTY FAR.
I GUESS... I'LL THINK ABOUT IT A BIT...
I'LL JUST TAKE A PIC.
SNAP
YOU'RE GOING TO COME NEXT WEEK, TOO? WOW.
OH, I DON'T KNOW YET... THERE'S THE TRAIN FARE AND EVERY-THING.
BUT THOUGH I CAN'T TRAVEL THROUGH TIME TO SEE THE OLD KOFUN ...
...I CAN TAKE THE TRAIN HERE!
HEH HEH HEH.
...

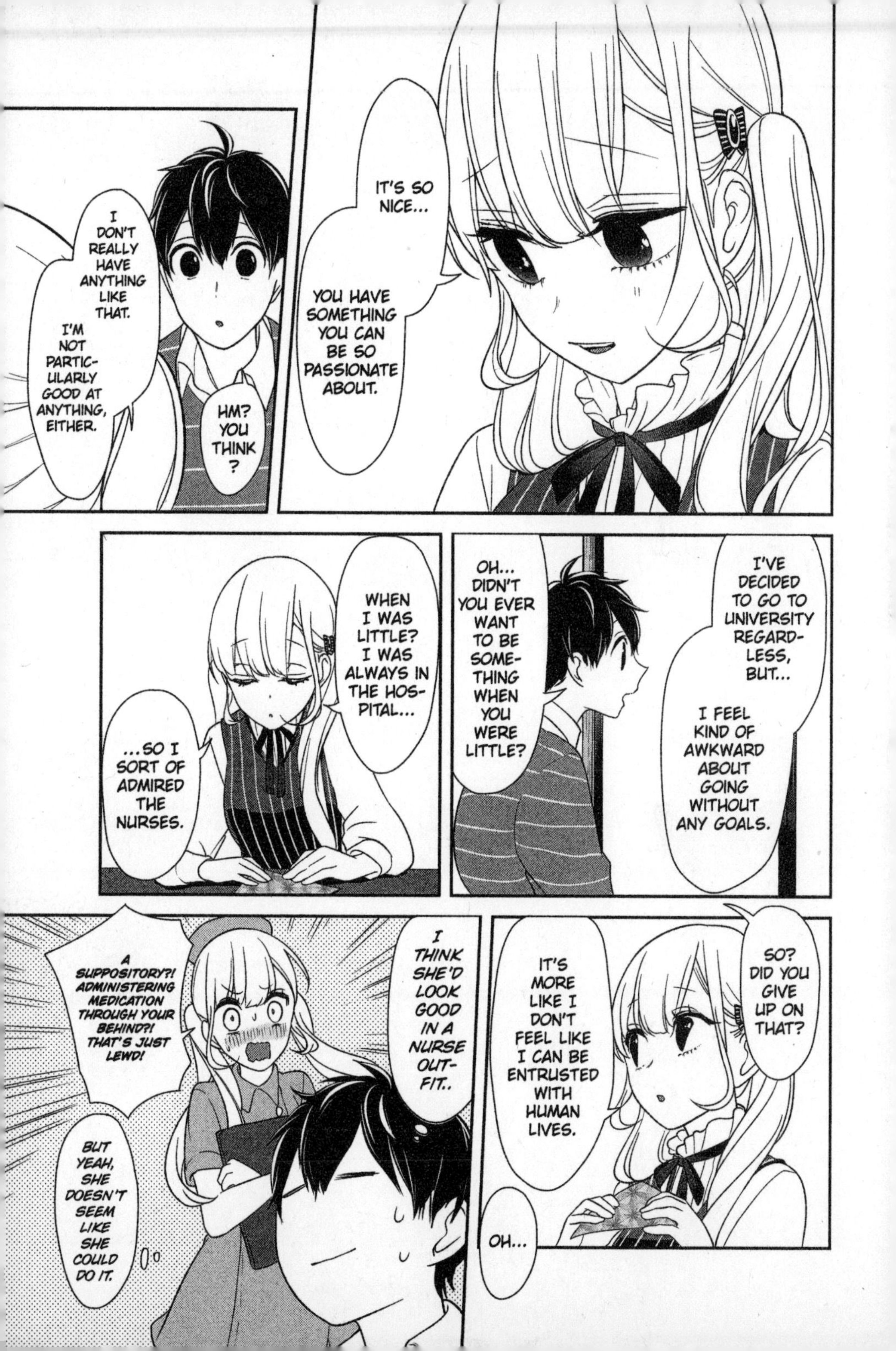
IT'S SO NICE...
YOU HAVE SOMETHING YOU CAN BE SO PASSIONATE ABOUT.
HM? YOU THINK?
I DON'T REALLY HAVE ANYTHING LIKE THAT.
I'M NOT PARTICULARLY GOOD AT ANYTHING, EITHER.
I'VE DECIDED TO GO TO UNIVERSITY REGARDLESS, BUT...
I FEEL KIND OF AWKWARD ABOUT GOING WITHOUT ANY GOALS.
OH... DIDN'T YOU EVER WANT TO BE SOMETHING WHEN YOU WERE LITTLE?
WHEN I WAS LITTLE? I WAS ALWAYS IN THE HOSPITAL...
...SO I SORT OF ADMIRED THE NURSES.
SO? DID YOU GIVE UP ON THAT?
IT'S MORE LIKE I DON'T FEEL LIKE I CAN BE ENTRUSTED WITH HUMAN LIVES.
OH...
I THINK SHE'D LOOK GOOD IN A NURSE OUTFIT..
A SUPPOSITORY?! ADMINISTERING MEDICATION THROUGH YOUR BEHIND?! THAT'S JUST LEWD!
BUT YEAH, SHE DOESN'T SEEM LIKE SHE COULD DO IT.

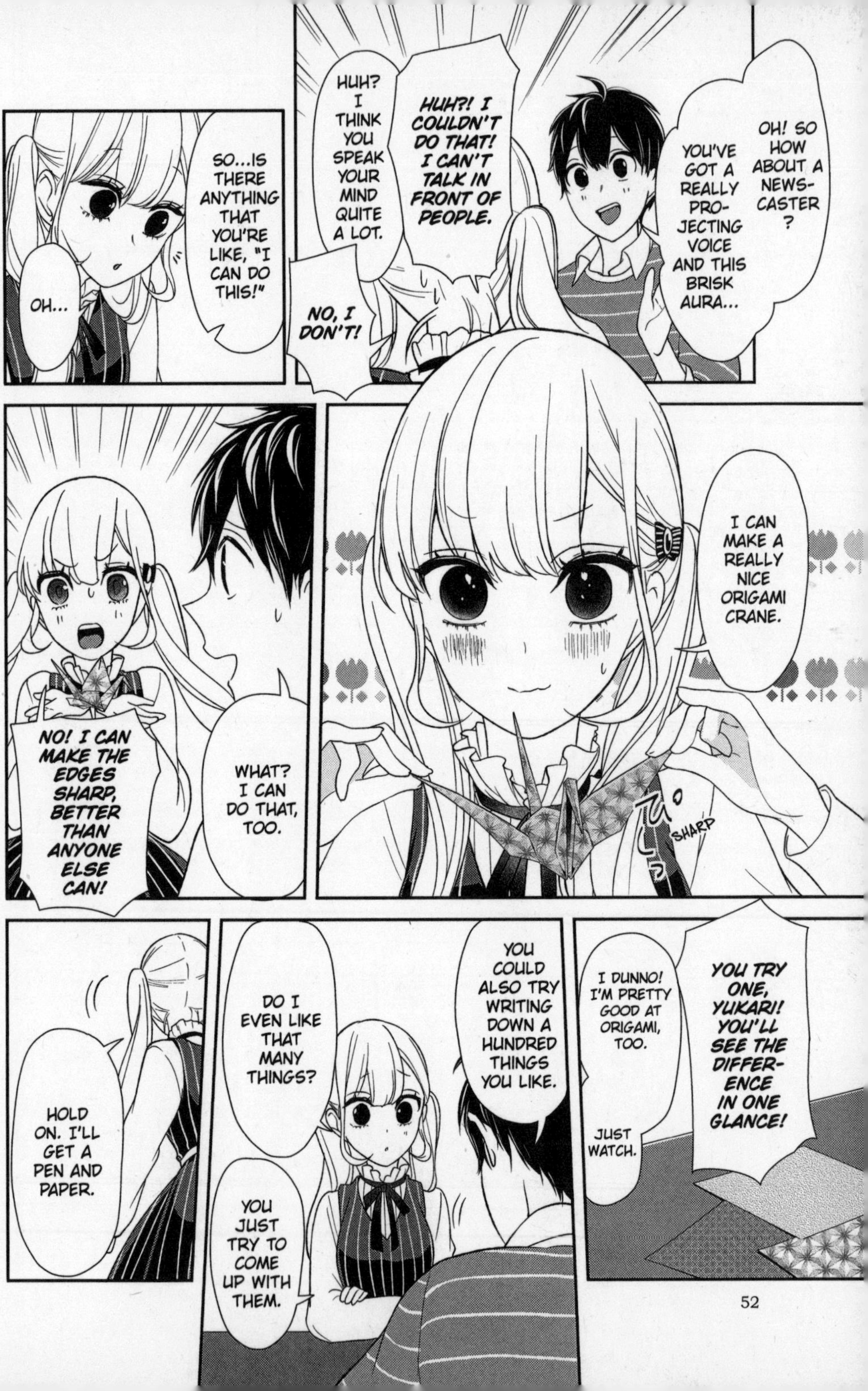
OH! SO HOW ABOUT A NEWS-CASTER?
YOU'VE GOT A REALLY PRO-JECTING VOICE AND THIS BRISK AURA...
HUH?! I COULDN'T DO THAT! I CAN'T TALK IN FRONT OF PEOPLE.
HUH? I THINK YOU SPEAK YOUR MIND QUITE A LOT.
NO, I DON'T!
SO...IS THERE ANYTHING THAT YOU'RE LIKE, "I CAN DO THIS!"
OH...
I CAN MAKE A REALLY NICE ORIGAMI CRANE.
SHARP
WHAT? I CAN DO THAT, TOO.
NO! I CAN MAKE THE EDGES SHARP, BETTER THAN ANYONE ELSE CAN!
YOU TRY ONE, YUKARI! YOU'LL SEE THE DIFFER-ENCE IN ONE GLANCE!
I DUNNO! I'M PRETTY GOOD AT ORIGAMI, TOO.
JUST WATCH.
YOU COULD ALSO TRY WRITING DOWN A HUNDRED THINGS YOU LIKE.
DO I EVEN LIKE THAT MANY THINGS?
YOU JUST TRY TO COME UP WITH THEM.
HOLD ON. I'LL GET A PEN AND PAPER.

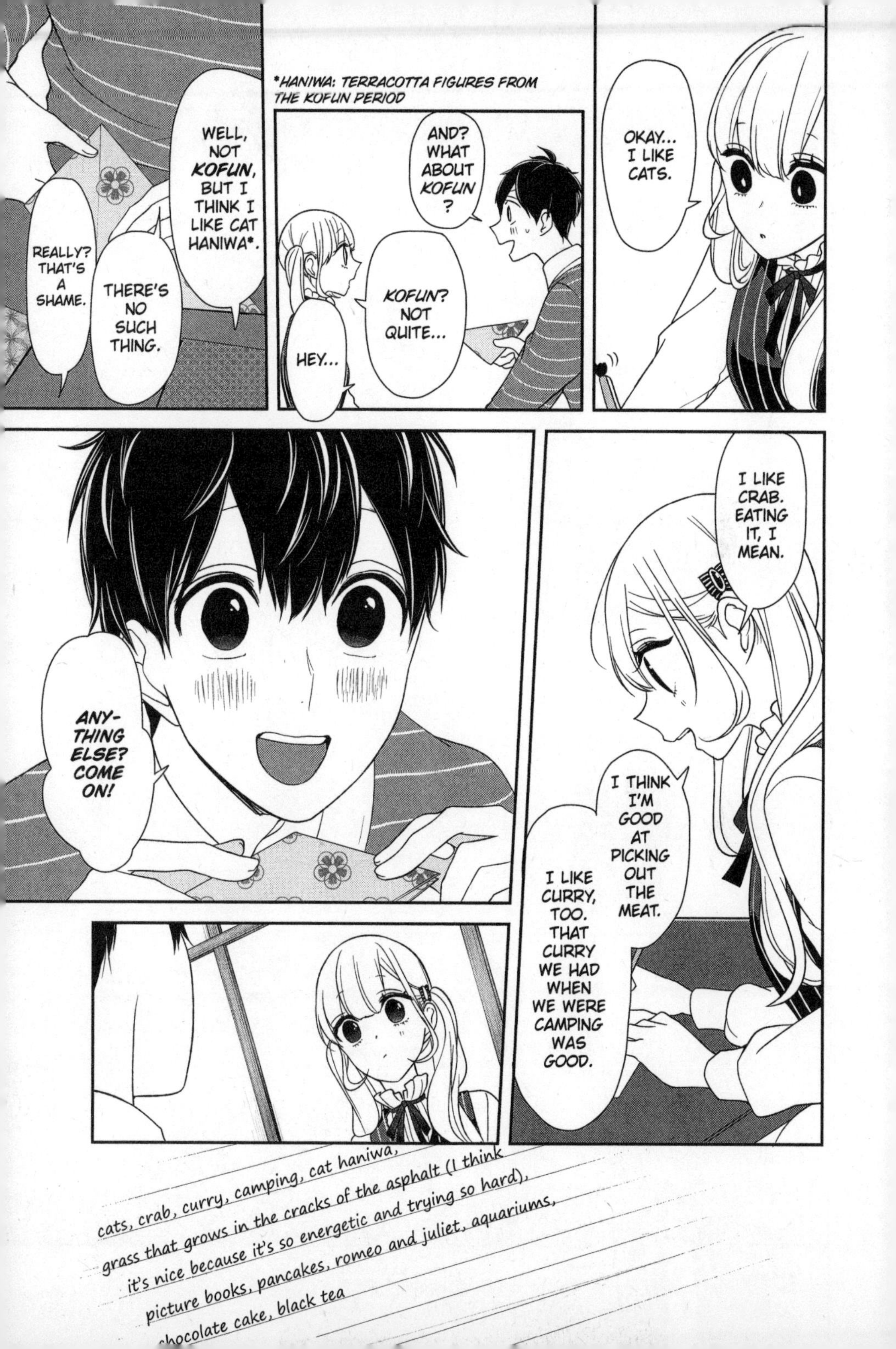
OKAY... I LIKE CATS.
*HANIWA: TERRACOTTA FIGURES FROM THE KOFUN PERIOD
AND? WHAT ABOUT KOFUN?
KOFUN? NOT QUITE...
HEY...
WELL, NOT KOFUN, BUT I THINK I LIKE CAT HANIWA*.
THERE'S NO SUCH THING.
REALLY? THAT'S A SHAME.
I LIKE CRAB. EATING IT, I MEAN.
I THINK I'M GOOD AT PICKING OUT THE MEAT.
I LIKE CURRY, TOO. THAT CURRY WE HAD WHEN WE WERE CAMPING WAS GOOD.
ANYTHING ELSE? COME ON!
cats, crab, curry, camping, cat haniwa,
grass that grows in the cracks of the asphalt (I think
it's nice because it's so energetic and trying so hard),
picture books, pancakes, romeo and juliet, aquariums,
chocolate cake, black tea

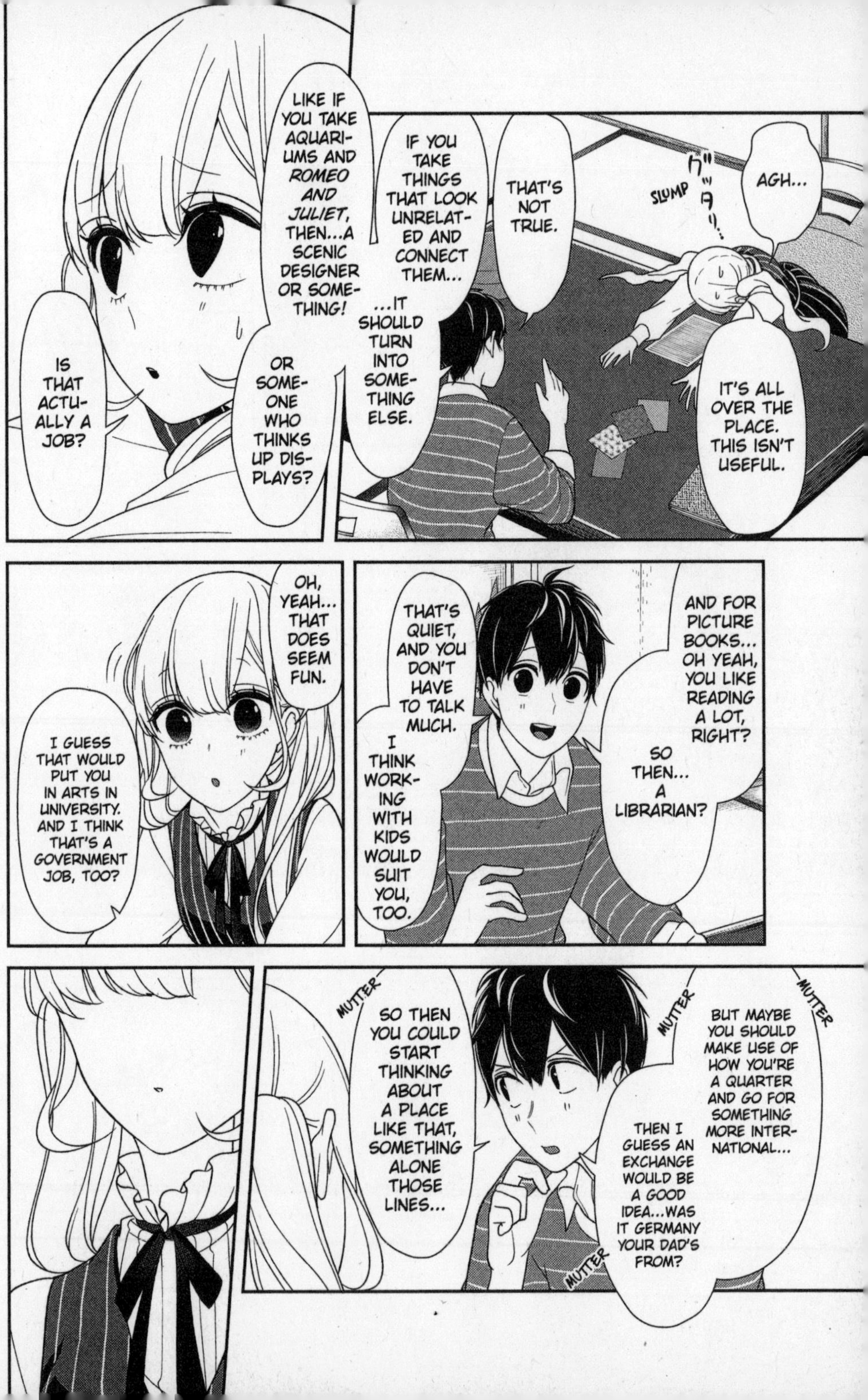
AGH...
SLUMP
IT'S ALL OVER THE PLACE. THIS ISN'T USEFUL.
THAT'S NOT TRUE.
IF YOU TAKE THINGS THAT LOOK UNRELATED AND CONNECT THEM...
...IT SHOULD TURN INTO SOMETHING ELSE.
LIKE IF YOU TAKE AQUARIUMS AND *ROMEO AND JULIET*, THEN...A SCENIC DESIGNER OR SOMETHING!
OR SOMEONE WHO THINKS UP DISPLAYS?
IS THAT ACTUALLY A JOB?
AND FOR PICTURE BOOKS... OH YEAH, YOU LIKE READING A LOT, RIGHT?
SO THEN... A LIBRARIAN?
THAT'S QUIET, AND YOU DON'T HAVE TO TALK MUCH.
I THINK WORKING WITH KIDS WOULD SUIT YOU, TOO.
OH, YEAH... THAT DOES SEEM FUN.
I GUESS THAT WOULD PUT YOU IN ARTS IN UNIVERSITY. AND I THINK THAT'S A GOVERNMENT JOB, TOO?
MUTTER
BUT MAYBE YOU SHOULD MAKE USE OF HOW YOU'RE A QUARTER AND GO FOR SOMETHING MORE INTERNATIONAL...
THEN I GUESS AN EXCHANGE WOULD BE A GOOD IDEA...WAS IT GERMANY YOUR DAD'S FROM?
MUTTER
SO THEN YOU COULD START THINKING ABOUT A PLACE LIKE THAT, SOMETHING ALONE THOSE LINES...
MUTTER
MUTTER

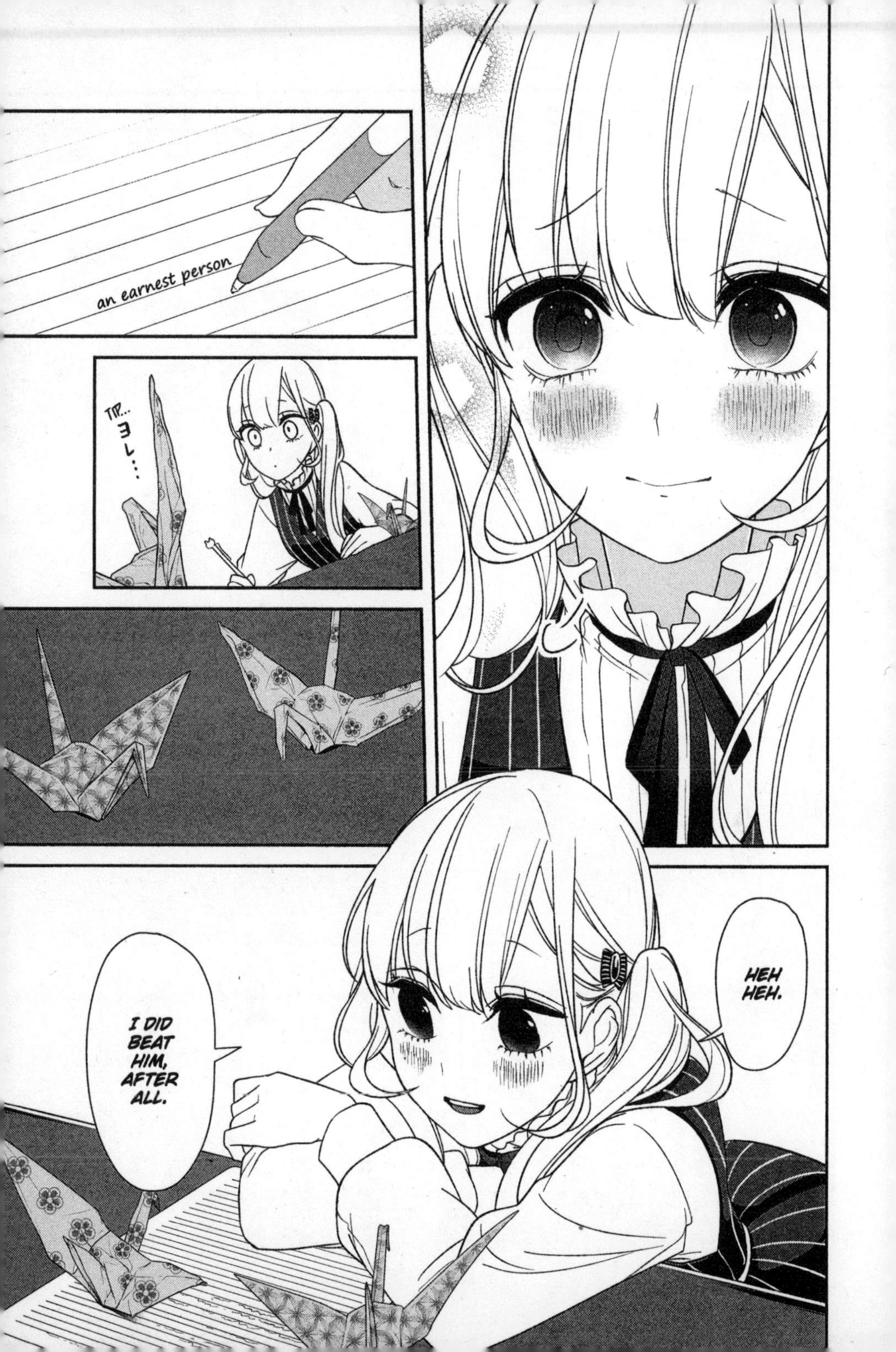
an earnest person
TIP...
ヨレ・・・
HEH HEH.
I DID BEAT HIM, AFTER ALL.

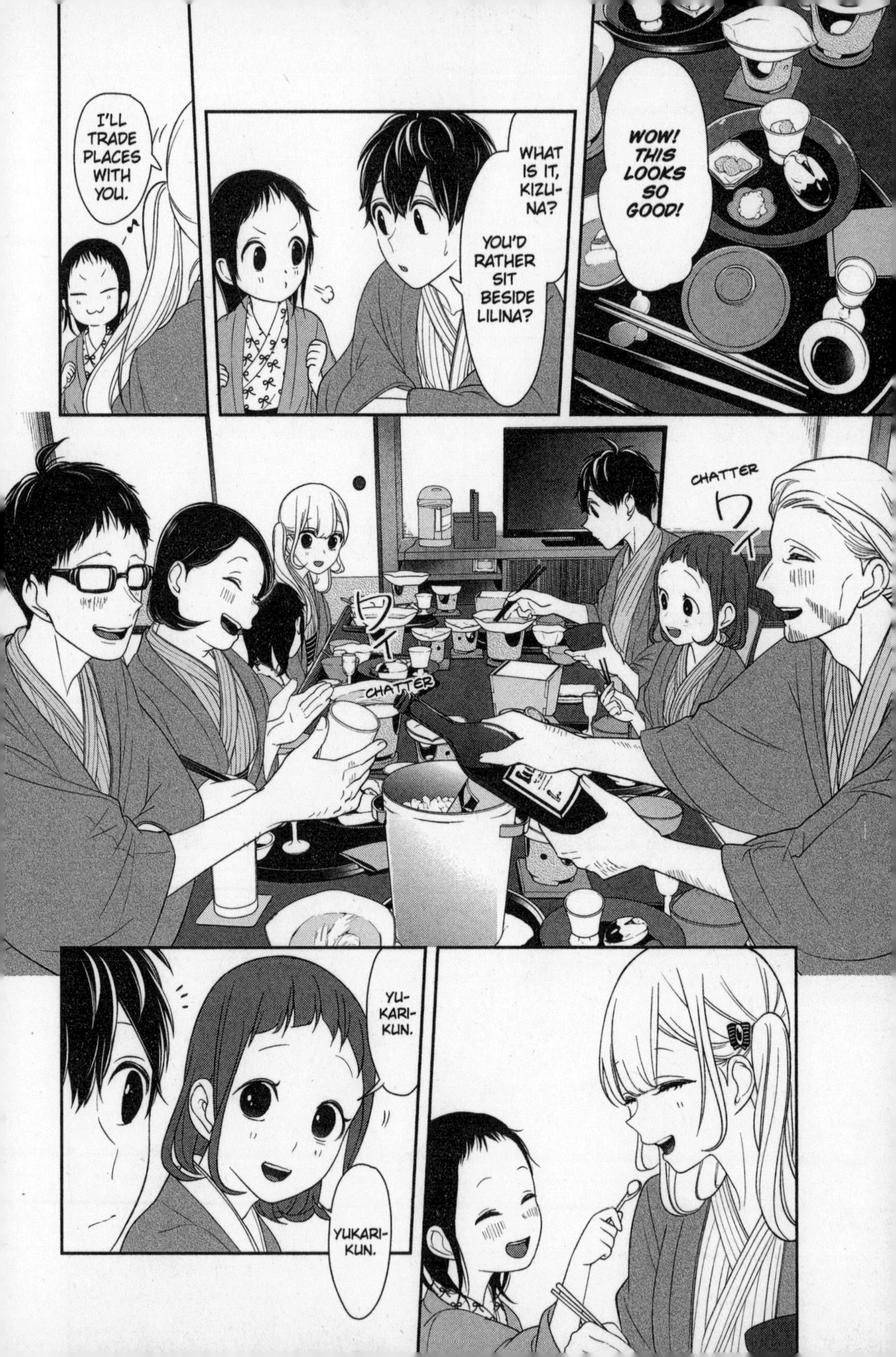
WOW! THIS LOOKS SO GOOD!
WHAT IS IT, KIZUNA?
YOU'D RATHER SIT BESIDE LILINA?
I'LL TRADE PLACES WITH YOU.
CHATTER
ワイ
ワイ
CHATTER
YU-KARI-KUN.
YUKARI-KUN.

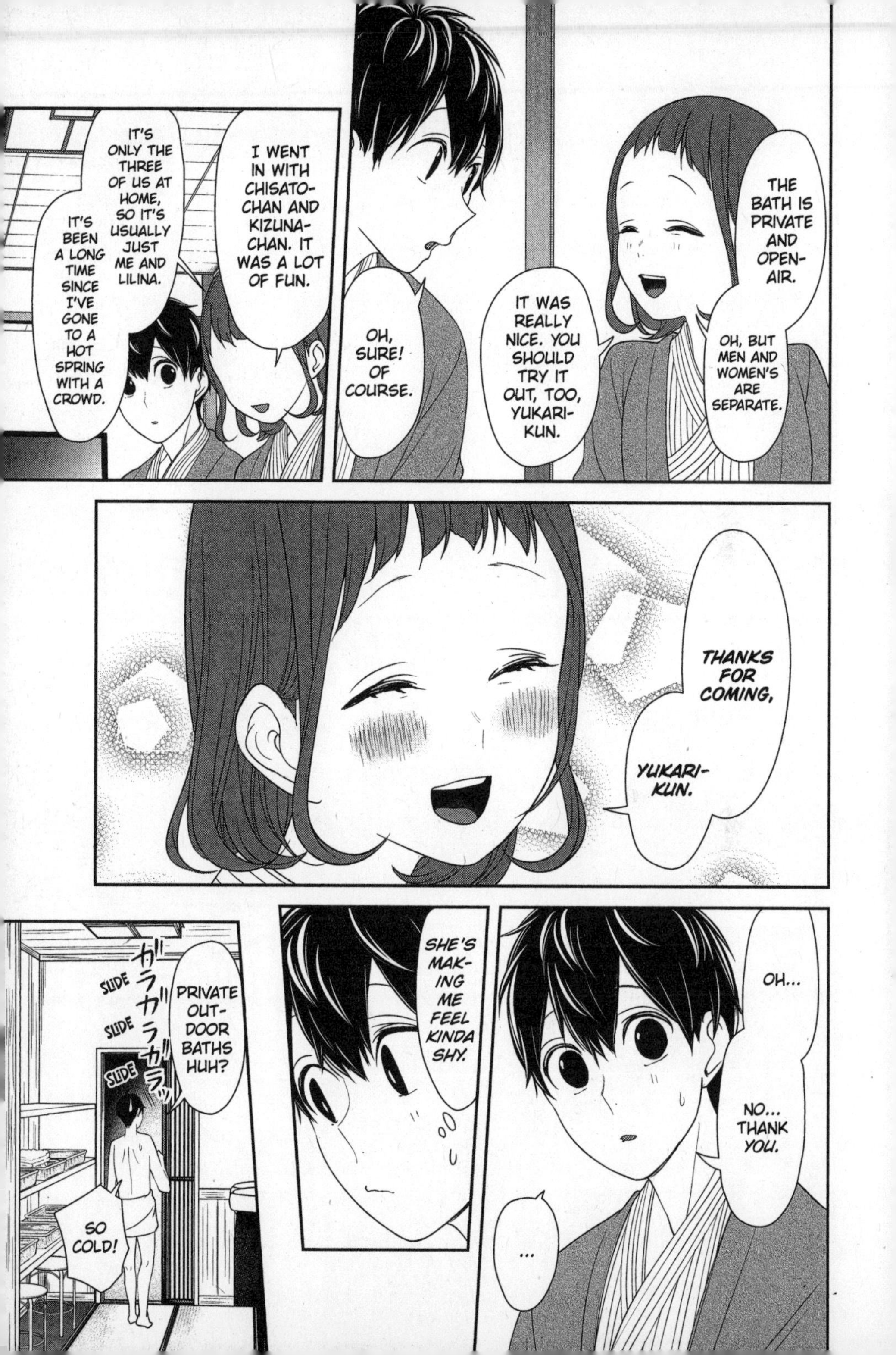
THE BATH IS PRIVATE AND OPEN-AIR.
OH, BUT MEN AND WOMEN'S ARE SEPARATE.
IT WAS REALLY NICE. YOU SHOULD TRY IT OUT, TOO, YUKARI-KUN.
OH, SURE! OF COURSE.
I WENT IN WITH CHISATO-CHAN AND KIZUNA-CHAN. IT WAS A LOT OF FUN.
IT'S ONLY THE THREE OF US AT HOME, SO IT'S USUALLY JUST ME AND LILINA.
IT'S BEEN A LONG TIME SINCE I'VE GONE TO A HOT SPRING WITH A CROWD.
THANKS FOR COMING,
YUKARI-KUN.
OH...
NO... THANK YOU.
...
SHE'S MAK-ING ME FEEL KINDA SHY.
ガラガラガラッ
SLIDE
SLIDE
SLIDE
PRIVATE OUT-DOOR BATHS HUH?
SO COLD!

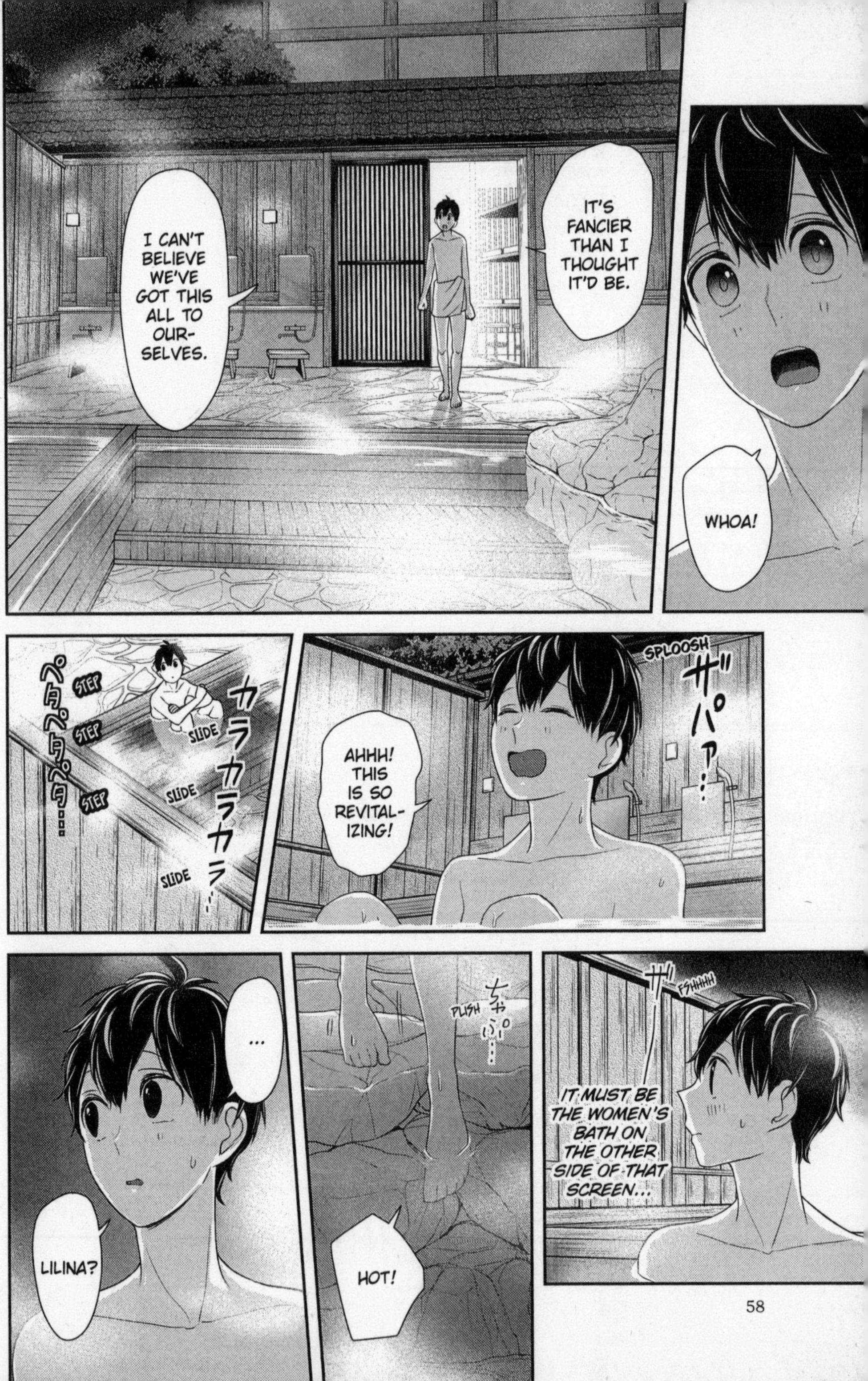
WHOA!
IT'S FANCIER THAN I THOUGHT IT'D BE.
I CAN'T BELIEVE WE'VE GOT THIS ALL TO OUR-SELVES.
SPLOOSH
ザパァ‥
AHHH! THIS IS SO REVITAL-IZING!
カラカラカラ‥
SLIDE
SLIDE
SLIDE
ペタペタペタ‥‥
STEP
STEP
STEP
ザ
FSHHHH
IT MUST BE THE WOMEN'S BATH ON THE OTHER SIDE OF THAT SCREEN...
ちゃぷ‥
PLISH
HOT!
...
LILINA?

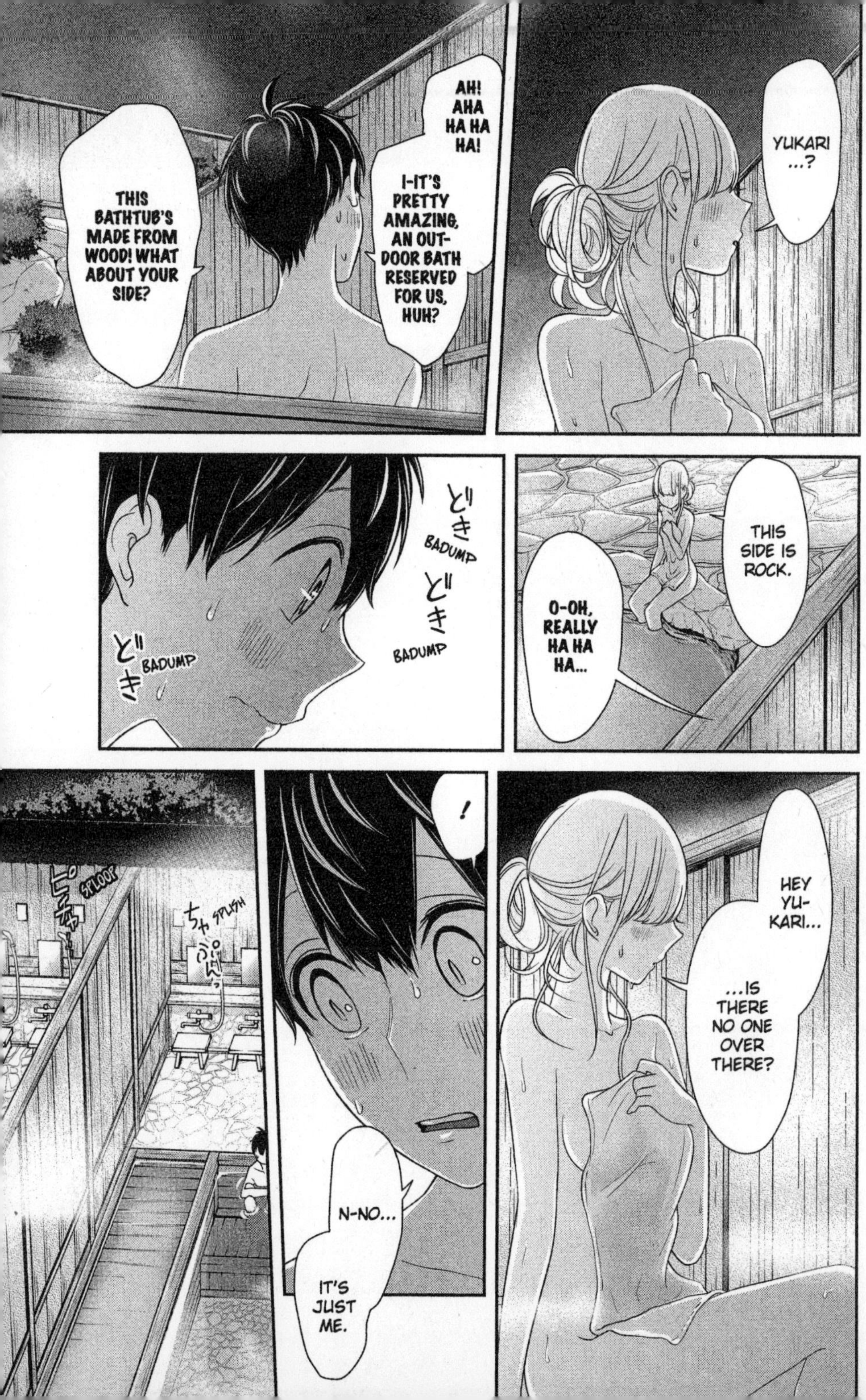
YUKARI ...?
AH! AHA HA HA HA!
I-IT'S PRETTY AMAZING, AN OUT-DOOR BATH RESERVED FOR US, HUH?
THIS BATHTUB'S MADE FROM WOOD! WHAT ABOUT YOUR SIDE?
THIS SIDE IS ROCK.
O-OH, REALLY HA HA HA...
どき BADUMP
どき BADUMP
どき BADUMP
HEY YU-KARI...
...IS THERE NO ONE OVER THERE?
!
N-NO...
IT'S JUST ME.
SPLOOP
SPLISH

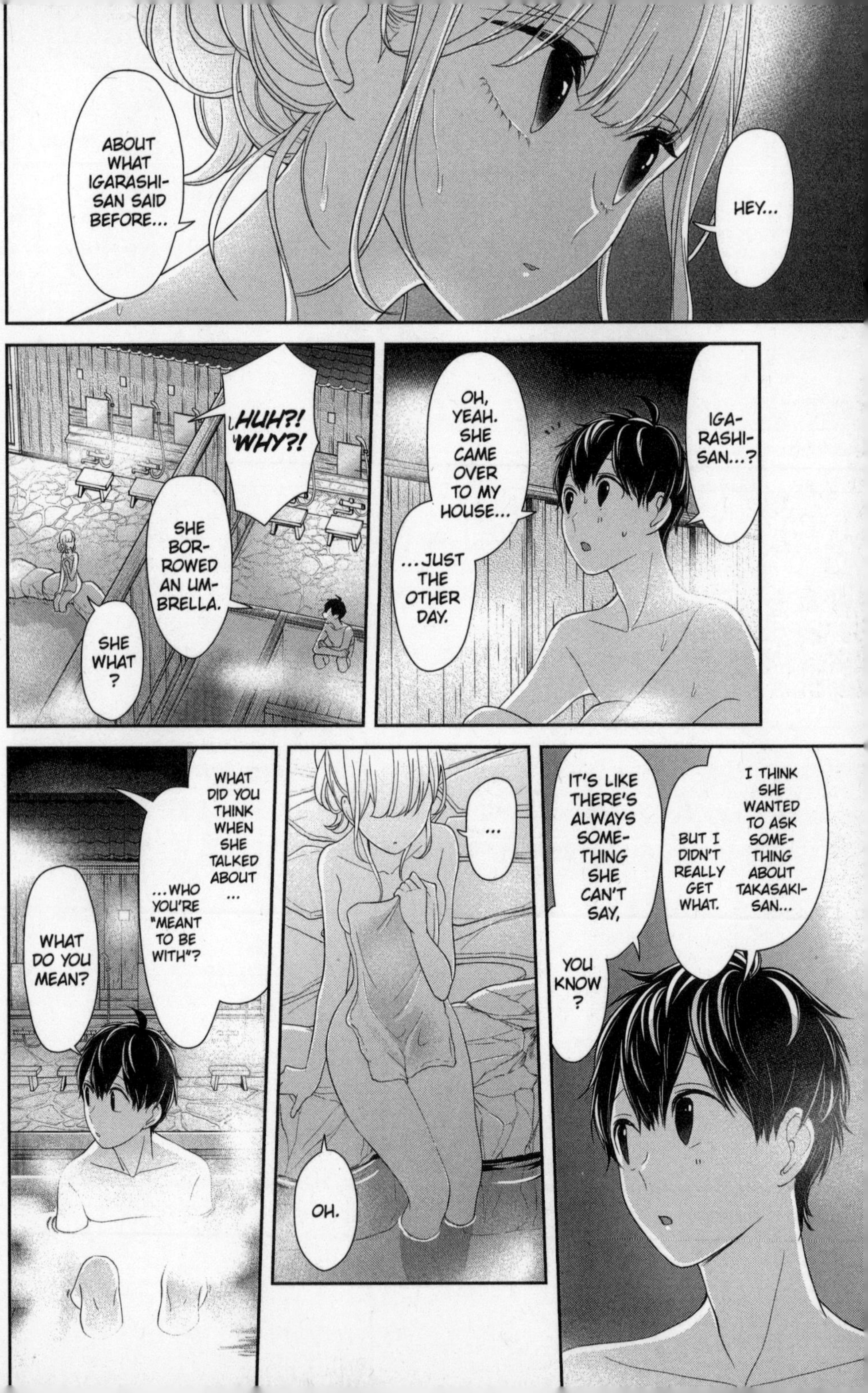
HEY...
ABOUT WHAT IGARASHI-SAN SAID BEFORE...
IGA-RASHI-SAN...?
OH, YEAH. SHE CAME OVER TO MY HOUSE...
...JUST THE OTHER DAY.
HUH?! WHY?!
SHE BOR-ROWED AN UM-BRELLA.
SHE WHAT?
I THINK SHE WANTED TO ASK SOME-THING ABOUT TAKASAKI-SAN...
BUT I DIDN'T REALLY GET WHAT.
IT'S LIKE THERE'S ALWAYS SOME-THING SHE CAN'T SAY,
YOU KNOW?
...
OH.
WHAT DID YOU THINK WHEN SHE TALKED ABOUT...
...WHO YOU'RE "MEANT TO BE WITH"?
WHAT DO YOU MEAN?

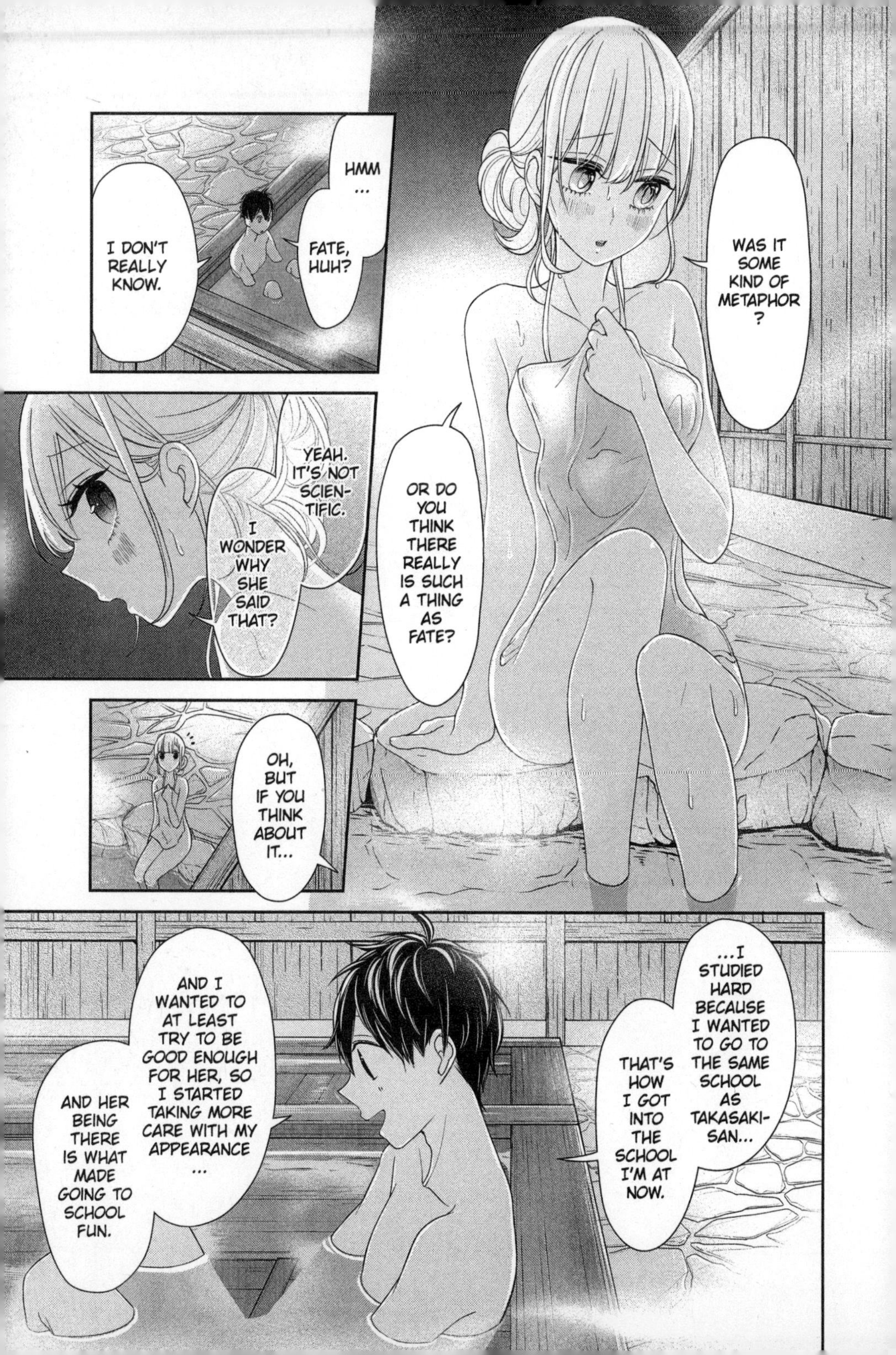
WAS IT SOME KIND OF METAPHOR?
OR DO YOU THINK THERE REALLY IS SUCH A THING AS FATE?
HMM... FATE, HUH?
I DON'T REALLY KNOW.
YEAH. IT'S NOT SCIEN-TIFIC.
I WONDER WHY SHE SAID THAT?
OH, BUT IF YOU THINK ABOUT IT...
...I STUDIED HARD BECAUSE I WANTED TO GO TO THE SAME SCHOOL AS TAKASAKI-SAN...
THAT'S HOW I GOT INTO THE SCHOOL I'M AT NOW.
AND I WANTED TO AT LEAST TRY TO BE GOOD ENOUGH FOR HER, SO I STARTED TAKING MORE CARE WITH MY APPEARANCE...
AND HER BEING THERE IS WHAT MADE GOING TO SCHOOL FUN.

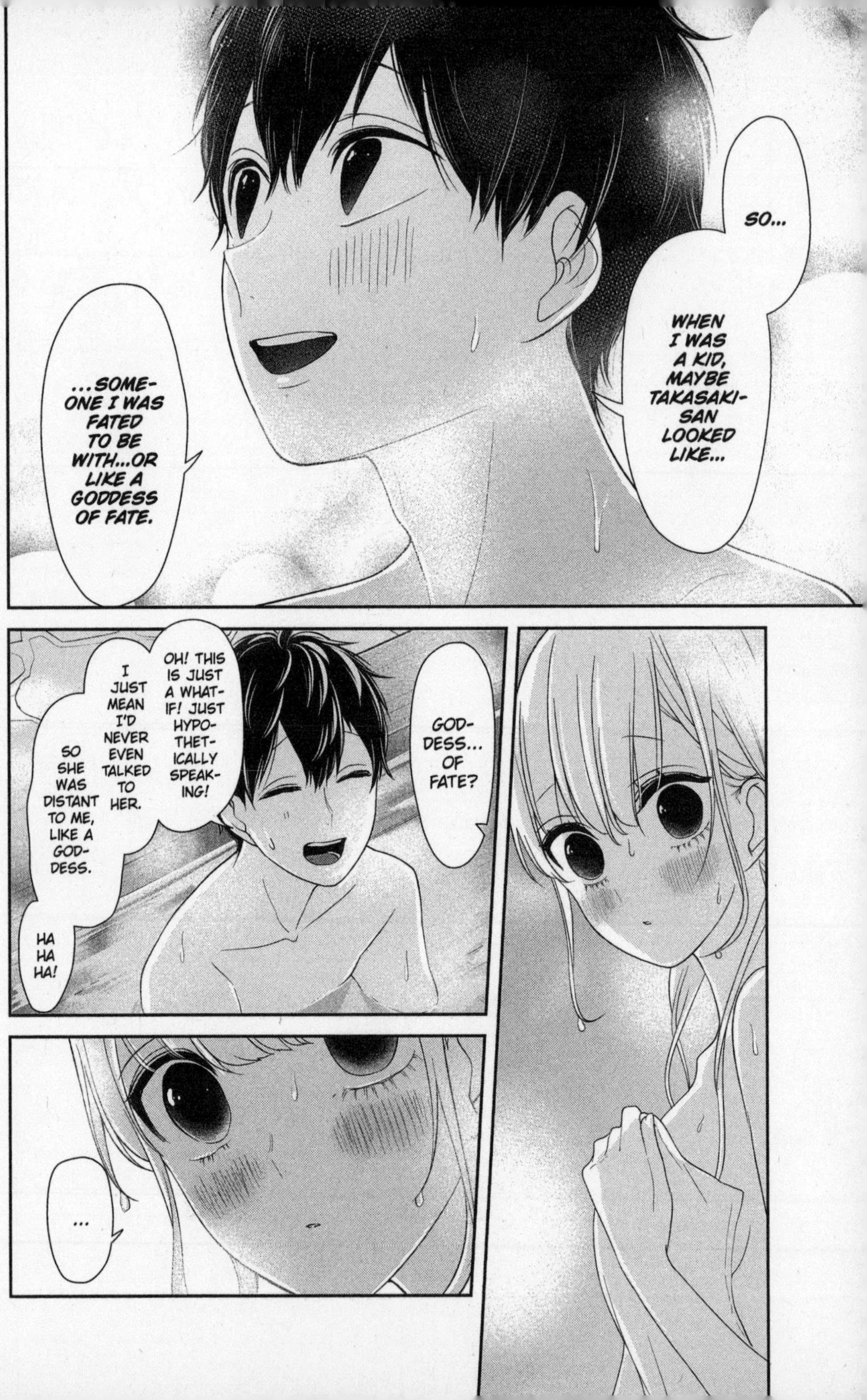
SO...
WHEN I WAS A KID, MAYBE TAKASAKI-SAN LOOKED LIKE...
...SOME-ONE I WAS FATED TO BE WITH...OR LIKE A GODDESS OF FATE.
GOD-DESS... OF FATE?
OH! THIS IS JUST A WHAT-IF! JUST HYPO-THET-ICALLY SPEAK-ING!
I JUST MEAN I'D NEVER EVEN TALKED TO HER.
SO SHE WAS DISTANT TO ME, LIKE A GOD-DESS.
HA HA HA!
...

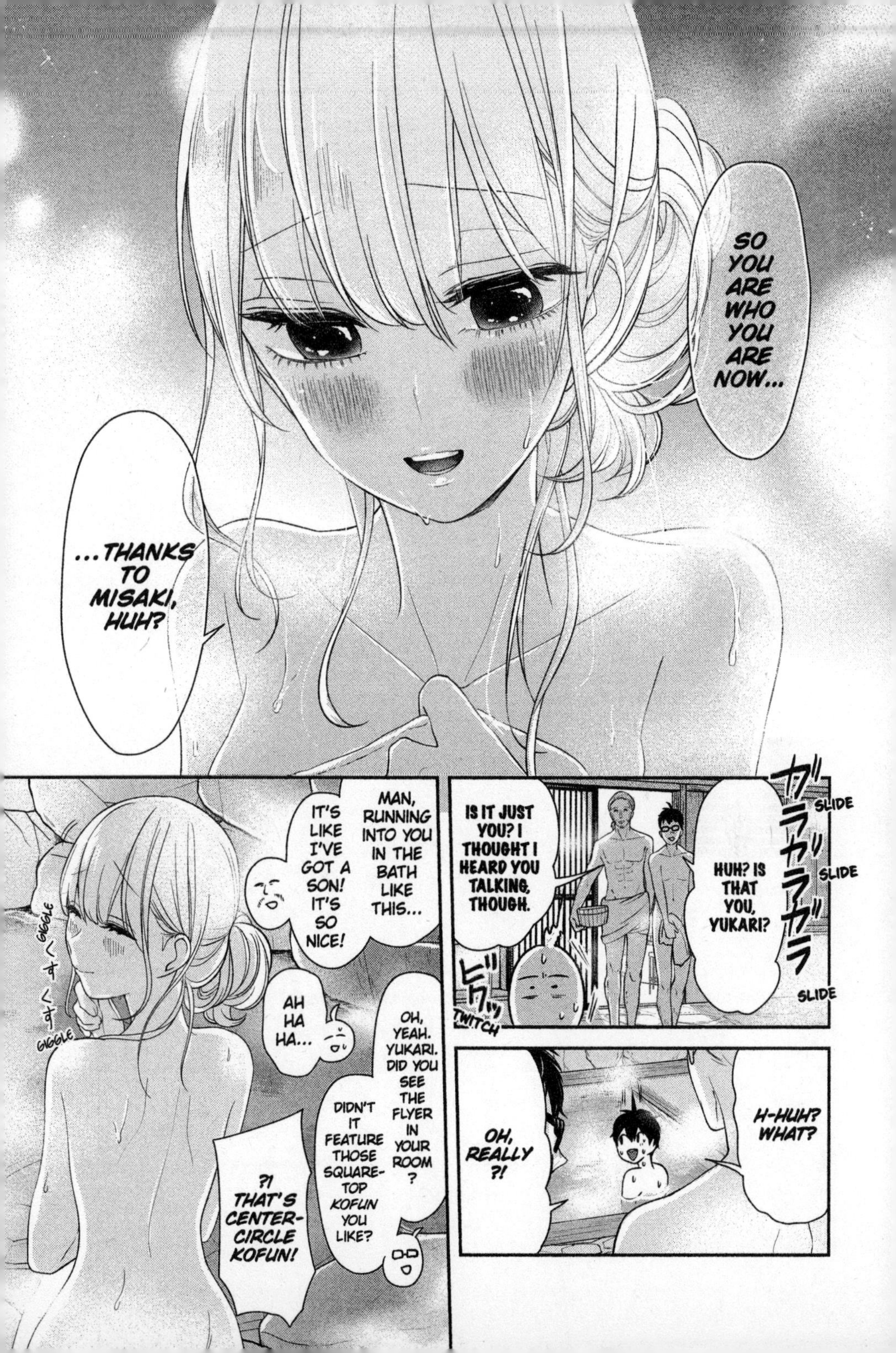
SO YOU ARE WHO YOU ARE NOW...
...THANKS TO MISAKI, HUH?
ガラガラガラ
SLIDE SLIDE SLIDE
HUH? IS THAT YOU, YUKARI?
IS IT JUST YOU? I THOUGHT I HEARD YOU TALKING, THOUGH.
ビクッ
TWITCH
H-HUH? WHAT?
OH, REALLY?!
MAN, RUNNING INTO YOU IN THE BATH LIKE THIS...
IT'S LIKE I'VE GOT A SON! IT'S SO NICE!
くすくす
GIGGLE GIGGLE
AH HA HA...
OH, YEAH. YUKARI. DID YOU SEE THE FLYER IN YOUR ROOM?
DIDN'T IT FEATURE THOSE SQUARE-TOP KOFUN YOU LIKE?
?! THAT'S CENTER-CIRCLE KOFUN!

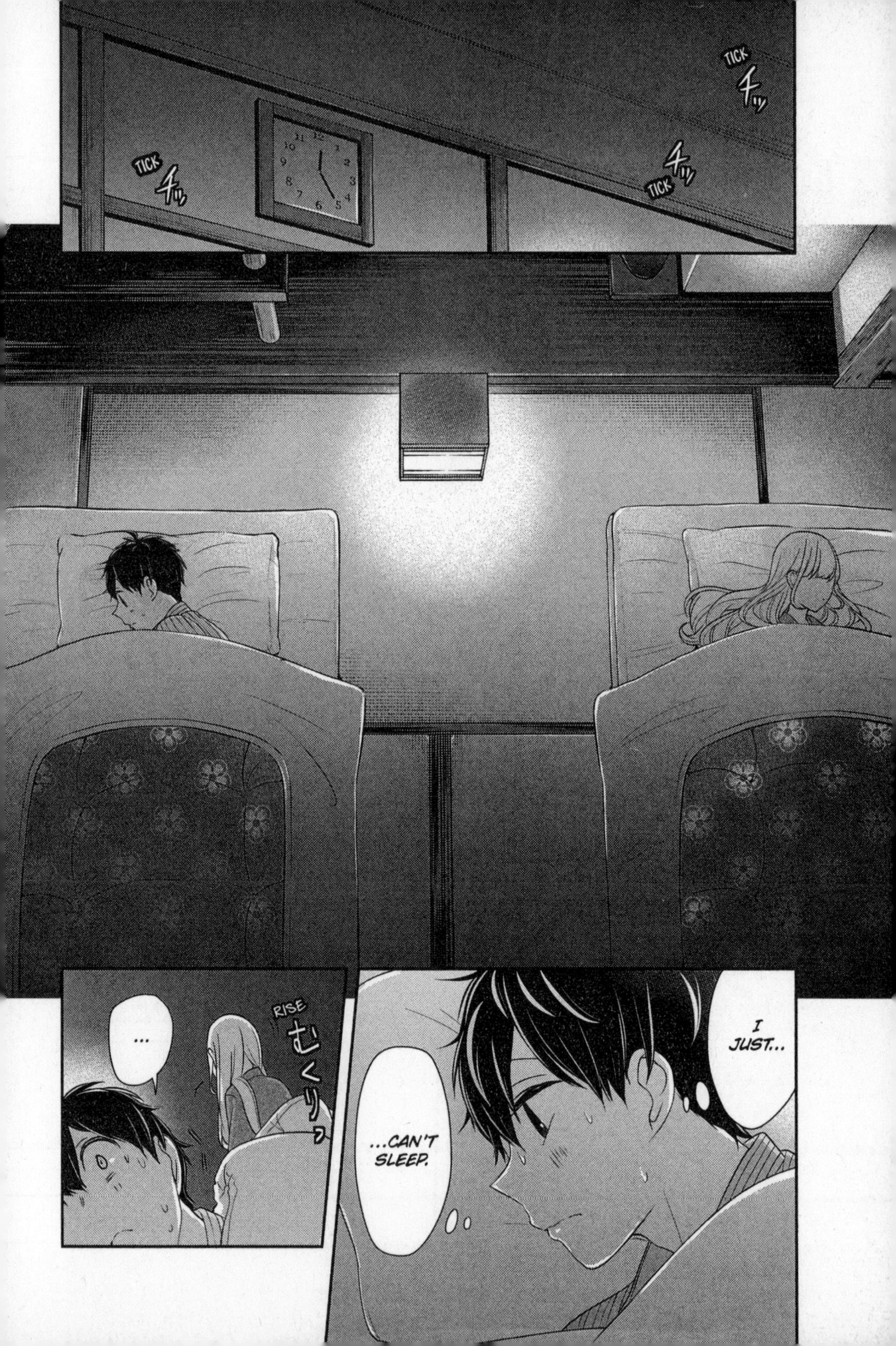
TICK
チッ
TICK
チッ
TICK
チッ
I JUST...
...CAN'T SLEEP.
...
RISE
むくりっ

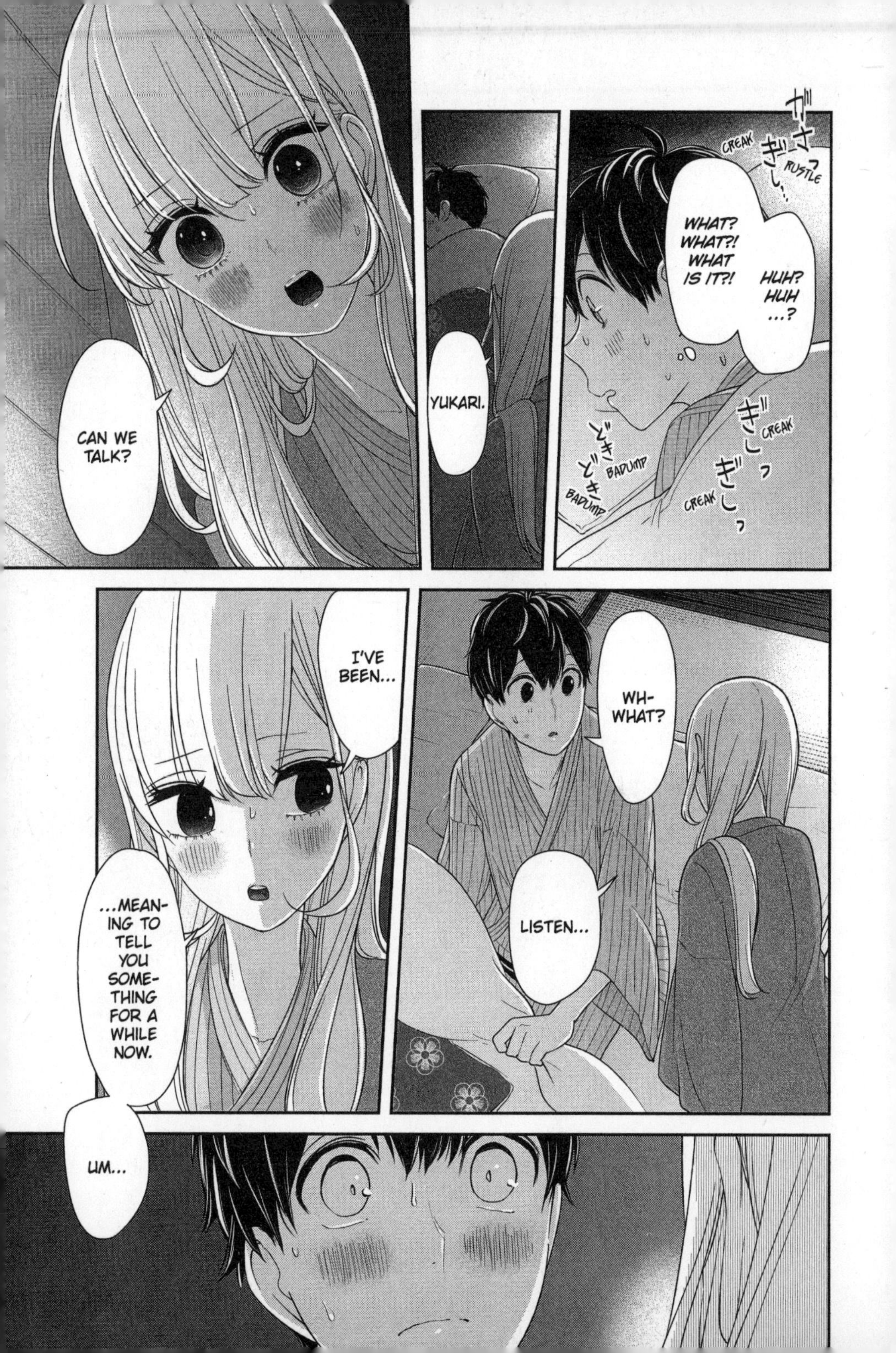
ガサッ
RUSTLE
ぎし…
CREAK
HUH? HUH …?
WHAT? WHAT?! WHAT IS IT?!
ぎしっ
CREAK
ぎしっ
CREAK
どき
BADUMP
どき
BADUMP
YUKARI.
CAN WE TALK?
WH-WHAT?
LISTEN…
I'VE BEEN…
…MEANING TO TELL YOU SOMETHING FOR A WHILE NOW.
UM…

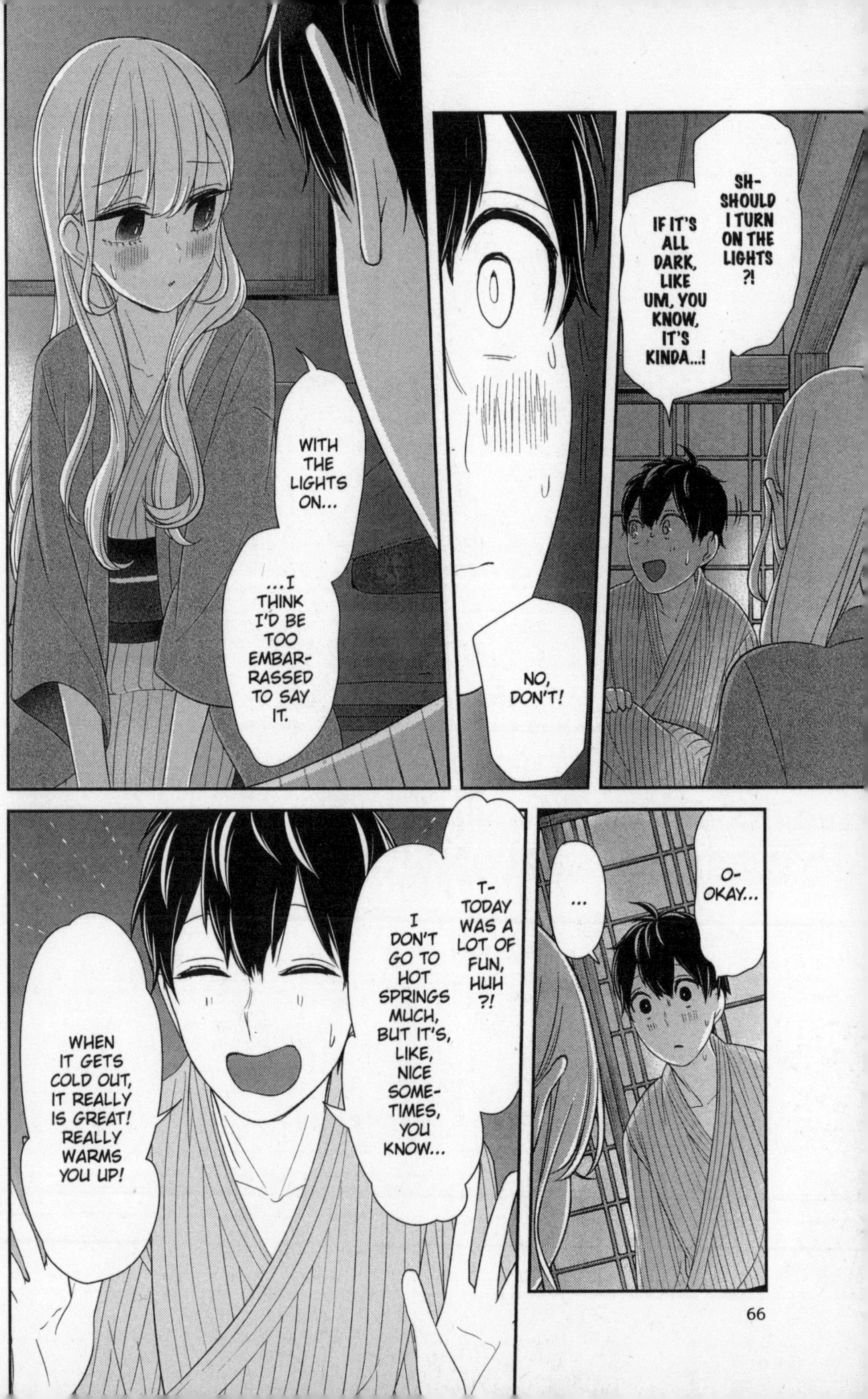

SH-SHOULD I TURN ON THE LIGHTS?!
IF IT'S ALL DARK, LIKE UM, YOU KNOW, IT'S KINDA...!
NO, DON'T!
WITH THE LIGHTS ON...
...I THINK I'D BE TOO EMBARRASSED TO SAY IT.
O-OKAY...
...
T-TODAY WAS A LOT OF FUN, HUH?!
I DON'T GO TO HOT SPRINGS MUCH, BUT IT'S, LIKE, NICE SOMETIMES, YOU KNOW...
WHEN IT GETS COLD OUT, IT REALLY IS GREAT! REALLY WARMS YOU UP!

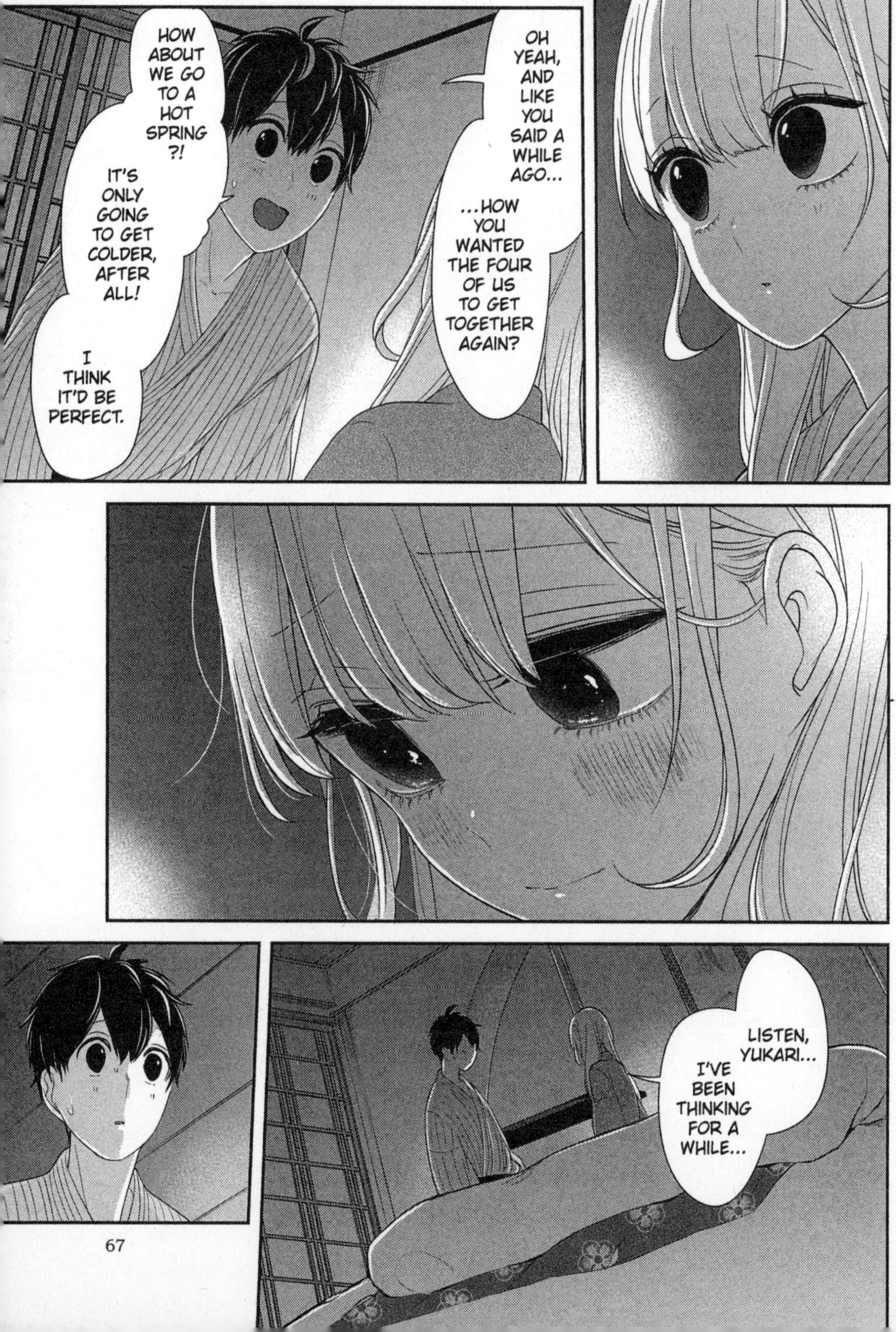
OH YEAH, AND LIKE YOU SAID A WHILE AGO...
...HOW YOU WANTED THE FOUR OF US TO GET TOGETHER AGAIN?
HOW ABOUT WE GO TO A HOT SPRING?!
IT'S ONLY GOING TO GET COLDER, AFTER ALL!
I THINK IT'D BE PERFECT.
LISTEN, YUKARI...
I'VE BEEN THINKING FOR A WHILE...

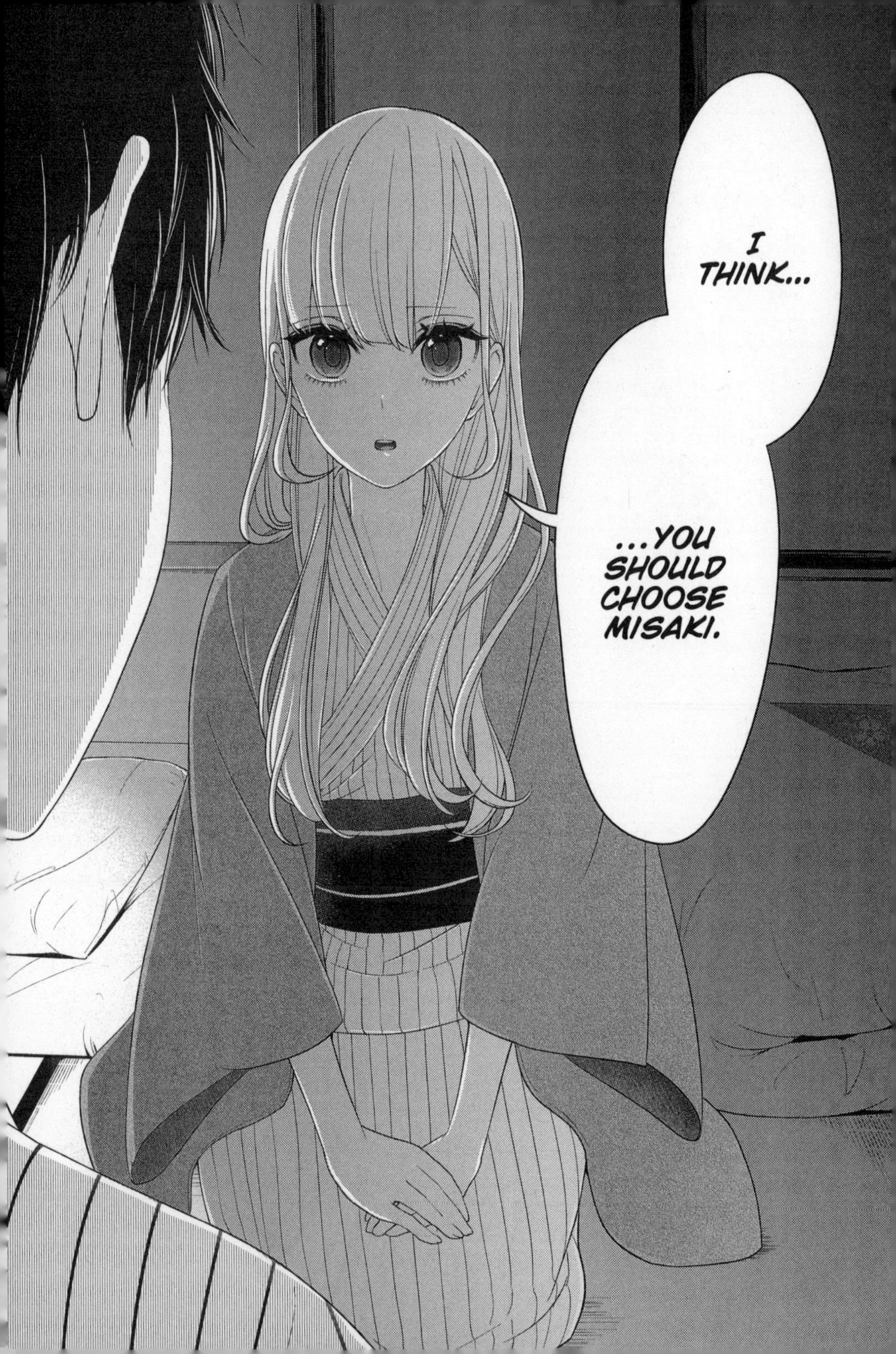
I THINK...
...YOU SHOULD CHOOSE MISAKI.

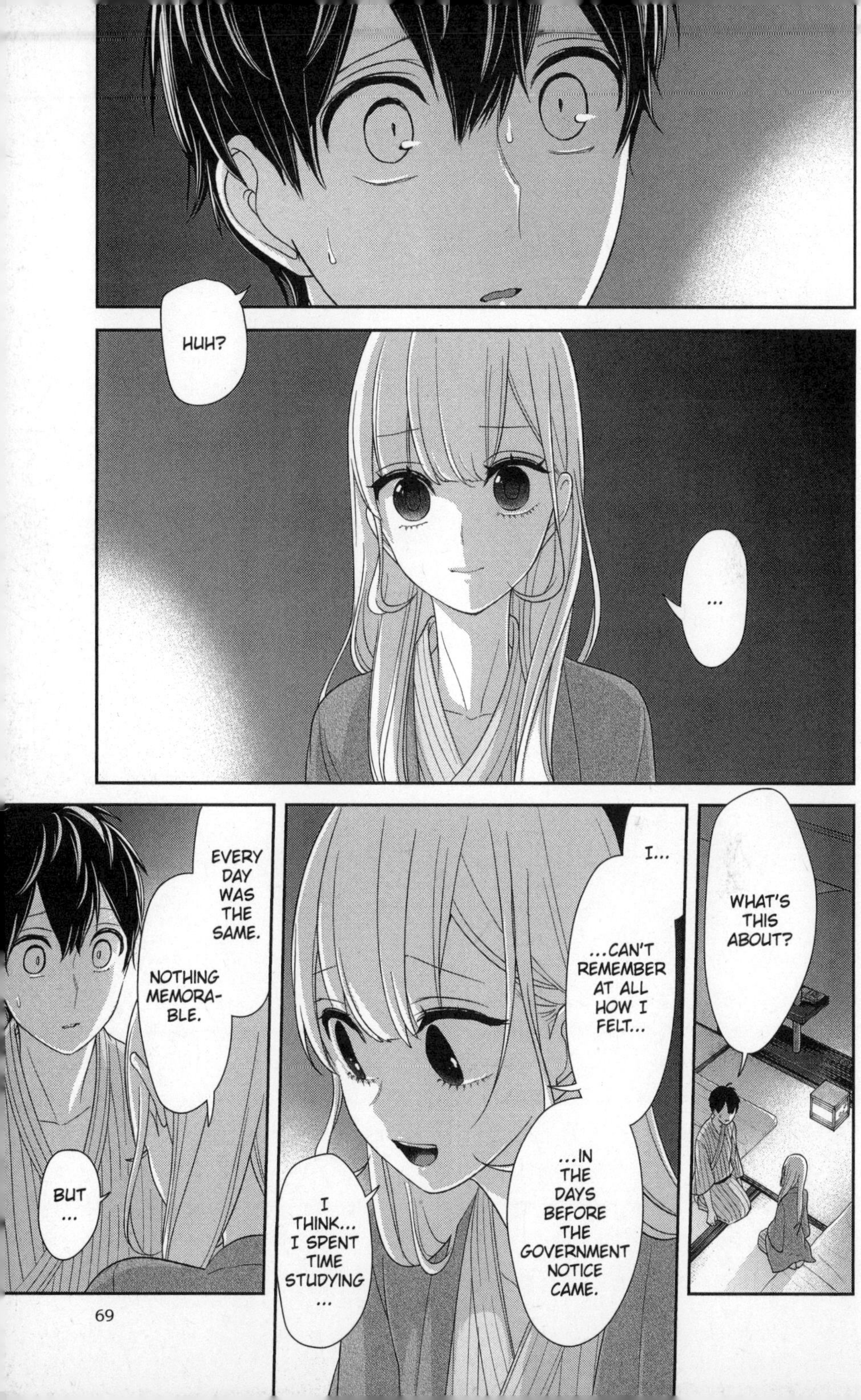
HUH?
...
WHAT'S THIS ABOUT?
I...
...CAN'T REMEMBER AT ALL HOW I FELT...
...IN THE DAYS BEFORE THE GOVERNMENT NOTICE CAME.
I THINK... I SPENT TIME STUDYING ...
EVERY DAY WAS THE SAME.
NOTHING MEMORABLE.
BUT ...

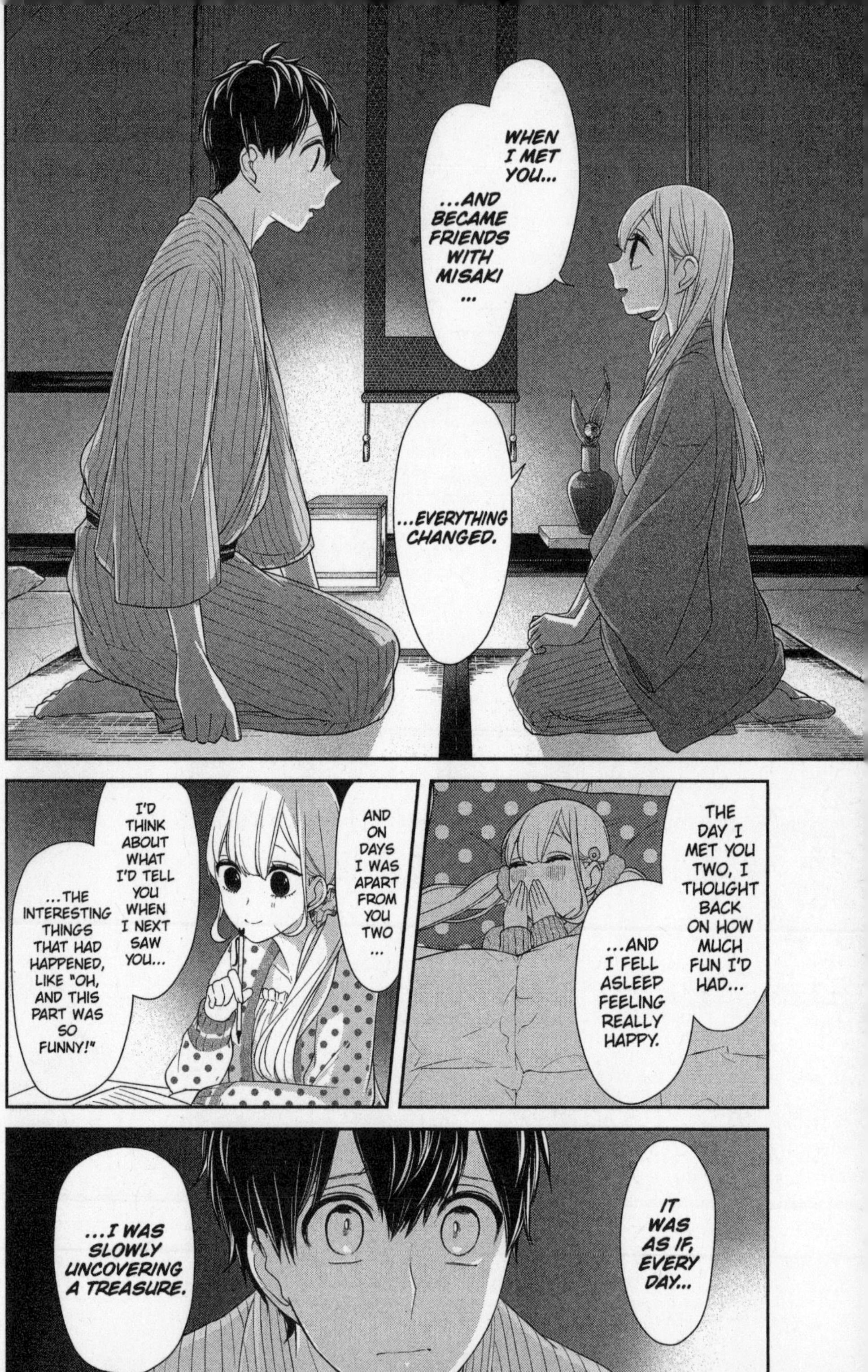
WHEN I MET YOU...
...AND BECAME FRIENDS WITH MISAKI...
...EVERYTHING CHANGED.
THE DAY I MET YOU TWO, I THOUGHT BACK ON HOW MUCH FUN I'D HAD...
...AND I FELL ASLEEP FEELING REALLY HAPPY.
AND ON DAYS I WAS APART FROM YOU TWO...
I'D THINK ABOUT WHAT I'D TELL YOU WHEN I NEXT SAW YOU...
...THE INTERESTING THINGS THAT HAD HAPPENED, LIKE "OH, AND THIS PART WAS SO FUNNY!"
IT WAS AS IF, EVERY DAY...
...I WAS SLOWLY UNCOVERING A TREASURE.

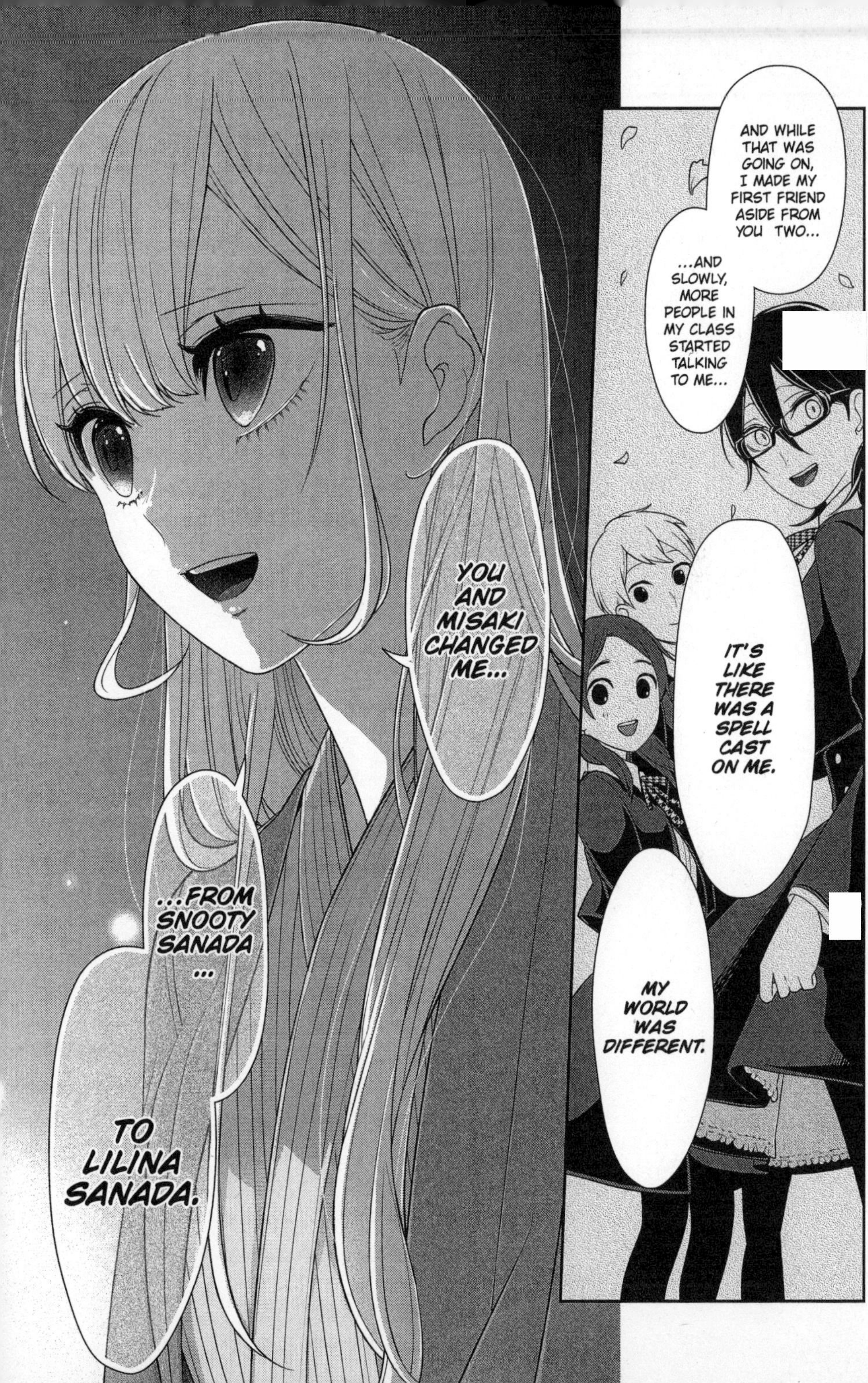
AND WHILE THAT WAS GOING ON, I MADE MY FIRST FRIEND ASIDE FROM YOU TWO...
...AND SLOWLY, MORE PEOPLE IN MY CLASS STARTED TALKING TO ME...
IT'S LIKE THERE WAS A SPELL CAST ON ME.
MY WORLD WAS DIFFERENT.
YOU AND MISAKI CHANGED ME...
...FROM SNOOTY SANADA ...
TO LILINA SANADA.

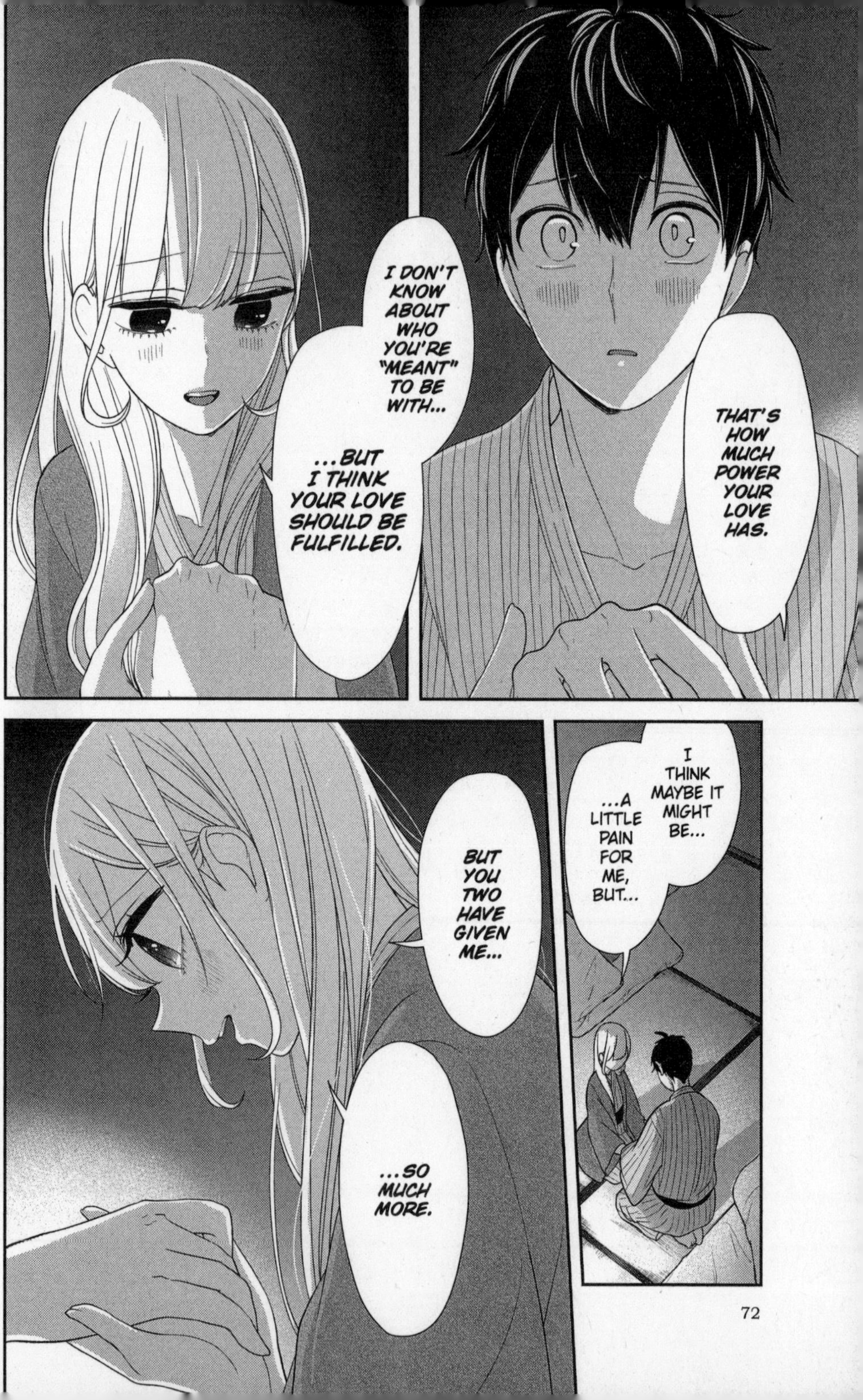
THAT'S HOW MUCH POWER YOUR LOVE HAS.
I DON'T KNOW ABOUT WHO YOU'RE "MEANT" TO BE WITH...
...BUT I THINK YOUR LOVE SHOULD BE FULFILLED.
I THINK MAYBE IT MIGHT BE...
...A LITTLE PAIN FOR ME, BUT...
BUT YOU TWO HAVE GIVEN ME...
...SO MUCH MORE.

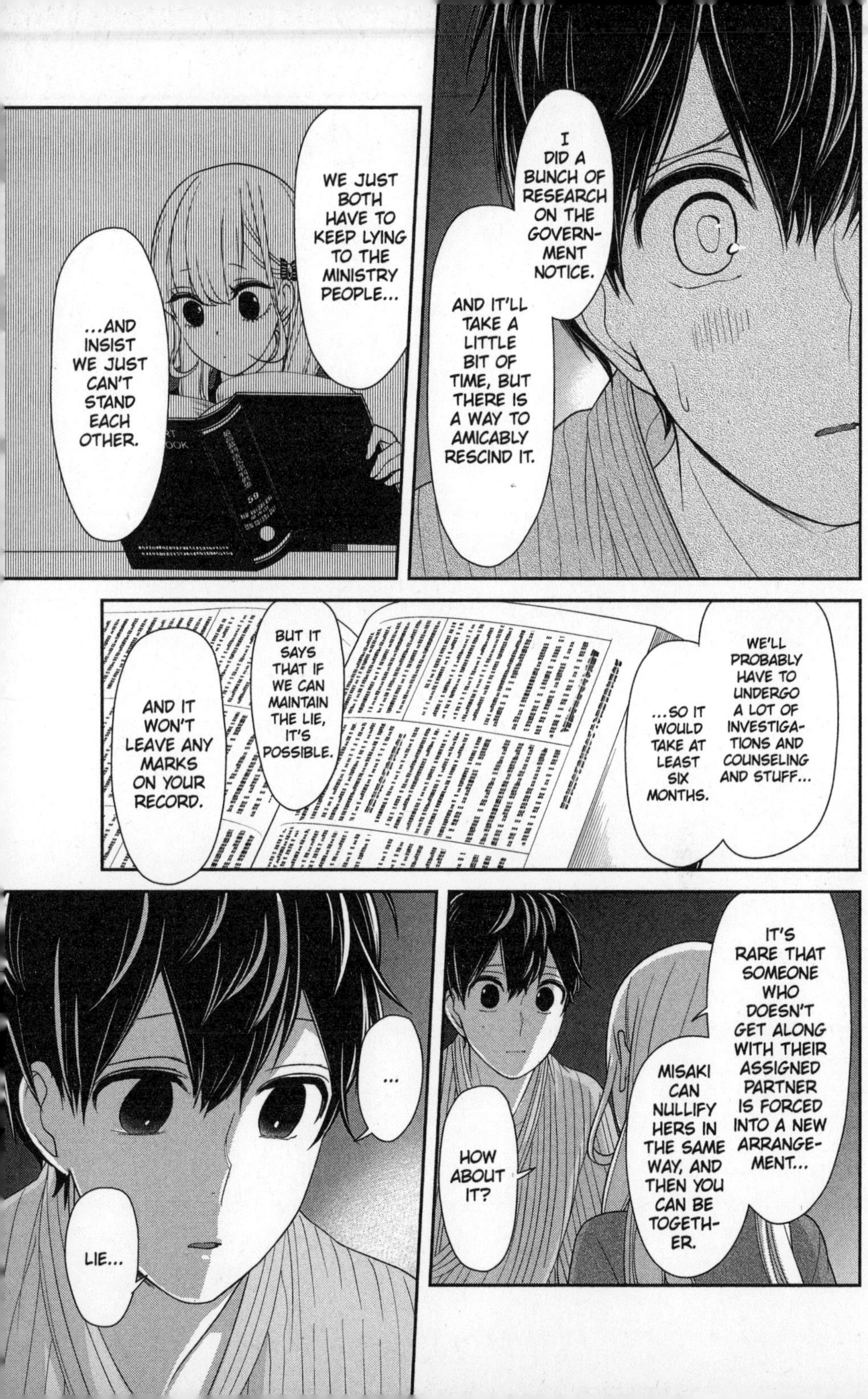
I DID A BUNCH OF RESEARCH ON THE GOVERNMENT NOTICE.
AND IT'LL TAKE A LITTLE BIT OF TIME, BUT THERE IS A WAY TO AMICABLY RESCIND IT.
WE JUST BOTH HAVE TO KEEP LYING TO THE MINISTRY PEOPLE...
...AND INSIST WE JUST CAN'T STAND EACH OTHER.
WE'LL PROBABLY HAVE TO UNDERGO A LOT OF INVESTIGATIONS AND COUNSELING AND STUFF...
...SO IT WOULD TAKE AT LEAST SIX MONTHS.
BUT IT SAYS THAT IF WE CAN MAINTAIN THE LIE, IT'S POSSIBLE.
AND IT WON'T LEAVE ANY MARKS ON YOUR RECORD.
IT'S RARE THAT SOMEONE WHO DOESN'T GET ALONG WITH THEIR ASSIGNED PARTNER IS FORCED INTO A NEW ARRANGEMENT...
MISAKI CAN NULLIFY HERS IN THE SAME WAY, AND THEN YOU CAN BE TOGETHER.
HOW ABOUT IT?
...
LIE...

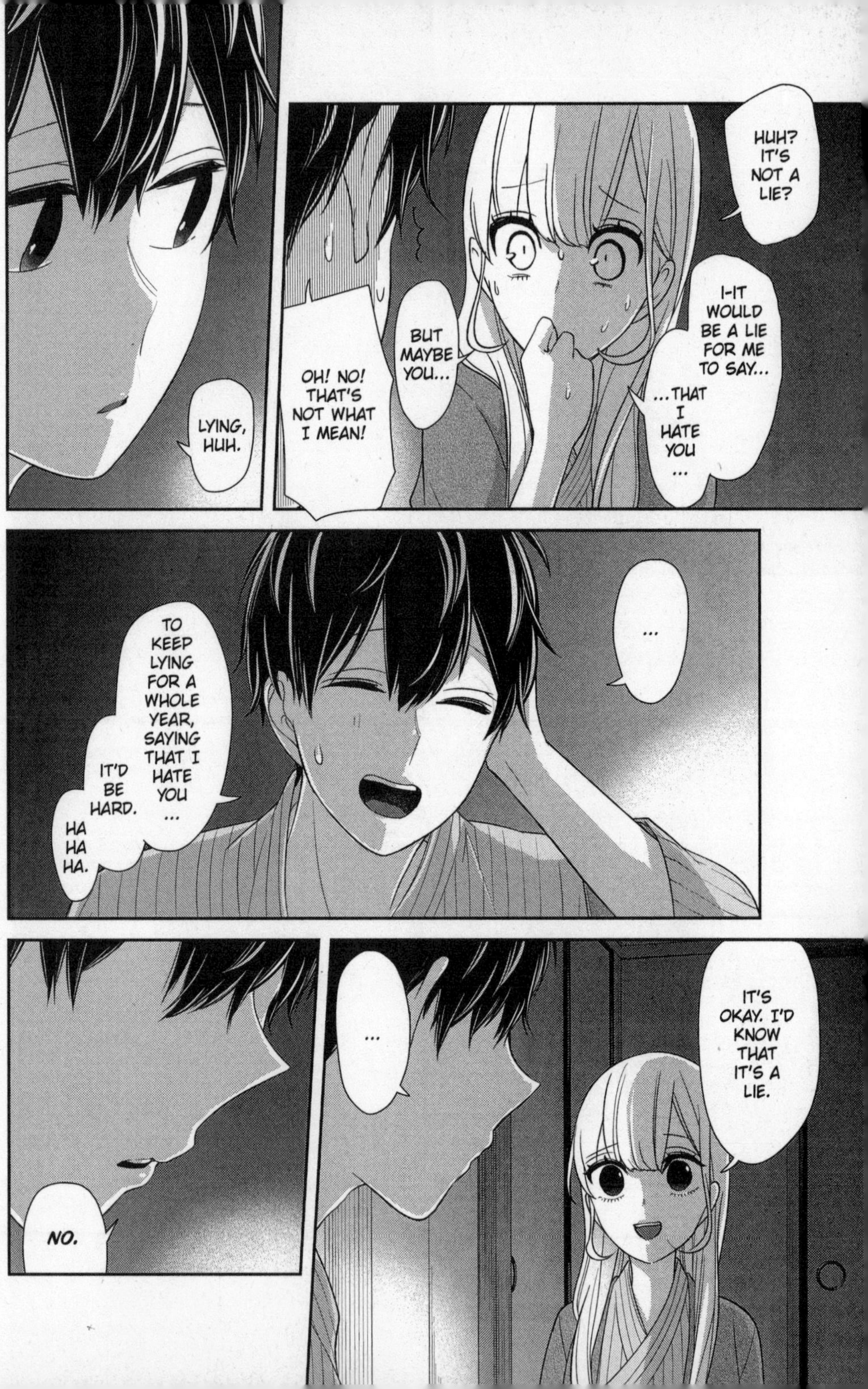

HUH? IT'S NOT A LIE?
I-IT WOULD BE A LIE FOR ME TO SAY...
...THAT I HATE YOU ...
BUT MAYBE YOU...
OH! NO! THAT'S NOT WHAT I MEAN!
LYING, HUH.
...
TO KEEP LYING FOR A WHOLE YEAR, SAYING THAT I HATE YOU ...
IT'D BE HARD.
HA HA HA.
IT'S OKAY. I'D KNOW THAT IT'S A LIE.
...
NO.

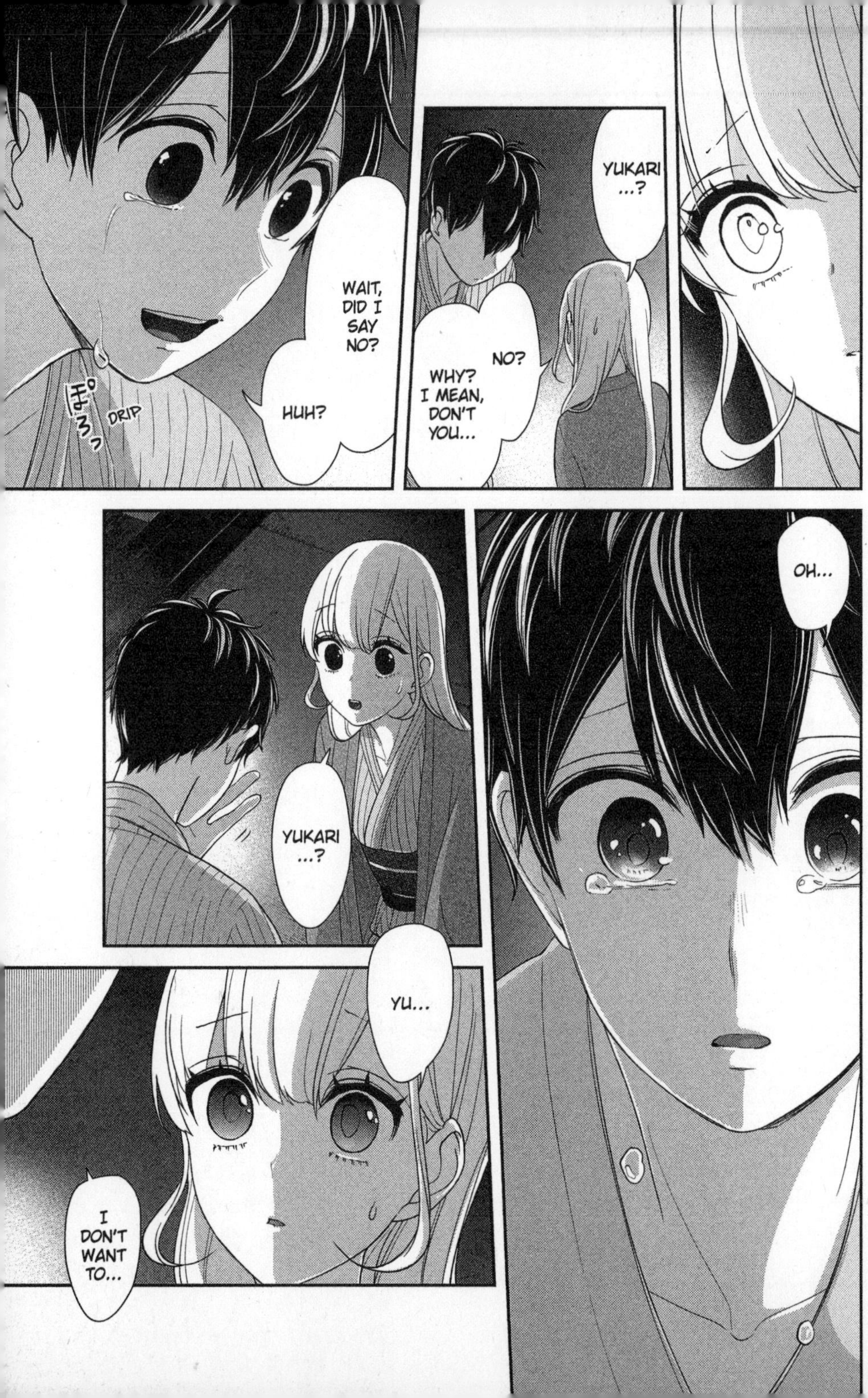
YUKARI ...?
NO? WHY? I MEAN, DON'T YOU...
WAIT, DID I SAY NO?
HUH?
ぽろっ DRIP
OH...
YUKARI ...?
YU...
I DON'T WANT TO...

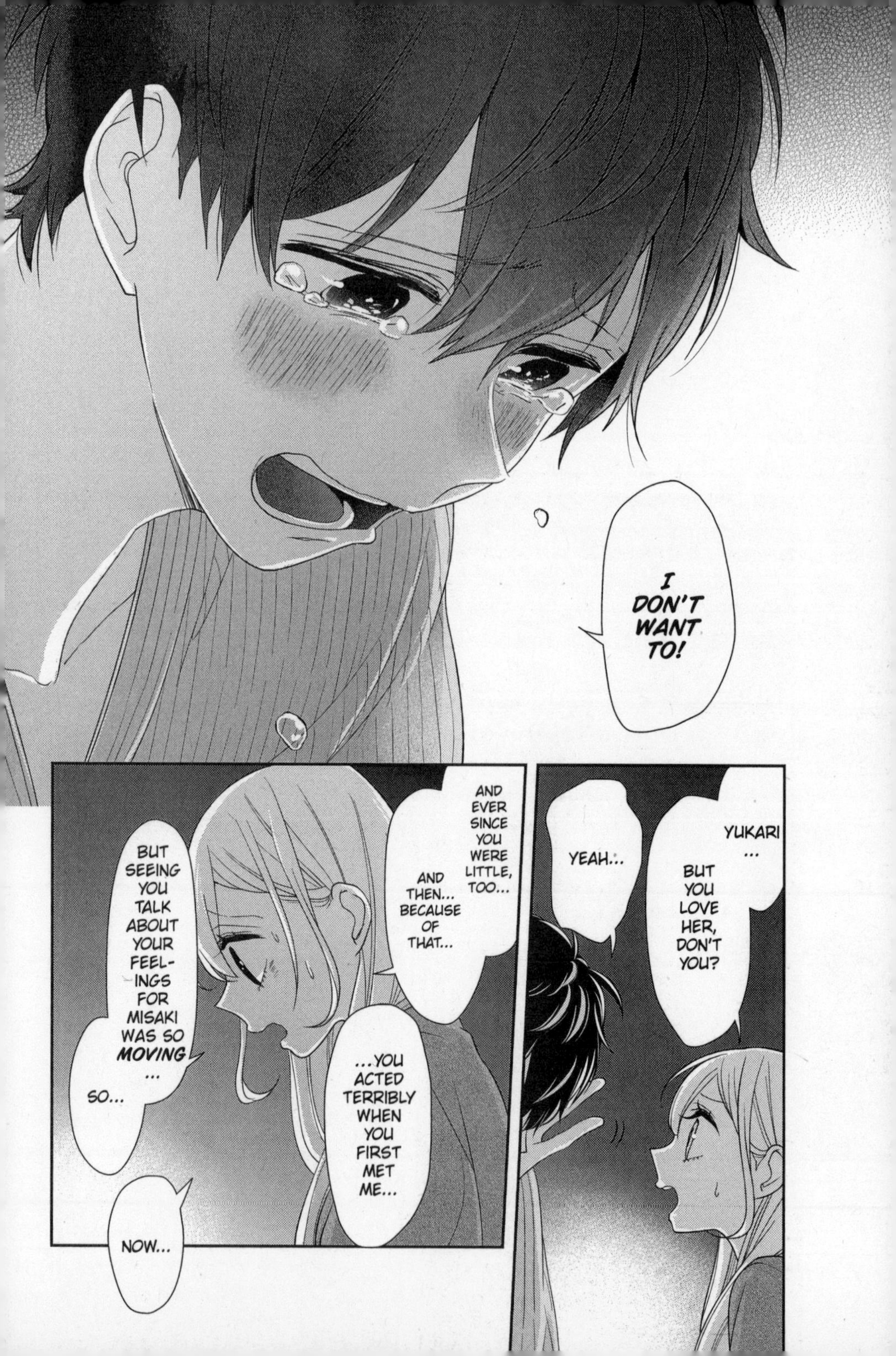
I DON'T WANT TO!
YUKARI...
BUT YOU LOVE HER, DON'T YOU?
YEAH...
AND EVER SINCE YOU WERE LITTLE, TOO...
AND THEN... BECAUSE OF THAT...
...YOU ACTED TERRIBLY WHEN YOU FIRST MET ME...
BUT SEEING YOU TALK ABOUT YOUR FEEL-INGS FOR MISAKI WAS SO *MOVING*...
SO...
NOW...

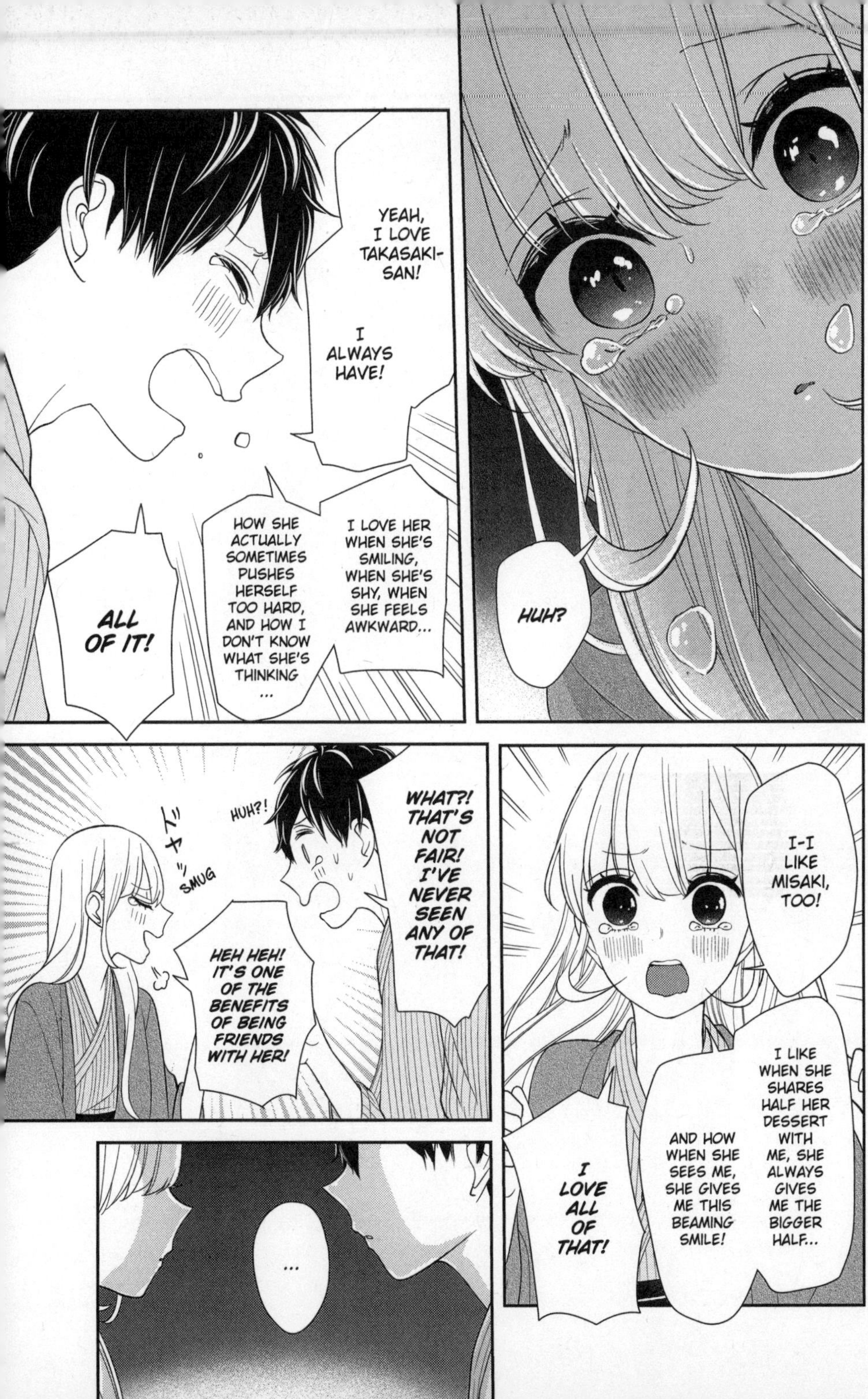
HUH?
YEAH, I LOVE TAKASAKI-SAN!
I ALWAYS HAVE!
I LOVE HER WHEN SHE'S SMILING, WHEN SHE'S SHY, WHEN SHE FEELS AWKWARD...
HOW SHE ACTUALLY SOMETIMES PUSHES HERSELF TOO HARD, AND HOW I DON'T KNOW WHAT SHE'S THINKING...
ALL OF IT!
I-I LIKE MISAKI, TOO!
I LIKE WHEN SHE SHARES HALF HER DESSERT WITH ME, SHE ALWAYS GIVES ME THE BIGGER HALF...
AND HOW WHEN SHE SEES ME, SHE GIVES ME THIS BEAMING SMILE!
I LOVE ALL OF THAT!
WHAT?! THAT'S NOT FAIR! I'VE NEVER SEEN ANY OF THAT!
HUH?!
ドヤッ
SMUG
HEH HEH! IT'S ONE OF THE BENEFITS OF BEING FRIENDS WITH HER!
...

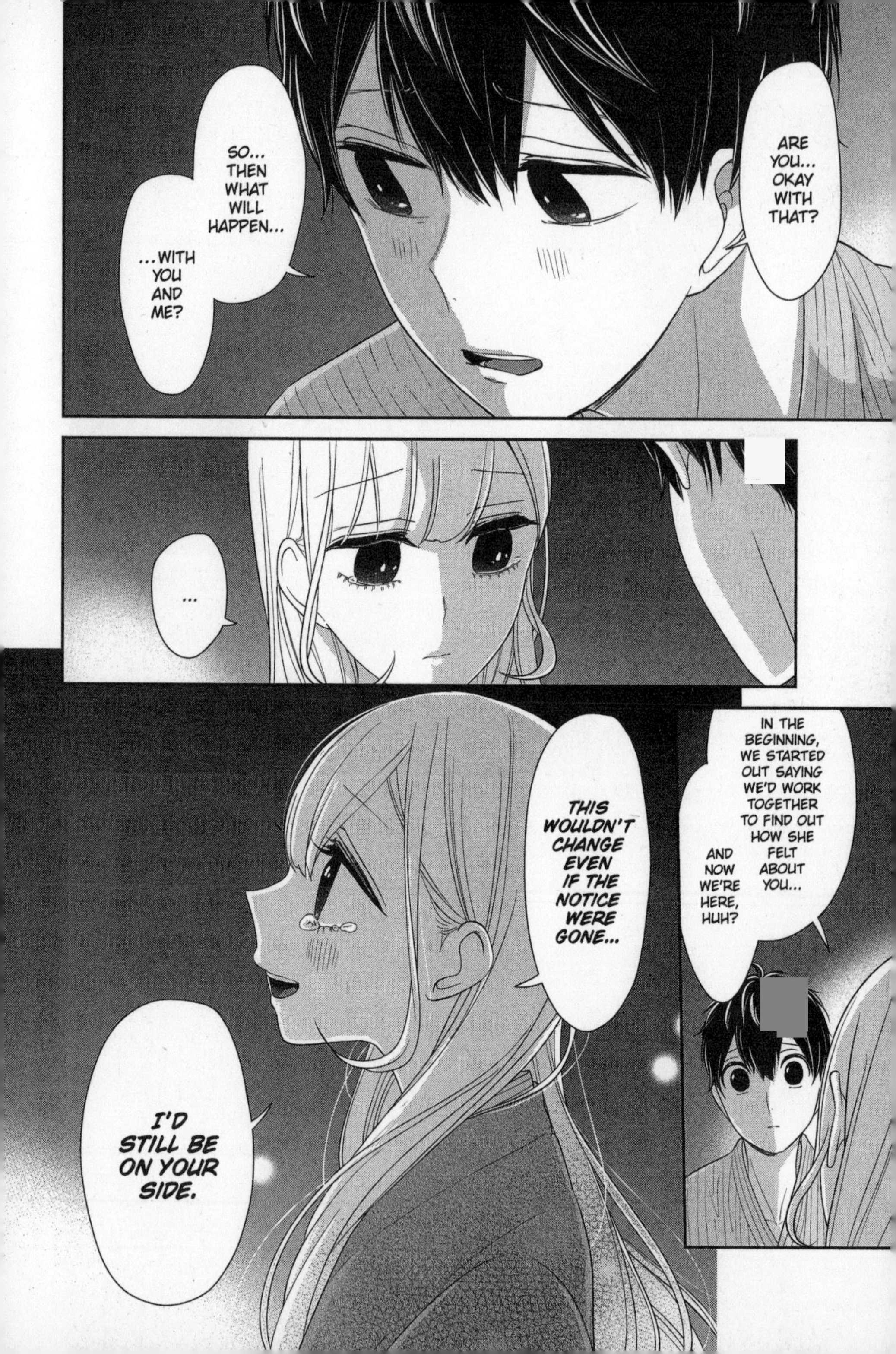
ARE YOU... OKAY WITH THAT?
SO... THEN WHAT WILL HAPPEN...
...WITH YOU AND ME?
...
IN THE BEGINNING, WE STARTED OUT SAYING WE'D WORK TOGETHER TO FIND OUT HOW SHE FELT ABOUT YOU...
AND NOW WE'RE HERE, HUH?
THIS WOULDN'T CHANGE EVEN IF THE NOTICE WERE GONE...
I'D STILL BE ON YOUR SIDE.

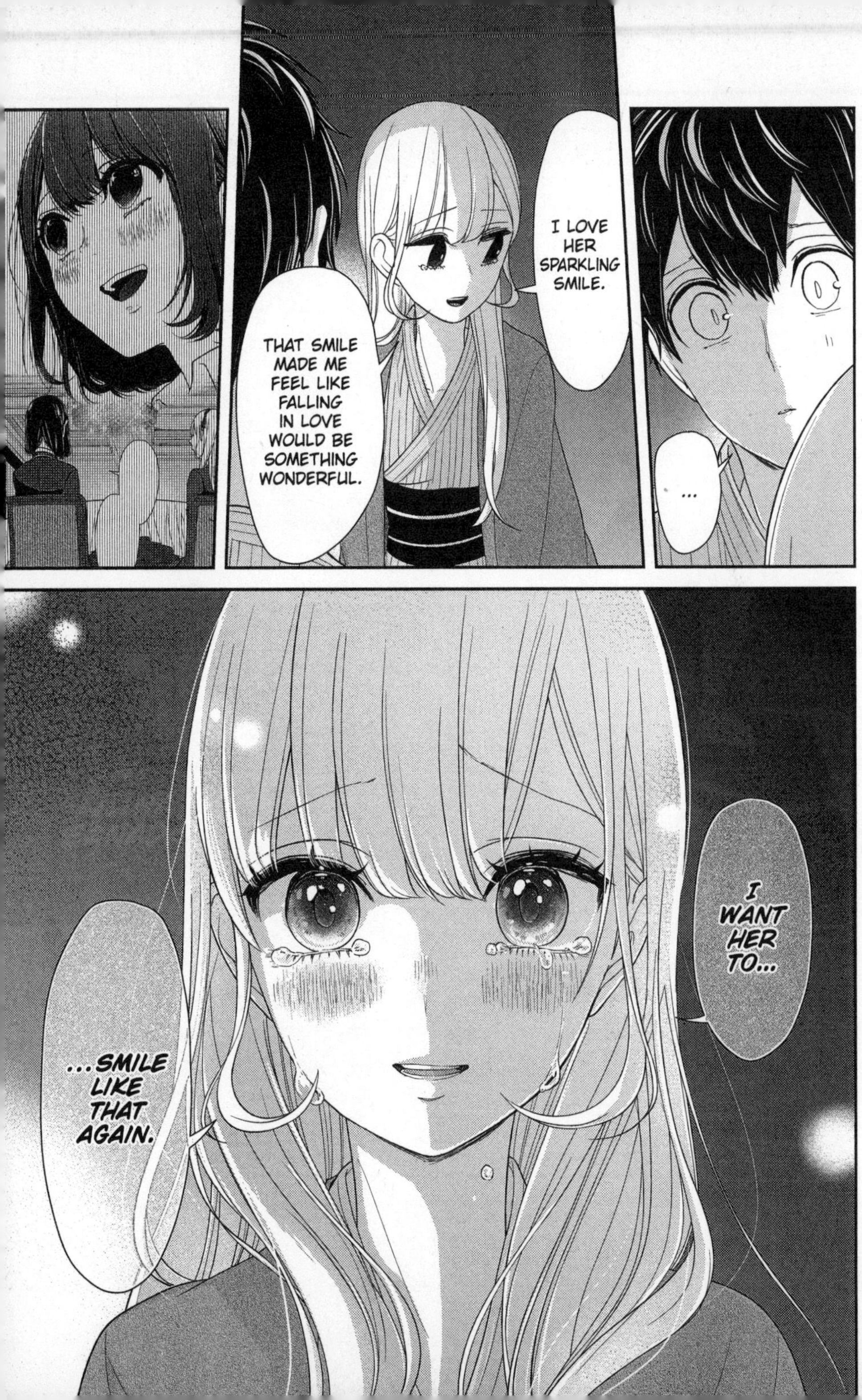
...
I LOVE HER SPARKLING SMILE.
THAT SMILE MADE ME FEEL LIKE FALLING IN LOVE WOULD BE SOMETHING WONDERFUL.
I WANT HER TO...
...SMILE LIKE THAT AGAIN.

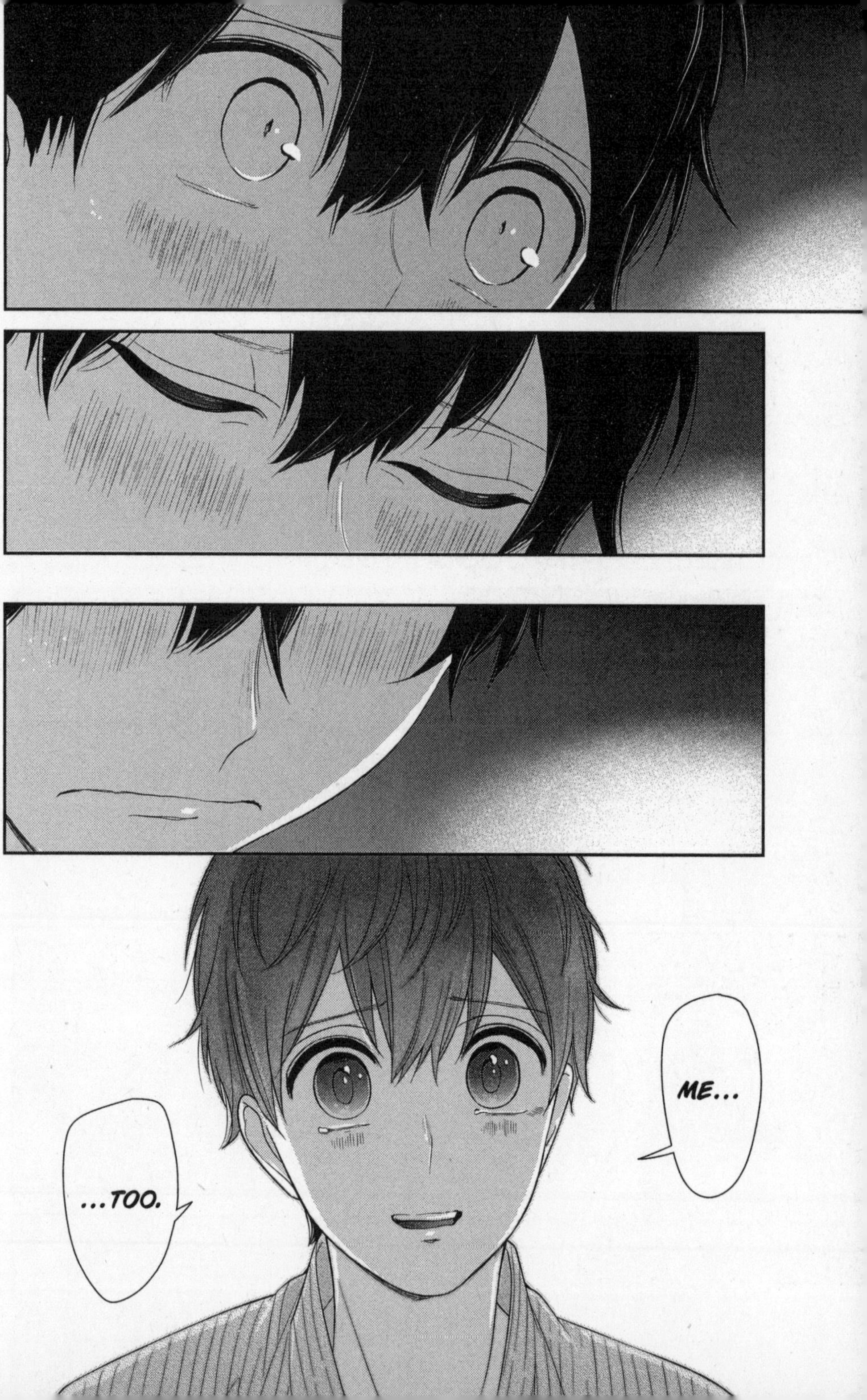
ME...
...TOO.

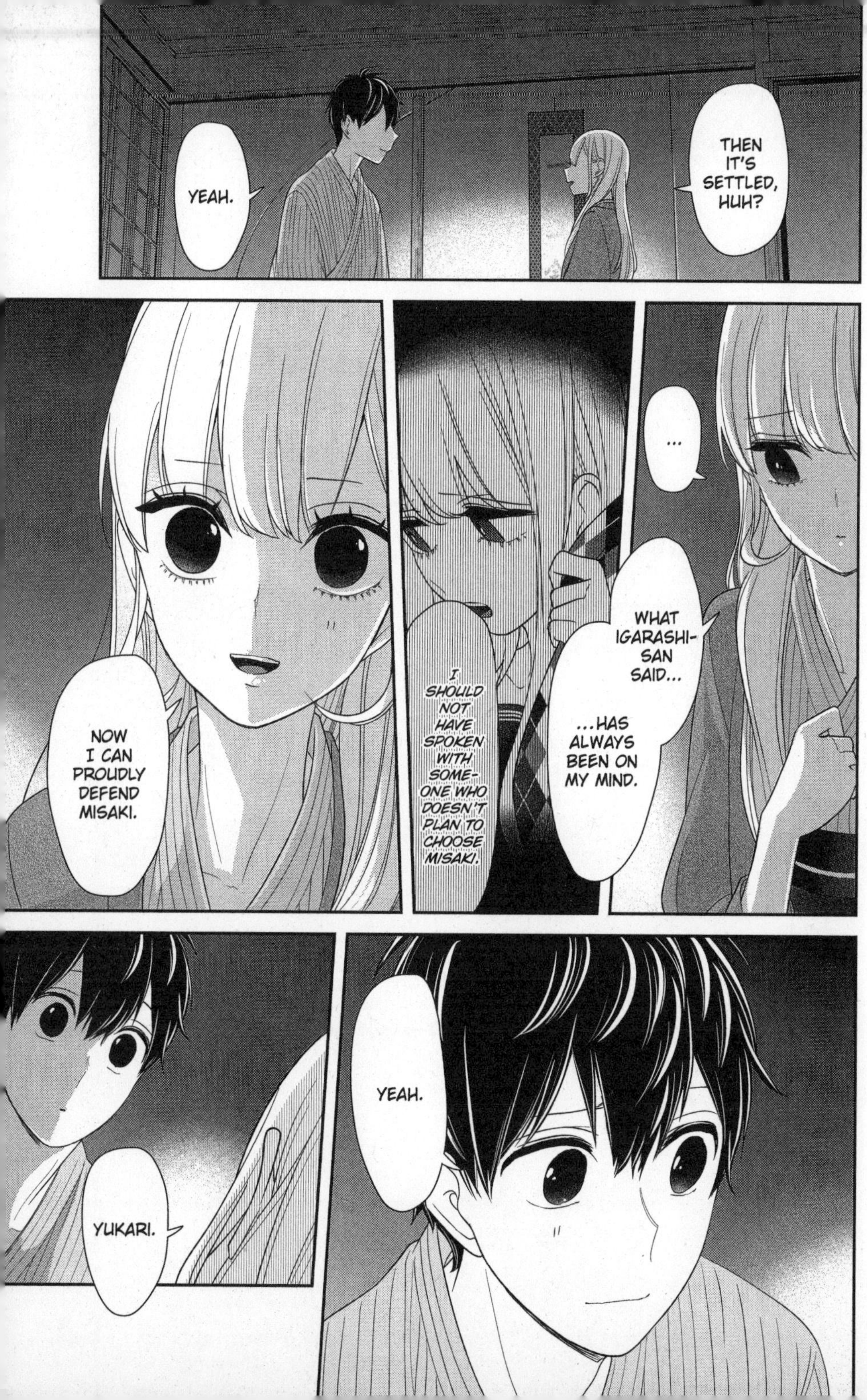
THEN IT'S SETTLED, HUH?
YEAH.
...
WHAT IGARASHI-SAN SAID...
...HAS ALWAYS BEEN ON MY MIND.
I SHOULD NOT HAVE SPOKEN WITH SOME-ONE WHO DOESN'T PLAN TO CHOOSE MISAKI.
NOW I CAN PROUDLY DEFEND MISAKI.
YEAH.
YUKARI.

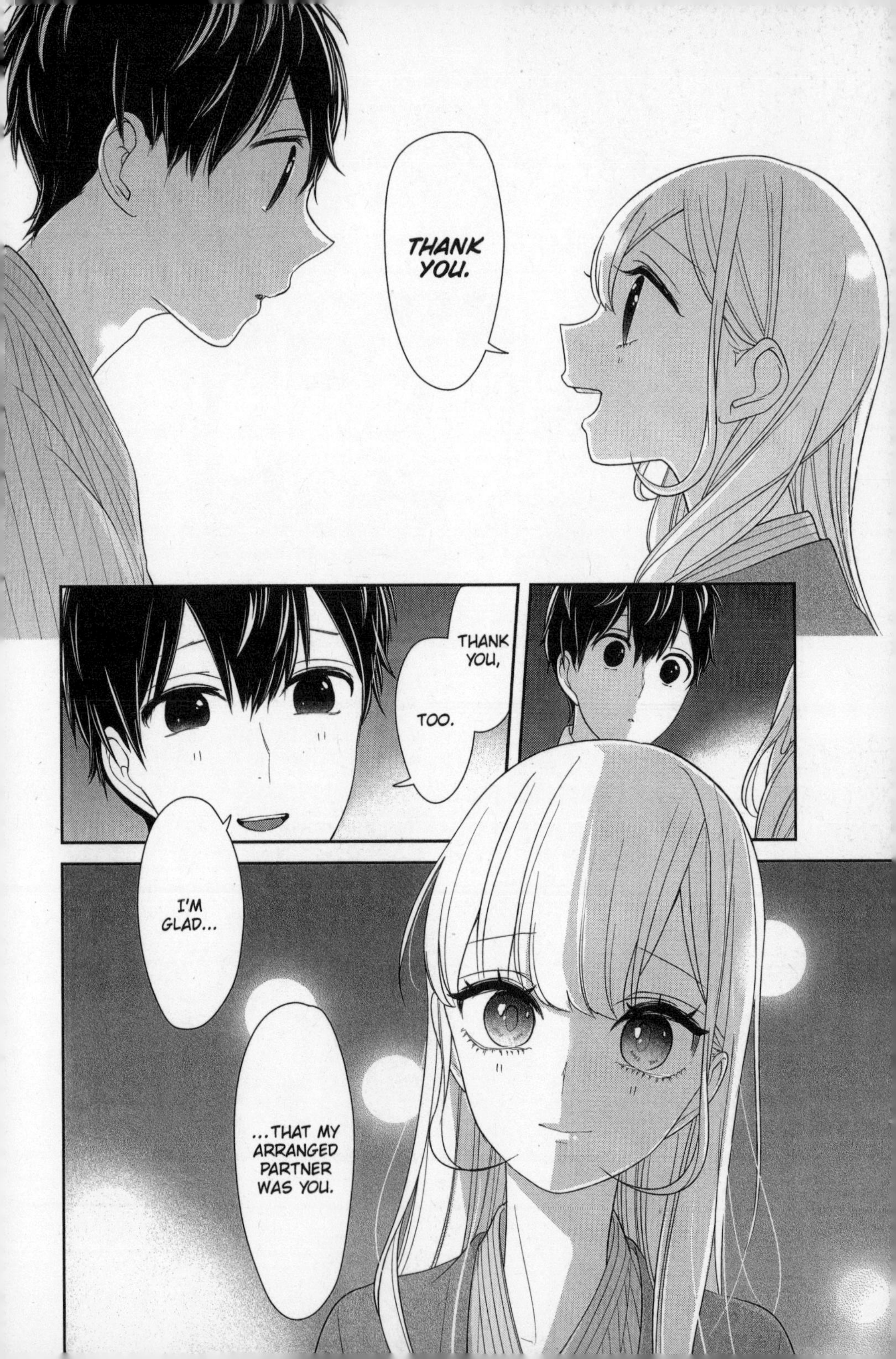
THANK YOU.
THANK YOU, TOO.
I'M GLAD...
...THAT MY ARRANGED PARTNER WAS YOU.

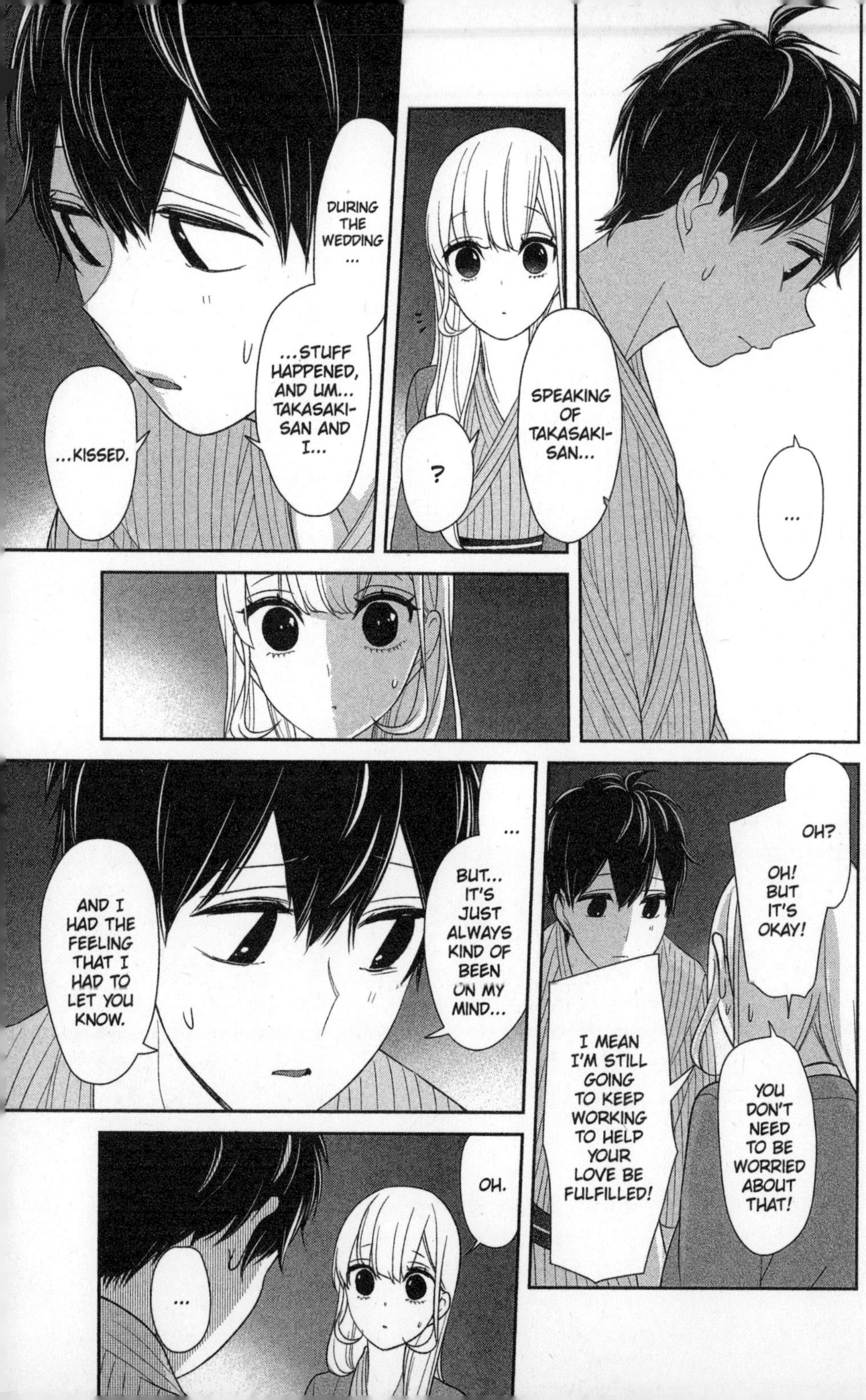
...
SPEAKING OF TAKASAKI-SAN...
?
DURING THE WEDDING...
...STUFF HAPPENED, AND UM... TAKASAKI-SAN AND I...
...KISSED.
OH?
OH! BUT IT'S OKAY!
YOU DON'T NEED TO BE WORRIED ABOUT THAT!
I MEAN I'M STILL GOING TO KEEP WORKING TO HELP YOUR LOVE BE FULFILLED!
...
BUT... IT'S JUST ALWAYS KIND OF BEEN ON MY MIND...
AND I HAD THE FEELING THAT I HAD TO LET YOU KNOW.
OH.
...

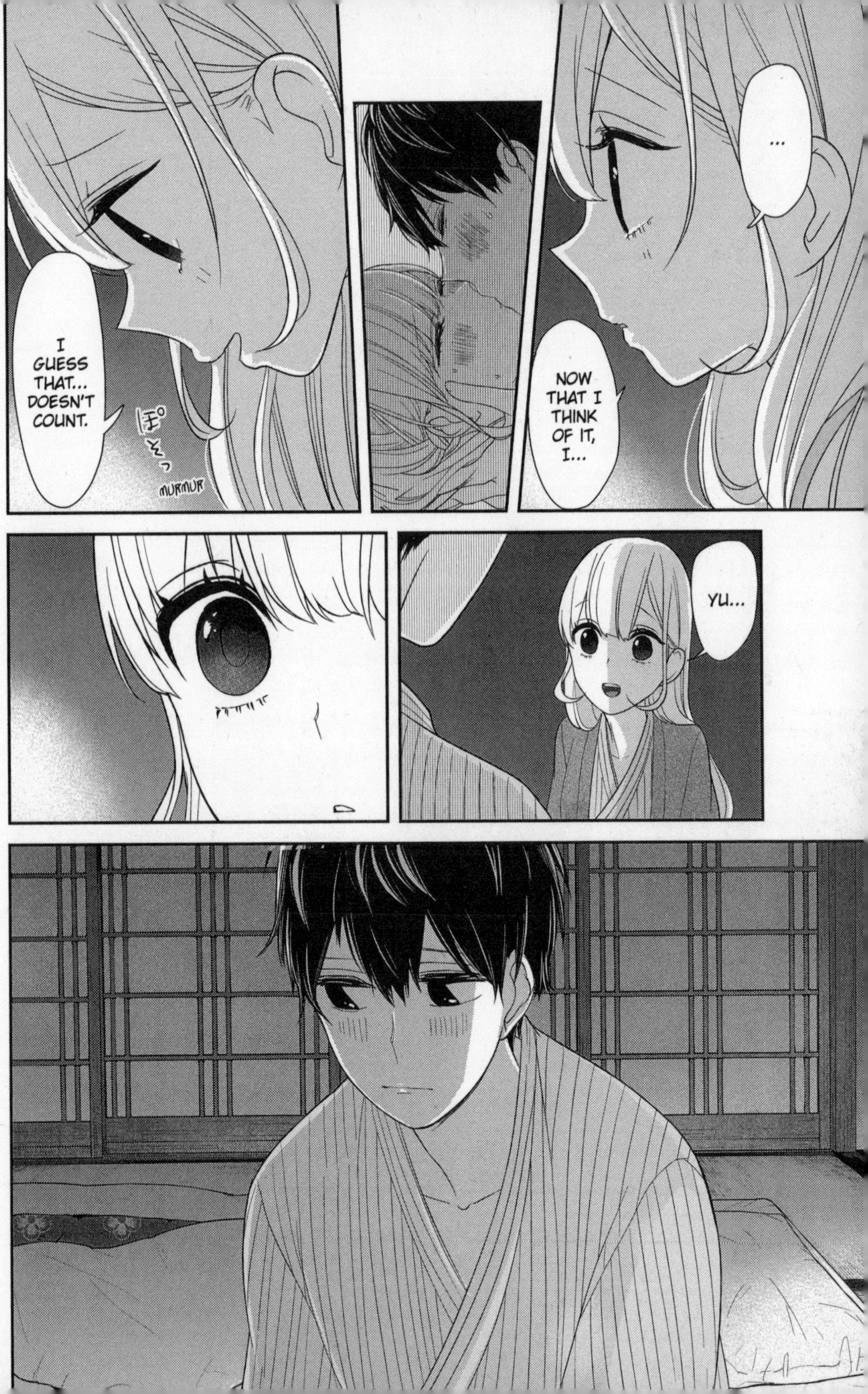
...
NOW THAT I THINK OF IT, I...
I GUESS THAT... DOESN'T COUNT.
ぽそっ
MURMUR
YU...

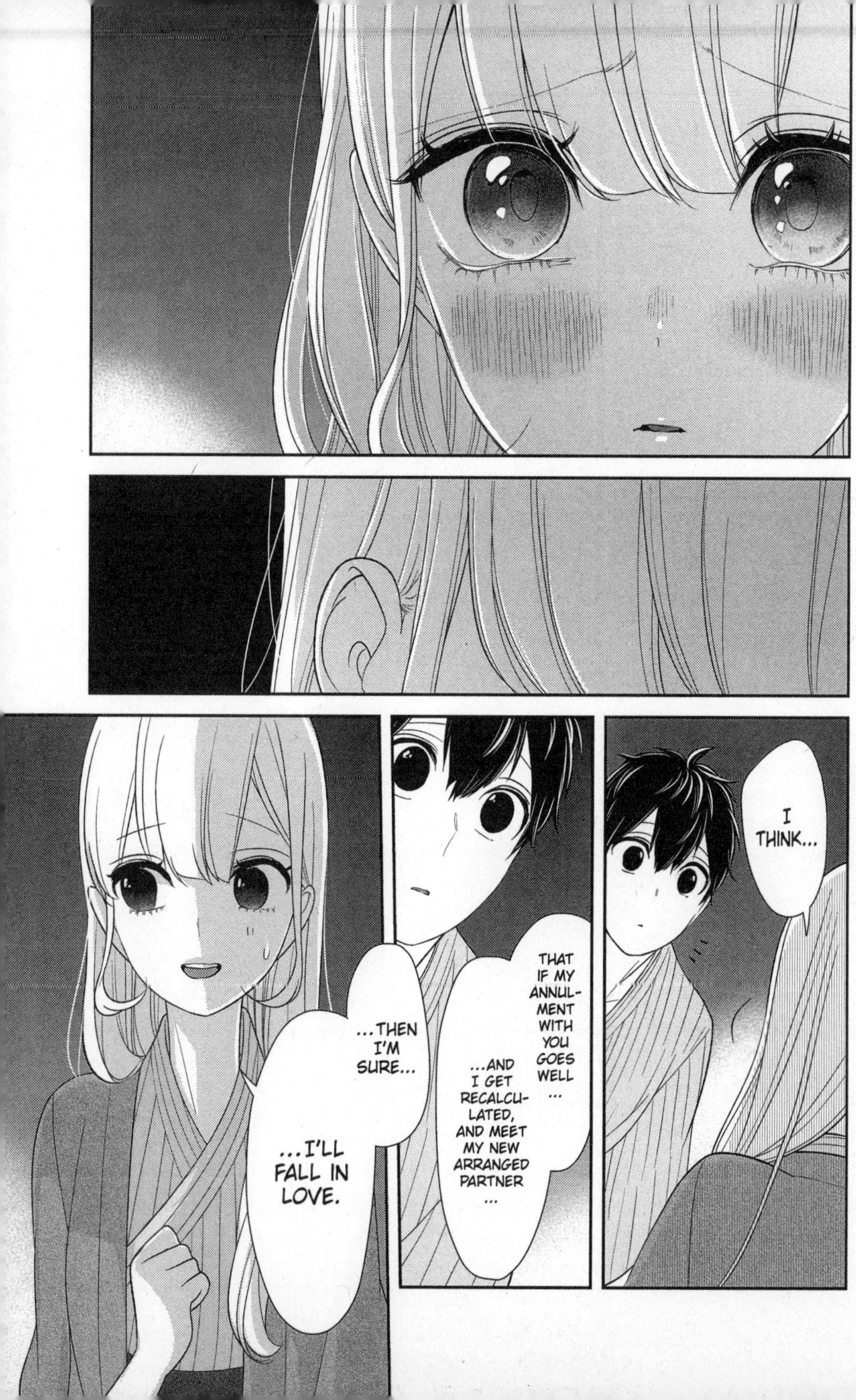
I THINK...
THAT IF MY ANNULMENT WITH YOU GOES WELL...
...AND I GET RECALCULATED, AND MEET MY NEW ARRANGED PARTNER...
...THEN I'M SURE...
...I'LL FALL IN LOVE.

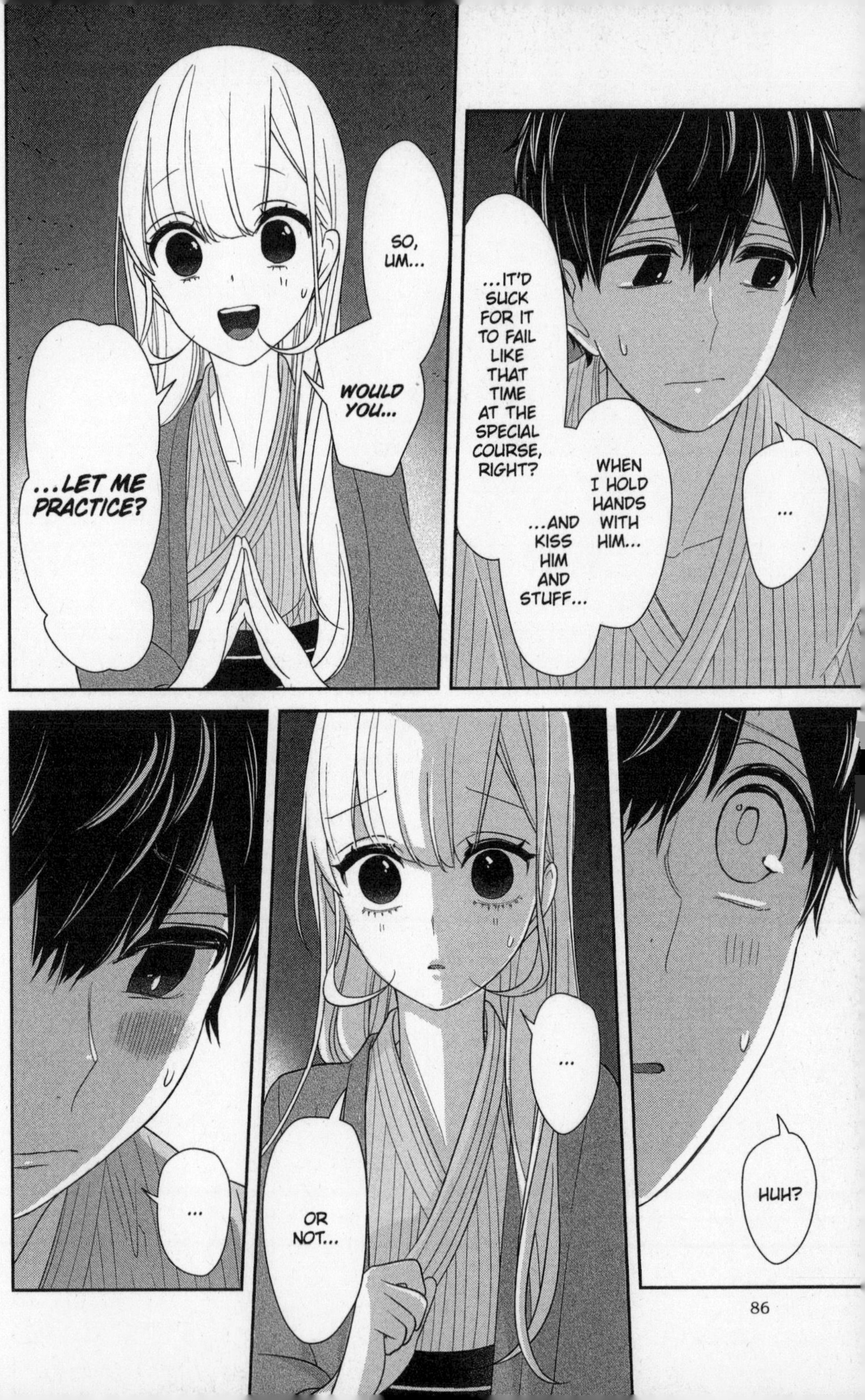
...IT'D SUCK FOR IT TO FAIL LIKE THAT TIME AT THE SPECIAL COURSE, RIGHT?
WHEN I HOLD HANDS WITH HIM...
...AND KISS HIM AND STUFF...
...
SO, UM...
WOULD YOU...
...LET ME PRACTICE?
HUH?
...
OR NOT...
...

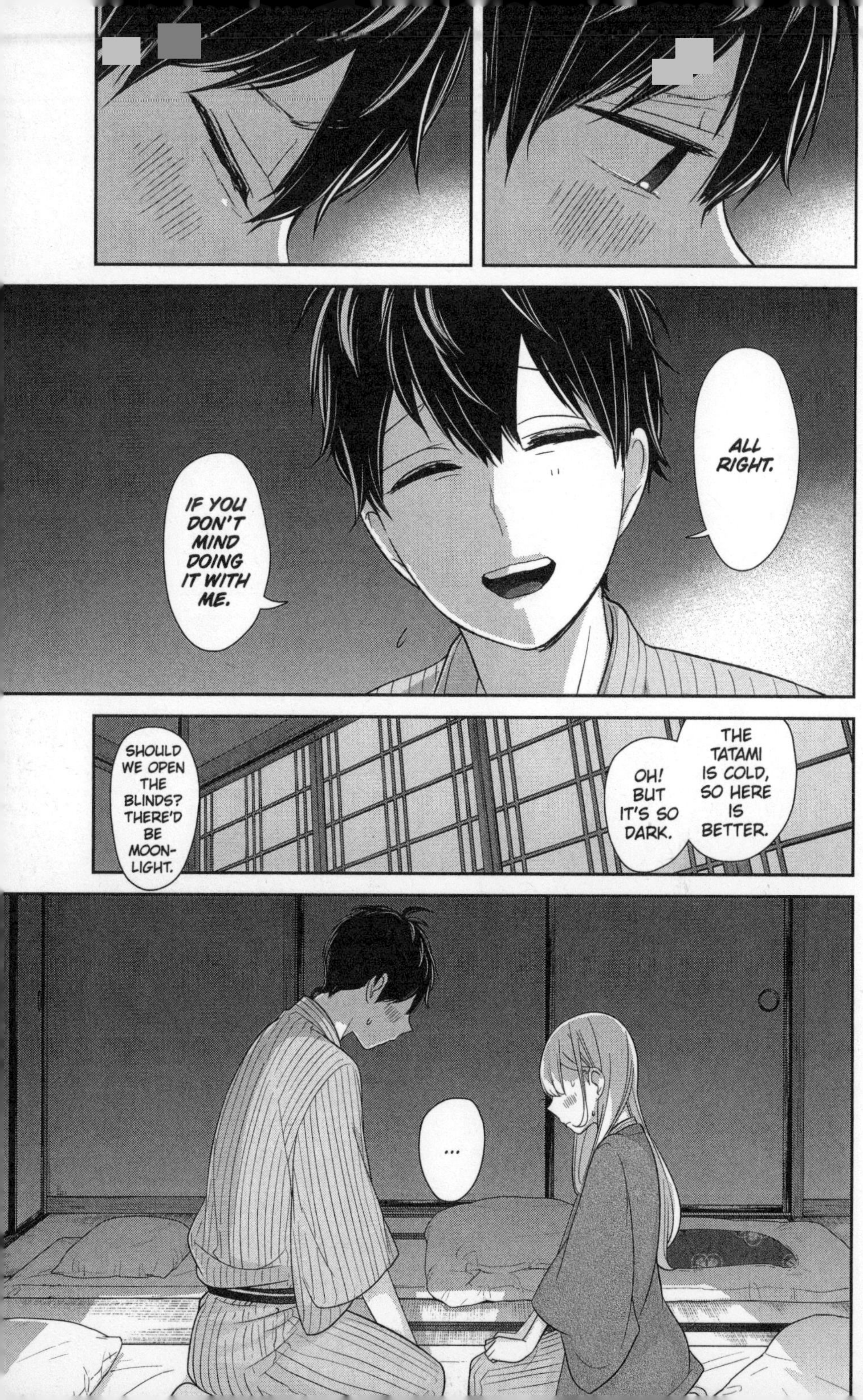
ALL RIGHT.
IF YOU DON'T MIND DOING IT WITH ME.
THE TATAMI IS COLD, SO HERE IS BETTER.
OH! BUT IT'S SO DARK.
SHOULD WE OPEN THE BLINDS? THERE'D BE MOON-LIGHT.
...

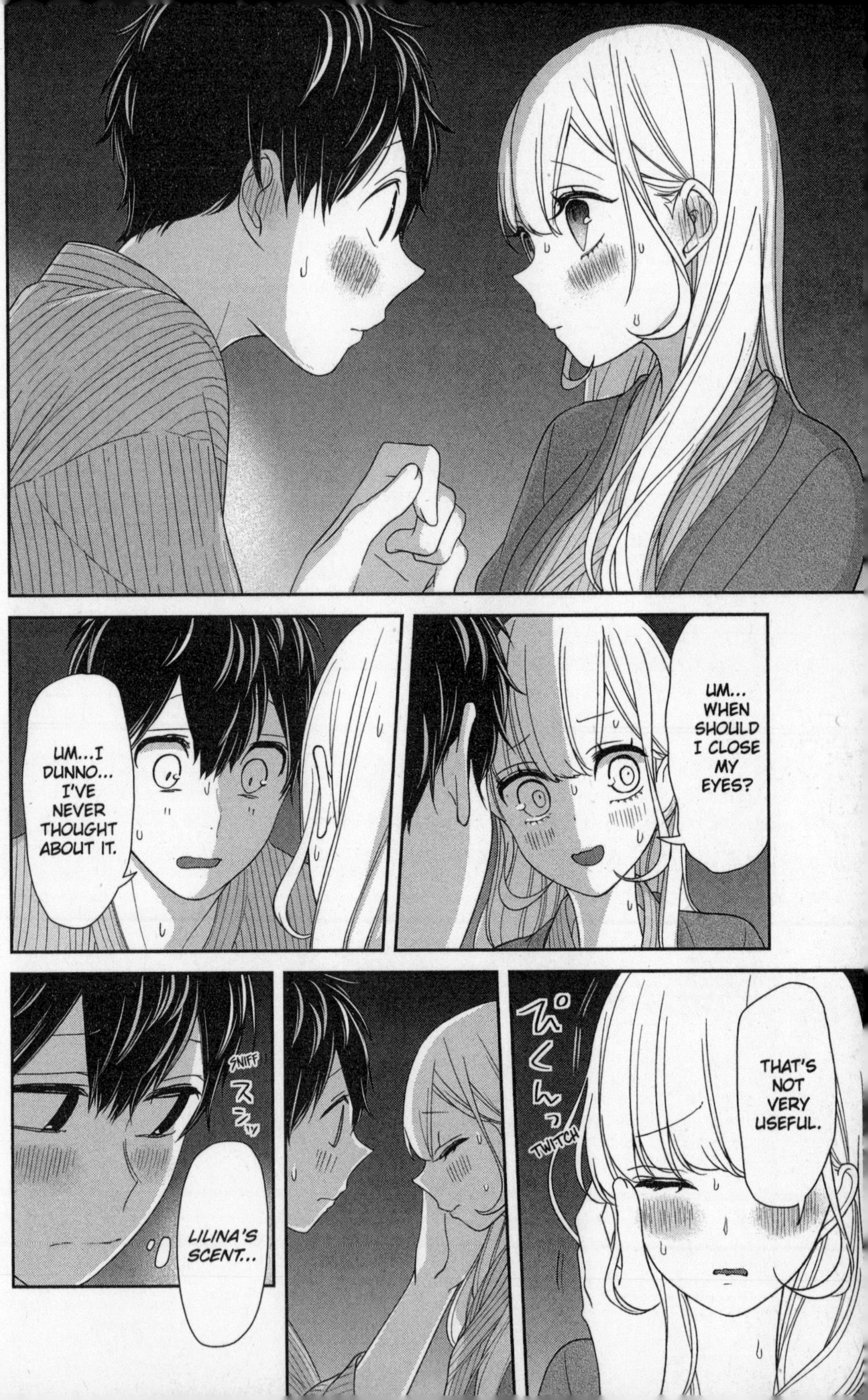
UM... WHEN SHOULD I CLOSE MY EYES?
UM...I DUNNO... I'VE NEVER THOUGHT ABOUT IT.
ぴくんっ
TWITCH
THAT'S NOT VERY USEFUL.
SNIFF
スンッ
LILINA'S SCENT...

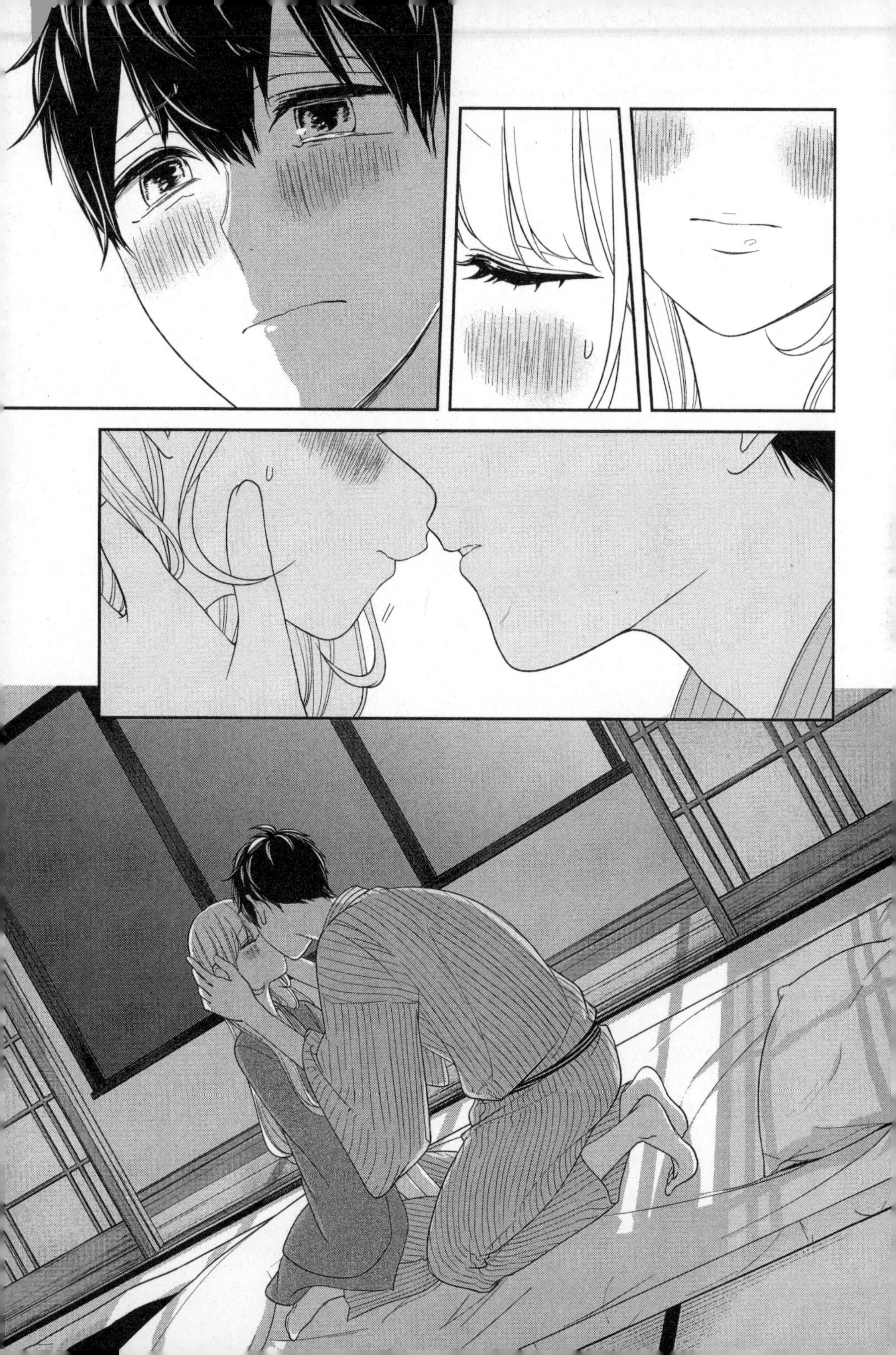

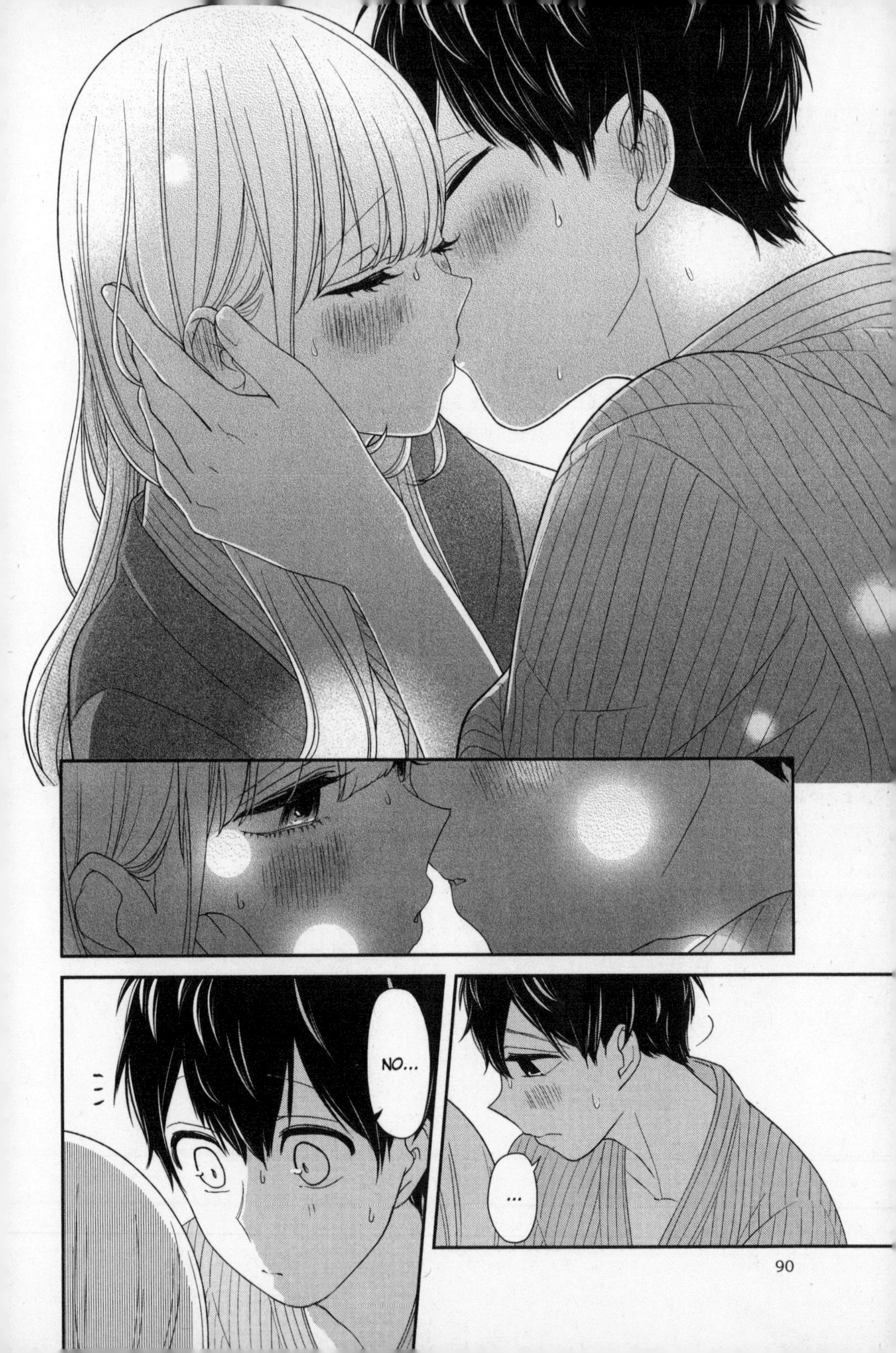
...
NO...

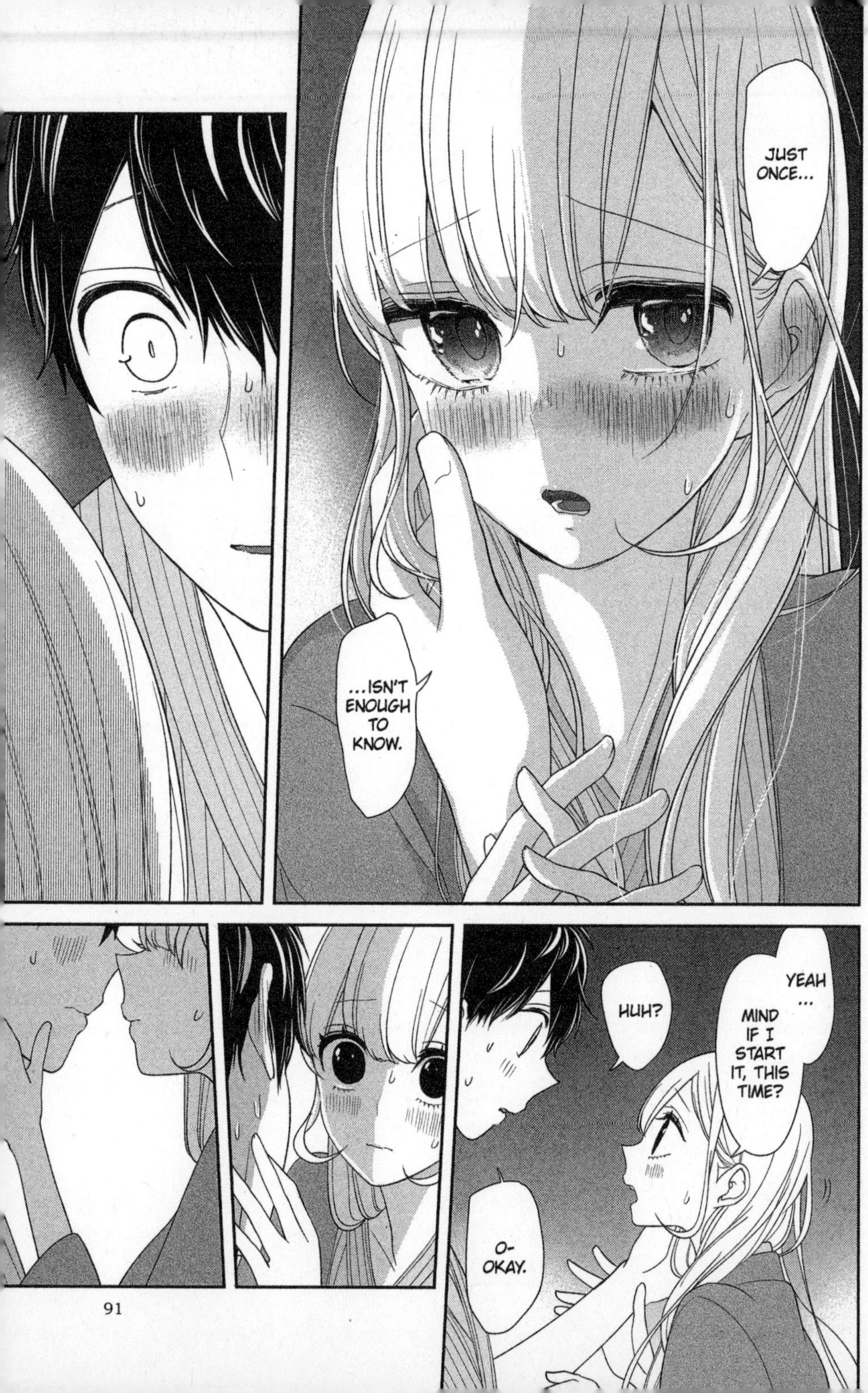
JUST ONCE...
...ISN'T ENOUGH TO KNOW.
YEAH... MIND IF I START IT, THIS TIME?
HUH?
O-OKAY.

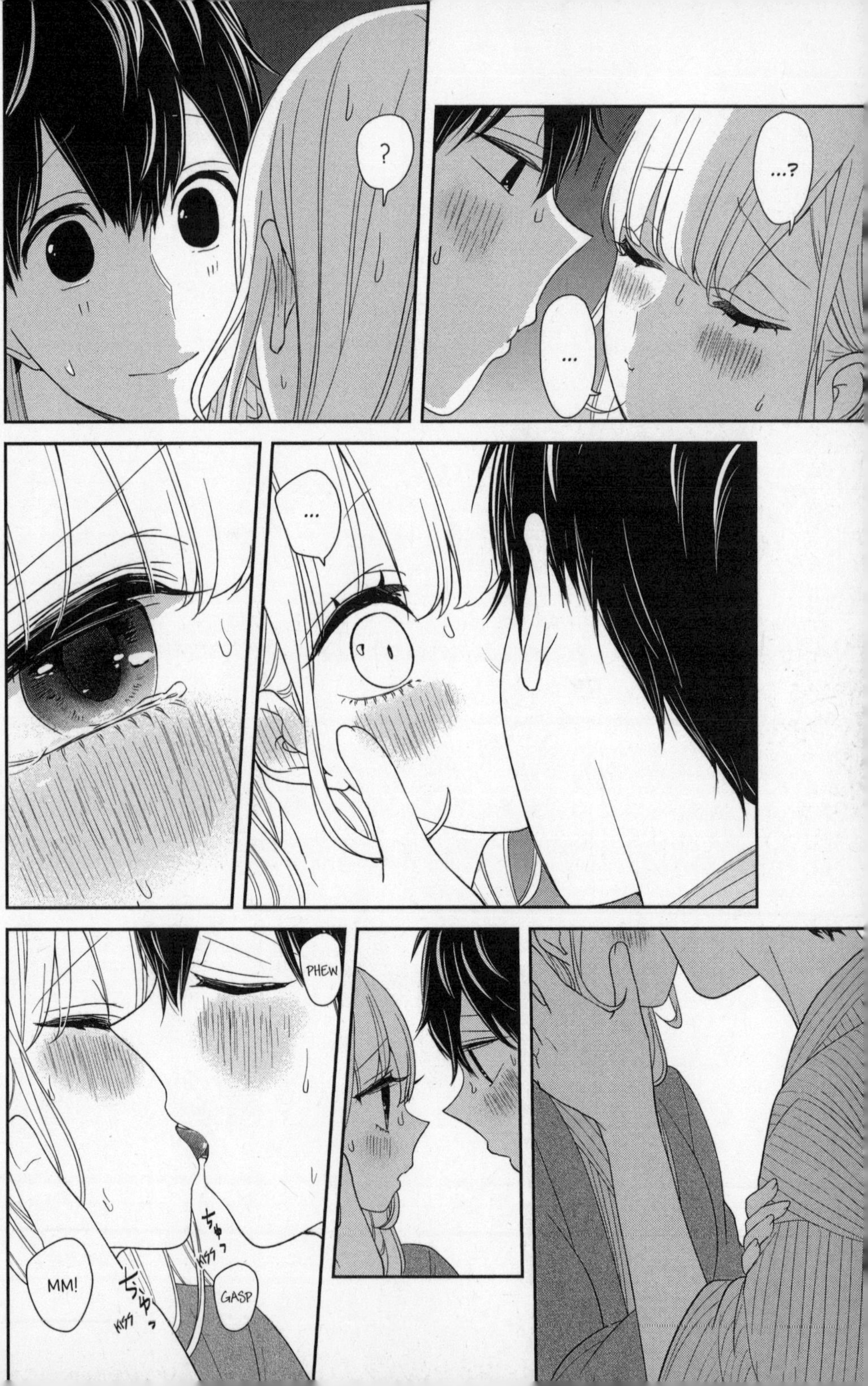

...?
...
?
...
PHEW
ちゅっ KISS
GASP
MM!
ちゅっ KISS

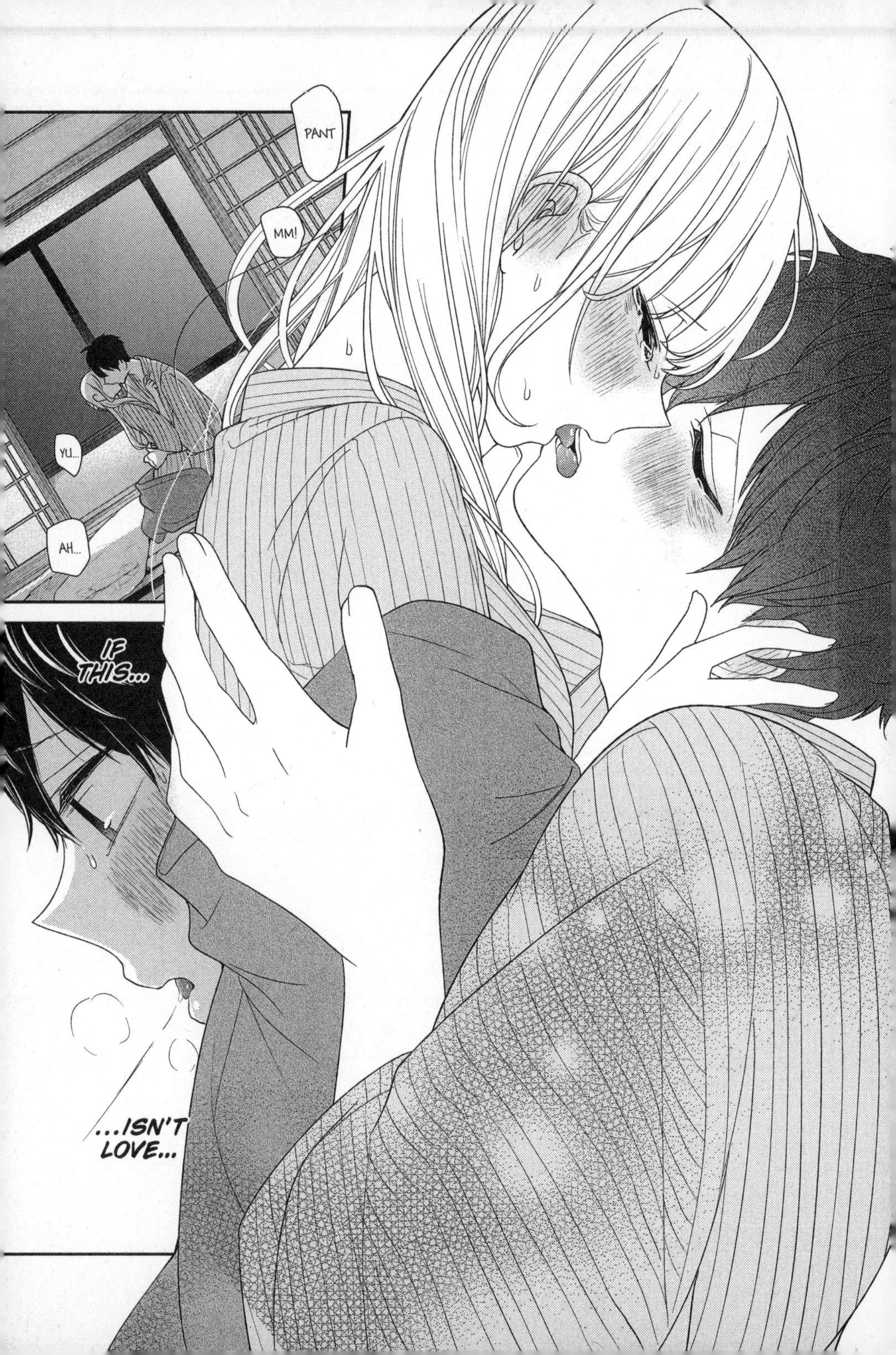
PANT
MM!
YU...
AH...
IF THIS...
...ISN'T LOVE...

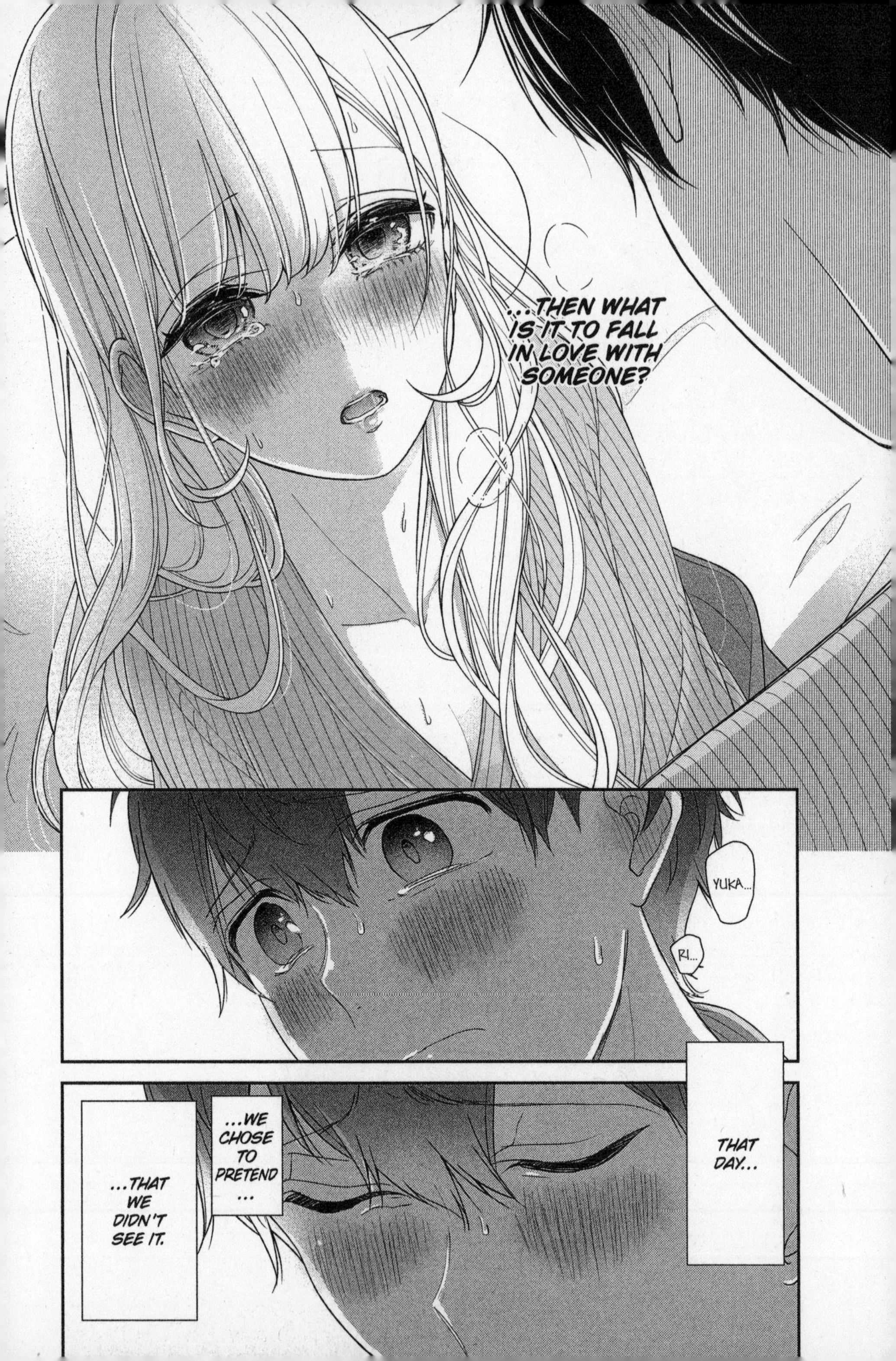
...THEN WHAT IS IT TO FALL IN LOVE WITH SOMEONE?
YUKA...
RI...
THAT DAY...
...WE CHOSE TO PRETEND...
...THAT WE DIDN'T SEE IT.

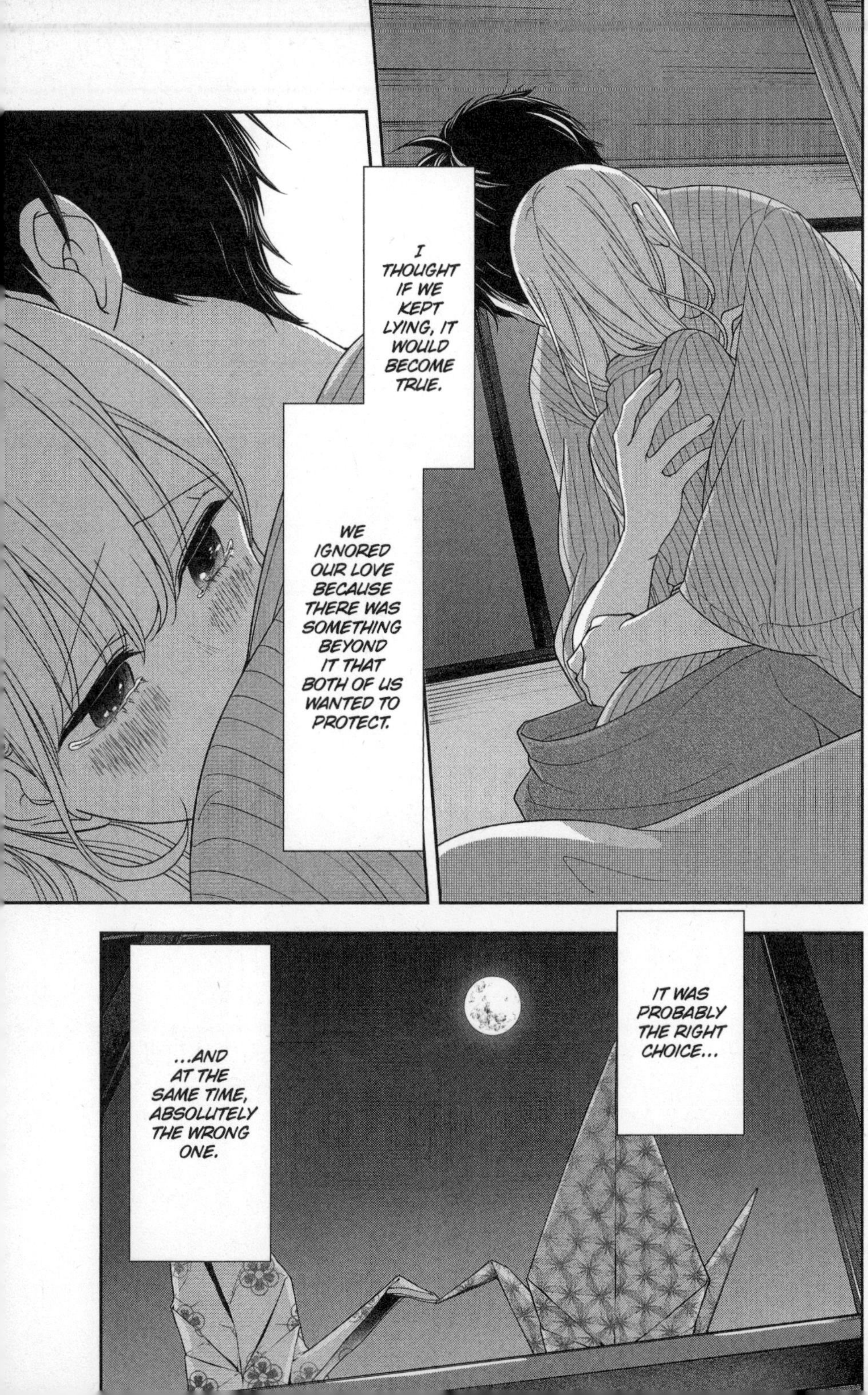
I THOUGHT IF WE KEPT LYING, IT WOULD BECOME TRUE.
WE IGNORED OUR LOVE BECAUSE THERE WAS SOMETHING BEYOND IT THAT BOTH OF US WANTED TO PROTECT.
IT WAS PROBABLY THE RIGHT CHOICE...
...AND AT THE SAME TIME, ABSOLUTELY THE WRONG ONE.

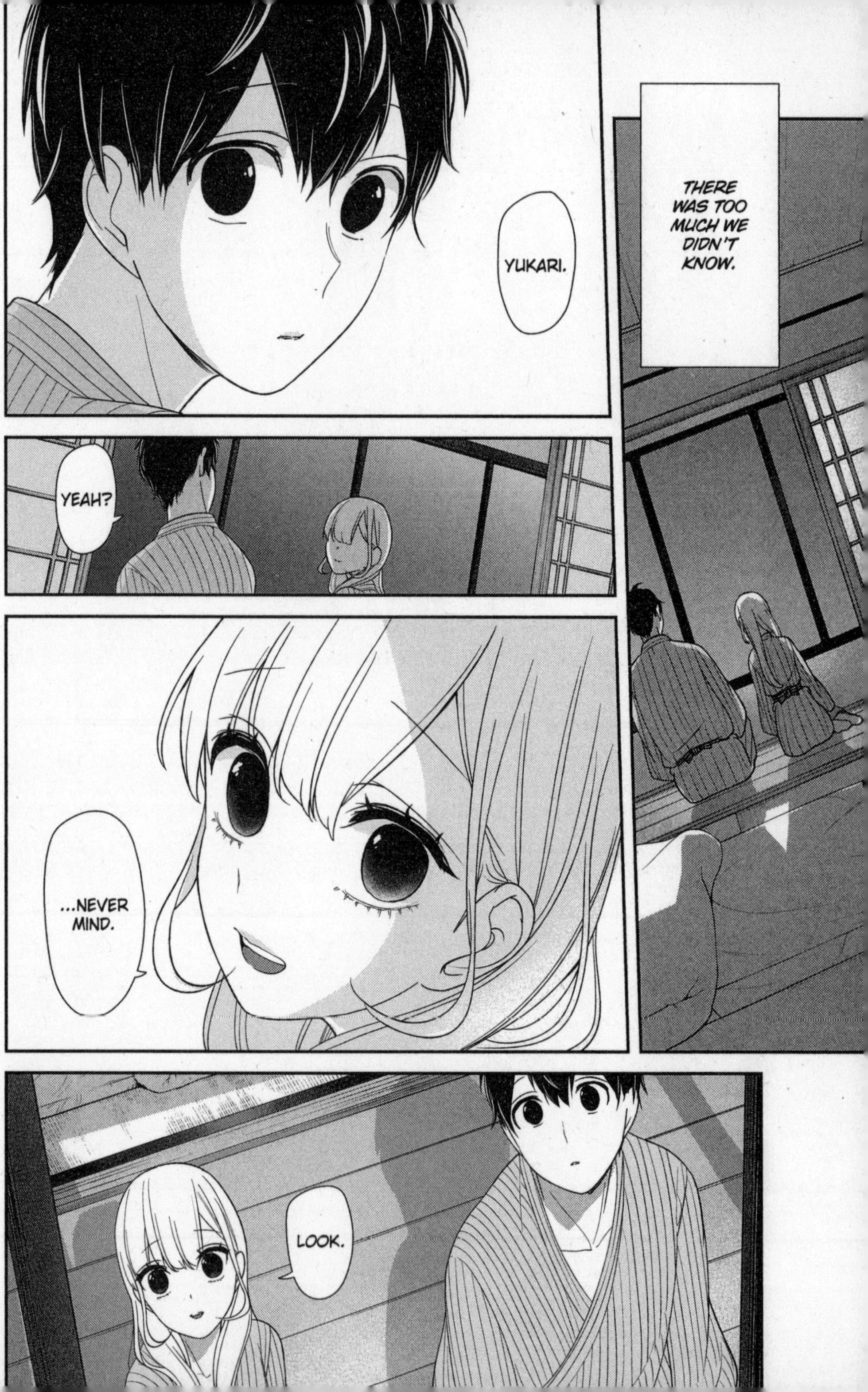
THERE WAS TOO MUCH WE DIDN'T KNOW.
YUKARI.
YEAH?
...NEVER MIND.
LOOK.

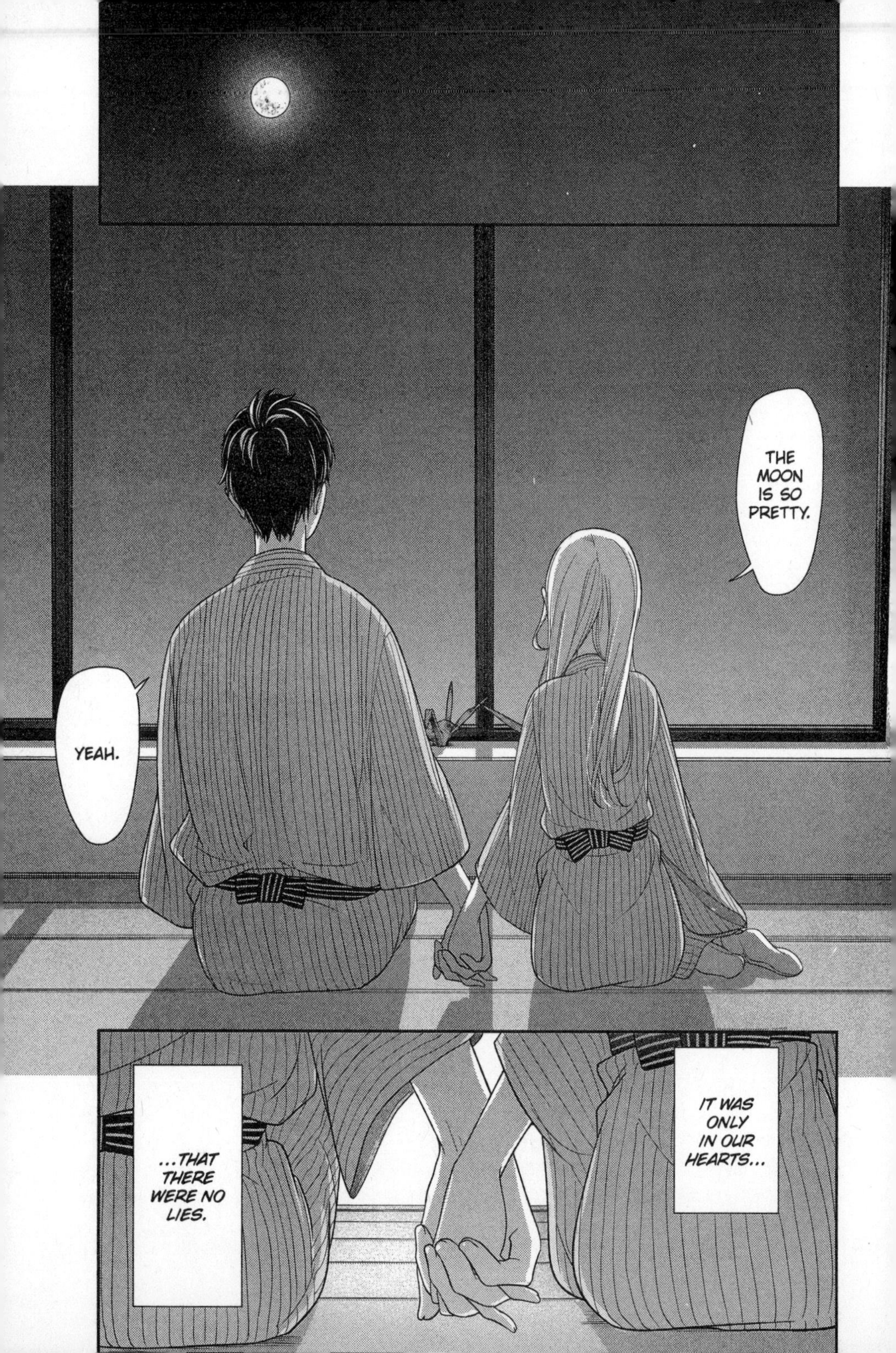
THE MOON IS SO PRETTY.
YEAH.
IT WAS ONLY IN OUR HEARTS...
...THAT THERE WERE NO LIES.

Love & Lies

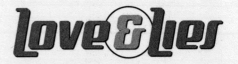

## Chapter 25: Chains of Love

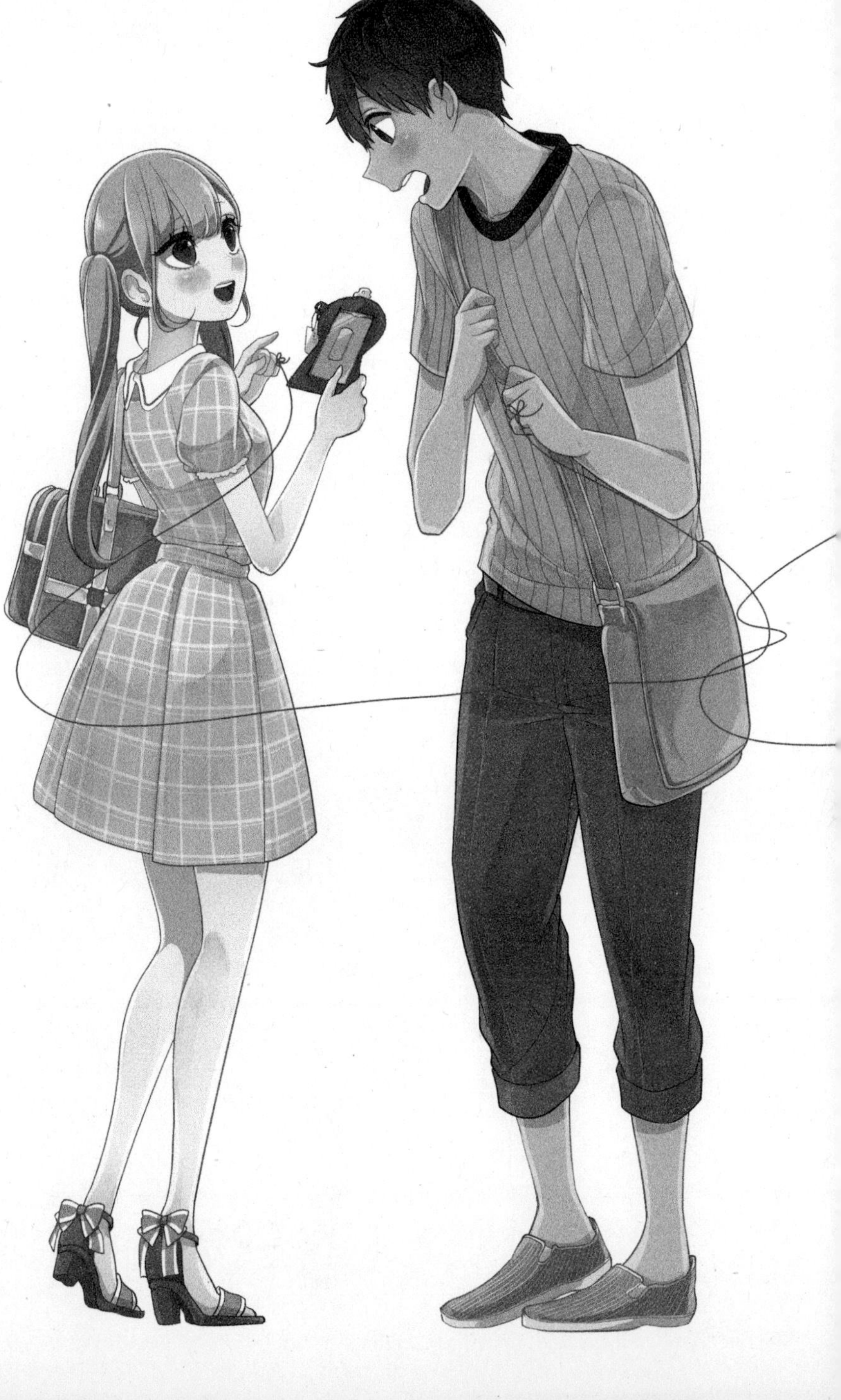

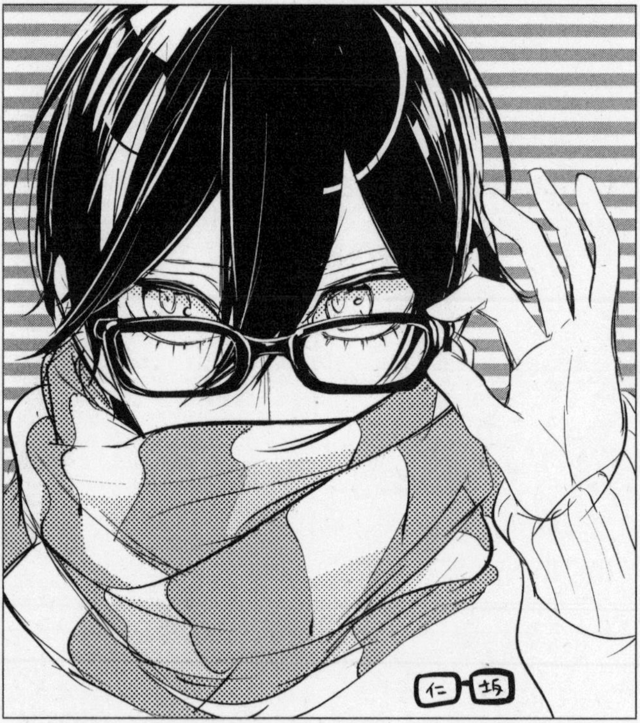
仁坂

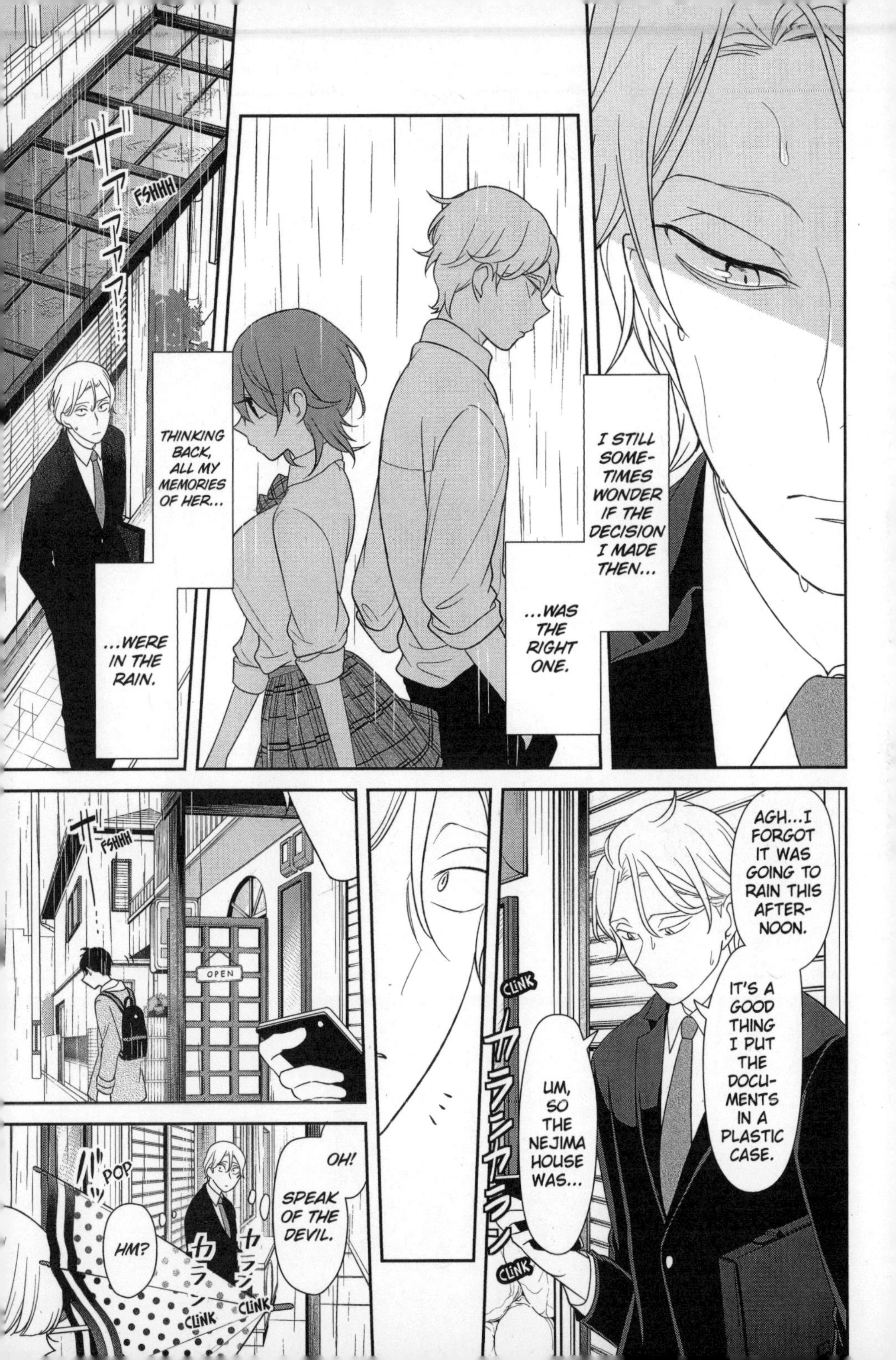
I STILL SOME-TIMES WONDER IF THE DECISION I MADE THEN...
...WAS THE RIGHT ONE.
THINKING BACK, ALL MY MEMORIES OF HER...
...WERE IN THE RAIN.
FSHHH
AGH...I FORGOT IT WAS GOING TO RAIN THIS AFTER-NOON.
IT'S A GOOD THING I PUT THE DOCU-MENTS IN A PLASTIC CASE.
UM, SO THE NEJIMA HOUSE WAS...
CLINK
CLINK
FSHHH
OPEN
OH!
SPEAK OF THE DEVIL.
POP
HM?
CLINK
CLINK

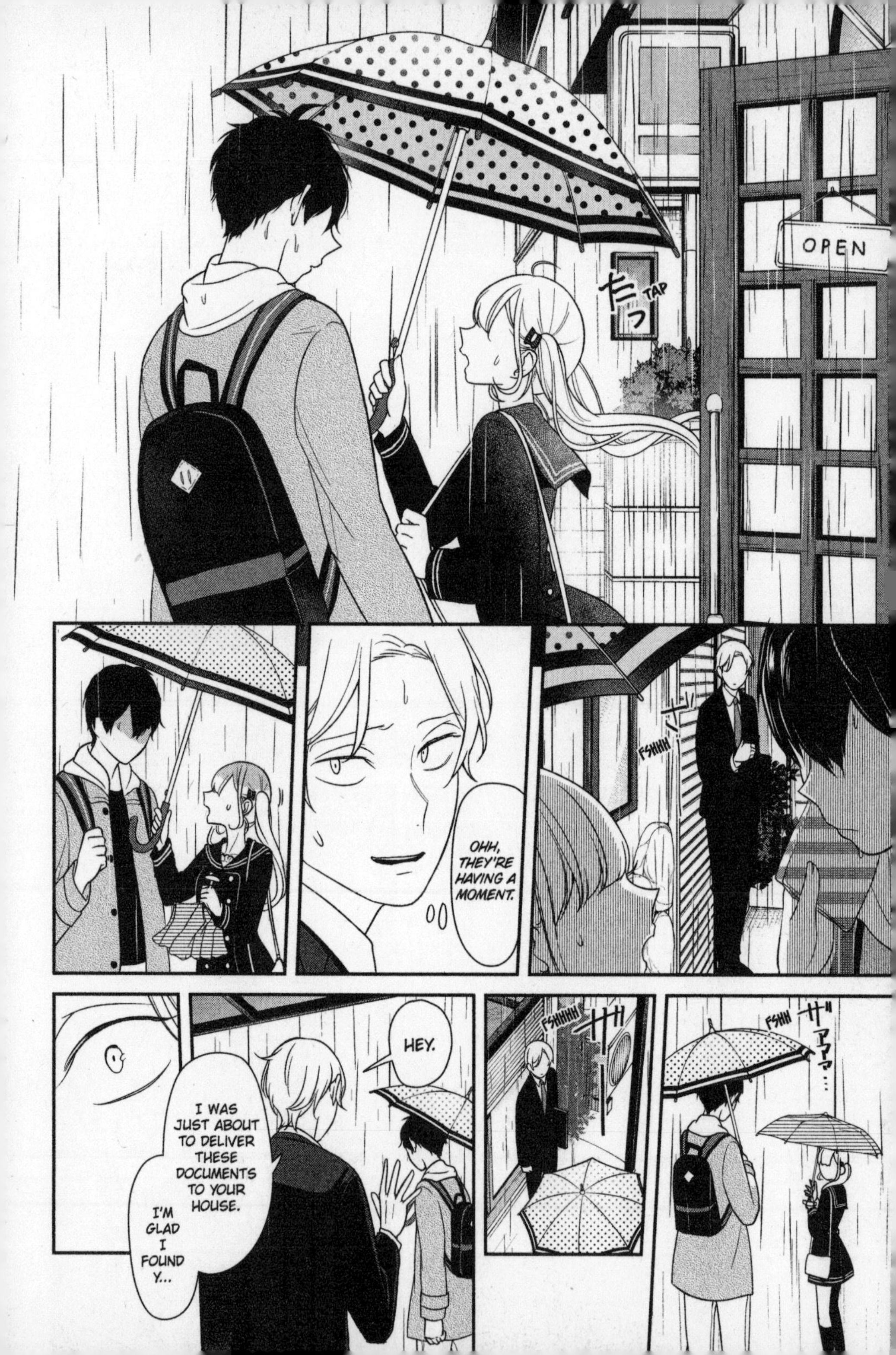
TAP
FSHHH
OHH, THEY'RE HAVING A MOMENT.
FSHH
FSHHHH
HEY.
I WAS JUST ABOUT TO DELIVER THESE DOCUMENTS TO YOUR HOUSE.
I'M GLAD I FOUND Y...

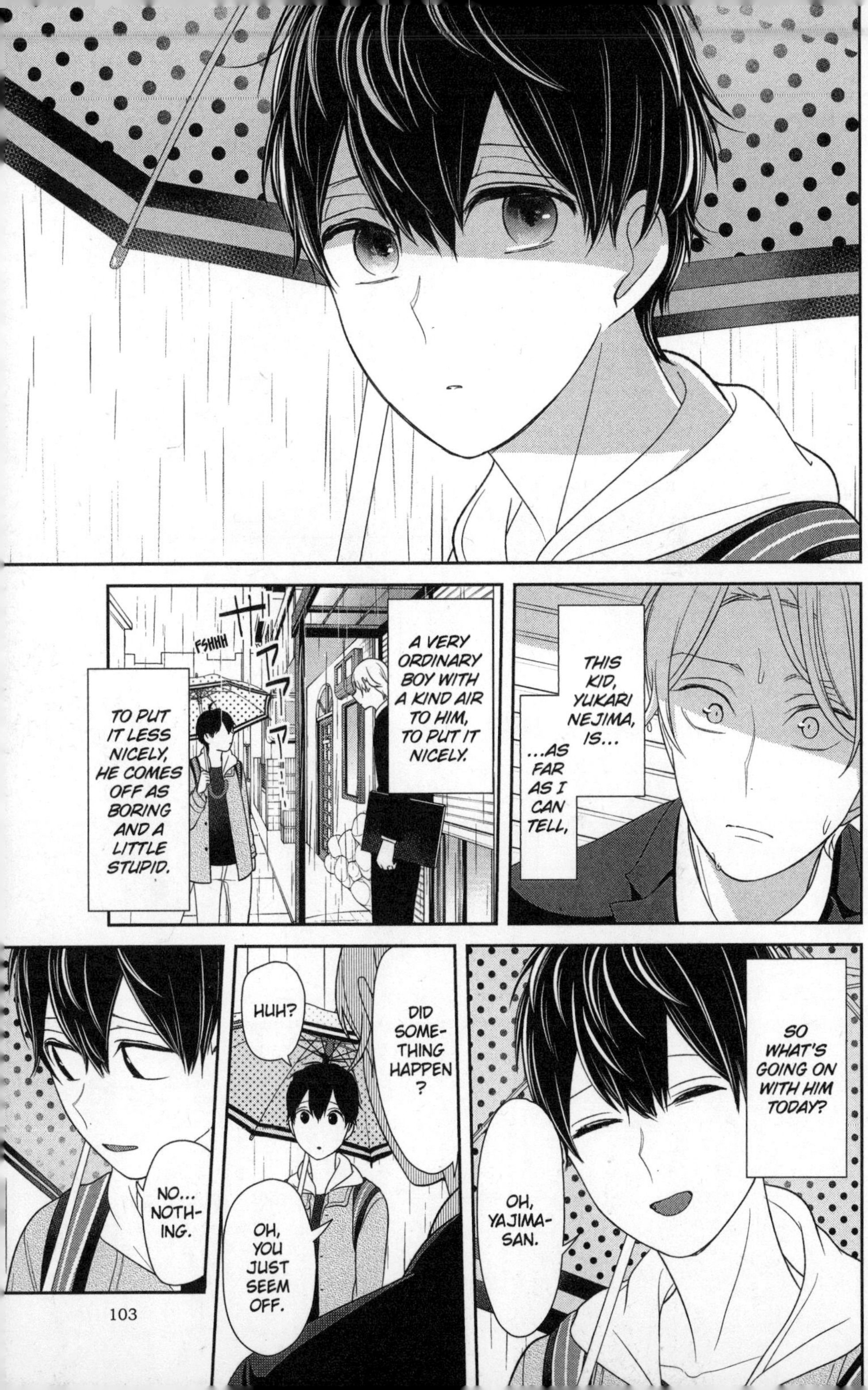
THIS KID, YUKARI NEJIMA, IS...
...AS FAR AS I CAN TELL,
A VERY ORDINARY BOY WITH A KIND AIR TO HIM, TO PUT IT NICELY.
FSHHH
TO PUT IT LESS NICELY, HE COMES OFF AS BORING AND A LITTLE STUPID.
SO WHAT'S GOING ON WITH HIM TODAY?
OH, YAJIMA-SAN.
DID SOME-THING HAPPEN?
HUH?
OH, YOU JUST SEEM OFF.
NO... NOTH-ING.

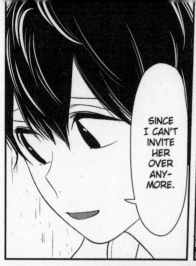

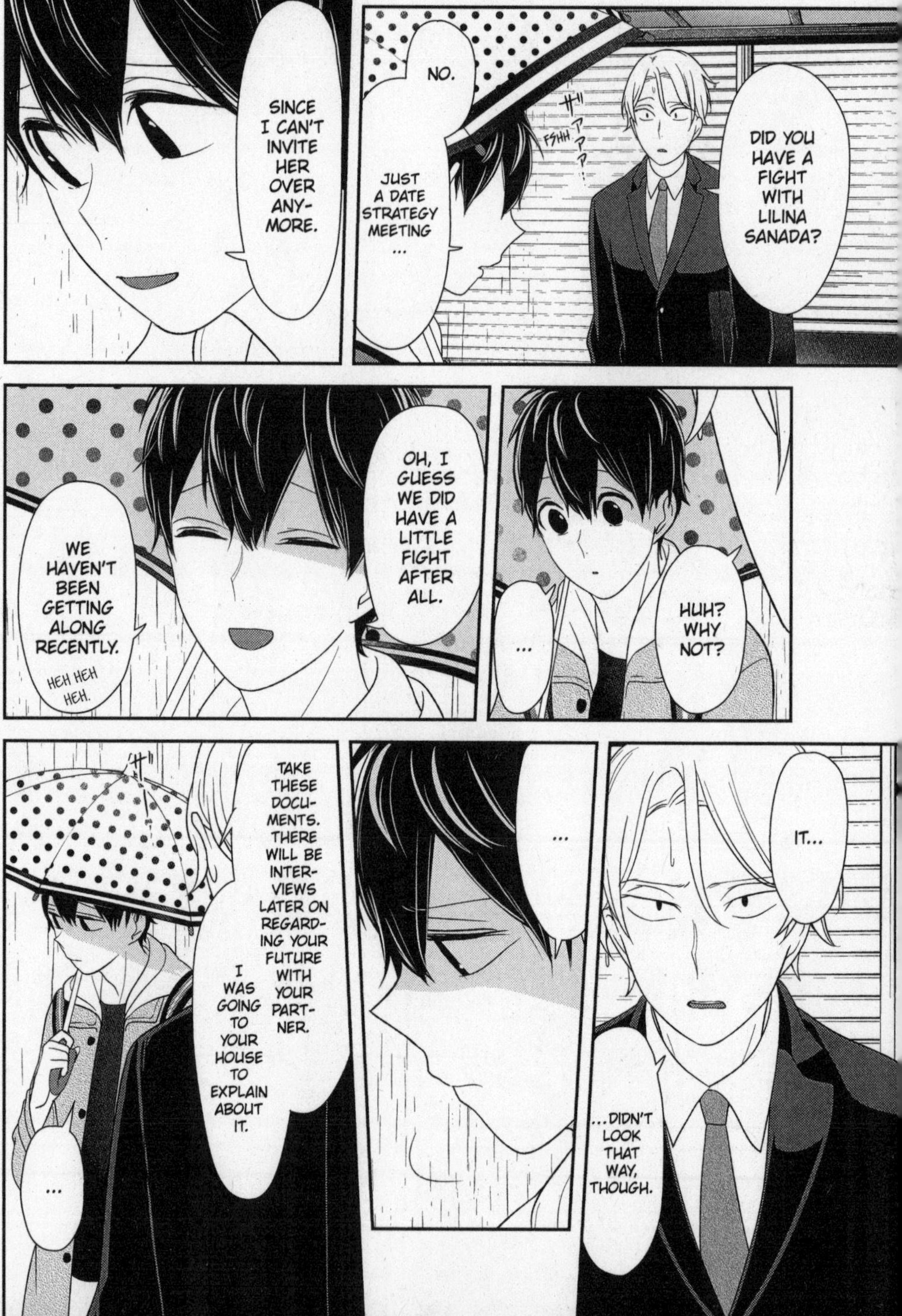
DID YOU HAVE A FIGHT WITH LILINA SANADA?
FSHH
NO.
JUST A DATE STRATEGY MEETING ...
SINCE I CAN'T INVITE HER OVER ANYMORE.
HUH? WHY NOT?
...
OH, I GUESS WE DID HAVE A LITTLE FIGHT AFTER ALL.
WE HAVEN'T BEEN GETTING ALONG RECENTLY.
HEH HEH HEH.
IT...
...DIDN'T LOOK THAT WAY, THOUGH.
...
TAKE THESE DOCUMENTS. THERE WILL BE INTERVIEWS LATER ON REGARDING YOUR FUTURE WITH YOUR PARTNER.
I WAS GOING TO YOUR HOUSE TO EXPLAIN ABOUT IT.
...

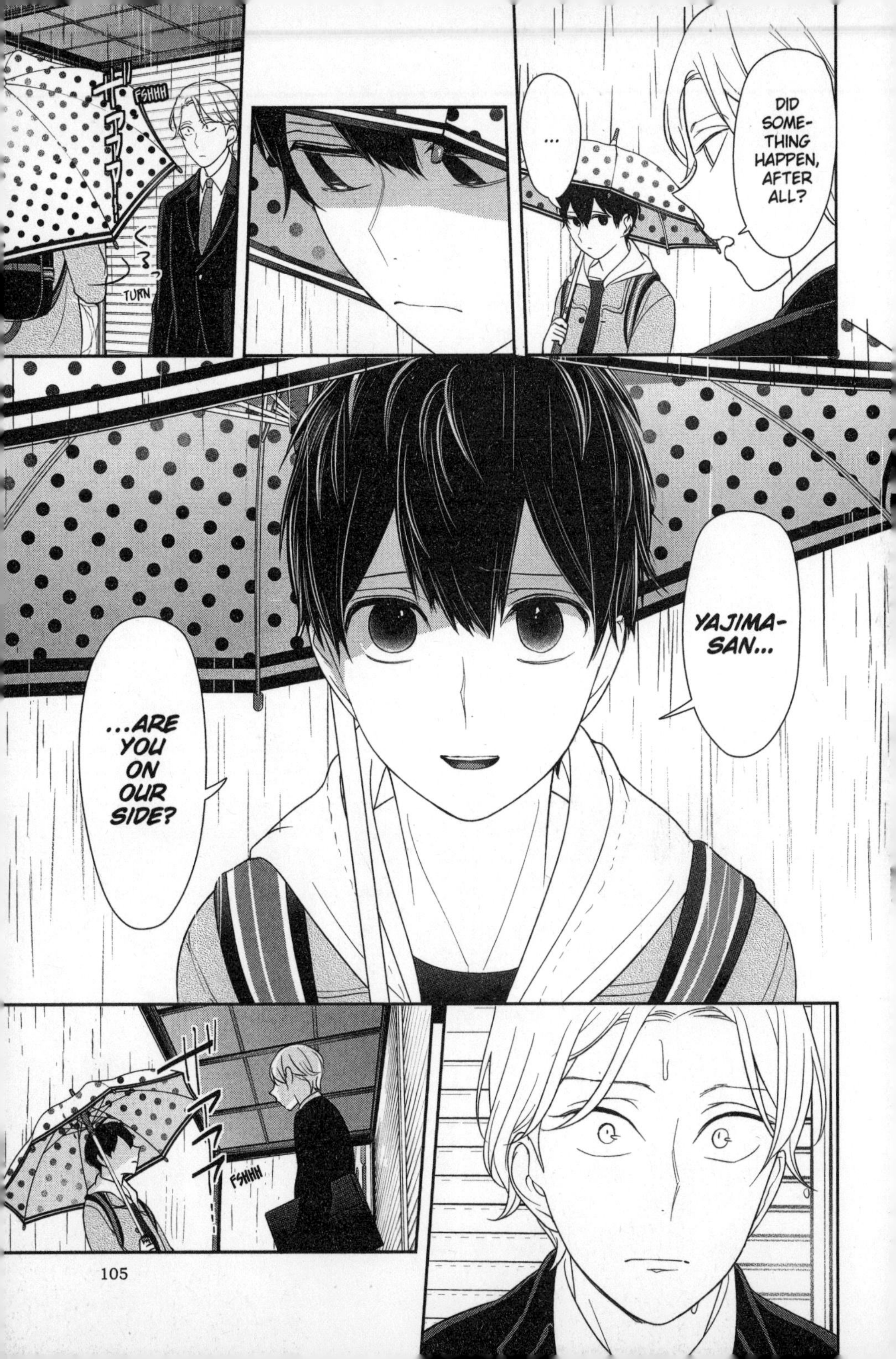
DID SOMETHING HAPPEN, AFTER ALL?
...
FSHHH
TURN
YAJIMA-SAN...
...ARE YOU ON OUR SIDE?
FSHHH

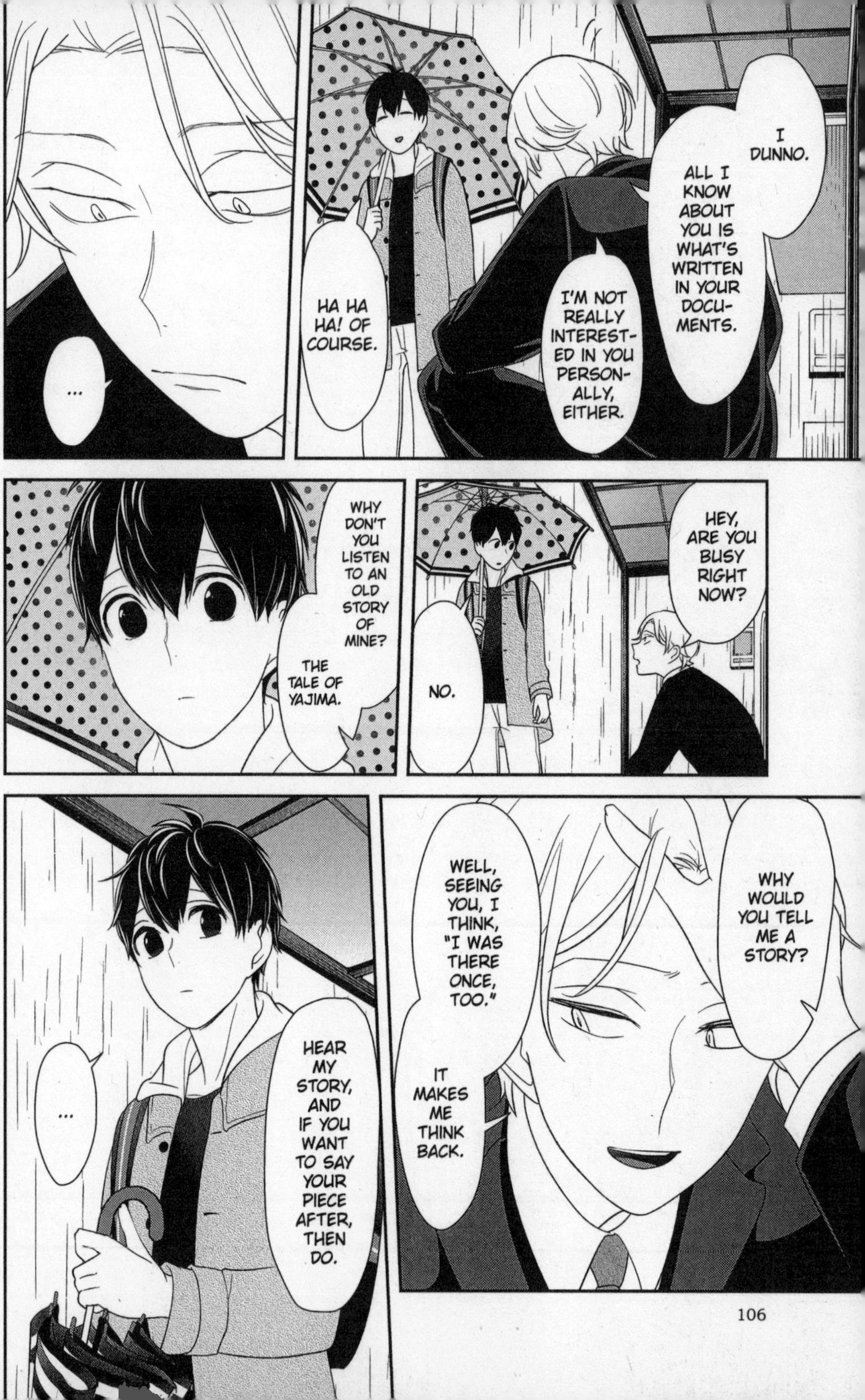
I DUNNO.
ALL I KNOW ABOUT YOU IS WHAT'S WRITTEN IN YOUR DOCU-MENTS.
I'M NOT REALLY INTEREST-ED IN YOU PERSON-ALLY, EITHER.
HA HA HA! OF COURSE.
...
HEY, ARE YOU BUSY RIGHT NOW?
NO.
WHY DON'T YOU LISTEN TO AN OLD STORY OF MINE?
THE TALE OF YAJIMA.
WHY WOULD YOU TELL ME A STORY?
WELL, SEEING YOU, I THINK, "I WAS THERE ONCE, TOO."
IT MAKES ME THINK BACK.
HEAR MY STORY, AND IF YOU WANT TO SAY YOUR PIECE AFTER, THEN DO.
...

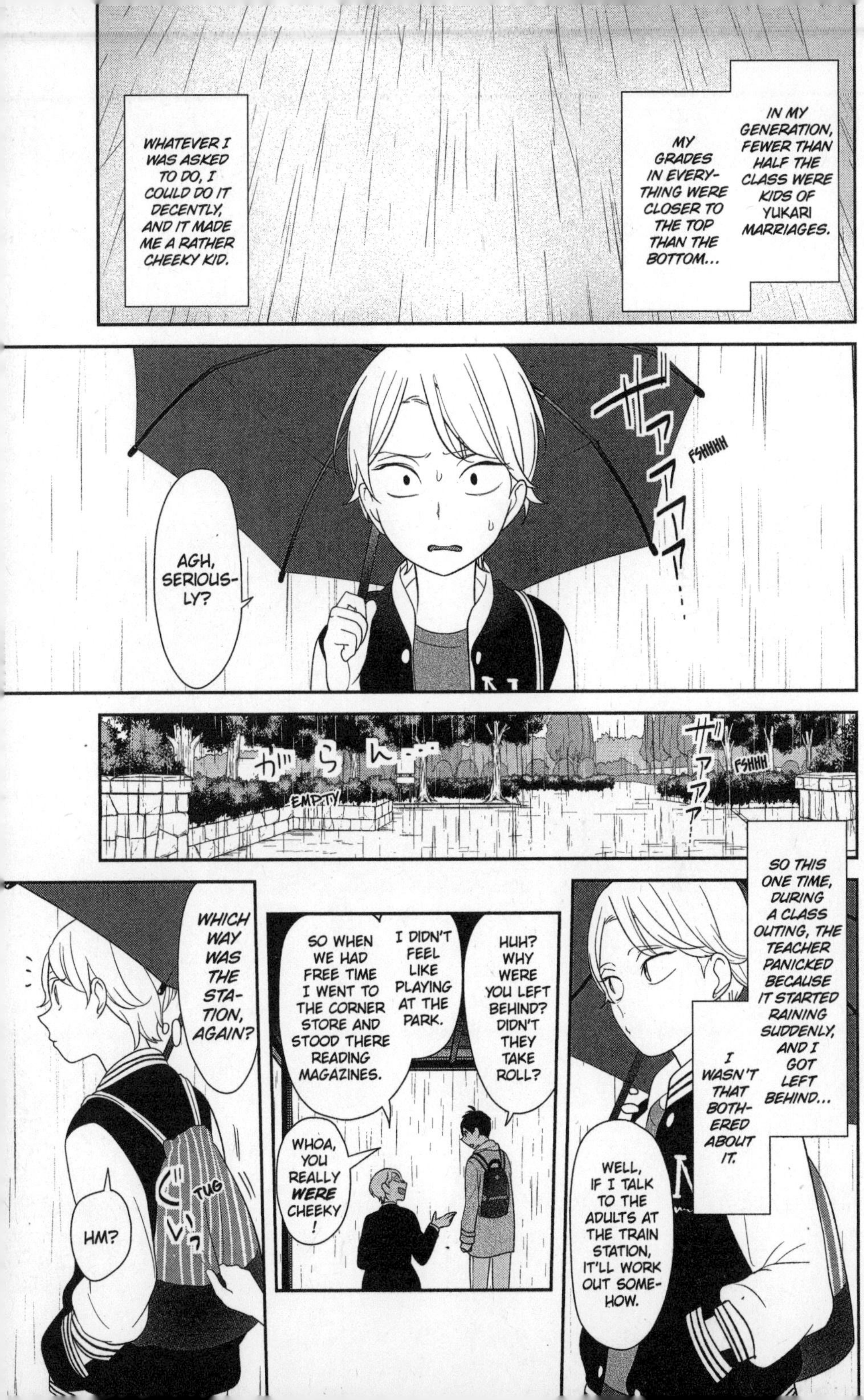
IN MY GENERATION, FEWER THAN HALF THE CLASS WERE KIDS OF YUKARI MARRIAGES.
MY GRADES IN EVERYTHING WERE CLOSER TO THE TOP THAN THE BOTTOM...
WHATEVER I WAS ASKED TO DO, I COULD DO IT DECENTLY, AND IT MADE ME A RATHER CHEEKY KID.
ザァァァ...
FSHHHH
AGH, SERIOUSLY?
ザァァァ
FSHHH
がらん...
EMPTY
SO THIS ONE TIME, DURING A CLASS OUTING, THE TEACHER PANICKED BECAUSE IT STARTED RAINING SUDDENLY, AND I GOT LEFT BEHIND...
I WASN'T THAT BOTHERED ABOUT IT.
WELL, IF I TALK TO THE ADULTS AT THE TRAIN STATION, IT'LL WORK OUT SOMEHOW.
HUH? WHY WERE YOU LEFT BEHIND? DIDN'T THEY TAKE ROLL?
I DIDN'T FEEL LIKE PLAYING AT THE PARK.
SO WHEN WE HAD FREE TIME I WENT TO THE CORNER STORE AND STOOD THERE READING MAGAZINES.
WHOA, YOU REALLY WERE CHEEKY!
WHICH WAY WAS THE STATION, AGAIN?
ぐいっ
TUG
HM?

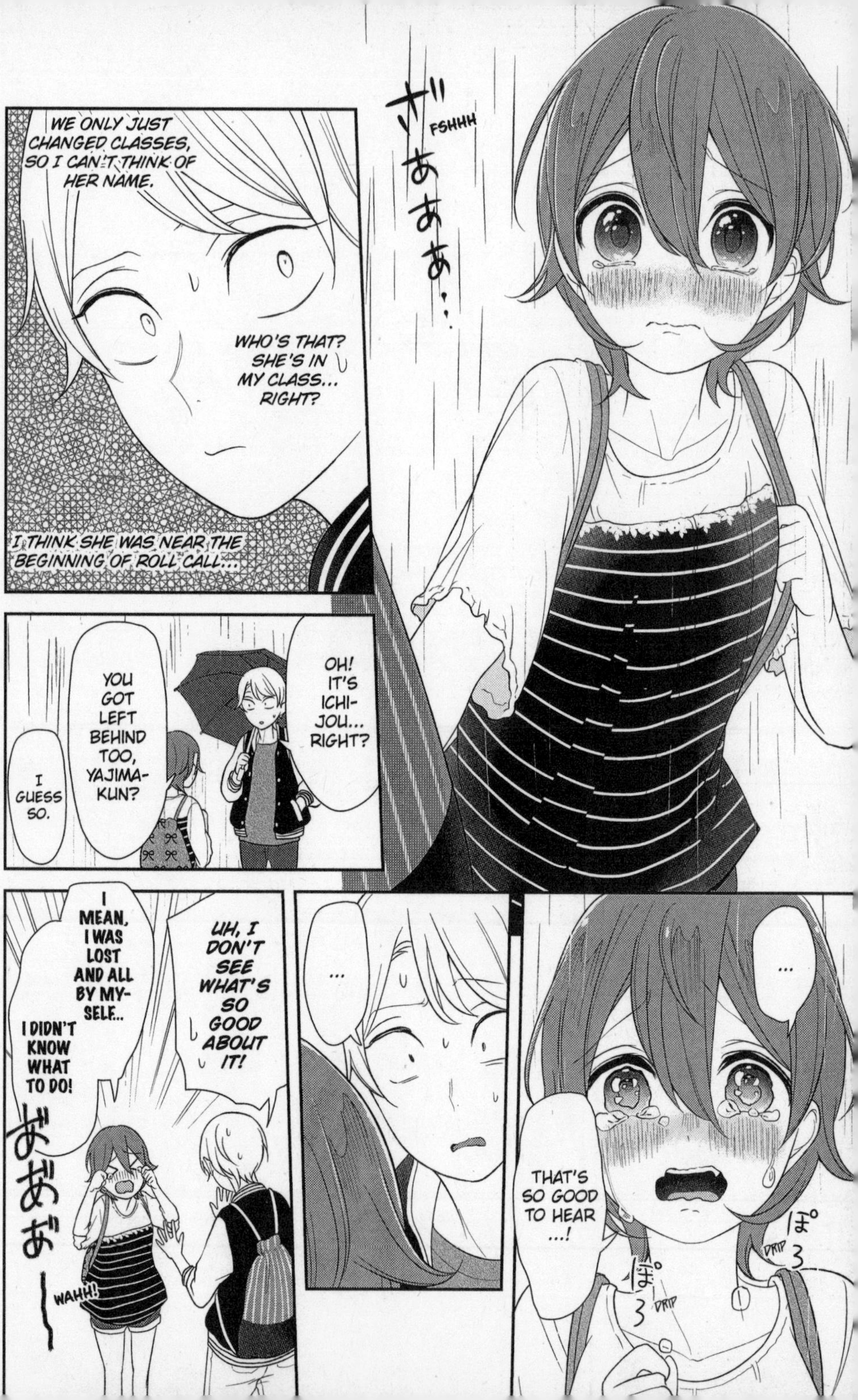

ざあああ・・・
FSHHH
WE ONLY JUST CHANGED CLASSES, SO I CAN'T THINK OF HER NAME.
WHO'S THAT? SHE'S IN MY CLASS... RIGHT?
I THINK SHE WAS NEAR THE BEGINNING OF ROLL CALL...
OH! IT'S ICHIJOU... RIGHT?
YOU GOT LEFT BEHIND TOO, YAJIMA-KUN?
I GUESS SO.
...
THAT'S SO GOOD TO HEAR ...!
ぽろ
DRIP
ぽろ
DRIP
...
UH, I DON'T SEE WHAT'S SO GOOD ABOUT IT!
I MEAN, I WAS LOST AND ALL BY MYSELF...
I DIDN'T KNOW WHAT TO DO!
おおぉ～
WAHH!

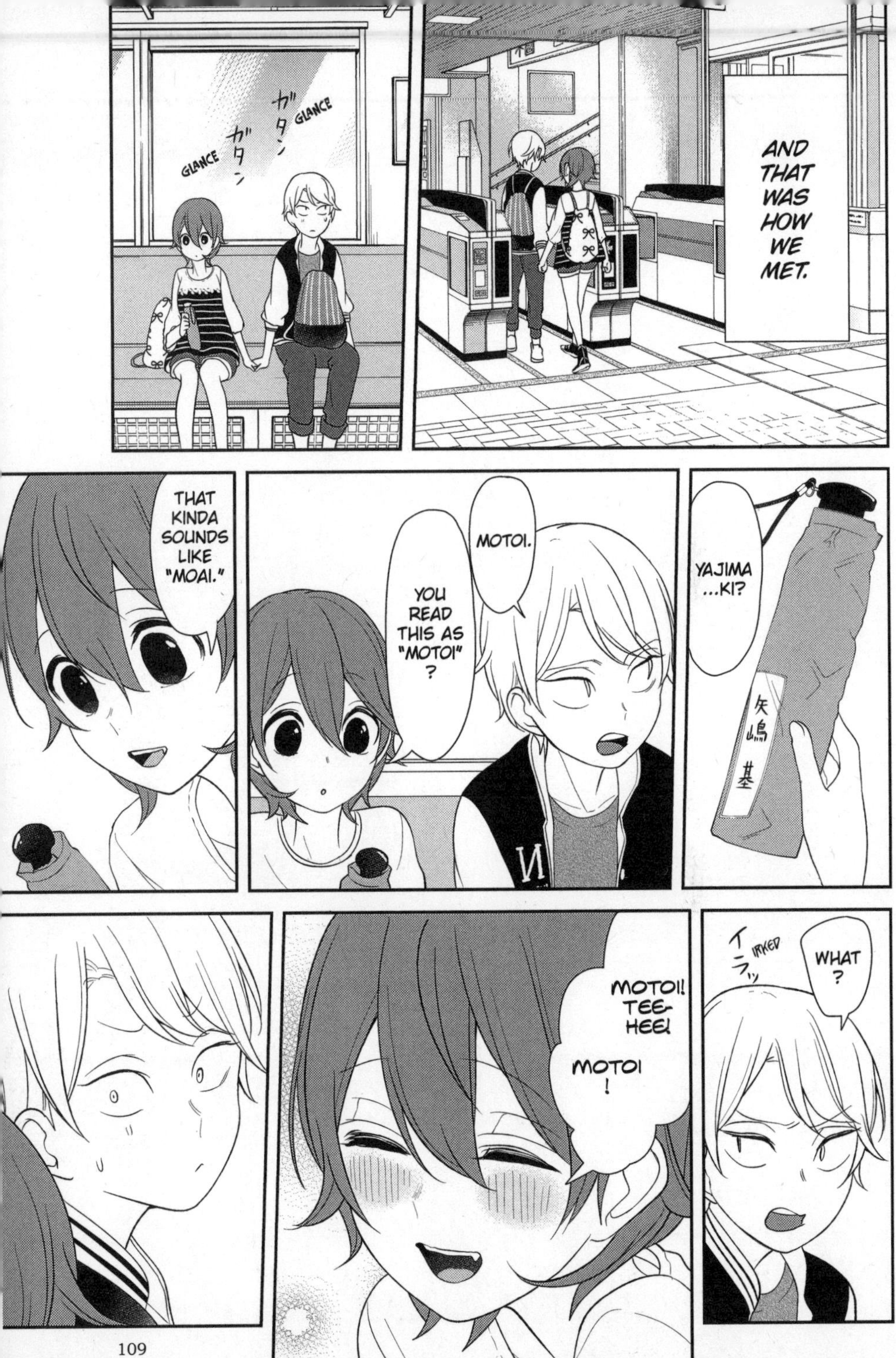
AND THAT WAS HOW WE MET.
ガタン
GLANCE
ガタン
GLANCE
YAJIMA ...KI?
矢嶋 基
MOTOI.
YOU READ THIS AS "MOTOI"?
THAT KINDA SOUNDS LIKE "MOAI."
イラッ
IRKED
WHAT?
MOTOI! TEE-HEE!
MOTOI!

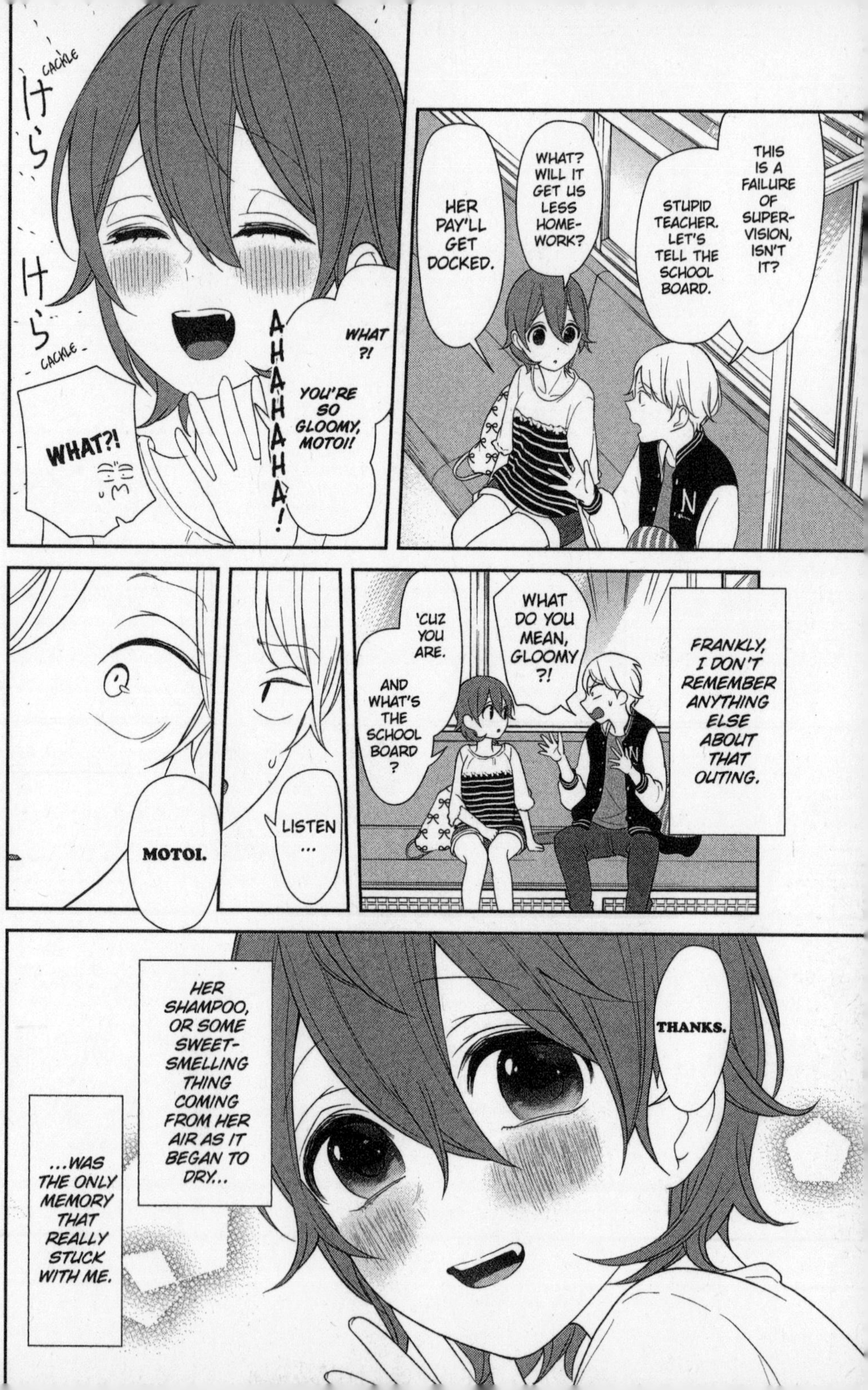THIS IS A FAILURE OF SUPER-VISION, ISN'T IT?
STUPID TEACHER. LET'S TELL THE SCHOOL BOARD.
WHAT? WILL IT GET US LESS HOME-WORK?
HER PAY'LL GET DOCKED.
けら CACKLE
けら CACKLE
AHAHAHA!
WHAT?!
YOU'RE SO GLOOMY, MOTOI!
WHAT?!
FRANKLY, I DON'T REMEMBER ANYTHING ELSE ABOUT THAT OUTING.
WHAT DO YOU MEAN, GLOOMY?!
'CUZ YOU ARE.
AND WHAT'S THE SCHOOL BOARD?
LISTEN...
MOTOI.
THANKS.
HER SHAMPOO, OR SOME SWEET-SMELLING THING COMING FROM HER AIR AS IT BEGAN TO DRY...
...WAS THE ONLY MEMORY THAT REALLY STUCK WITH ME.

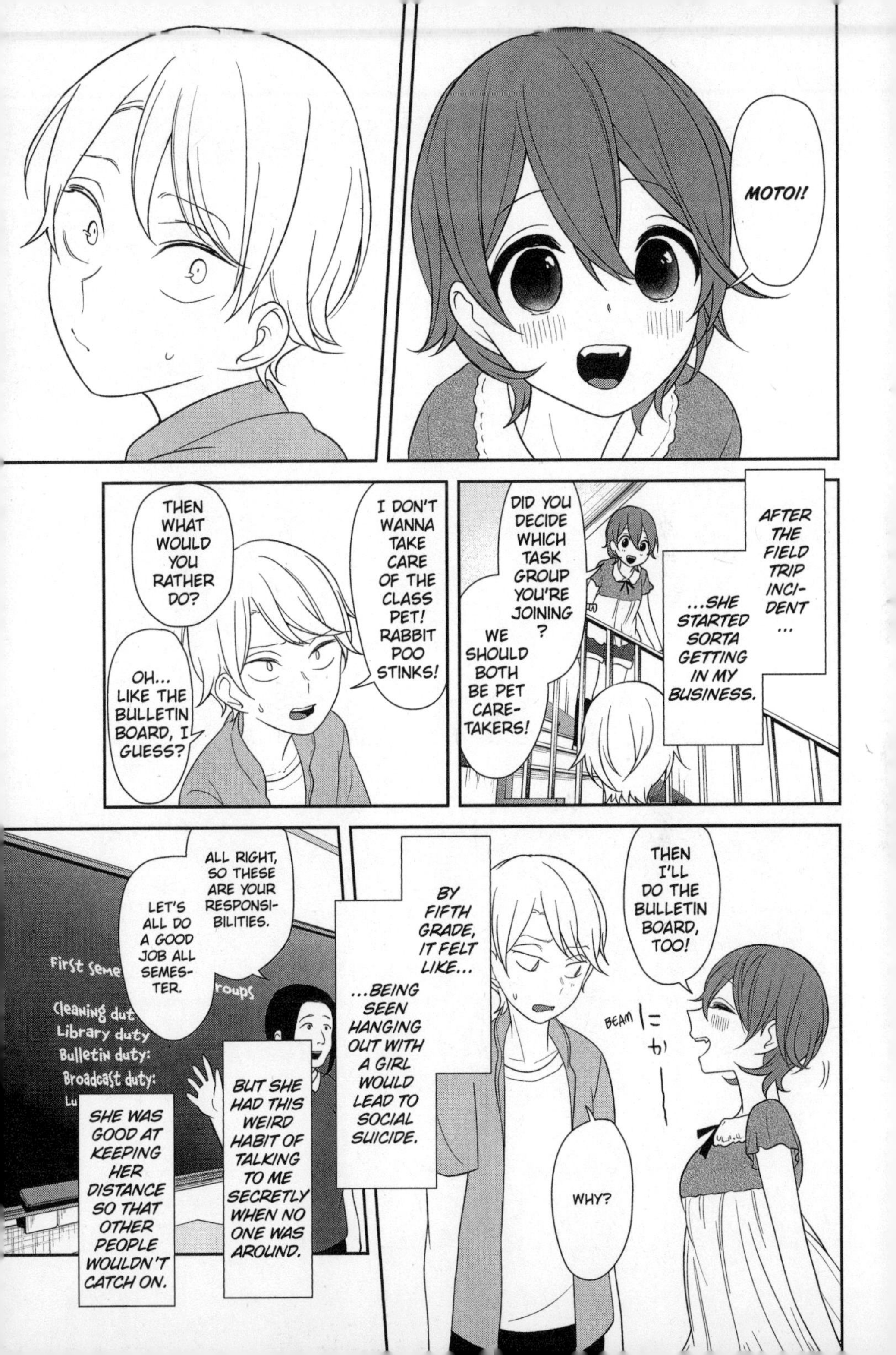
MOTOI!
AFTER THE FIELD TRIP INCIDENT...
...SHE STARTED SORTA GETTING IN MY BUSINESS.
DID YOU DECIDE WHICH TASK GROUP YOU'RE JOINING?
WE SHOULD BOTH BE PET CARETAKERS!
I DON'T WANNA TAKE CARE OF THE CLASS PET! RABBIT POO STINKS!
THEN WHAT WOULD YOU RATHER DO?
OH... LIKE THE BULLETIN BOARD, I GUESS?
THEN I'LL DO THE BULLETIN BOARD, TOO!
BEAM
BY FIFTH GRADE, IT FELT LIKE...
...BEING SEEN HANGING OUT WITH A GIRL WOULD LEAD TO SOCIAL SUICIDE.
WHY?
ALL RIGHT, SO THESE ARE YOUR RESPONSIBILITIES.
LET'S ALL DO A GOOD JOB ALL SEMESTER.
Library duty
Bulletin duty:
Broadcast duty:
BUT SHE HAD THIS WEIRD HABIT OF TALKING TO ME SECRETLY WHEN NO ONE WAS AROUND.
SHE WAS GOOD AT KEEPING HER DISTANCE SO THAT OTHER PEOPLE WOULDN'T CATCH ON.

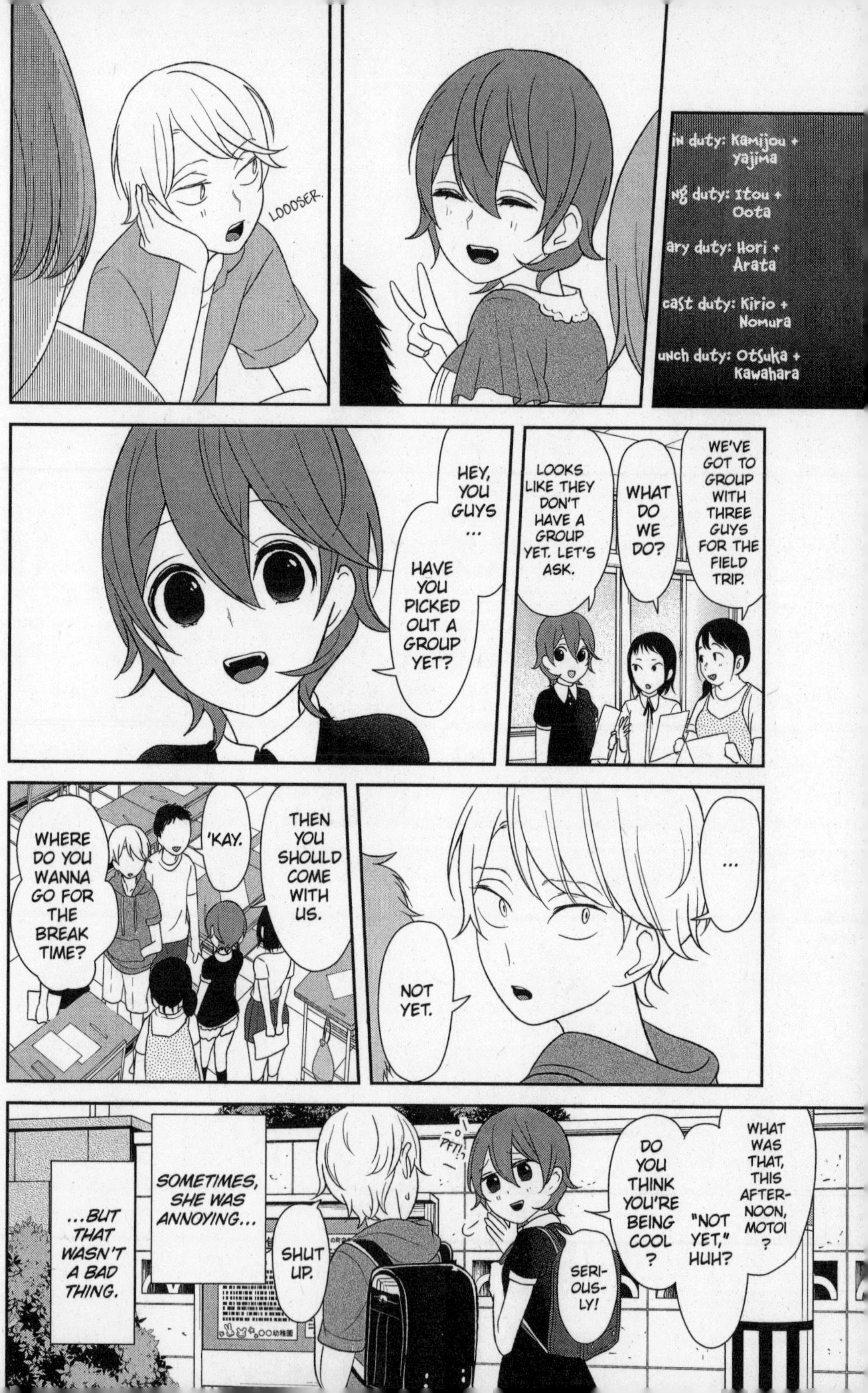

in duty: Kamijou + Yajima
ng duty: Itou + Oota
ary duty: Hori + Arata
cast duty: Kirio + Nomura
unch duty: Otsuka + Kawahara
LOOOSER.
WE'VE GOT TO GROUP WITH THREE GUYS FOR THE FIELD TRIP.
WHAT DO WE DO?
LOOKS LIKE THEY DON'T HAVE A GROUP YET. LET'S ASK.
HEY, YOU GUYS...
HAVE YOU PICKED OUT A GROUP YET?
...
NOT YET.
THEN YOU SHOULD COME WITH US.
'KAY.
WHERE DO YOU WANNA GO FOR THE BREAK TIME?
WHAT WAS THAT, THIS AFTERNOON, MOTOI?
"NOT YET," HUH?
DO YOU THINK YOU'RE BEING COOL?
PFT!
SERIOUSLY!
SHUT UP.
SOMETIMES, SHE WAS ANNOYING...
...BUT THAT WASN'T A BAD THING.

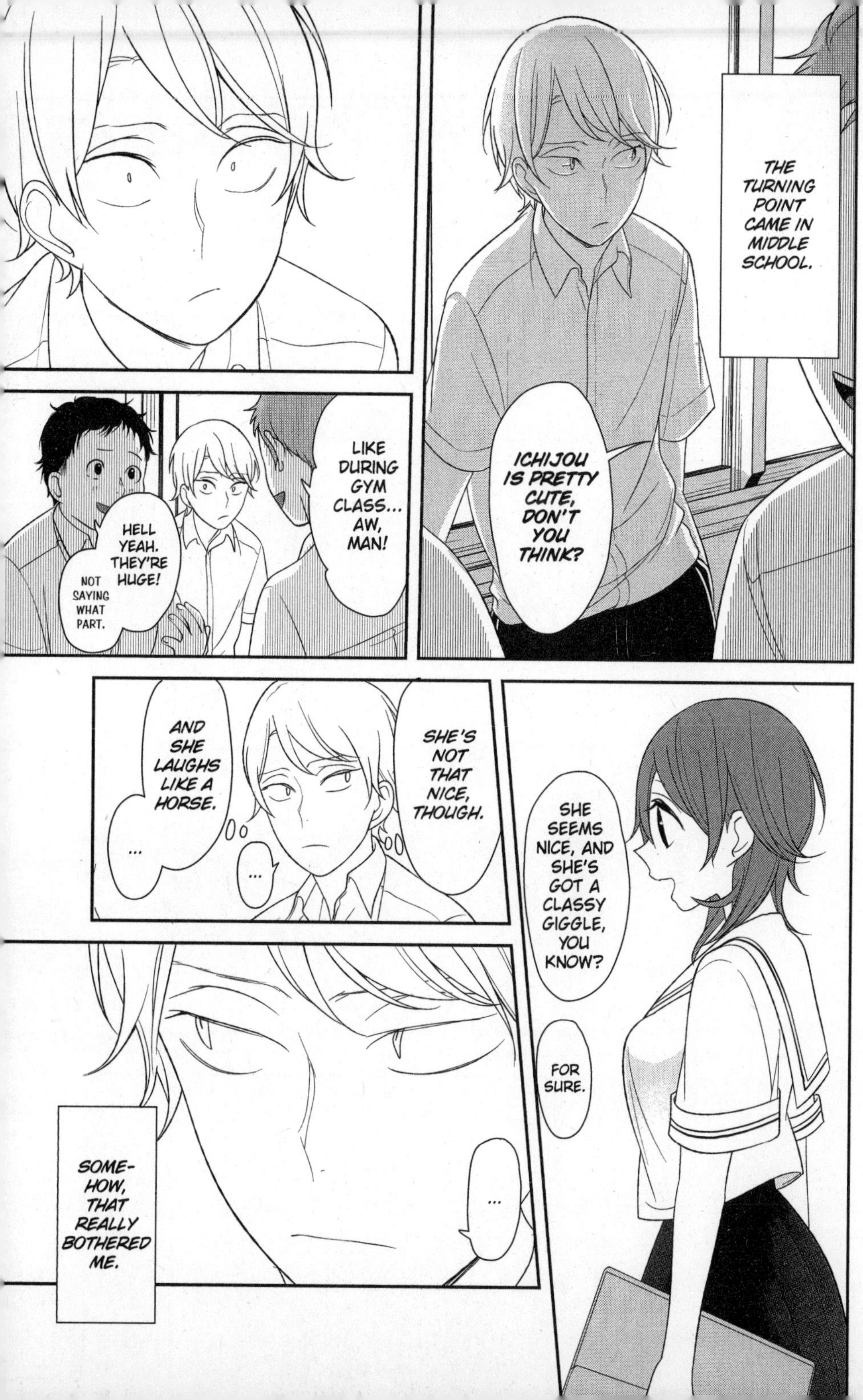
THE TURNING POINT CAME IN MIDDLE SCHOOL.
ICHIJOU IS PRETTY CUTE, DON'T YOU THINK?
LIKE DURING GYM CLASS... AW, MAN!
HELL YEAH. THEY'RE HUGE!
NOT SAYING WHAT PART.
SHE SEEMS NICE, AND SHE'S GOT A CLASSY GIGGLE, YOU KNOW?
FOR SURE.
SHE'S NOT THAT NICE, THOUGH.
...
AND SHE LAUGHS LIKE A HORSE.
...
...
SOME-HOW, THAT REALLY BOTHERED ME.

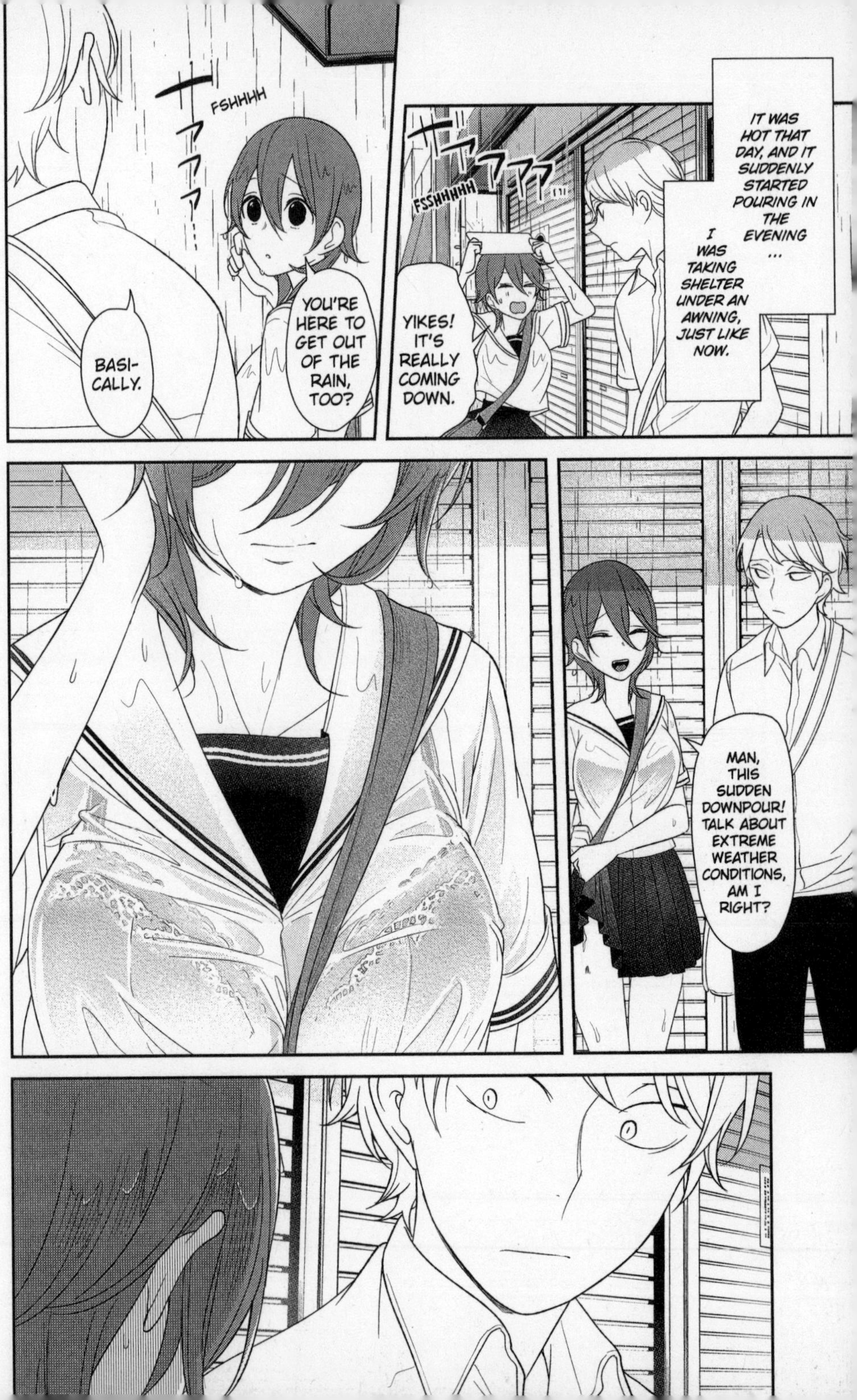
IT WAS HOT THAT DAY, AND IT SUDDENLY STARTED POURING IN THE EVENING...
I WAS TAKING SHELTER UNDER AN AWNING, JUST LIKE NOW.
FSSHHHHHH
YIKES! IT'S REALLY COMING DOWN.
FSHHHH
YOU'RE HERE TO GET OUT OF THE RAIN, TOO?
BASI-CALLY.
MAN, THIS SUDDEN DOWNPOUR! TALK ABOUT EXTREME WEATHER CONDITIONS, AM I RIGHT?

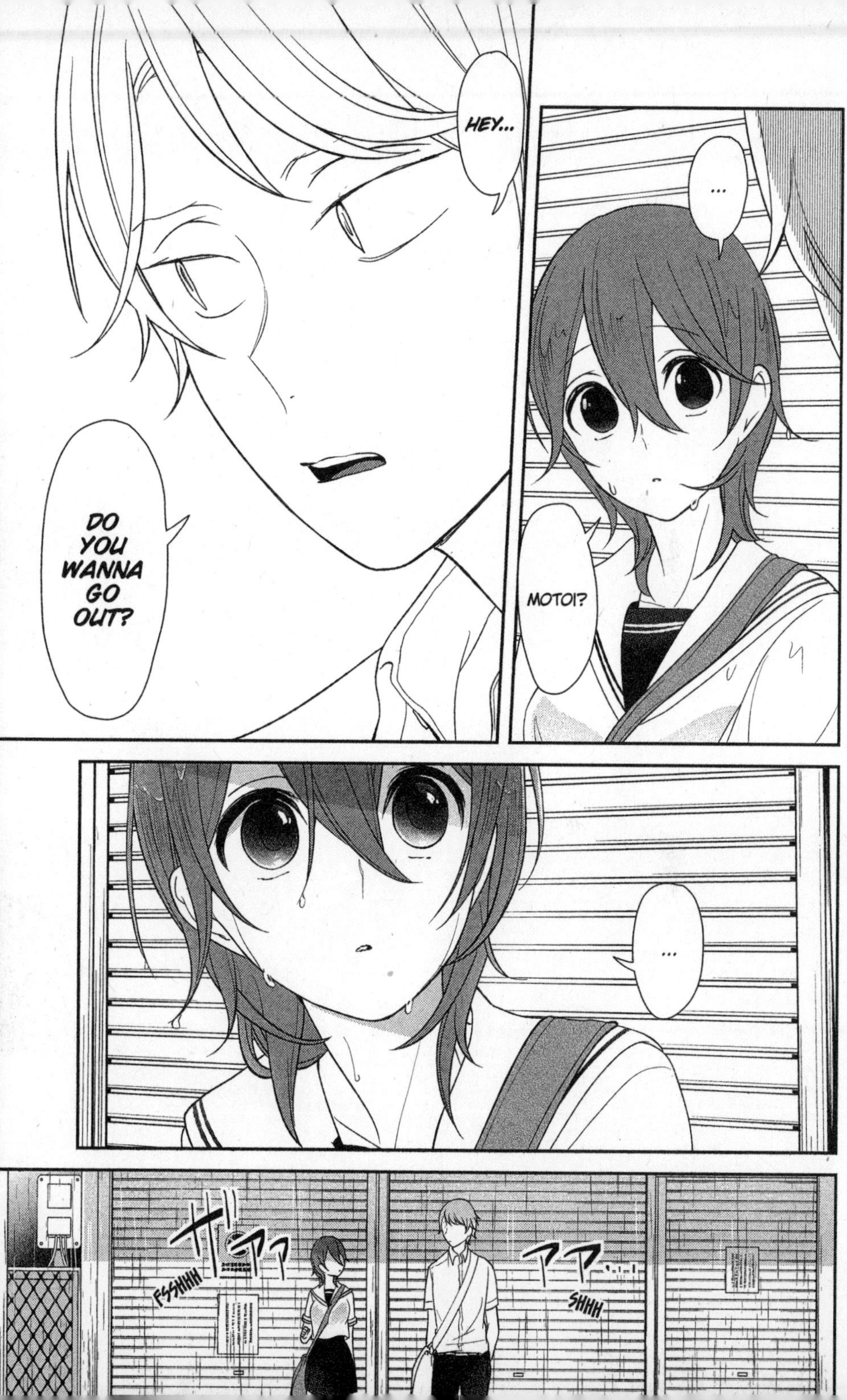
...
MOTOI?
HEY...
DO YOU WANNA GO OUT?
...
SHHH
FSSHHH

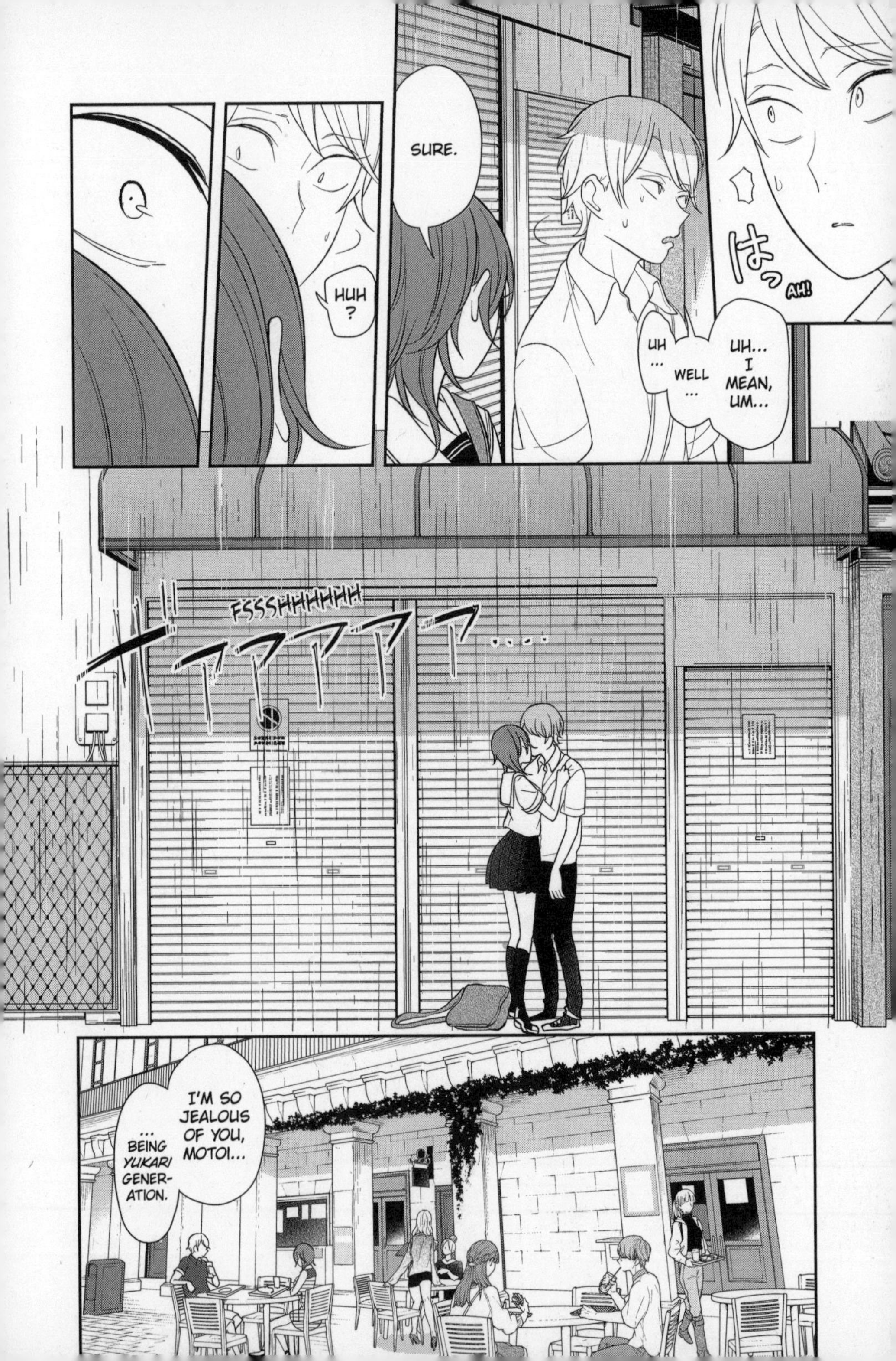
はっ
AH!
UH... I MEAN, UM...
WELL ...
UH ...
SURE.
HUH ?
ザアアアアア
FSSSHHHHHH
I'M SO JEALOUS OF YOU, MOTOI...
... BEING *YUKARI* GENERATION.

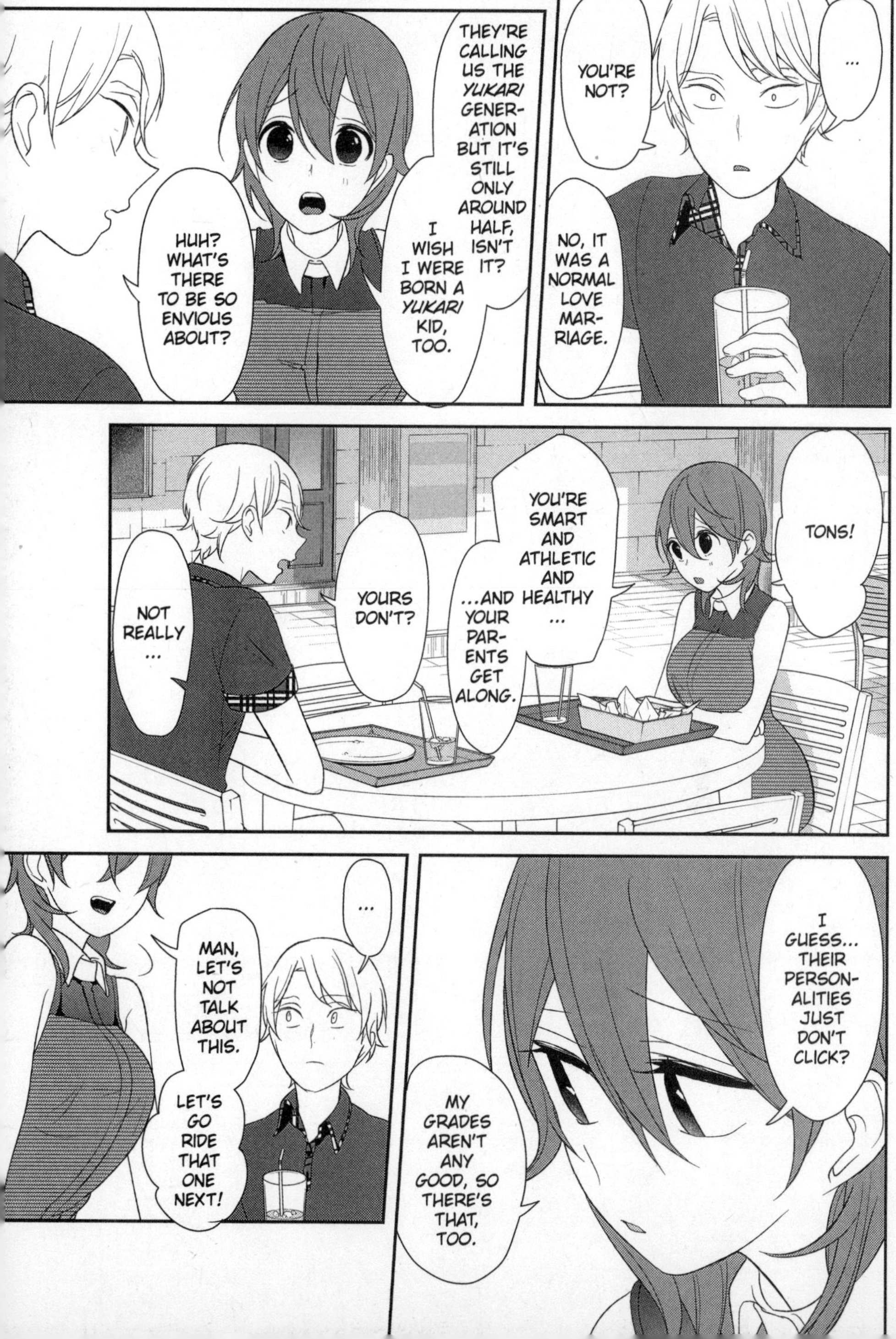
...
YOU'RE NOT?
NO, IT WAS A NORMAL LOVE MARRIAGE.
THEY'RE CALLING US THE *YUKARI* GENERATION BUT IT'S STILL ONLY AROUND HALF, ISN'T IT?
I WISH I WERE BORN A *YUKARI* KID, TOO.
HUH? WHAT'S THERE TO BE SO ENVIOUS ABOUT?
TONS!
YOU'RE SMART AND ATHLETIC AND HEALTHY ...
...AND YOUR PARENTS GET ALONG.
YOURS DON'T?
NOT REALLY ...
I GUESS... THEIR PERSONALITIES JUST DON'T CLICK?
MY GRADES AREN'T ANY GOOD, SO THERE'S THAT, TOO.
...
MAN, LET'S NOT TALK ABOUT THIS.
LET'S GO RIDE THAT ONE NEXT!

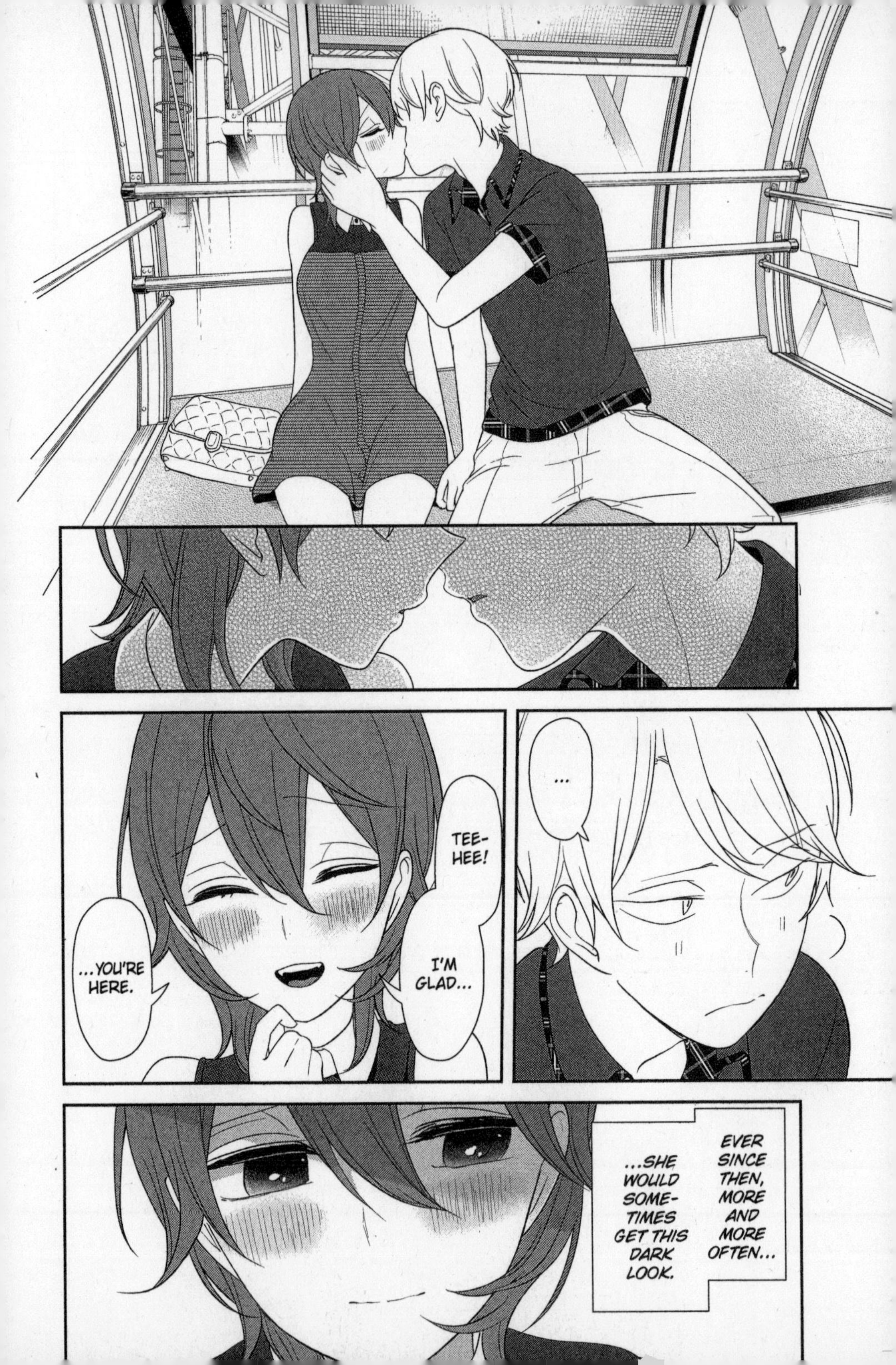
...
TEE-HEE!
I'M GLAD...
...YOU'RE HERE.
EVER SINCE THEN, MORE AND MORE OFTEN...
...SHE WOULD SOME-TIMES GET THIS DARK LOOK.

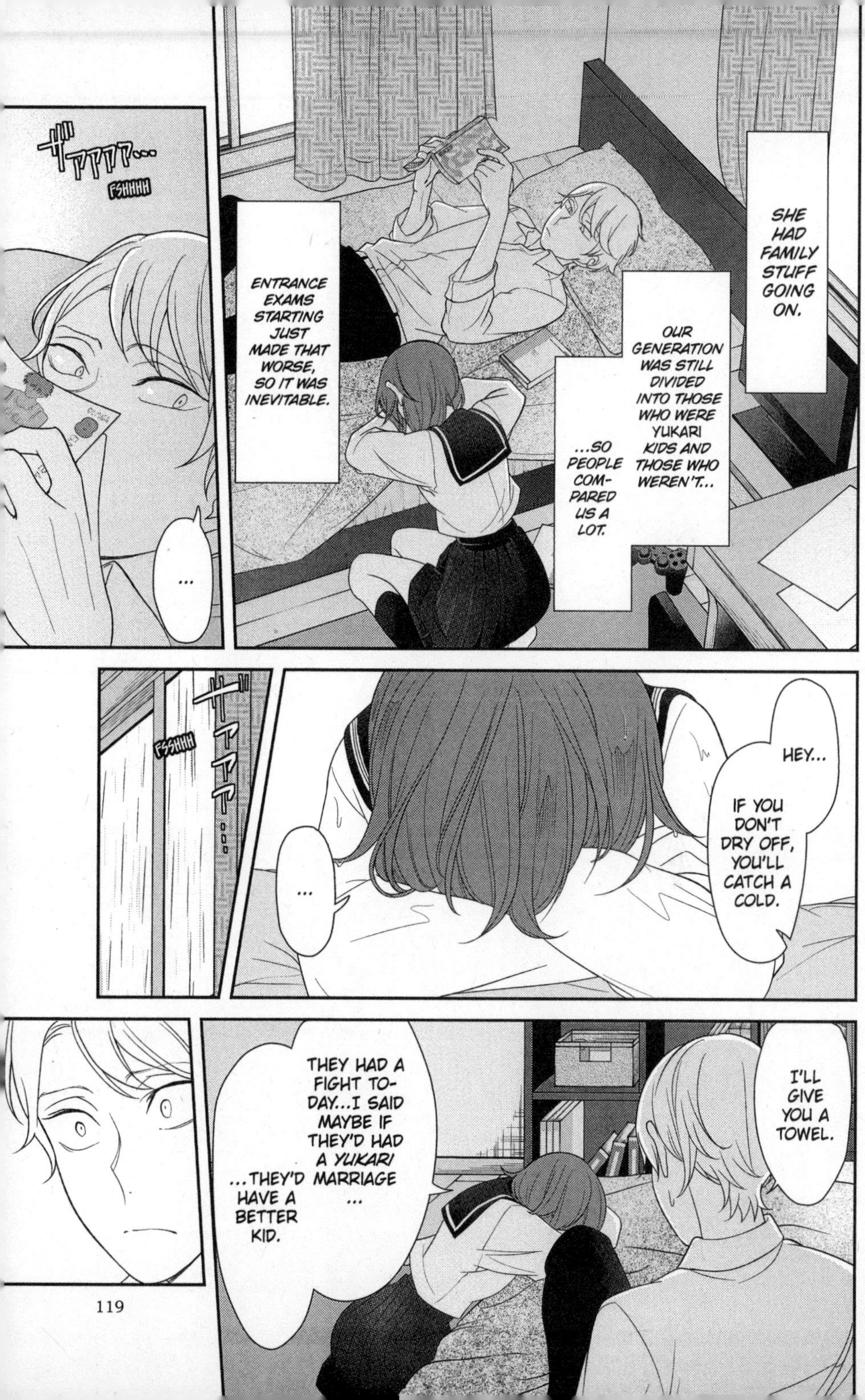
SHE HAD FAMILY STUFF GOING ON.
OUR GENERATION WAS STILL DIVIDED INTO THOSE WHO WERE YUKARI KIDS AND THOSE WHO WEREN'T...
...SO PEOPLE COMPARED US A LOT.
ENTRANCE EXAMS STARTING JUST MADE THAT WORSE, SO IT WAS INEVITABLE.
ザァァァ…
FSHHHH
...
HEY...
IF YOU DON'T DRY OFF, YOU'LL CATCH A COLD.
...
ザァァァ…
FSSHHH
I'LL GIVE YOU A TOWEL.
THEY HAD A FIGHT TODAY...I SAID MAYBE IF THEY'D HAD A *YUKARI* MARRIAGE...
...THEY'D HAVE A BETTER KID.

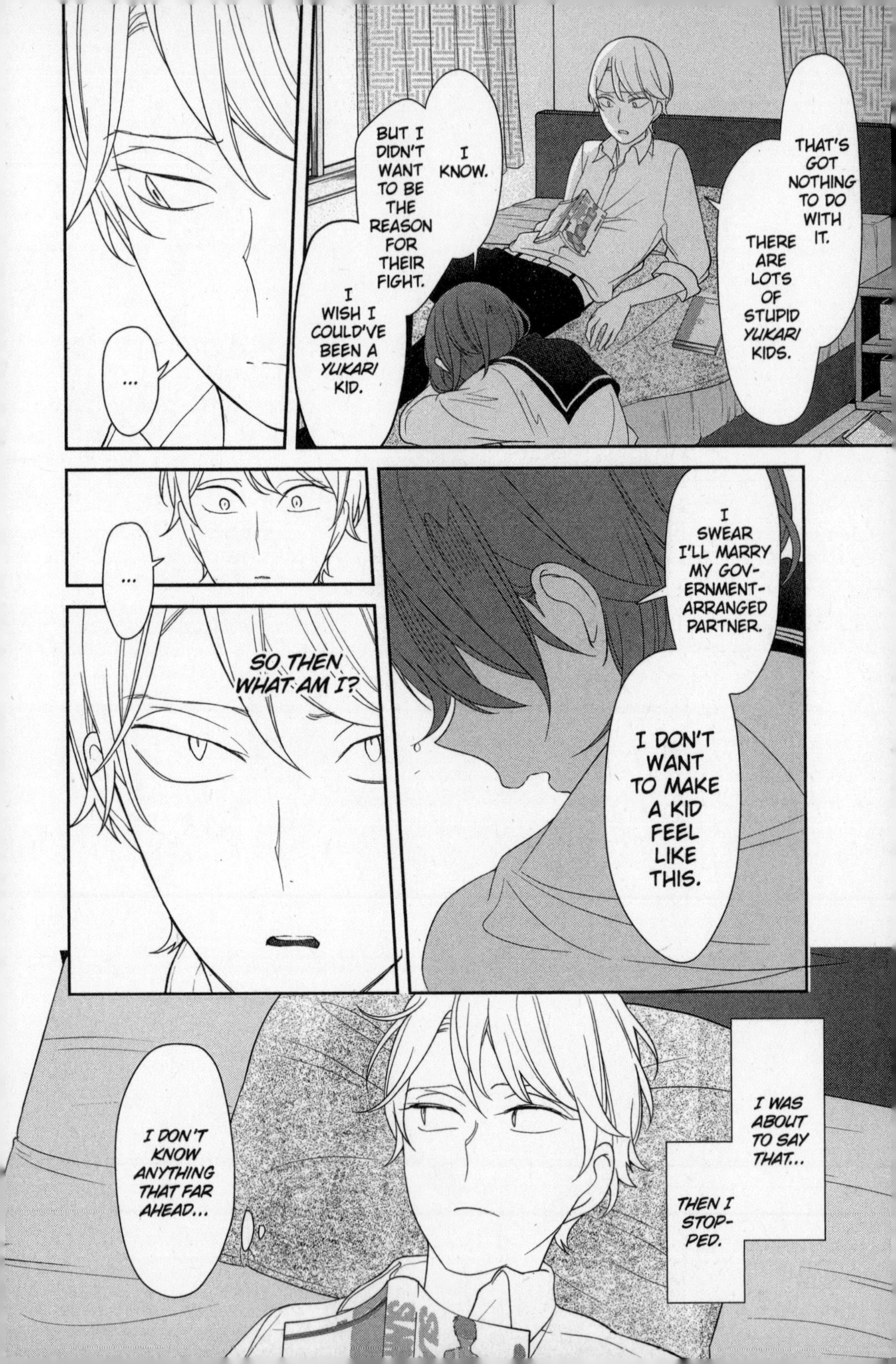

THAT'S GOT NOTHING TO DO WITH IT.
THERE ARE LOTS OF STUPID *YUKARI* KIDS.
I KNOW.
BUT I DIDN'T WANT TO BE THE REASON FOR THEIR FIGHT.
I WISH I COULD'VE BEEN A *YUKARI* KID.
...
I SWEAR I'LL MARRY MY GOV-ERNMENT-ARRANGED PARTNER.
I DON'T WANT TO MAKE A KID FEEL LIKE THIS.
...
SO THEN WHAT AM I?
I WAS ABOUT TO SAY THAT...
THEN I STOP-PED.
I DON'T KNOW ANYTHING THAT FAR AHEAD...

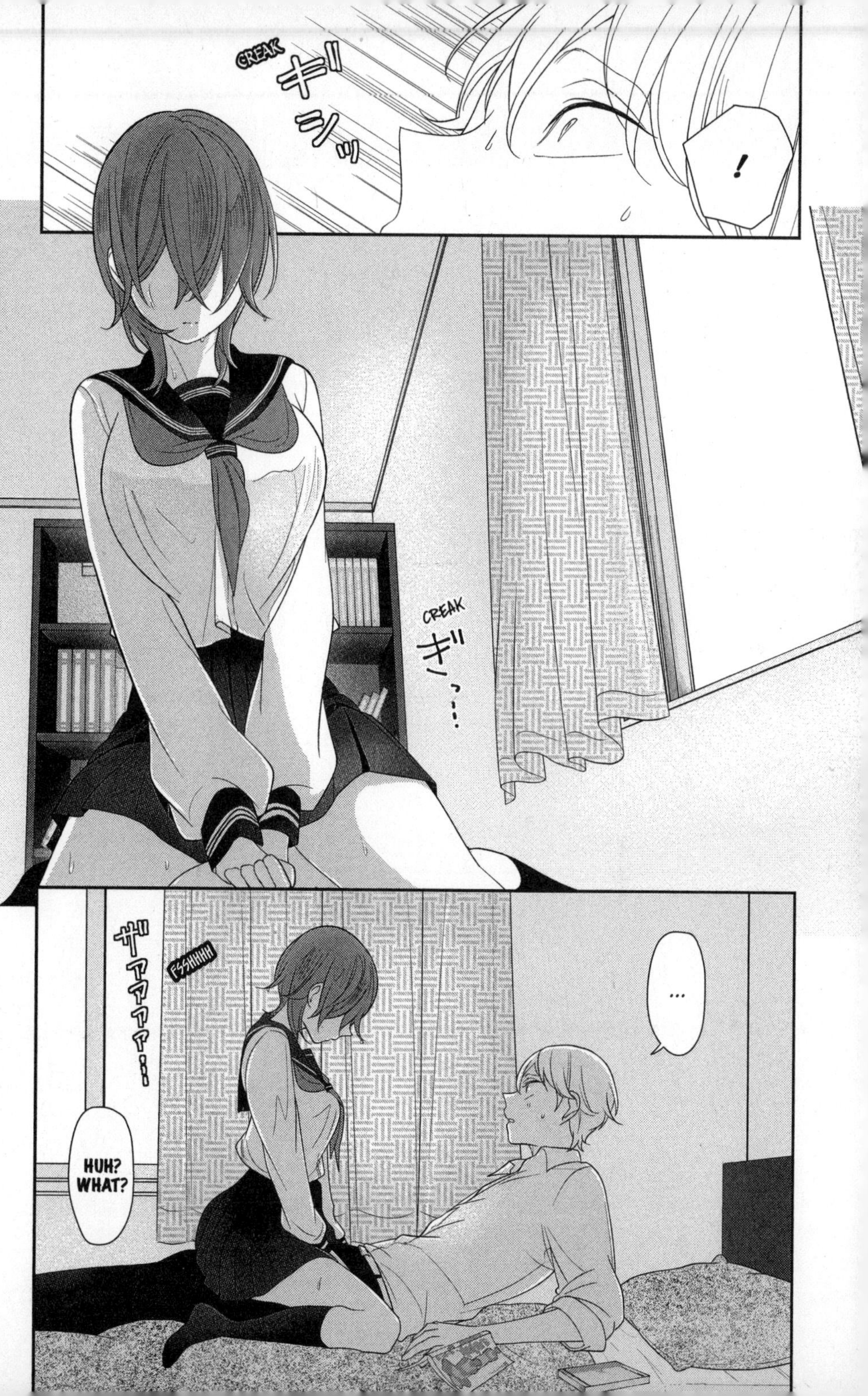
!
CREAK
ギシッ
CREAK
ぎっ…
…
ザァァァァ…
FSSHHHH
HUH? WHAT?

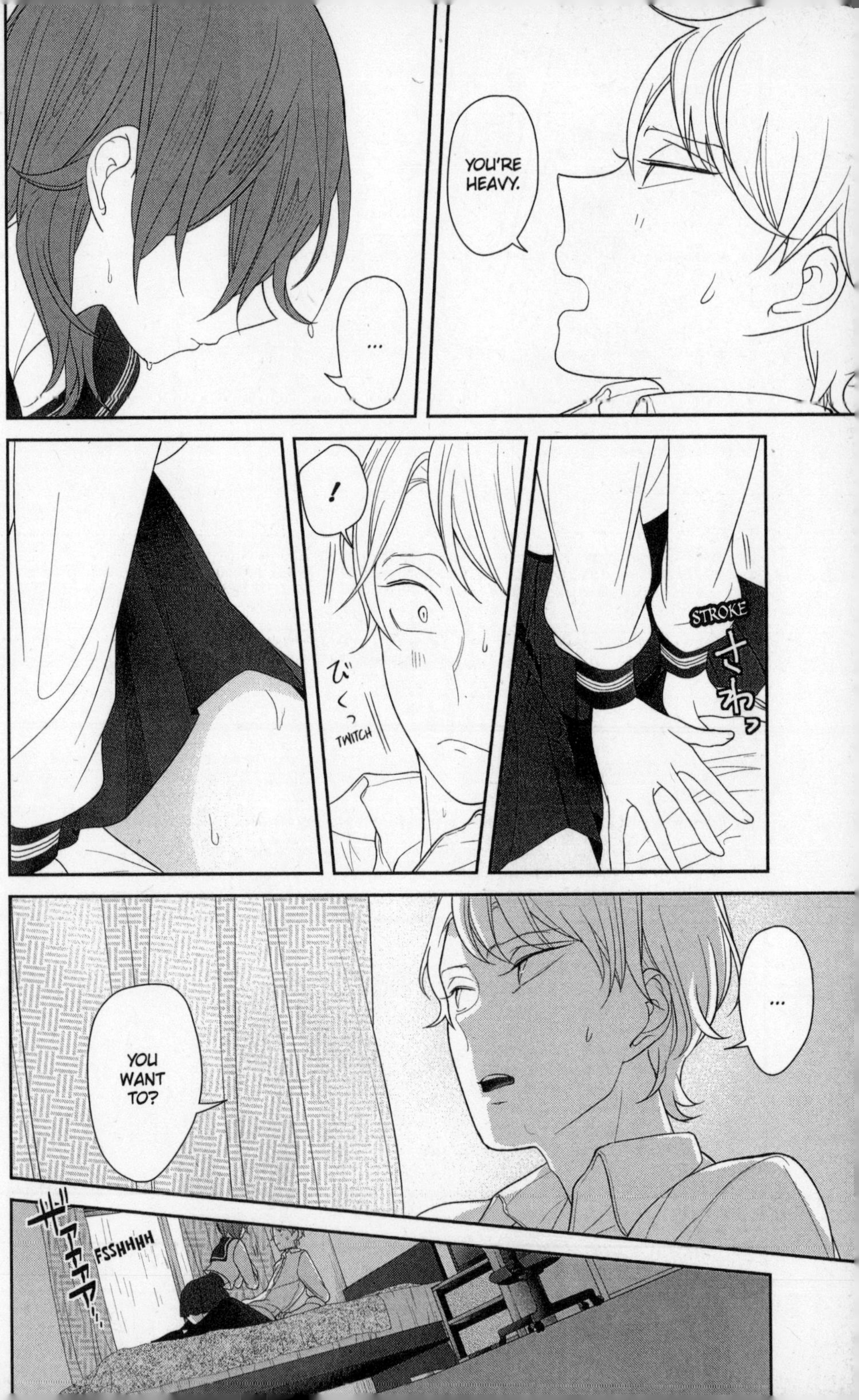
YOU'RE HEAVY.
...
STROKE
さわっ
!
びくっ
TWITCH
...
YOU WANT TO?
ザァァァ…
FSSHHHH

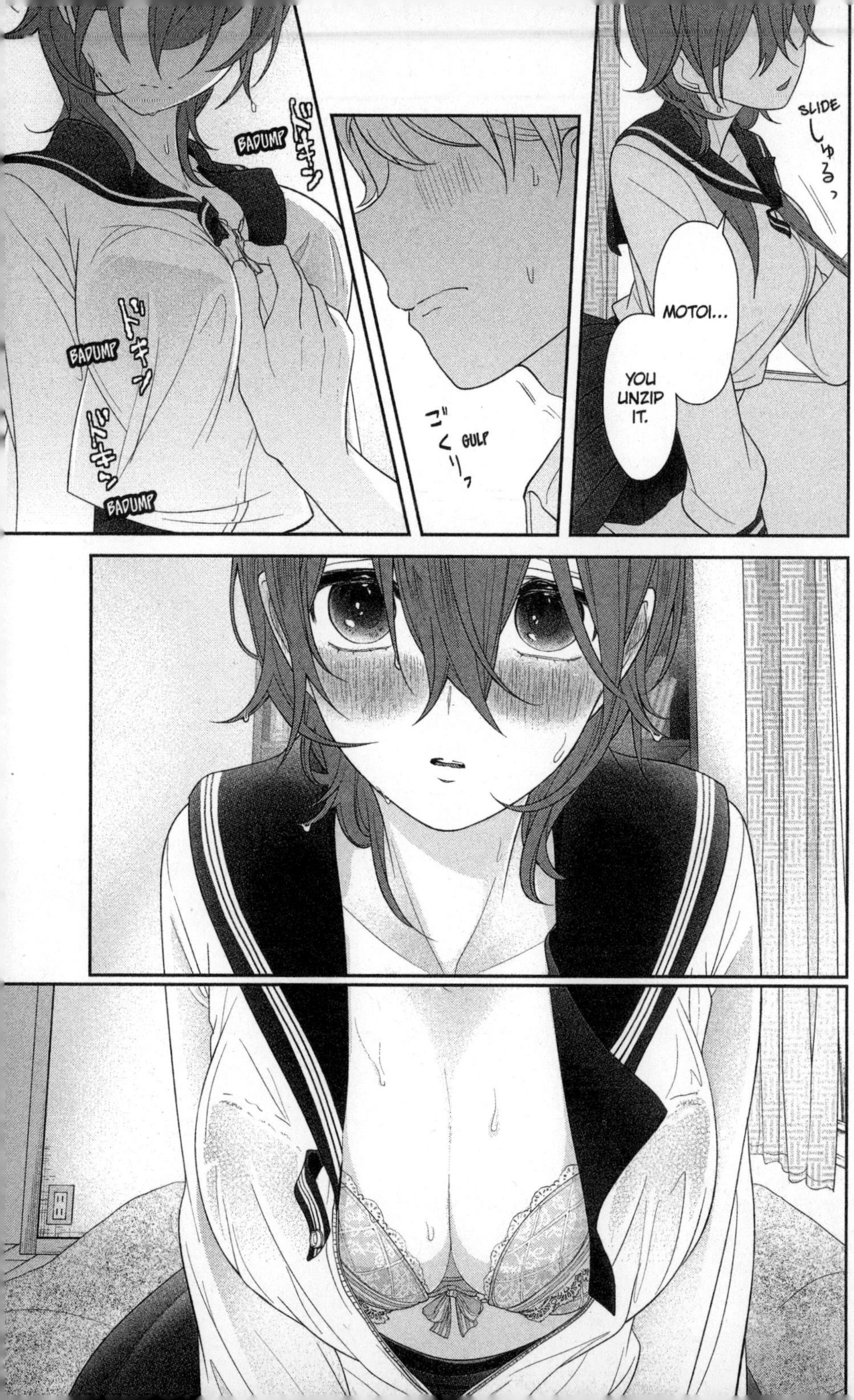
SLIDE
しゅるっ
MOTOI...
YOU UNZIP IT.
ごくりっ
GULP
BADUMP
BADUMP
BADUMP

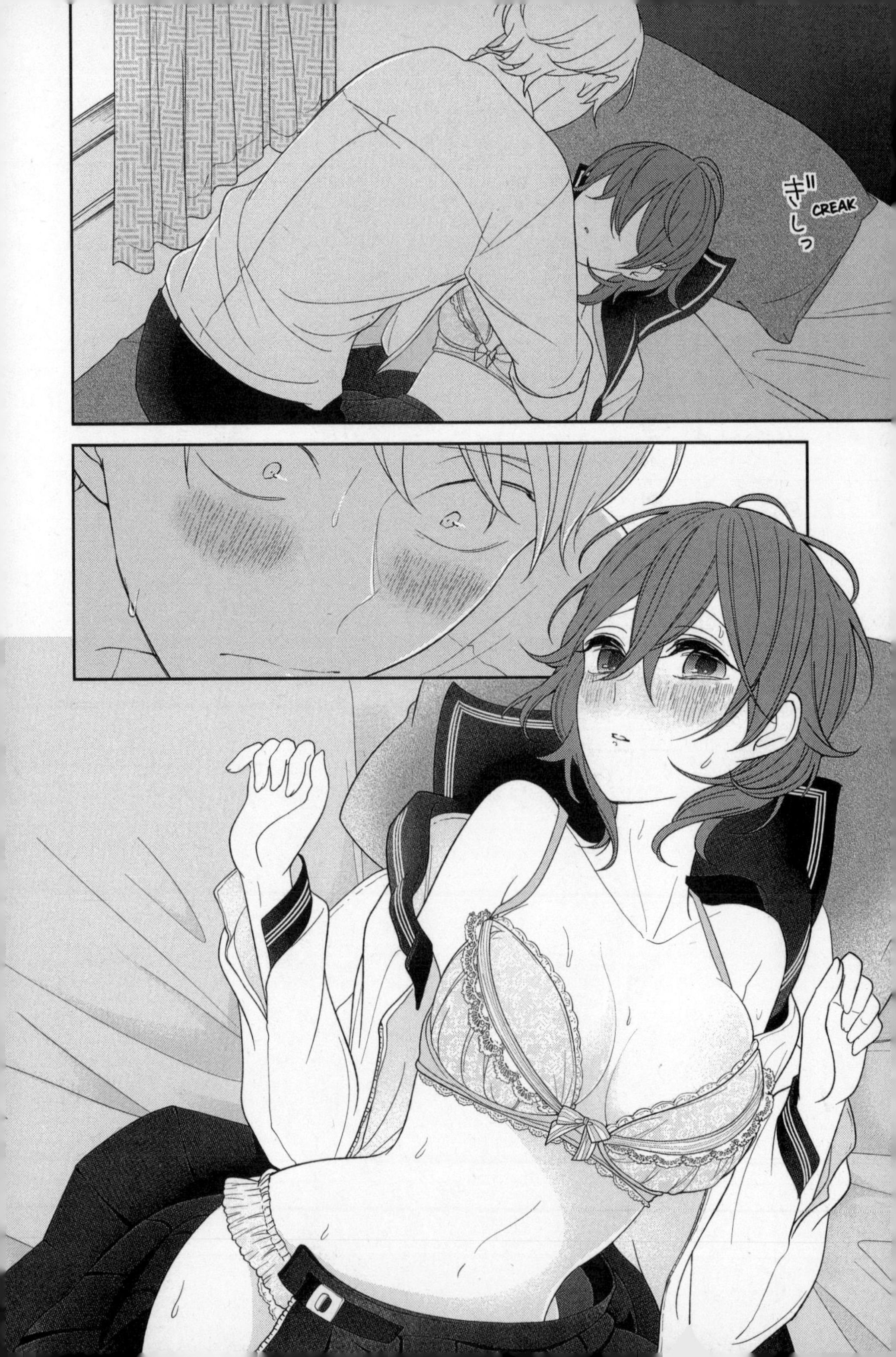
ぎしっ
CREAK

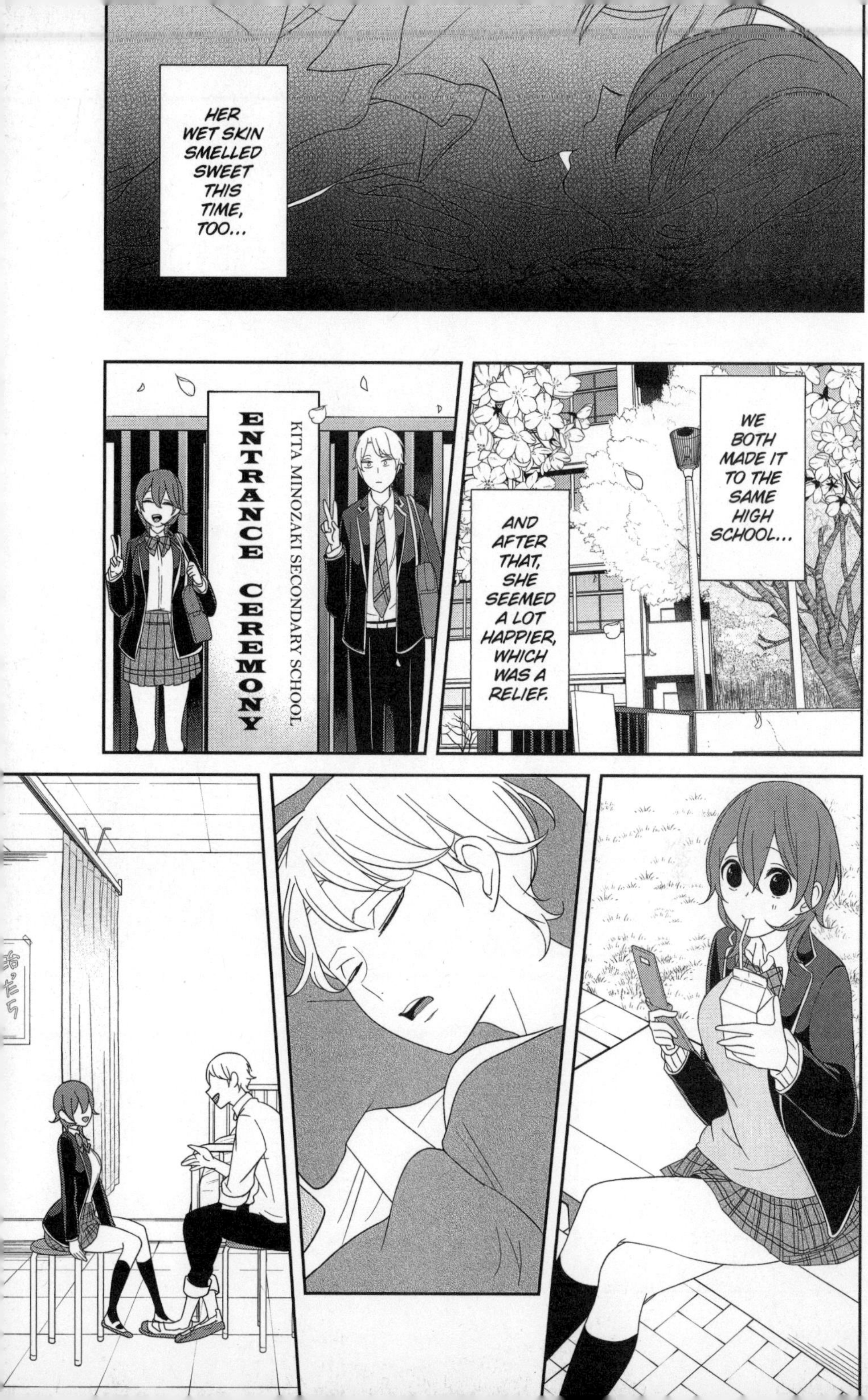
HER WET SKIN SMELLED SWEET THIS TIME, TOO...
WE BOTH MADE IT TO THE SAME HIGH SCHOOL...
AND AFTER THAT, SHE SEEMED A LOT HAPPIER, WHICH WAS A RELIEF.
KITA MINOZAKI SECONDARY SCHOOL
ENTRANCE CEREMONY

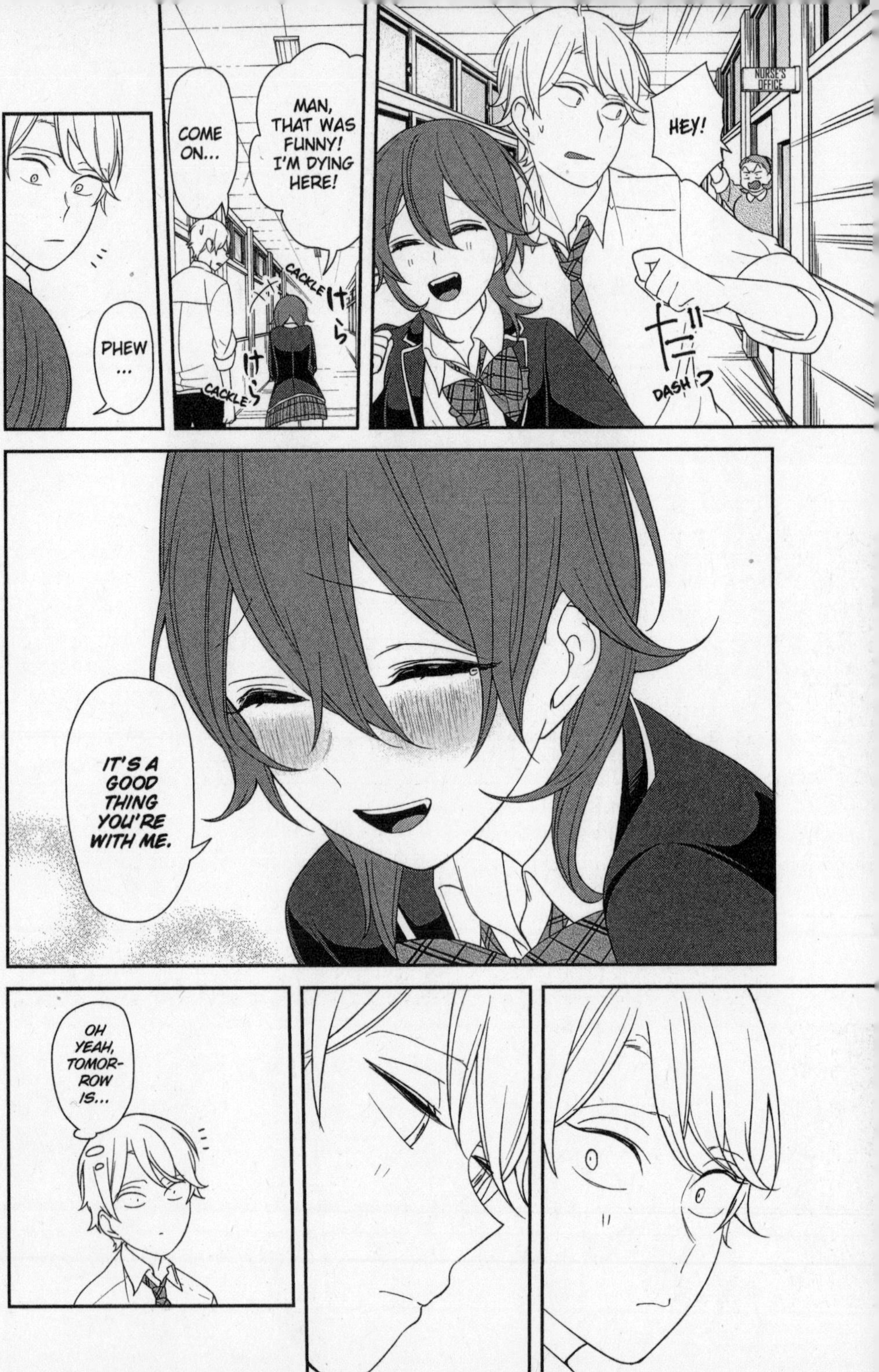
NURSE'S OFFICE
HEY!
DASH
MAN, THAT WAS FUNNY! I'M DYING HERE!
COME ON...
CACKLE
けら
CACKLE
けら
PHEW ...
IT'S A GOOD THING YOU'RE WITH ME.
OH YEAH, TOMORROW IS...

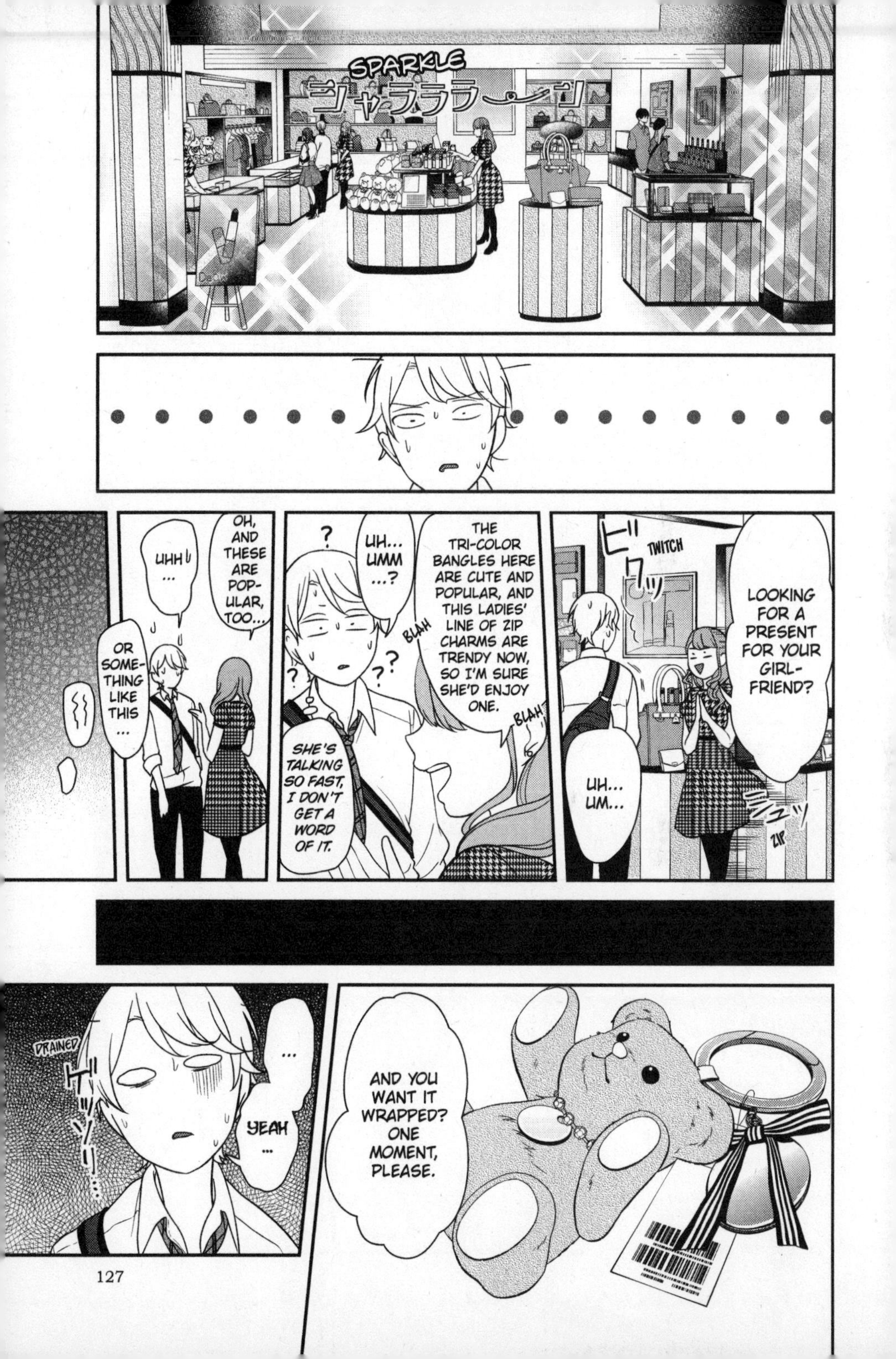
SPARKLE
LOOKING FOR A PRESENT FOR YOUR GIRL-FRIEND?
TWITCH
UH... UM...
ZIP
THE TRI-COLOR BANGLES HERE ARE CUTE AND POPULAR, AND THIS LADIES' LINE OF ZIP CHARMS ARE TRENDY NOW, SO I'M SURE SHE'D ENJOY ONE.
UH... UMM ...?
BLAH
BLAH
SHE'S TALKING SO FAST, I DON'T GET A WORD OF IT.
OH, AND THESE ARE POP-ULAR, TOO...
UHHH ...
OR SOME-THING LIKE THIS ...
AND YOU WANT IT WRAPPED? ONE MOMENT, PLEASE.
...
YEAH ...
DRAINED

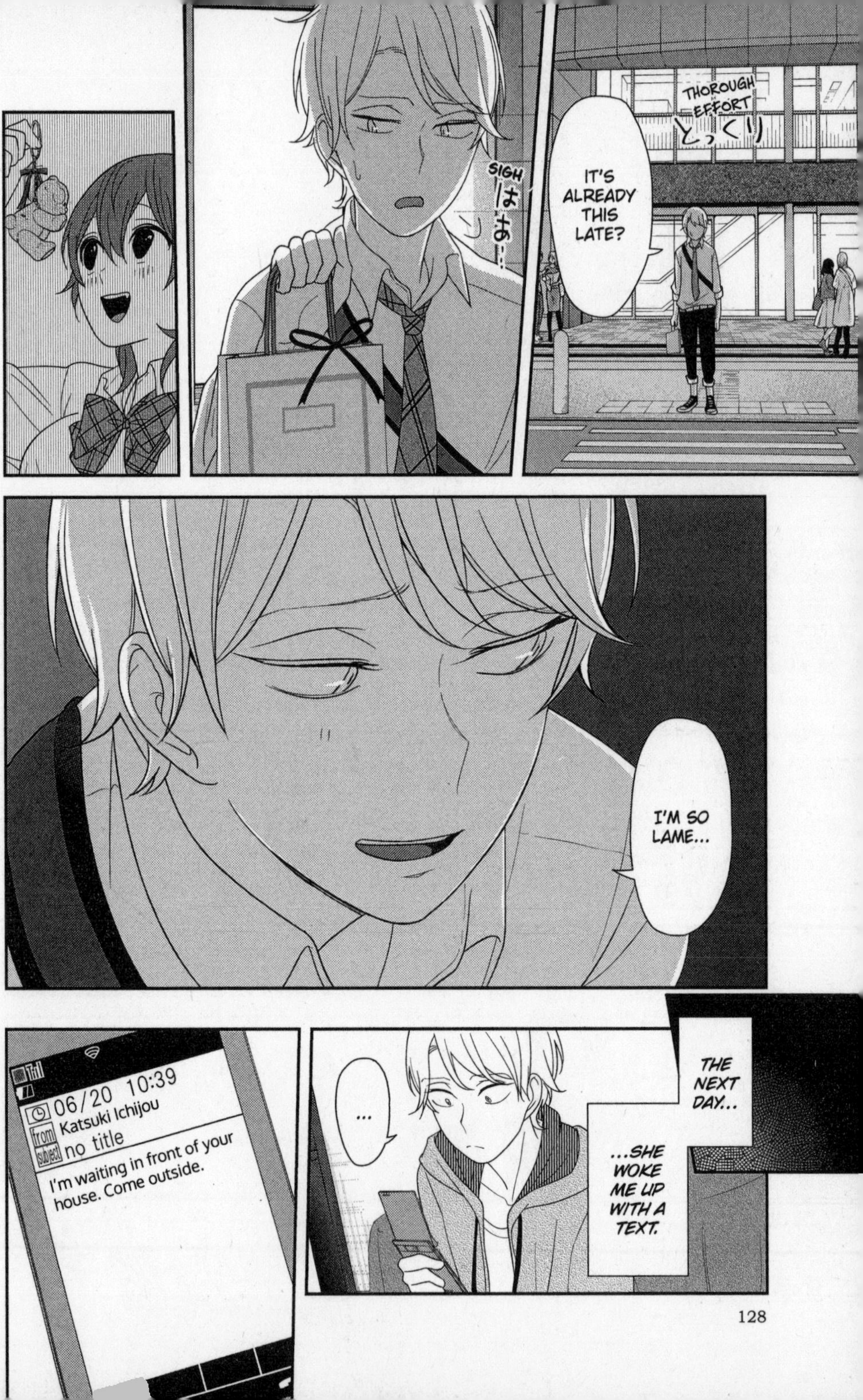
THOROUGH EFFORT
とっくり
IT'S ALREADY THIS LATE?
SIGH
はぁ…
I'M SO LAME...
THE NEXT DAY...
...SHE WOKE ME UP WITH A TEXT.
...
06/20 10:39
Katsuki Ichijou
from
subject
no title
I'm waiting in front of your house. Come outside.

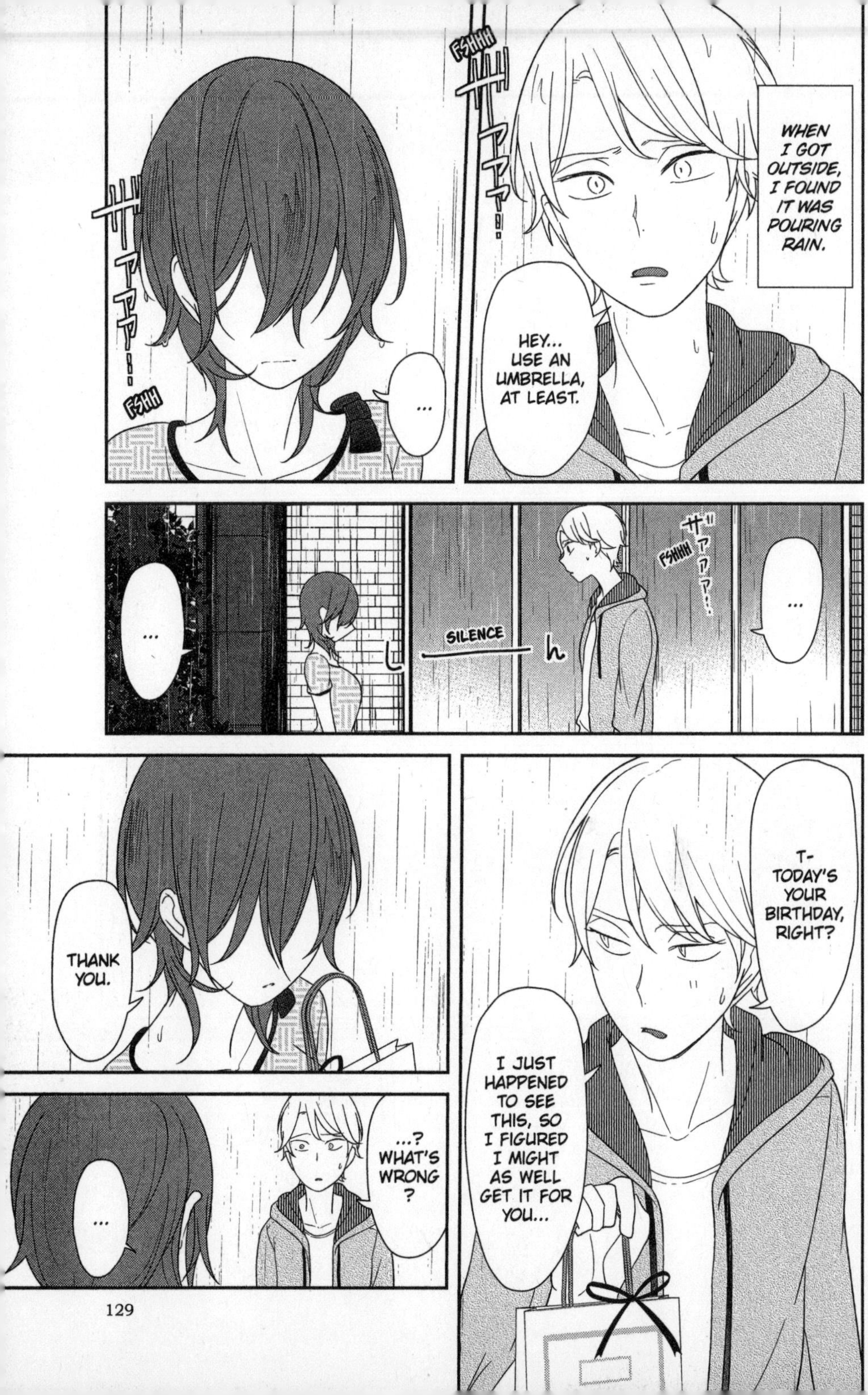

WHEN I GOT OUTSIDE, I FOUND IT WAS POURING RAIN.
FSHHH
ザァァァ!!
HEY... USE AN UMBRELLA, AT LEAST.
ザァァァ!!
FSHH
...
...
FSHHH
ザァァ...
SILENCE
し―ん
...
T- TODAY'S YOUR BIRTHDAY, RIGHT?
I JUST HAPPENED TO SEE THIS, SO I FIGURED I MIGHT AS WELL GET IT FOR YOU...
THANK YOU.
...? WHAT'S WRONG?
...

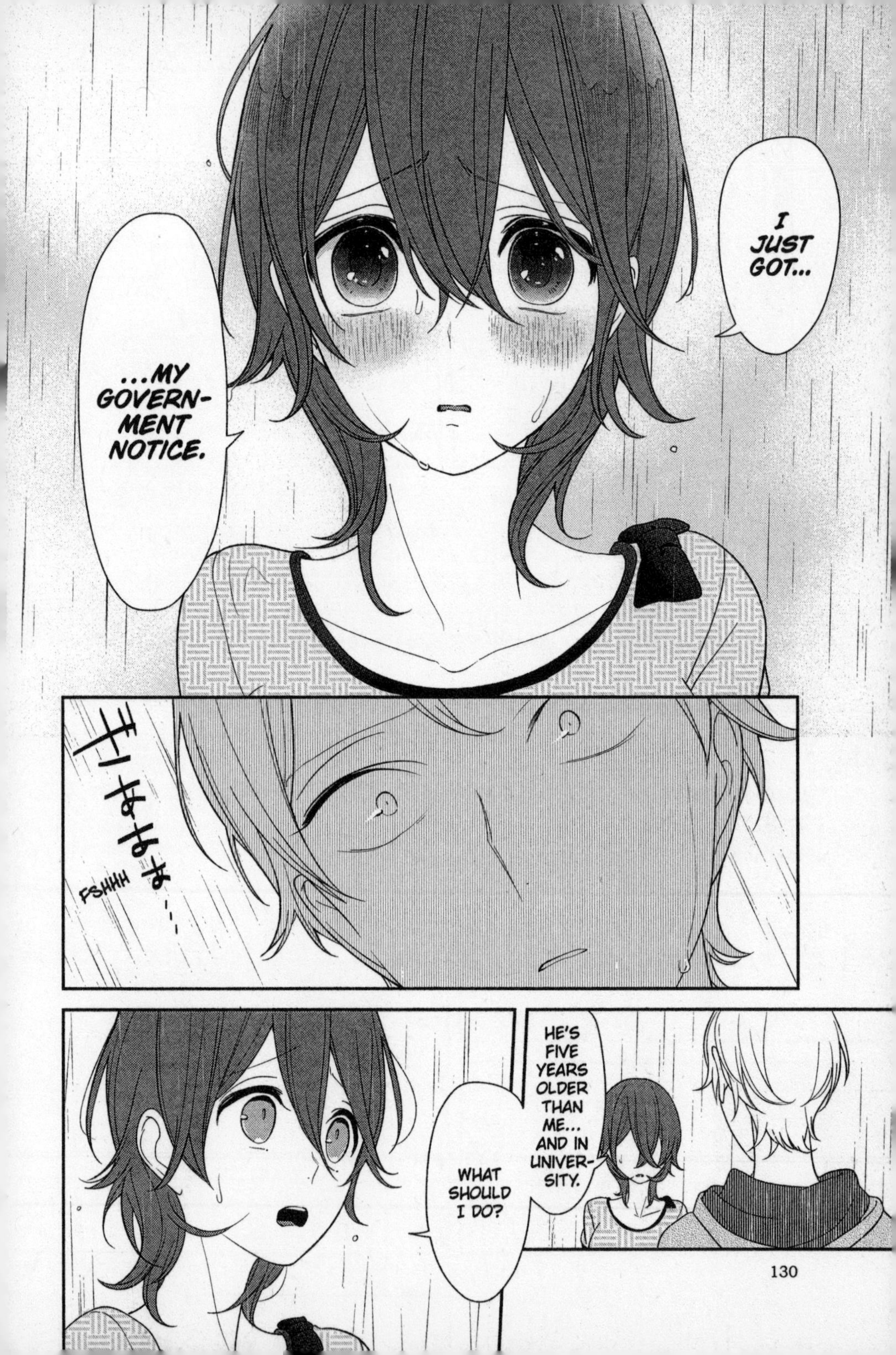
I JUST GOT...
...MY GOVERNMENT NOTICE.
FSHHH
HE'S FIVE YEARS OLDER THAN ME... AND IN UNIVERSITY.
WHAT SHOULD I DO?

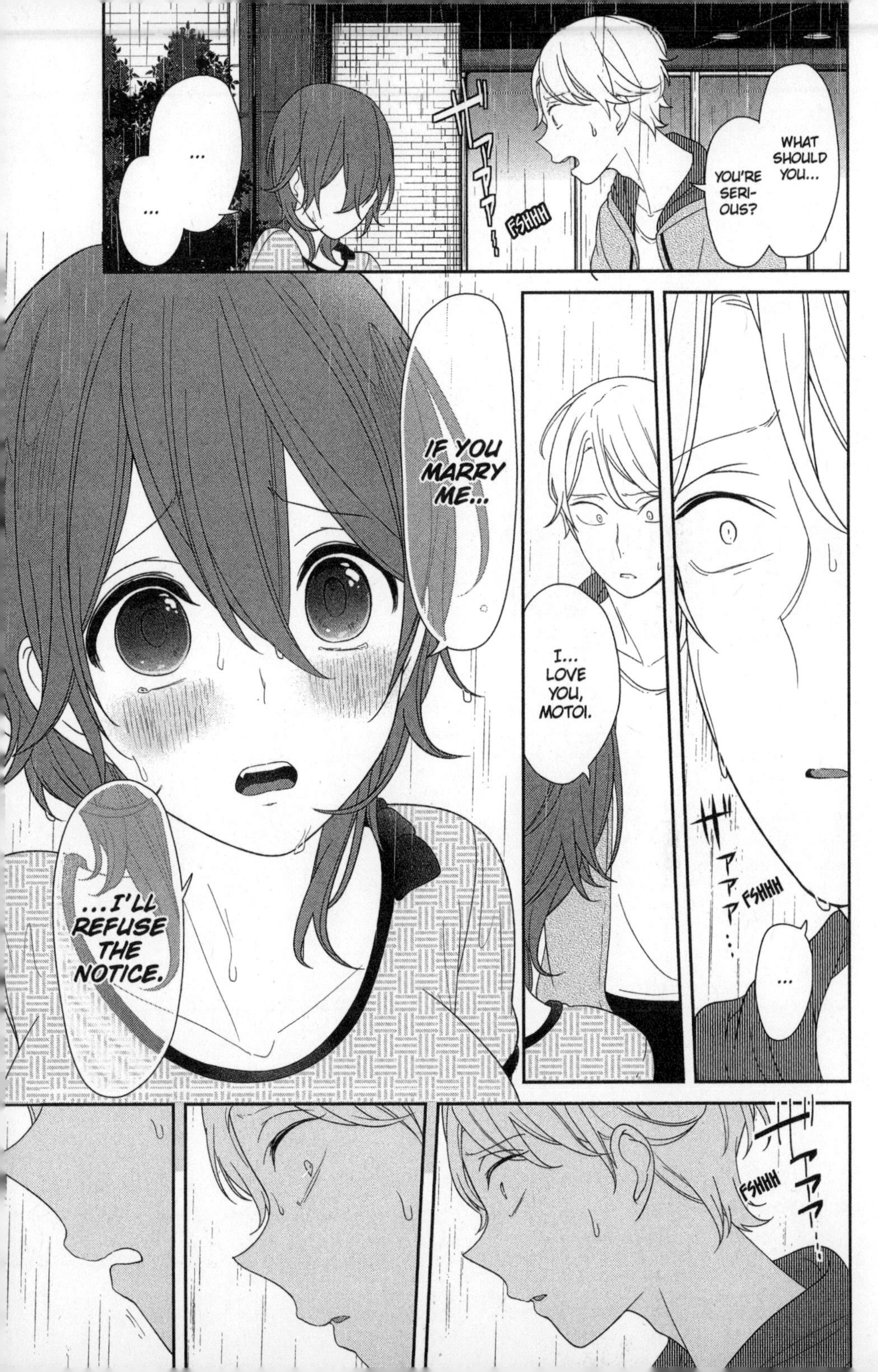
WHAT SHOULD YOU...
YOU'RE SERI-OUS?
FSHHH
...
...
FSHHH
...
I... LOVE YOU, MOTOI.
IF YOU MARRY ME...
...I'LL REFUSE THE NOTICE.
FSHHH

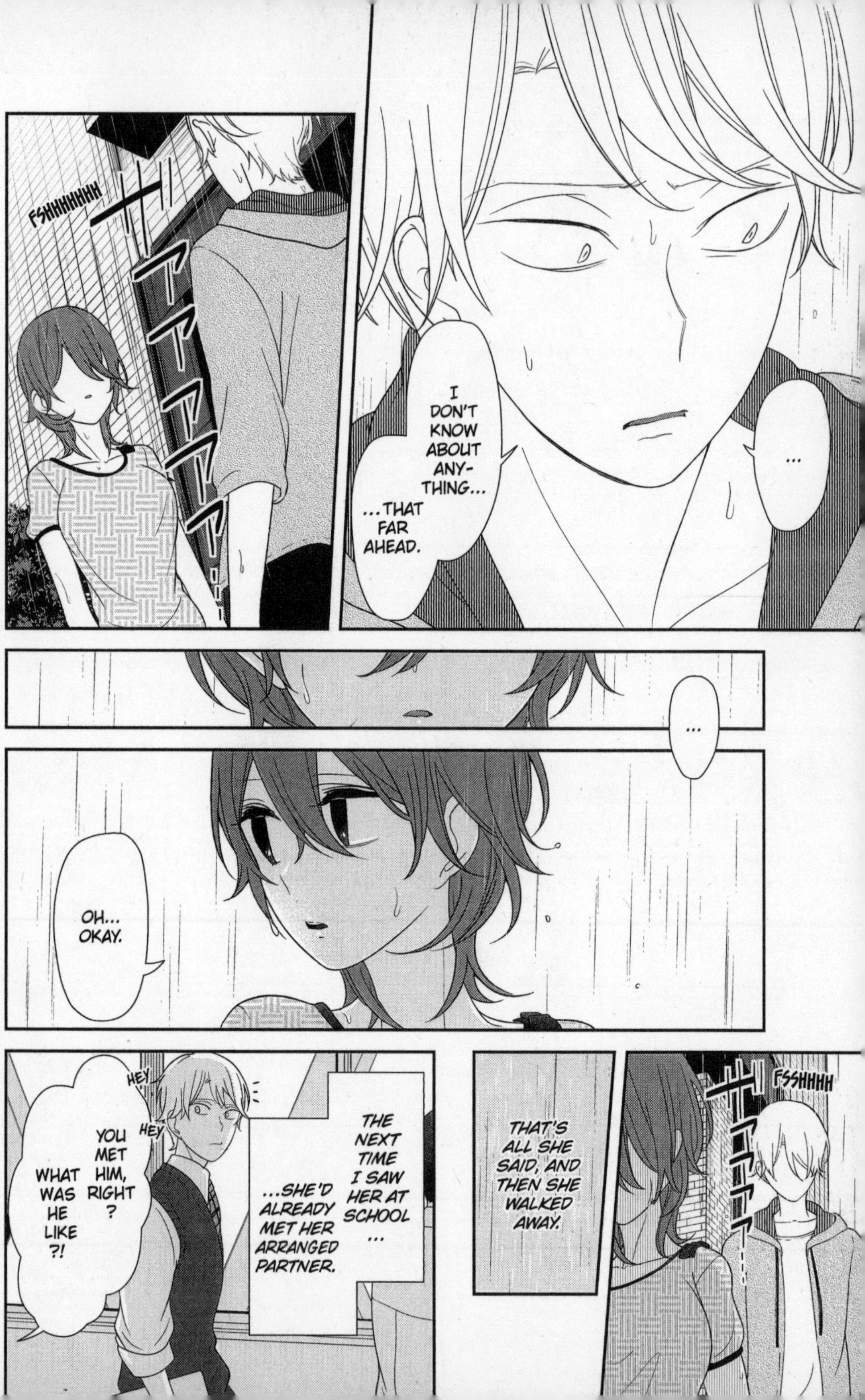
I DON'T KNOW ABOUT ANY-THING...
...THAT FAR AHEAD.
...
FSHHHHHHH
...
OH... OKAY.
THAT'S ALL SHE SAID, AND THEN SHE WALKED AWAY.
FSSHHHH
THE NEXT TIME I SAW HER AT SCHOOL...
...SHE'D ALREADY MET HER ARRANGED PARTNER.
HEY
HEY
YOU MET HIM, RIGHT? WHAT WAS HE LIKE?!

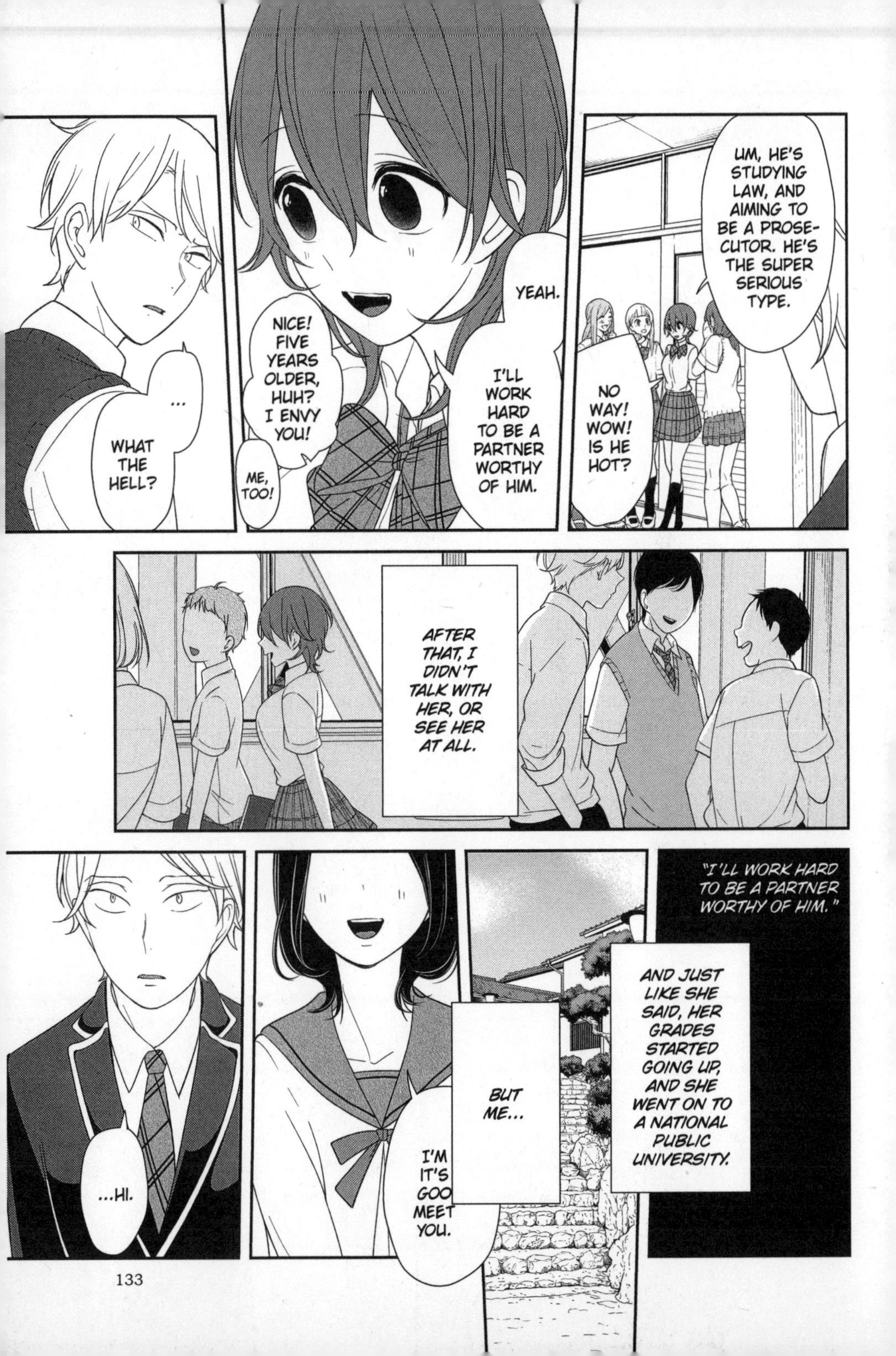
UM, HE'S STUDYING LAW, AND AIMING TO BE A PROSE-CUTOR. HE'S THE SUPER SERIOUS TYPE.
NO WAY! WOW! IS HE HOT?
YEAH.
I'LL WORK HARD TO BE A PARTNER WORTHY OF HIM.
NICE! FIVE YEARS OLDER, HUH? I ENVY YOU!
ME, TOO!
...
WHAT THE HELL?
AFTER THAT, I DIDN'T TALK WITH HER, OR SEE HER AT ALL.
"I'LL WORK HARD TO BE A PARTNER WORTHY OF HIM."
AND JUST LIKE SHE SAID, HER GRADES STARTED GOING UP, AND SHE WENT ON TO A NATIONAL PUBLIC UNIVERSITY.
BUT ME...
I'M
IT'S GOO
MEET YOU.
...HI.

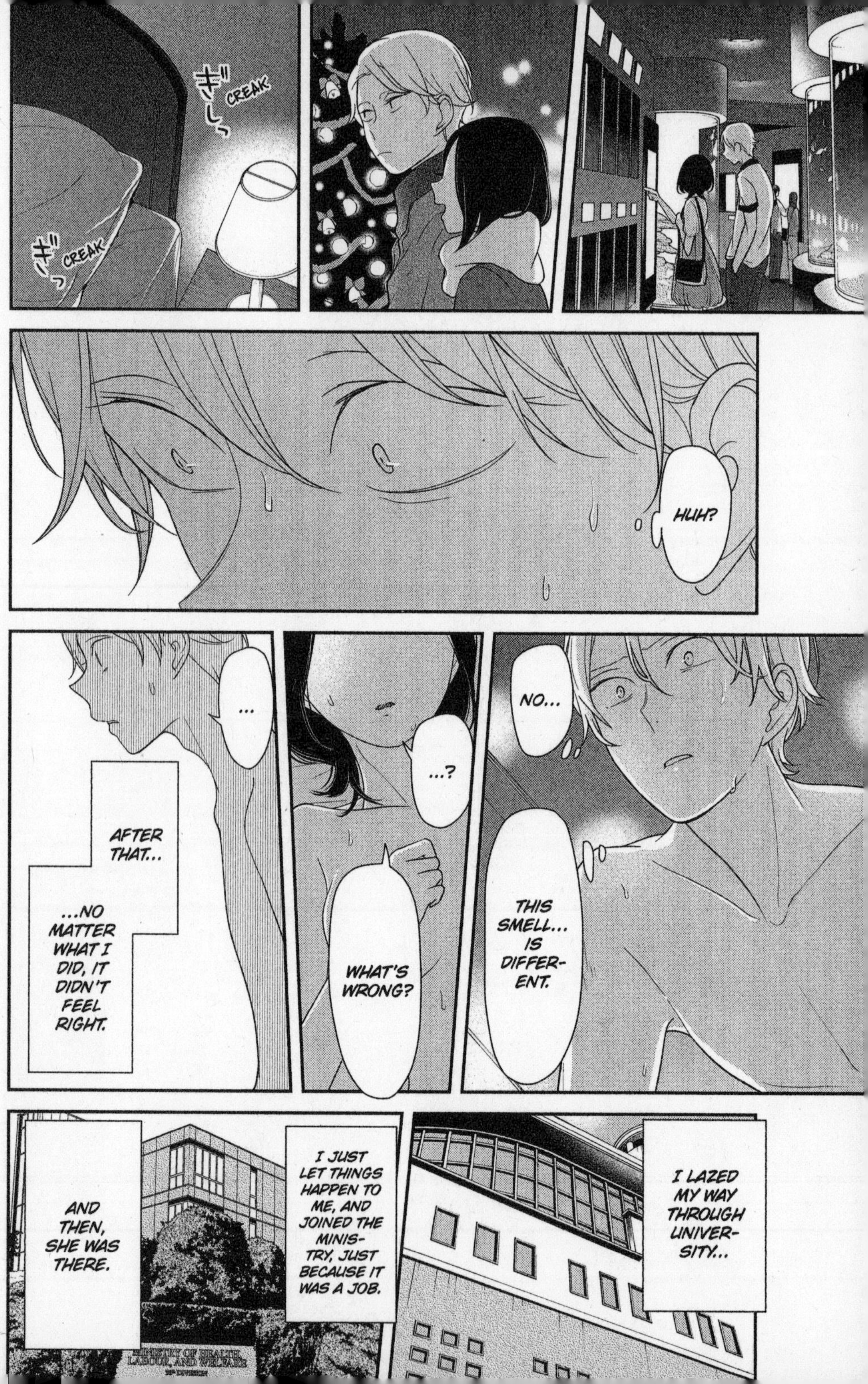
ぎし
CREAK
ぎっ
CREAK
HUH?
NO...
THIS SMELL... IS DIFFERENT.
...?
WHAT'S WRONG?
...
AFTER THAT...
...NO MATTER WHAT I DID, IT DIDN'T FEEL RIGHT.
I LAZED MY WAY THROUGH UNIVERSITY...
I JUST LET THINGS HAPPEN TO ME, AND JOINED THE MINISTRY, JUST BECAUSE IT WAS A JOB.
AND THEN, SHE WAS THERE.
MINISTRY OF HEALTH, LABOUR, AND WELFARE

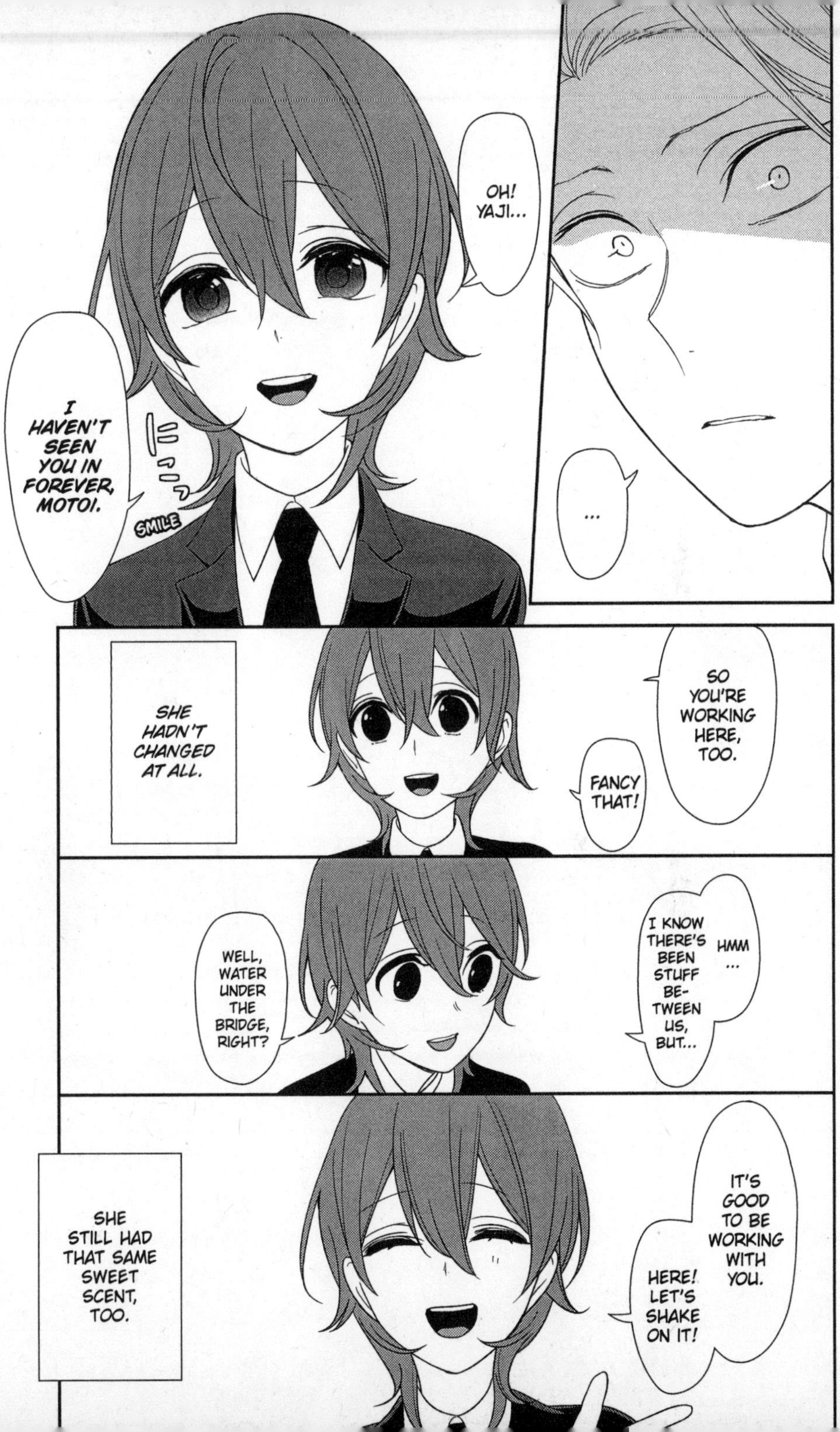
OH! YAJI...
...
I HAVEN'T SEEN YOU IN FOREVER, MOTOI.
SMILE
SO YOU'RE WORKING HERE, TOO.
FANCY THAT!
SHE HADN'T CHANGED AT ALL.
HMM...
I KNOW THERE'S BEEN STUFF BE-TWEEN US, BUT...
WELL, WATER UNDER THE BRIDGE, RIGHT?
IT'S GOOD TO BE WORKING WITH YOU.
HERE! LET'S SHAKE ON IT!
SHE STILL HAD THAT SAME SWEET SCENT, TOO.

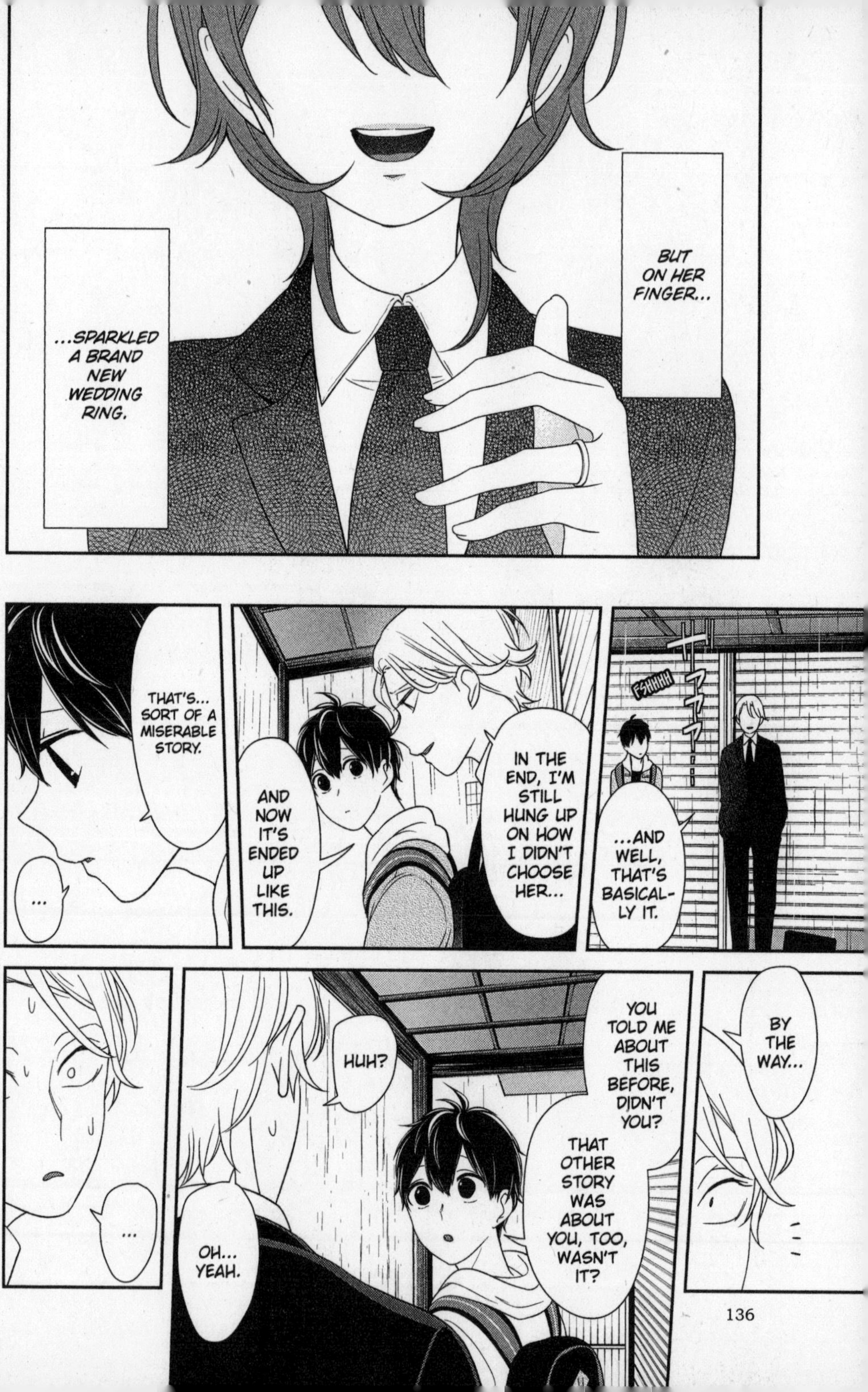
BUT ON HER FINGER...
...SPARKLED A BRAND NEW WEDDING RING.
FSHHHH
...AND WELL, THAT'S BASICAL-LY IT.
IN THE END, I'M STILL HUNG UP ON HOW I DIDN'T CHOOSE HER...
AND NOW IT'S ENDED UP LIKE THIS.
THAT'S... SORT OF A MISERABLE STORY.
...
BY THE WAY...
YOU TOLD ME ABOUT THIS BEFORE, DIDN'T YOU?
THAT OTHER STORY WAS ABOUT YOU, TOO, WASN'T IT?
HUH?
OH... YEAH.
...

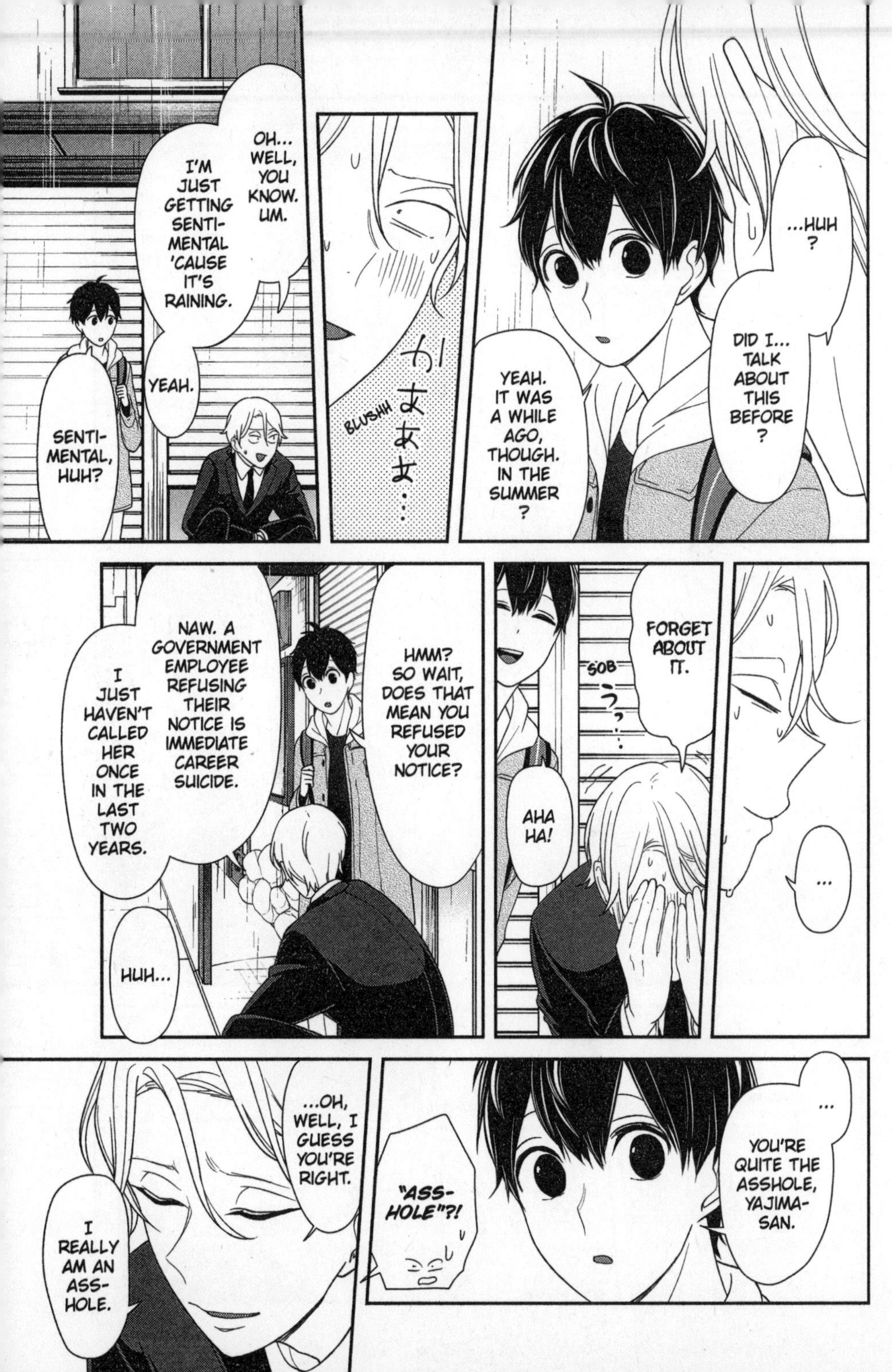
...HUH?
DID I... TALK ABOUT THIS BEFORE?
YEAH. IT WAS A WHILE AGO, THOUGH. IN THE SUMMER?
BLUSHH
OH... WELL, YOU KNOW. UM.
I'M JUST GETTING SENTIMENTAL 'CAUSE IT'S RAINING.
YEAH.
SENTIMENTAL, HUH?
...
FORGET ABOUT IT.
SOB
AHA HA!
HMM? SO WAIT, DOES THAT MEAN YOU REFUSED YOUR NOTICE?
NAW. A GOVERNMENT EMPLOYEE REFUSING THEIR NOTICE IS IMMEDIATE CAREER SUICIDE.
I JUST HAVEN'T CALLED HER ONCE IN THE LAST TWO YEARS.
HUH...
...
YOU'RE QUITE THE ASSHOLE, YAJIMA-SAN.
"ASSHOLE"?!
...OH, WELL, I GUESS YOU'RE RIGHT.
I REALLY AM AN ASSHOLE.

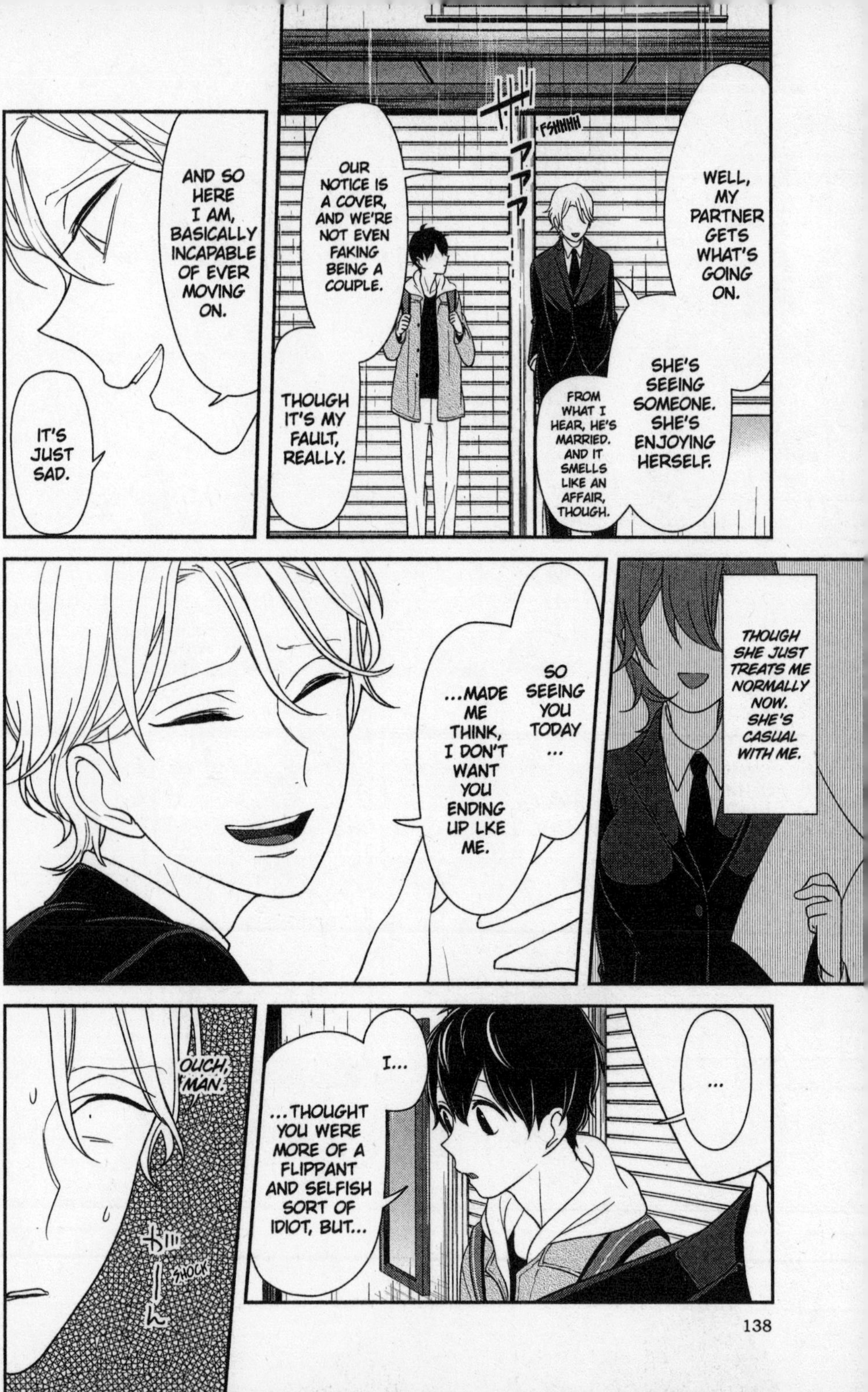
WELL, MY PARTNER GETS WHAT'S GOING ON.
SHE'S SEEING SOMEONE. SHE'S ENJOYING HERSELF.
FROM WHAT I HEAR, HE'S MARRIED. AND IT SMELLS LIKE AN AFFAIR, THOUGH.
FSHHHH
OUR NOTICE IS A COVER, AND WE'RE NOT EVEN FAKING BEING A COUPLE.
THOUGH IT'S MY FAULT, REALLY.
AND SO HERE I AM, BASICALLY INCAPABLE OF EVER MOVING ON.
IT'S JUST SAD.
THOUGH SHE JUST TREATS ME NORMALLY NOW. SHE'S CASUAL WITH ME.
SO SEEING YOU TODAY...
...MADE ME THINK, I DON'T WANT YOU ENDING UP LIKE ME.
...
I...
...THOUGHT YOU WERE MORE OF A FLIPPANT AND SELFISH SORT OF IDIOT, BUT...
OUCH, MAN.
SHOCK

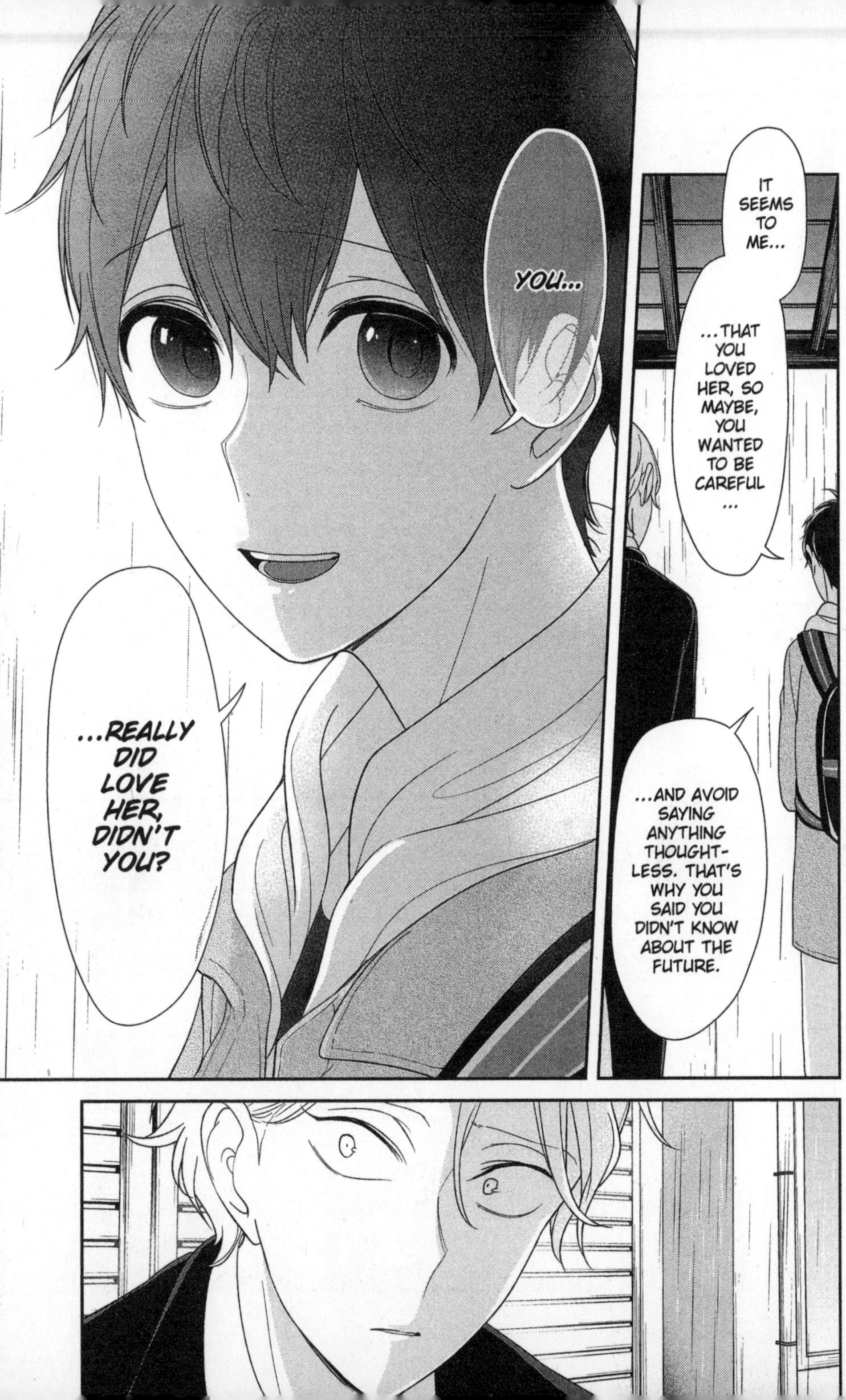
IT SEEMS TO ME...
...THAT YOU LOVED HER, SO MAYBE, YOU WANTED TO BE CAREFUL ...
...AND AVOID SAYING ANYTHING THOUGHTLESS. THAT'S WHY YOU SAID YOU DIDN'T KNOW ABOUT THE FUTURE.
YOU...
...REALLY DID LOVE HER, DIDN'T YOU?

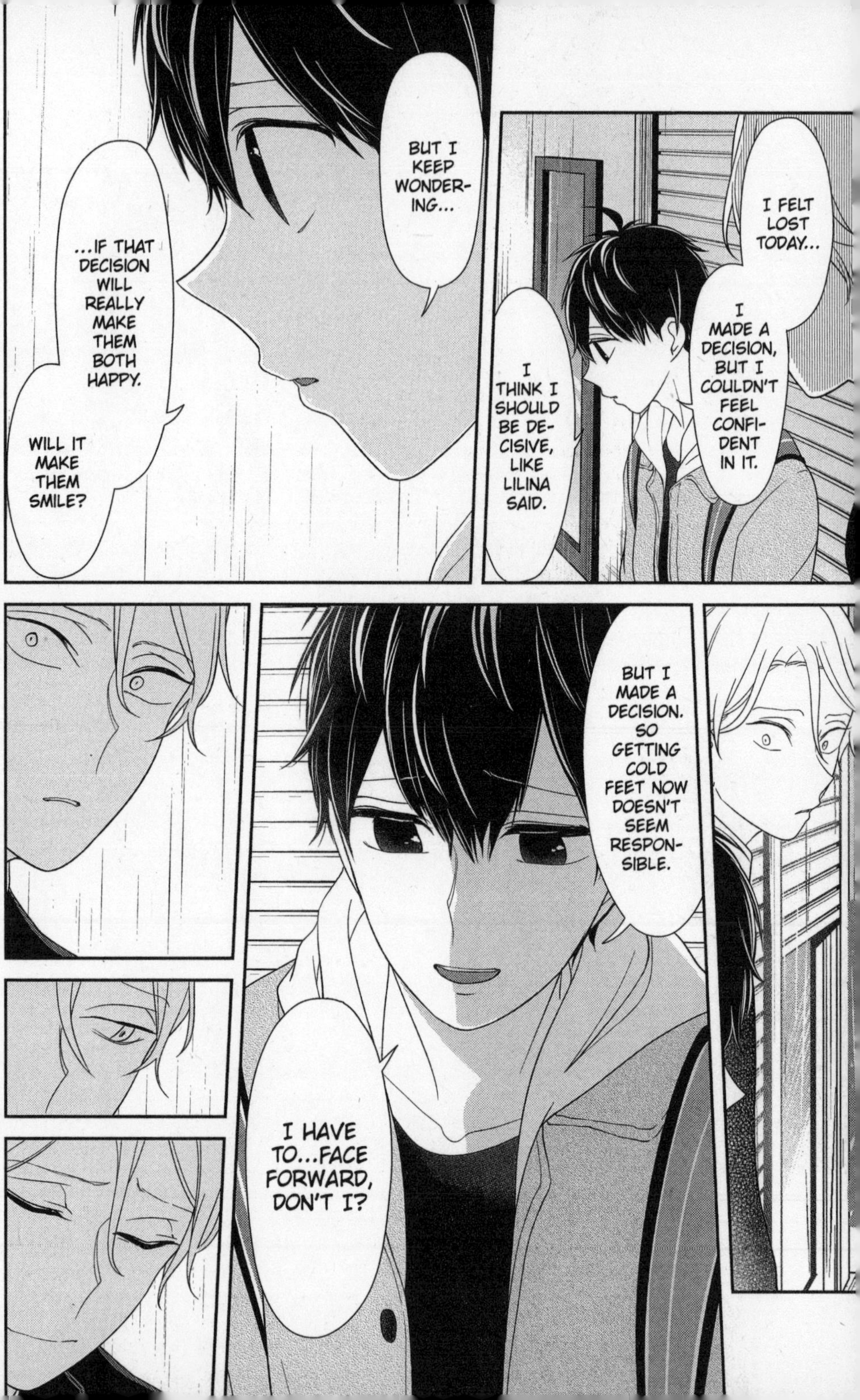
I FELT LOST TODAY...
I MADE A DECISION, BUT I COULDN'T FEEL CONFIDENT IN IT.
I THINK I SHOULD BE DECISIVE, LIKE LILINA SAID.
BUT I KEEP WONDERING...
...IF THAT DECISION WILL REALLY MAKE THEM BOTH HAPPY.
WILL IT MAKE THEM SMILE?
BUT I MADE A DECISION. SO GETTING COLD FEET NOW DOESN'T SEEM RESPONSIBLE.
I HAVE TO...FACE FORWARD, DON'T I?

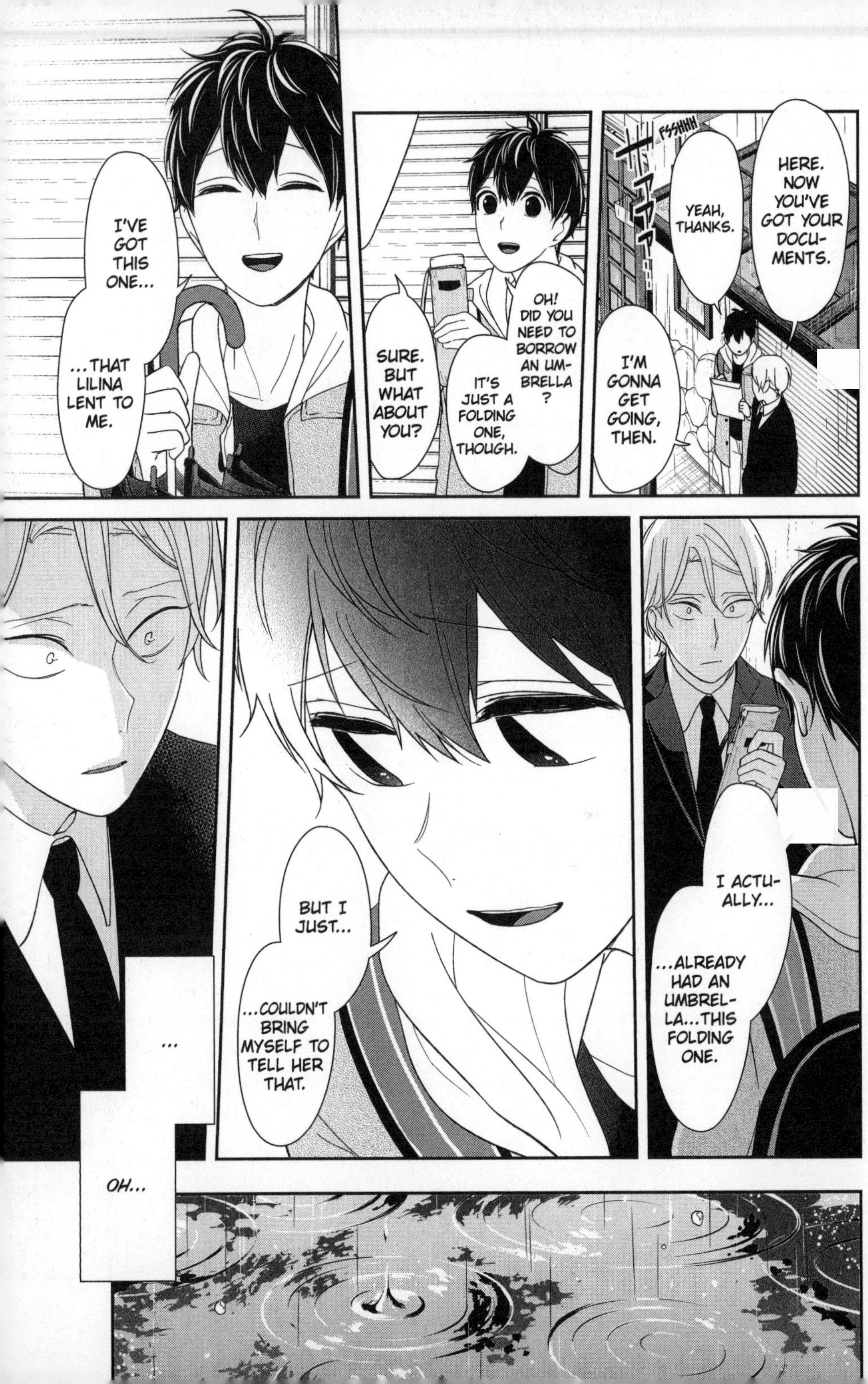
HERE. NOW YOU'VE GOT YOUR DOCU-MENTS.
FSSHHH
YEAH, THANKS.
I'M GONNA GET GOING, THEN.
OH! DID YOU NEED TO BORROW AN UM-BRELLA?
IT'S JUST A FOLDING ONE, THOUGH.
SURE. BUT WHAT ABOUT YOU?
I'VE GOT THIS ONE...
...THAT LILINA LENT TO ME.
I ACTU-ALLY...
...ALREADY HAD AN UMBREL-LA...THIS FOLDING ONE.
BUT I JUST...
...COULDN'T BRING MYSELF TO TELL HER THAT.
...
OH...

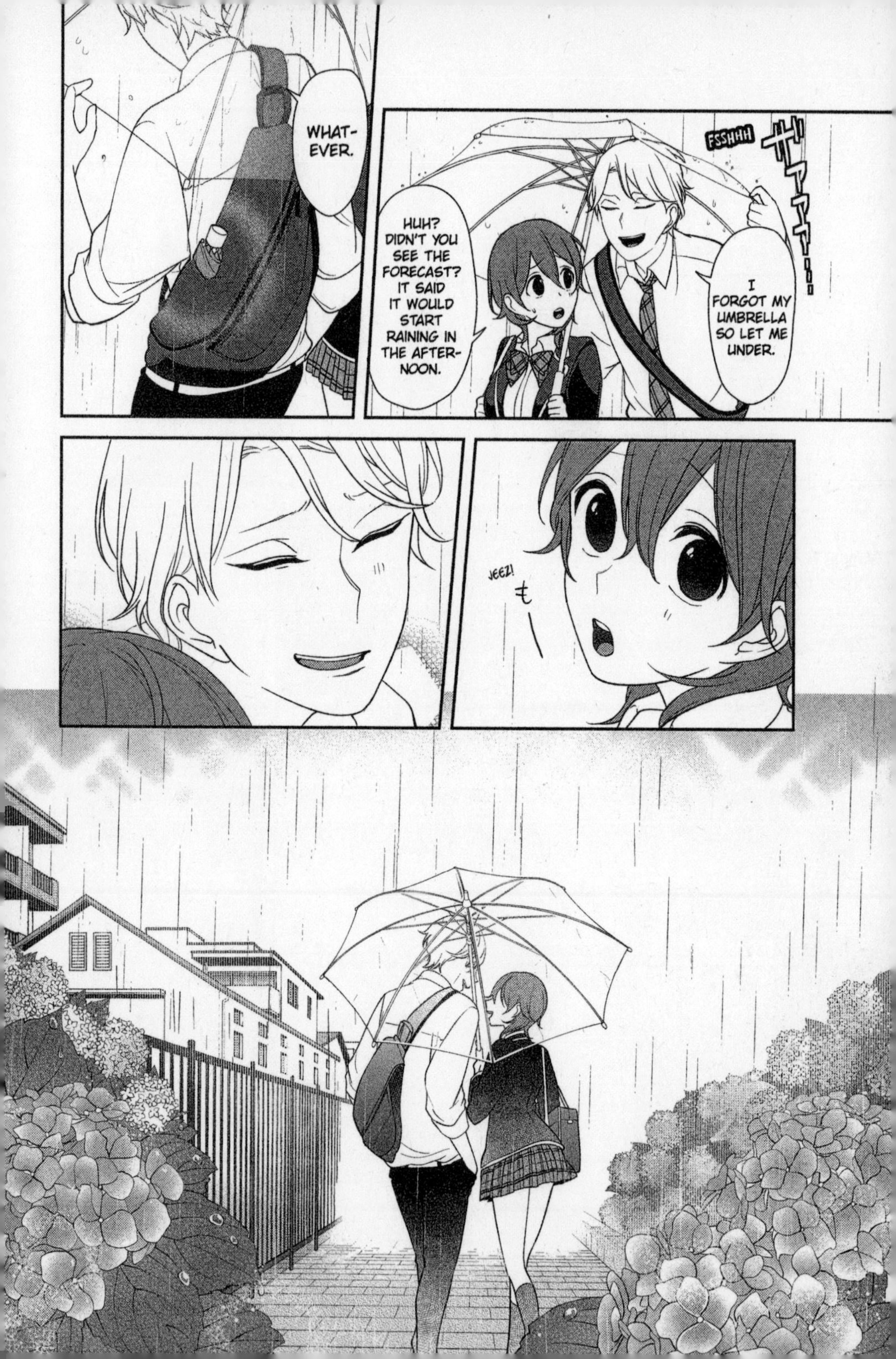
FSSHHH
I FORGOT MY UMBRELLA SO LET ME UNDER.
HUH? DIDN'T YOU SEE THE FORECAST? IT SAID IT WOULD START RAINING IN THE AFTER-NOON.
WHAT-EVER.
JEEZ!

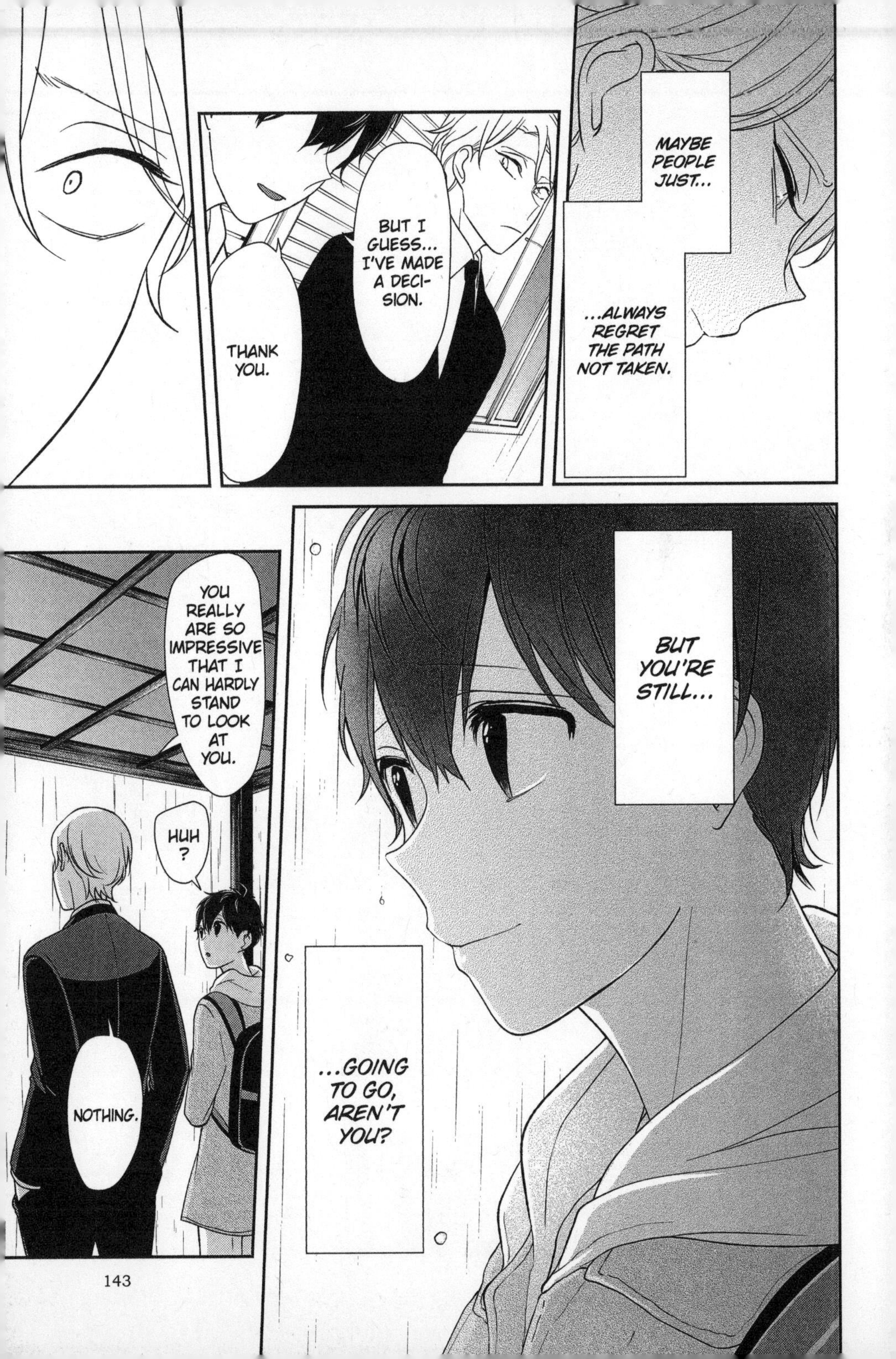
MAYBE PEOPLE JUST...
...ALWAYS REGRET THE PATH NOT TAKEN.
BUT I GUESS... I'VE MADE A DECISION.
THANK YOU.
BUT YOU'RE STILL...
...GOING TO GO, AREN'T YOU?
YOU REALLY ARE SO IMPRESSIVE THAT I CAN HARDLY STAND TO LOOK AT YOU.
HUH?
NOTHING.

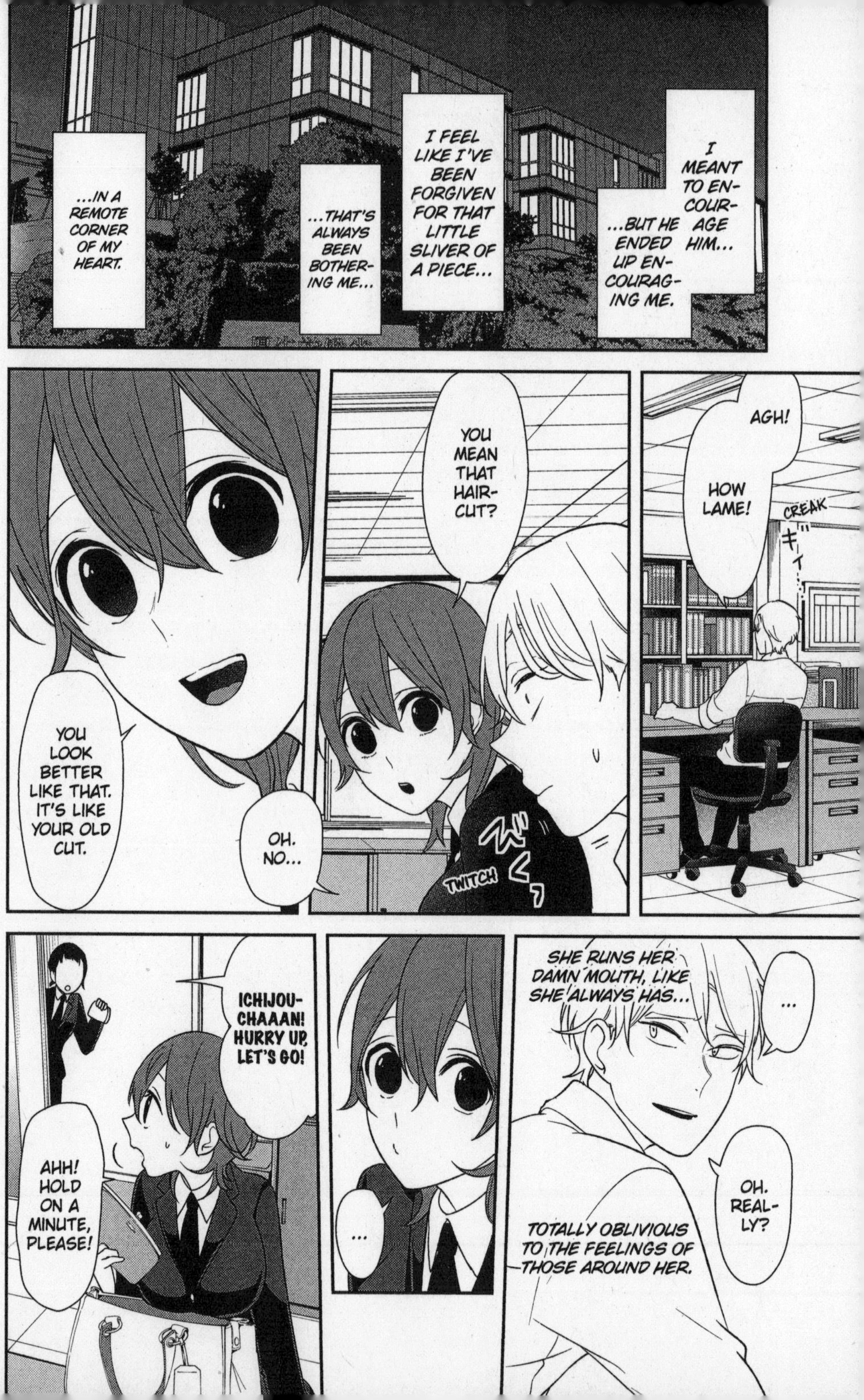
I MEANT TO ENCOURAGE HIM...
...BUT HE ENDED UP ENCOURAGING ME.
I FEEL LIKE I'VE BEEN FORGIVEN FOR THAT LITTLE SLIVER OF A PIECE...
...THAT'S ALWAYS BEEN BOTHERING ME...
...IN A REMOTE CORNER OF MY HEART.
AGH!
HOW LAME!
CREAK
YOU MEAN THAT HAIRCUT?
TWITCH
YOU LOOK BETTER LIKE THAT. IT'S LIKE YOUR OLD CUT.
OH. NO...
SHE RUNS HER DAMN MOUTH, LIKE SHE ALWAYS HAS...
...
OH. REALLY?
TOTALLY OBLIVIOUS TO THE FEELINGS OF THOSE AROUND HER.
...
ICHIJOU-CHAAAN! HURRY UP, LET'S GO!
AHH! HOLD ON A MINUTE, PLEASE!

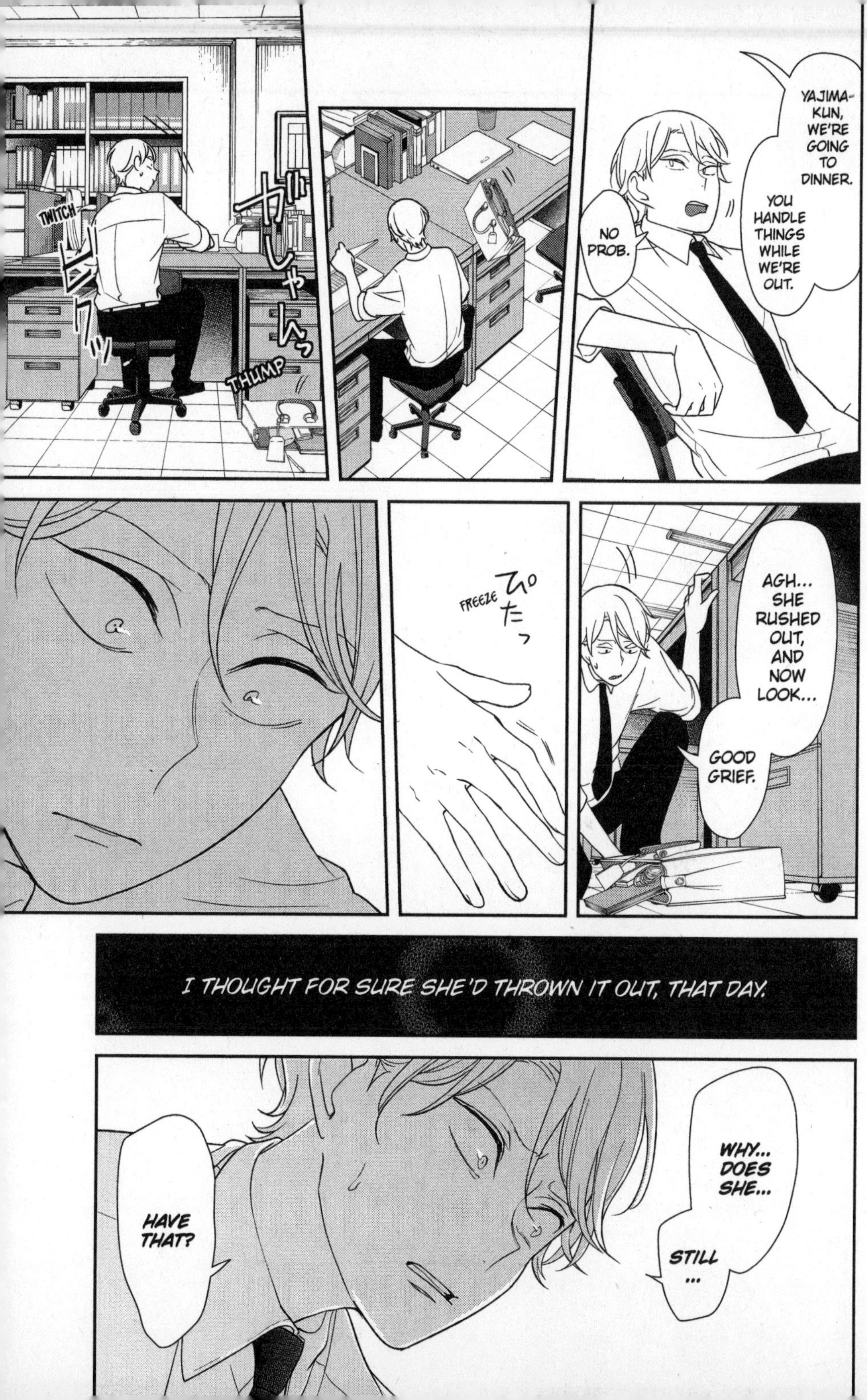
YAJIMA-KUN, WE'RE GOING TO DINNER.
YOU HANDLE THINGS WHILE WE'RE OUT.
NO PROB.
がしゃんっ
THUMP
TWITCH
ビクッ
AGH... SHE RUSHED OUT, AND NOW LOOK...
GOOD GRIEF.
ぴたっ
FREEZE
I THOUGHT FOR SURE SHE'D THROWN IT OUT, THAT DAY.
WHY... DOES SHE...
STILL ...
HAVE THAT?

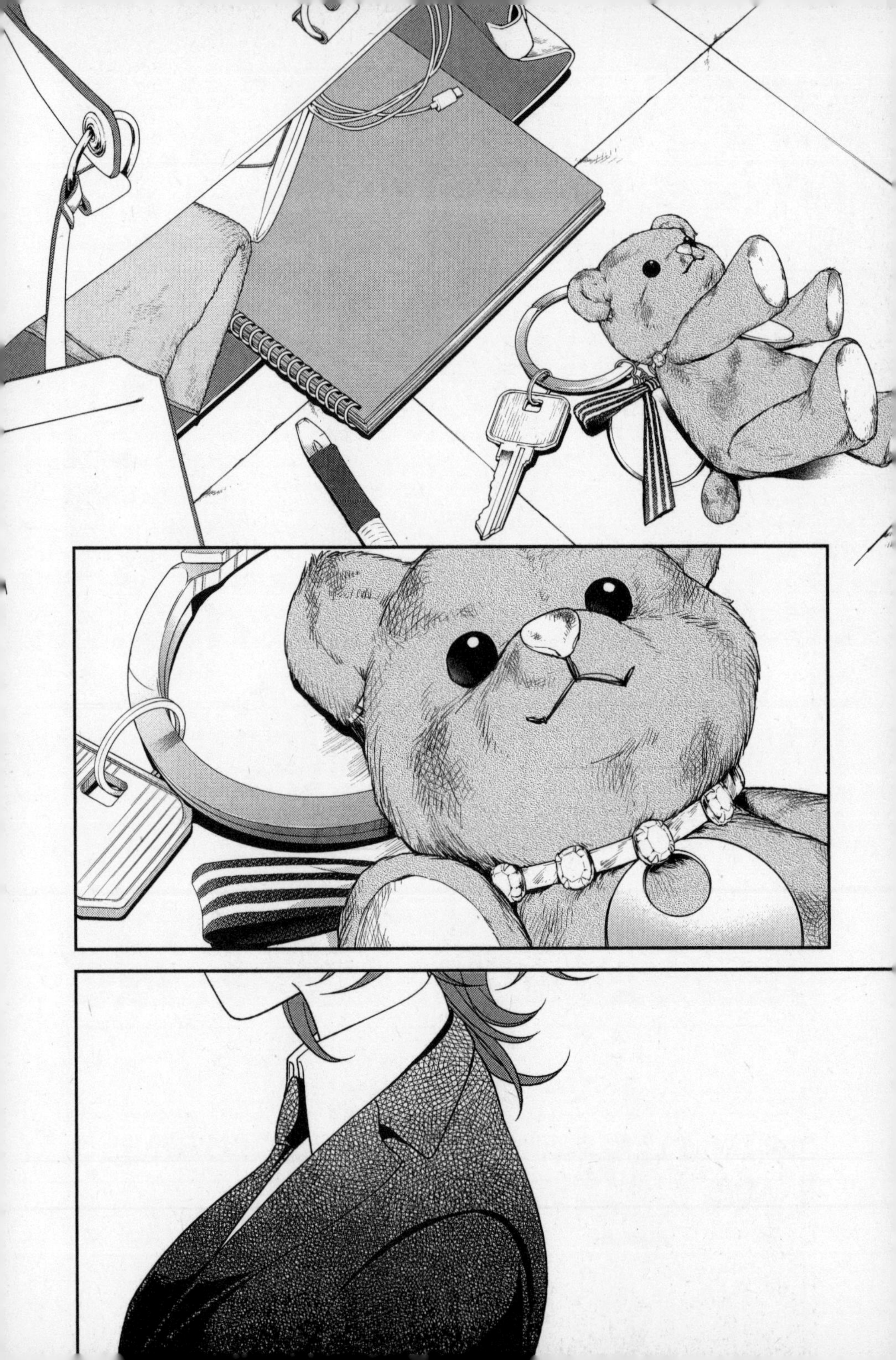

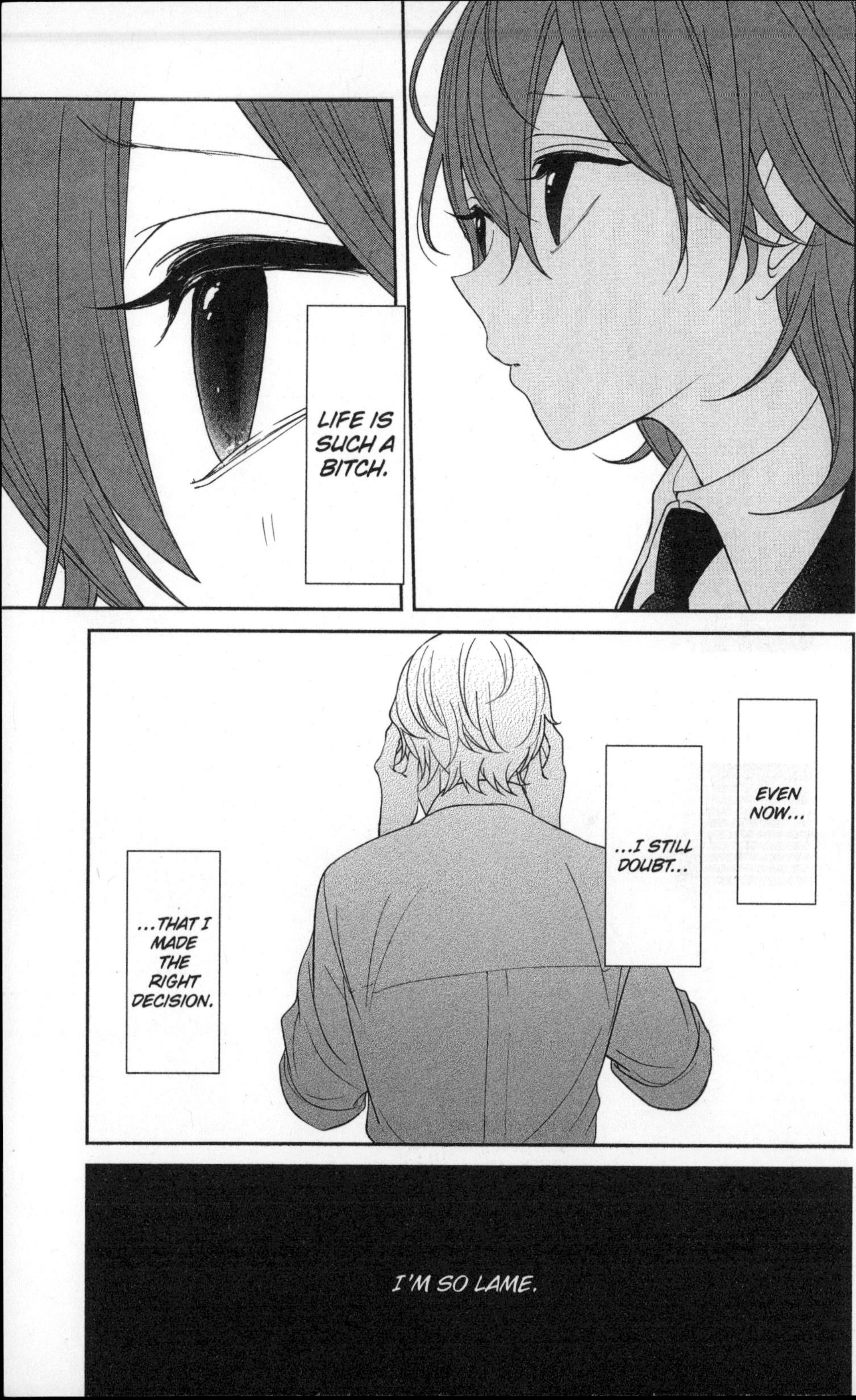
LIFE IS SUCH A BITCH.
EVEN NOW...
...I STILL DOUBT...
...THAT I MADE THE RIGHT DECISION.
I'M SO LAME.

Love & Lies

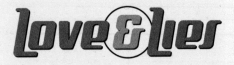

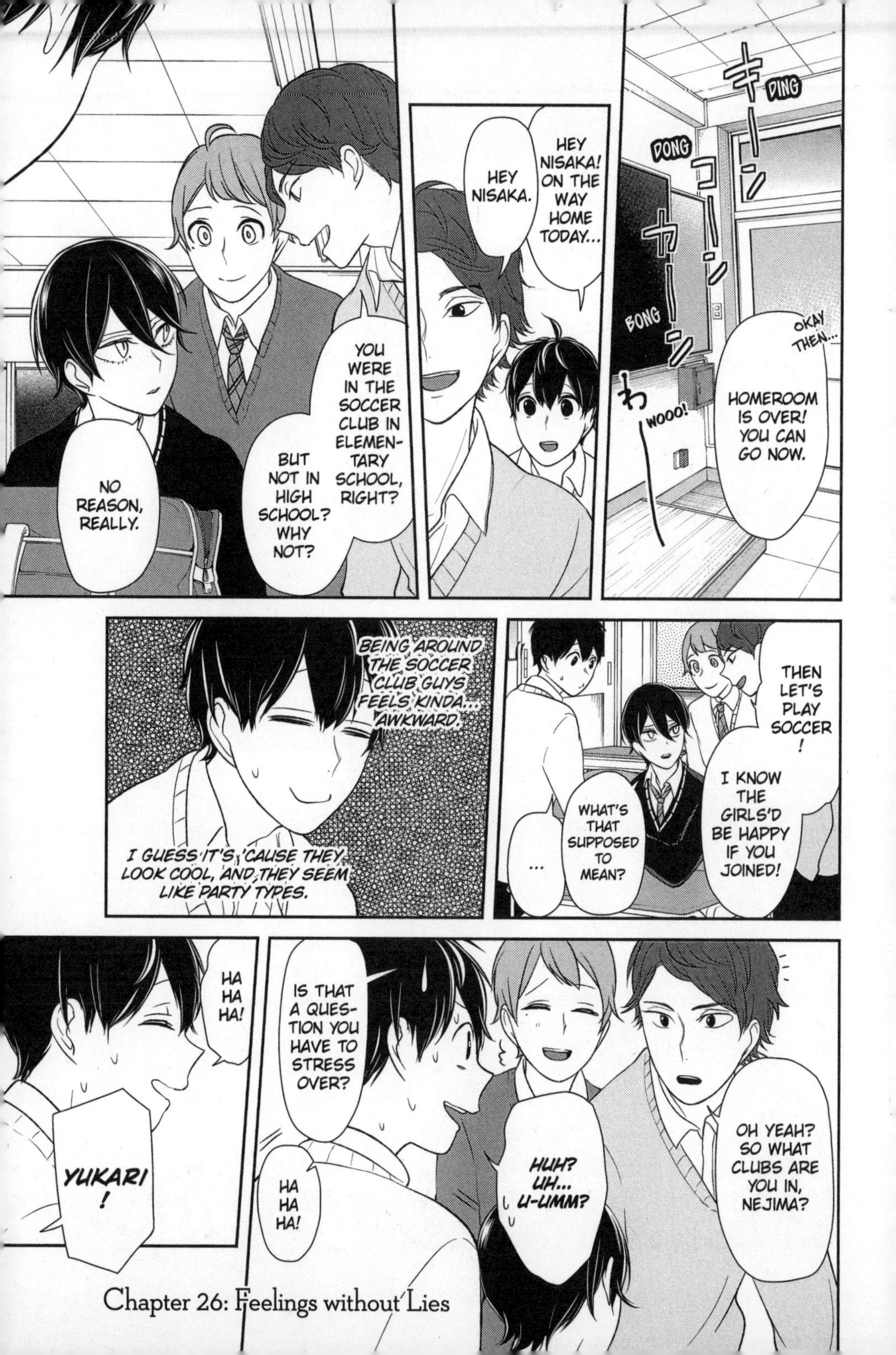
DING
DONG
BONG
WOOO!
OKAY THEN...
HOMEROOM IS OVER! YOU CAN GO NOW.
HEY NISAKA! ON THE WAY HOME TODAY...
HEY NISAKA.
YOU WERE IN THE SOCCER CLUB IN ELEMENTARY SCHOOL, RIGHT?
BUT NOT IN HIGH SCHOOL? WHY NOT?
NO REASON, REALLY.
THEN LET'S PLAY SOCCER!
I KNOW THE GIRLS'D BE HAPPY IF YOU JOINED!
WHAT'S THAT SUPPOSED TO MEAN?
...
BEING AROUND THE SOCCER CLUB GUYS FEELS KINDA... AWKWARD.
I GUESS IT'S 'CAUSE THEY LOOK COOL, AND THEY SEEM LIKE PARTY TYPES.
OH YEAH? SO WHAT CLUBS ARE YOU IN, NEJIMA?
HUH? UH... U-UMM?
IS THAT A QUESTION YOU HAVE TO STRESS OVER?
HA HA HA!
HA HA HA!
YUKARI!

Chapter 26: Feelings without Lies

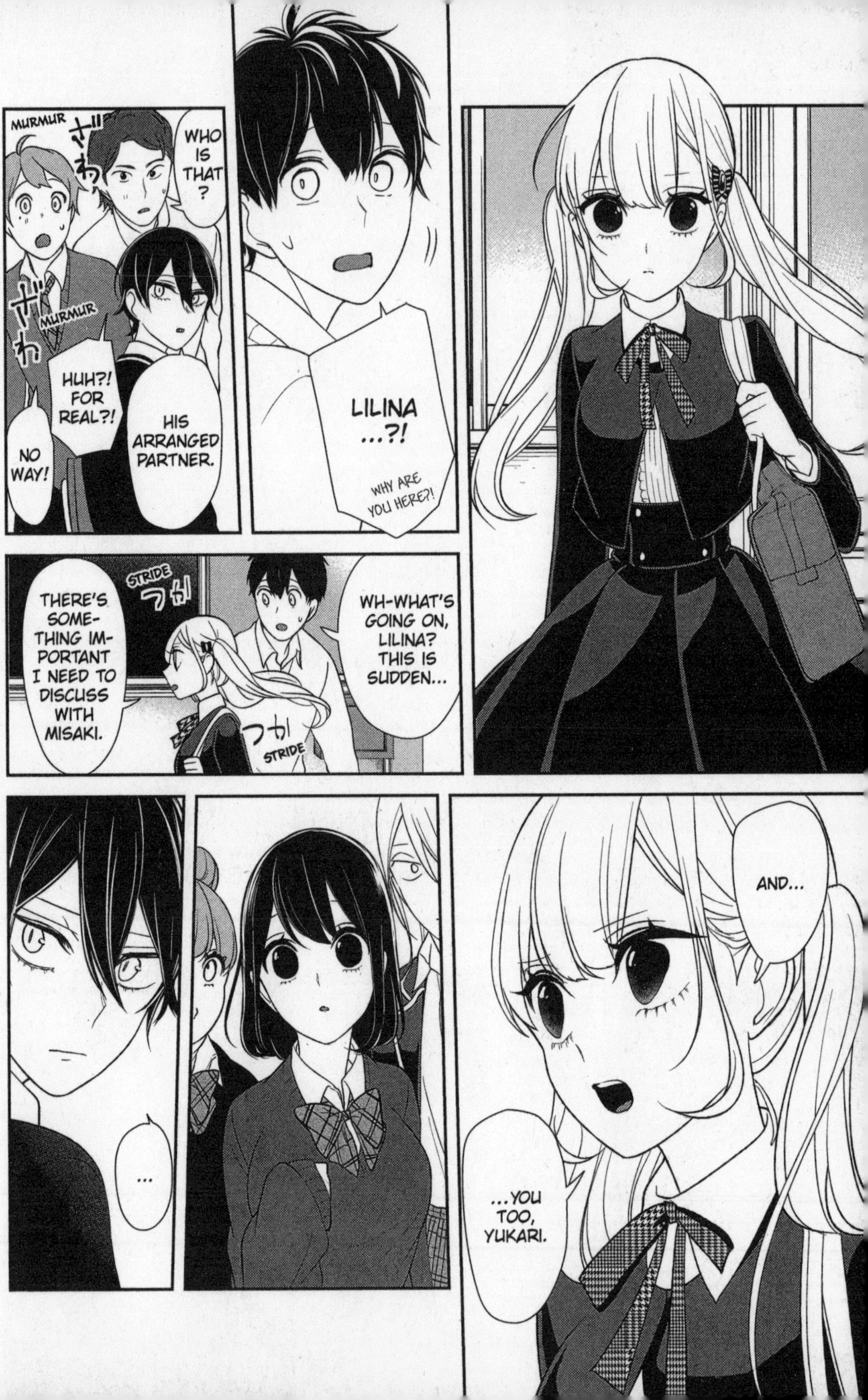
LILINA ...?!
WHY ARE YOU HERE?!
WHO IS THAT?
MURMUR ざわ
HIS ARRANGED PARTNER.
HUH?! FOR REAL?!
MURMUR ざわ
NO WAY!
WH-WHAT'S GOING ON, LILINA? THIS IS SUDDEN...
STRIDE ツカ
STRIDE ツカ
THERE'S SOME-THING IM-PORTANT I NEED TO DISCUSS WITH MISAKI.
AND...
...YOU TOO, YUKARI.
...

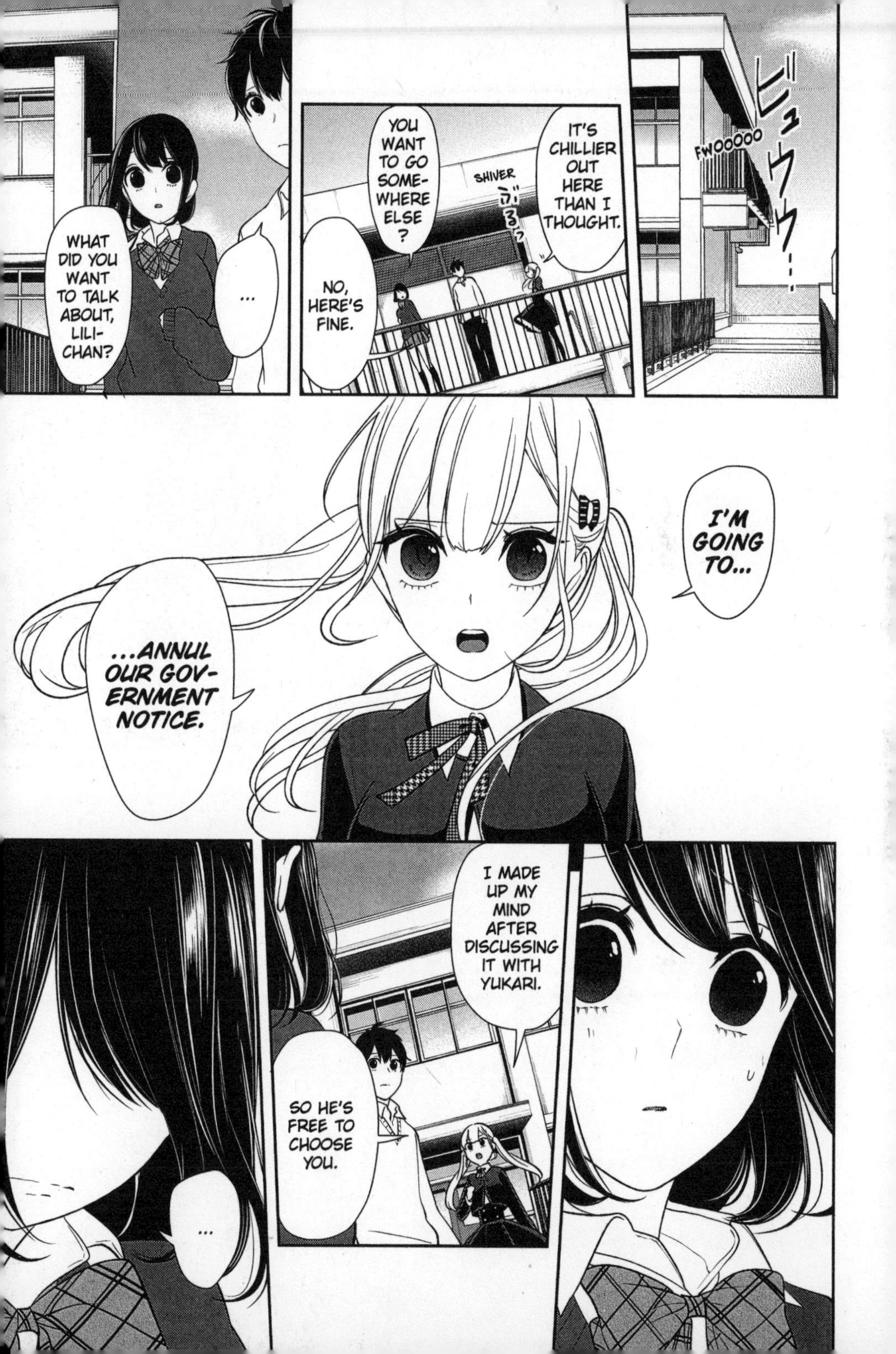
FWOOOOO
IT'S CHILLIER OUT HERE THAN I THOUGHT.
SHIVER
YOU WANT TO GO SOME-WHERE ELSE?
NO, HERE'S FINE.
...
WHAT DID YOU WANT TO TALK ABOUT, LILI-CHAN?
I'M GOING TO...
...ANNUL OUR GOV-ERNMENT NOTICE.
I MADE UP MY MIND AFTER DISCUSSING IT WITH YUKARI.
SO HE'S FREE TO CHOOSE YOU.
...

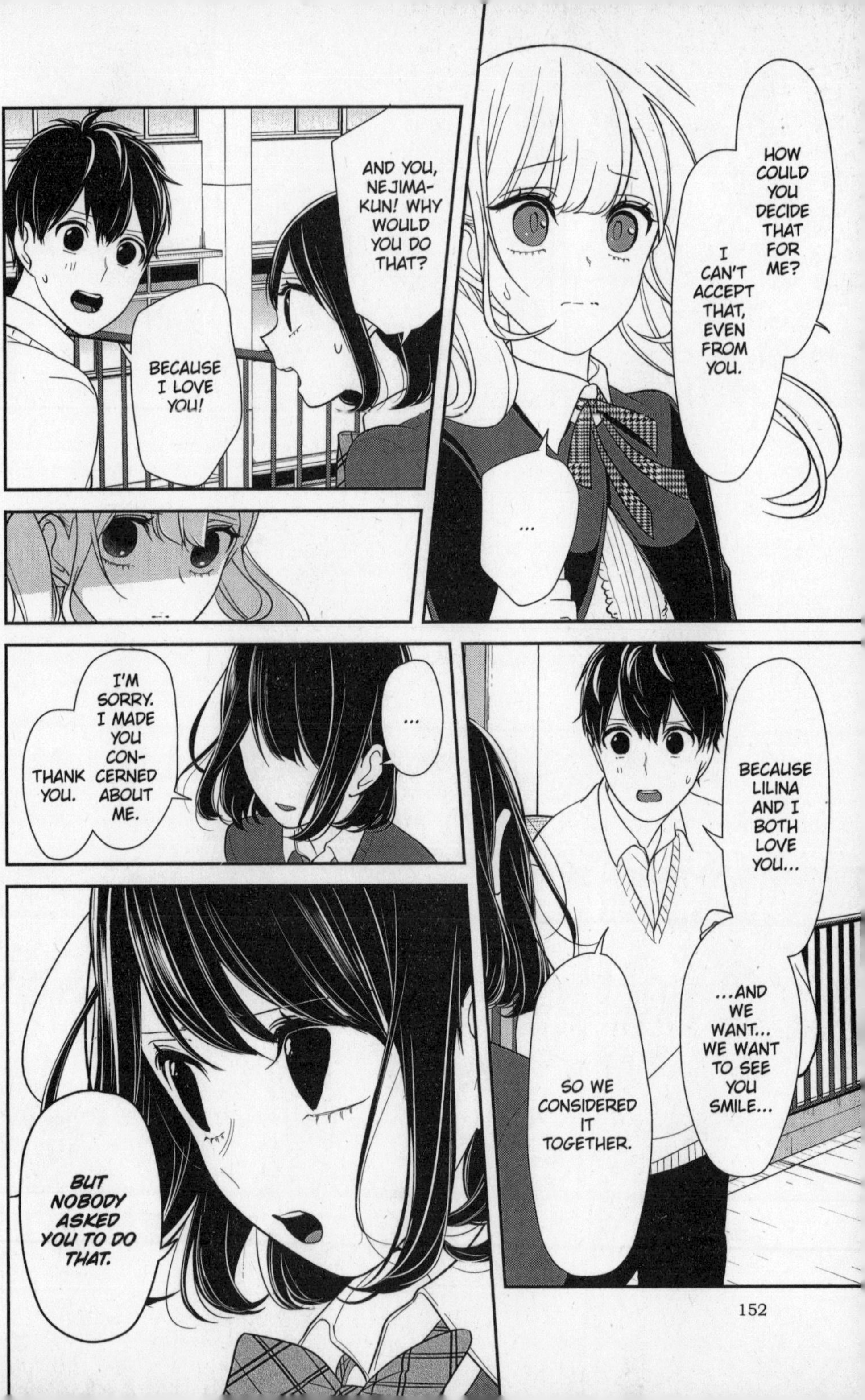
HOW COULD YOU DECIDE THAT FOR ME?
I CAN'T ACCEPT THAT, EVEN FROM YOU.
...
AND YOU, NEJIMA-KUN! WHY WOULD YOU DO THAT?
BECAUSE I LOVE YOU!
BECAUSE LILINA AND I BOTH LOVE YOU...
...AND WE WANT... WE WANT TO SEE YOU SMILE...
SO WE CONSIDERED IT TOGETHER.
...
I'M SORRY. I MADE YOU CONCERNED ABOUT ME.
THANK YOU.
BUT NOBODY ASKED YOU TO DO THAT.

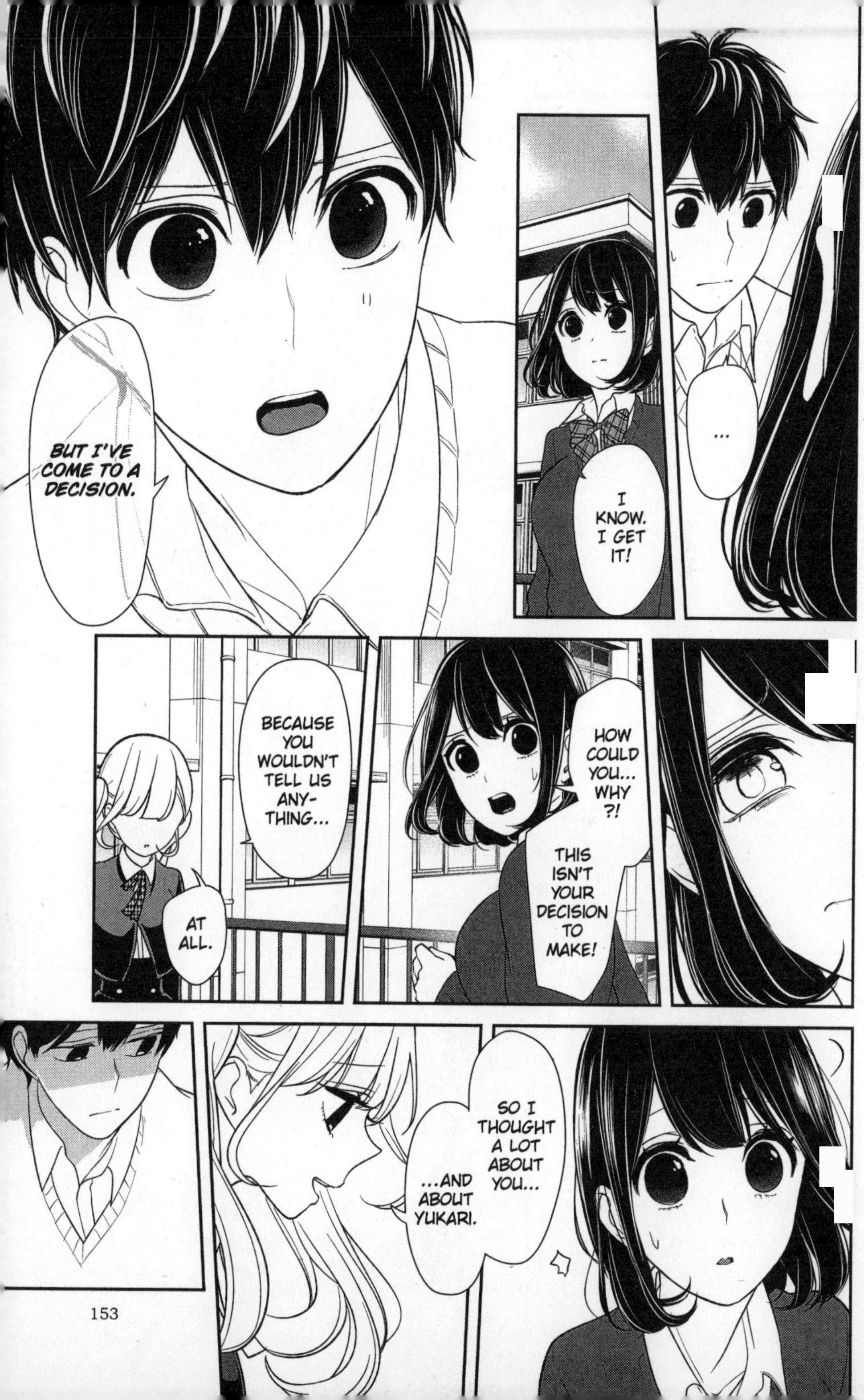
...
I KNOW. I GET IT!
BUT I'VE COME TO A DECISION.
HOW COULD YOU... WHY?!
THIS ISN'T YOUR DECISION TO MAKE!
BECAUSE YOU WOULDN'T TELL US ANY-THING...
AT ALL.
SO I THOUGHT A LOT ABOUT YOU...
...AND ABOUT YUKARI.

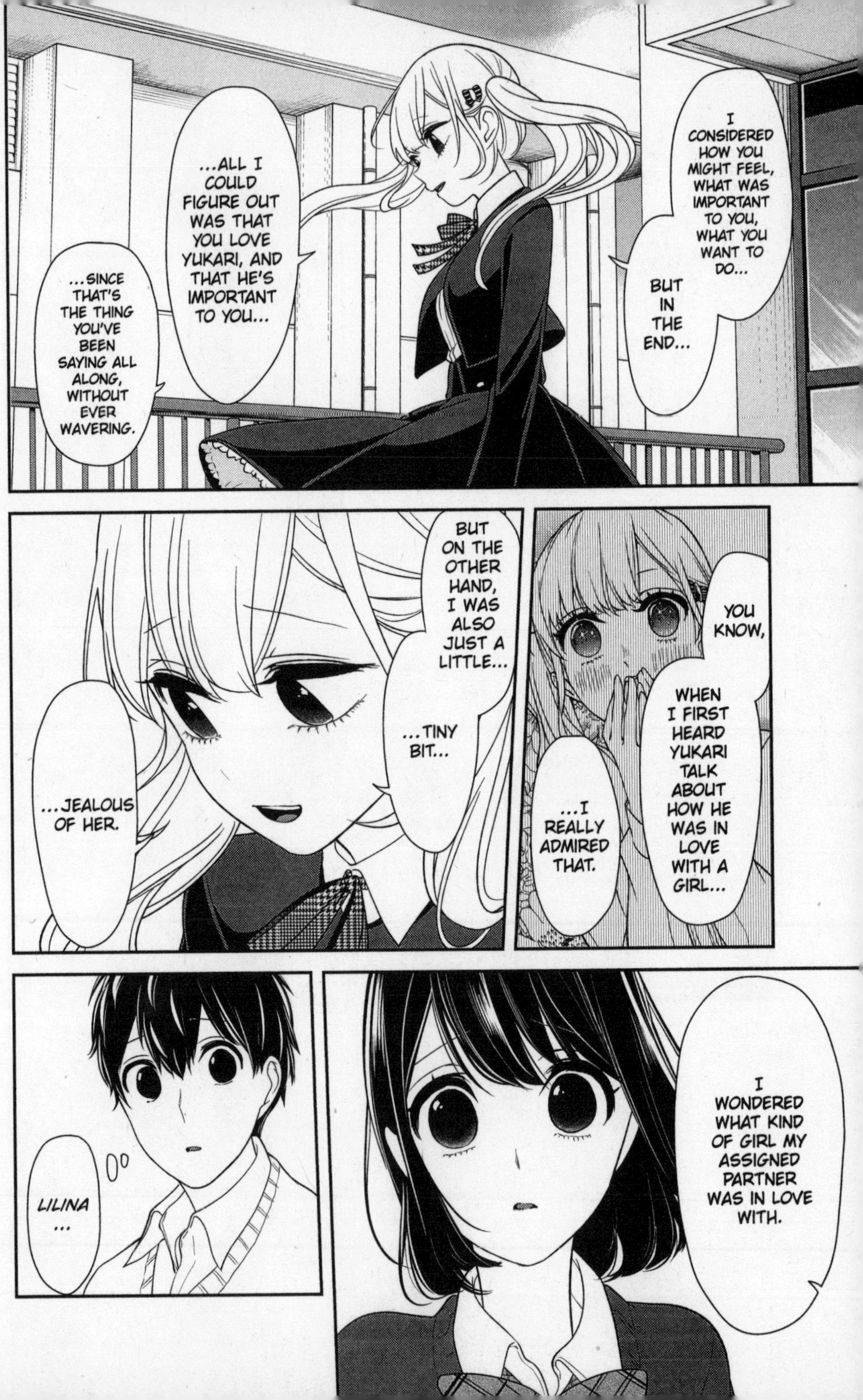
I CONSIDERED HOW YOU MIGHT FEEL, WHAT WAS IMPORTANT TO YOU, WHAT YOU WANT TO DO...
BUT IN THE END...
...ALL I COULD FIGURE OUT WAS THAT YOU LOVE YUKARI, AND THAT HE'S IMPORTANT TO YOU...
...SINCE THAT'S THE THING YOU'VE BEEN SAYING ALL ALONG, WITHOUT EVER WAVERING.
YOU KNOW,
WHEN I FIRST HEARD YUKARI TALK ABOUT HOW HE WAS IN LOVE WITH A GIRL...
...I REALLY ADMIRED THAT.
BUT ON THE OTHER HAND, I WAS ALSO JUST A LITTLE...
...TINY BIT...
...JEALOUS OF HER.
I WONDERED WHAT KIND OF GIRL MY ASSIGNED PARTNER WAS IN LOVE WITH.
LILINA ...

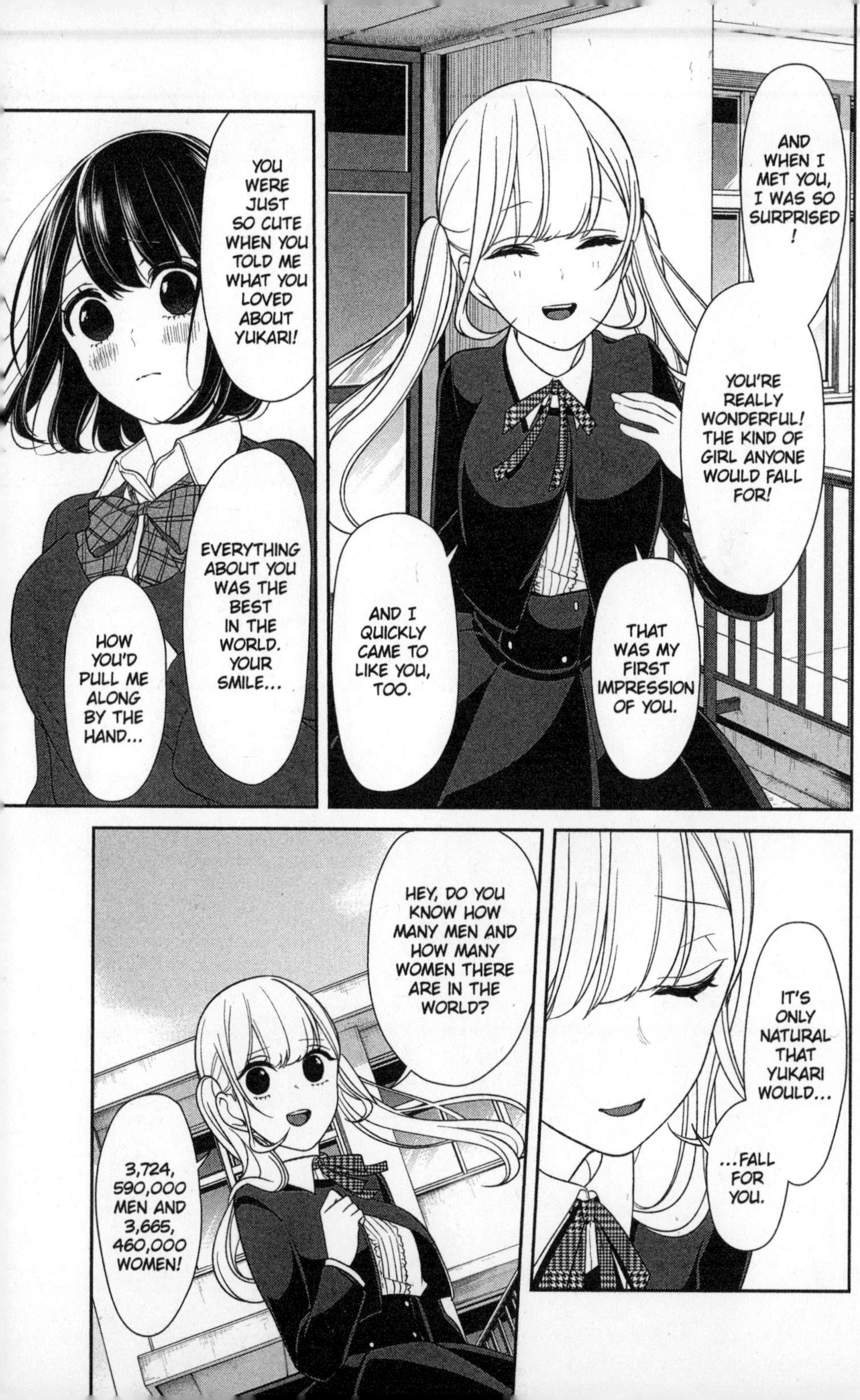
AND WHEN I MET YOU, I WAS SO SURPRISED!
YOU'RE REALLY WONDERFUL! THE KIND OF GIRL ANYONE WOULD FALL FOR!
THAT WAS MY FIRST IMPRESSION OF YOU.
AND I QUICKLY CAME TO LIKE YOU, TOO.
YOU WERE JUST SO CUTE WHEN YOU TOLD ME WHAT YOU LOVED ABOUT YUKARI!
EVERYTHING ABOUT YOU WAS THE BEST IN THE WORLD. YOUR SMILE...
HOW YOU'D PULL ME ALONG BY THE HAND...
IT'S ONLY NATURAL THAT YUKARI WOULD...
...FALL FOR YOU.
HEY, DO YOU KNOW HOW MANY MEN AND HOW MANY WOMEN THERE ARE IN THE WORLD?
3,724,590,000 MEN AND 3,665,460,000 WOMEN!

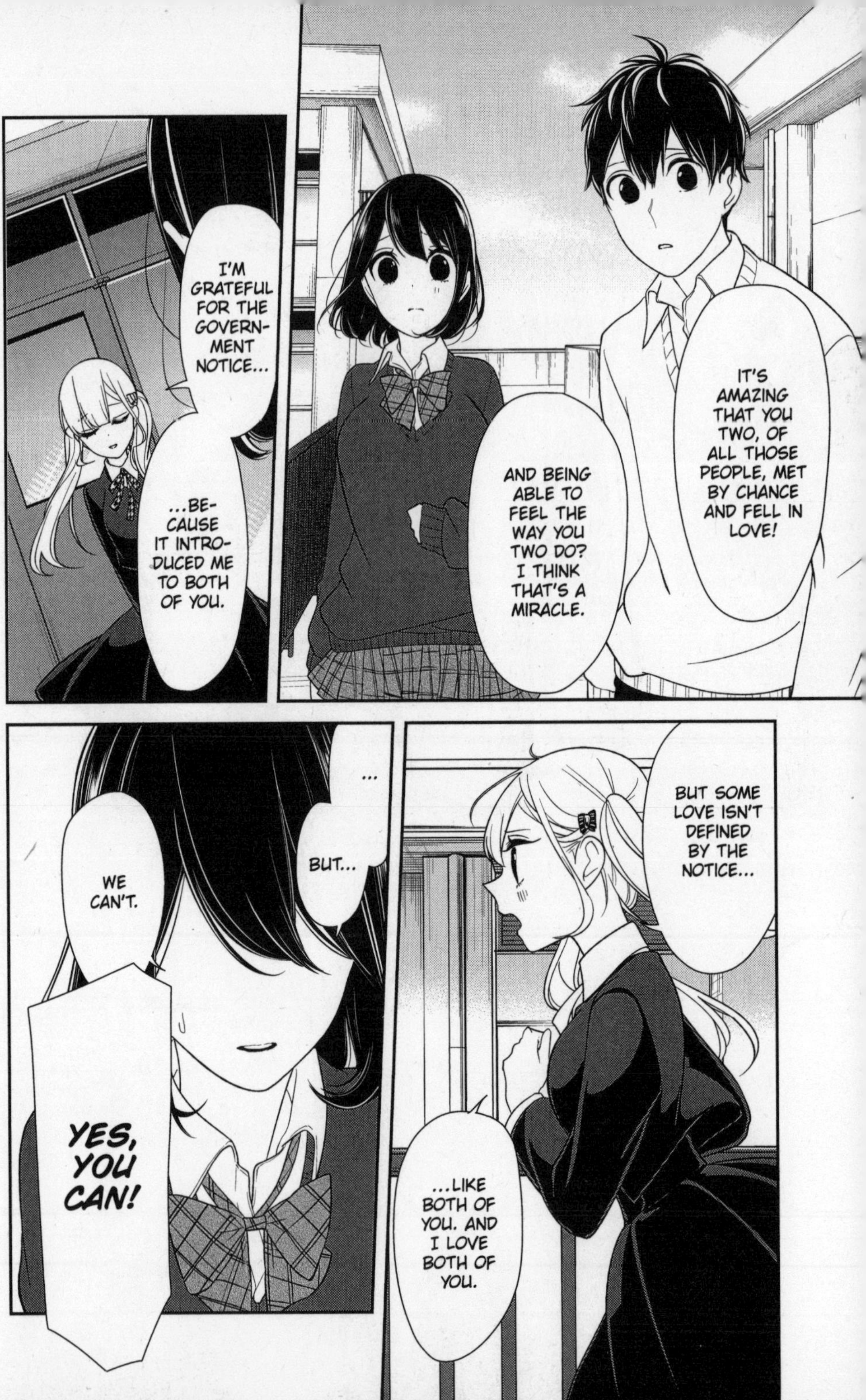
IT'S AMAZING THAT YOU TWO, OF ALL THOSE PEOPLE, MET BY CHANCE AND FELL IN LOVE!
AND BEING ABLE TO FEEL THE WAY YOU TWO DO? I THINK THAT'S A MIRACLE.
I'M GRATEFUL FOR THE GOVERNMENT NOTICE...
...BECAUSE IT INTRODUCED ME TO BOTH OF YOU.
BUT SOME LOVE ISN'T DEFINED BY THE NOTICE...
...LIKE BOTH OF YOU. AND I LOVE BOTH OF YOU.
...
BUT...
WE CAN'T.
YES, YOU CAN!

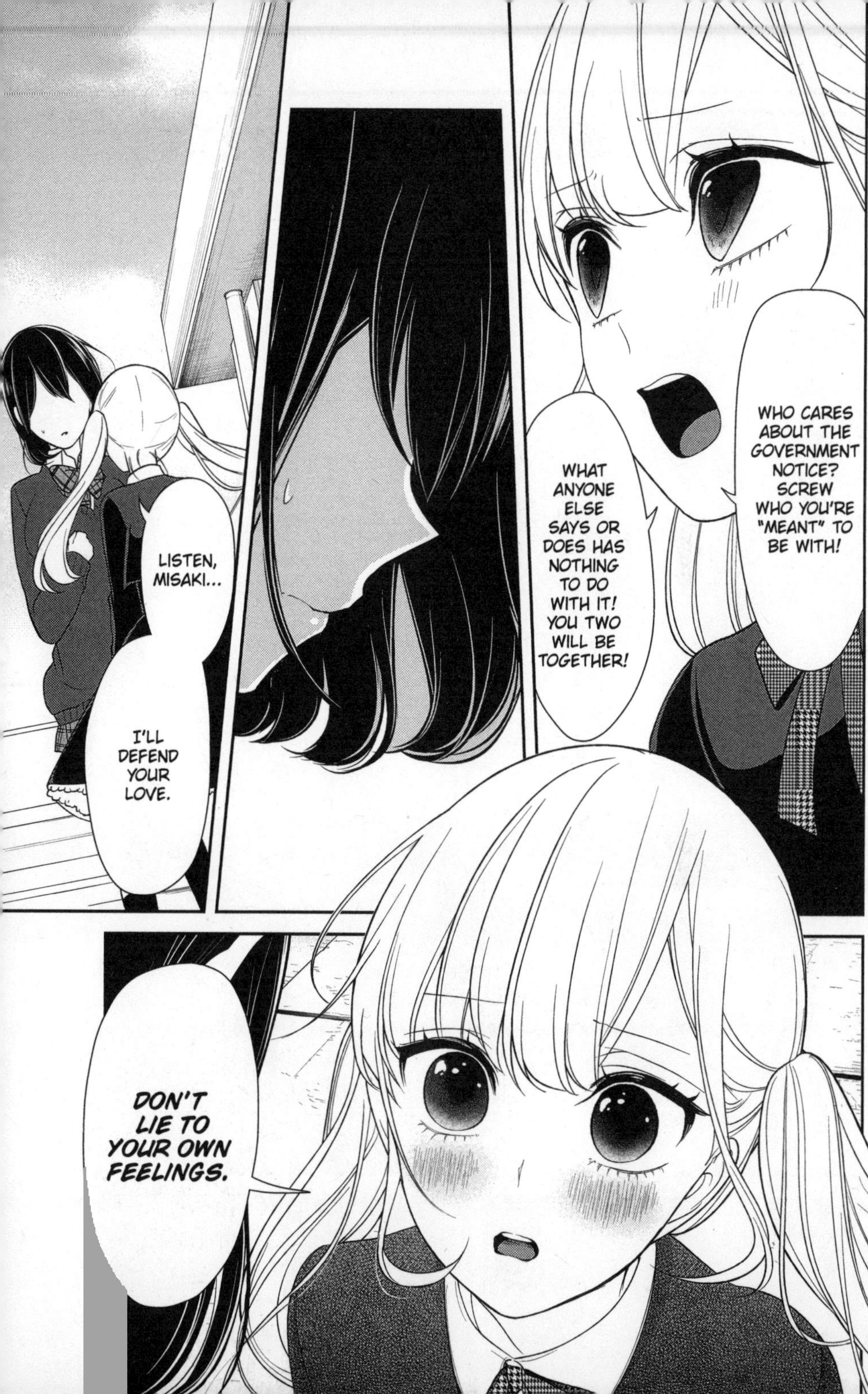
WHO CARES ABOUT THE GOVERNMENT NOTICE? SCREW WHO YOU'RE "MEANT" TO BE WITH!
WHAT ANYONE ELSE SAYS OR DOES HAS NOTHING TO DO WITH IT! YOU TWO WILL BE TOGETHER!
LISTEN, MISAKI...
I'LL DEFEND YOUR LOVE.
DON'T LIE TO YOUR OWN FEELINGS.

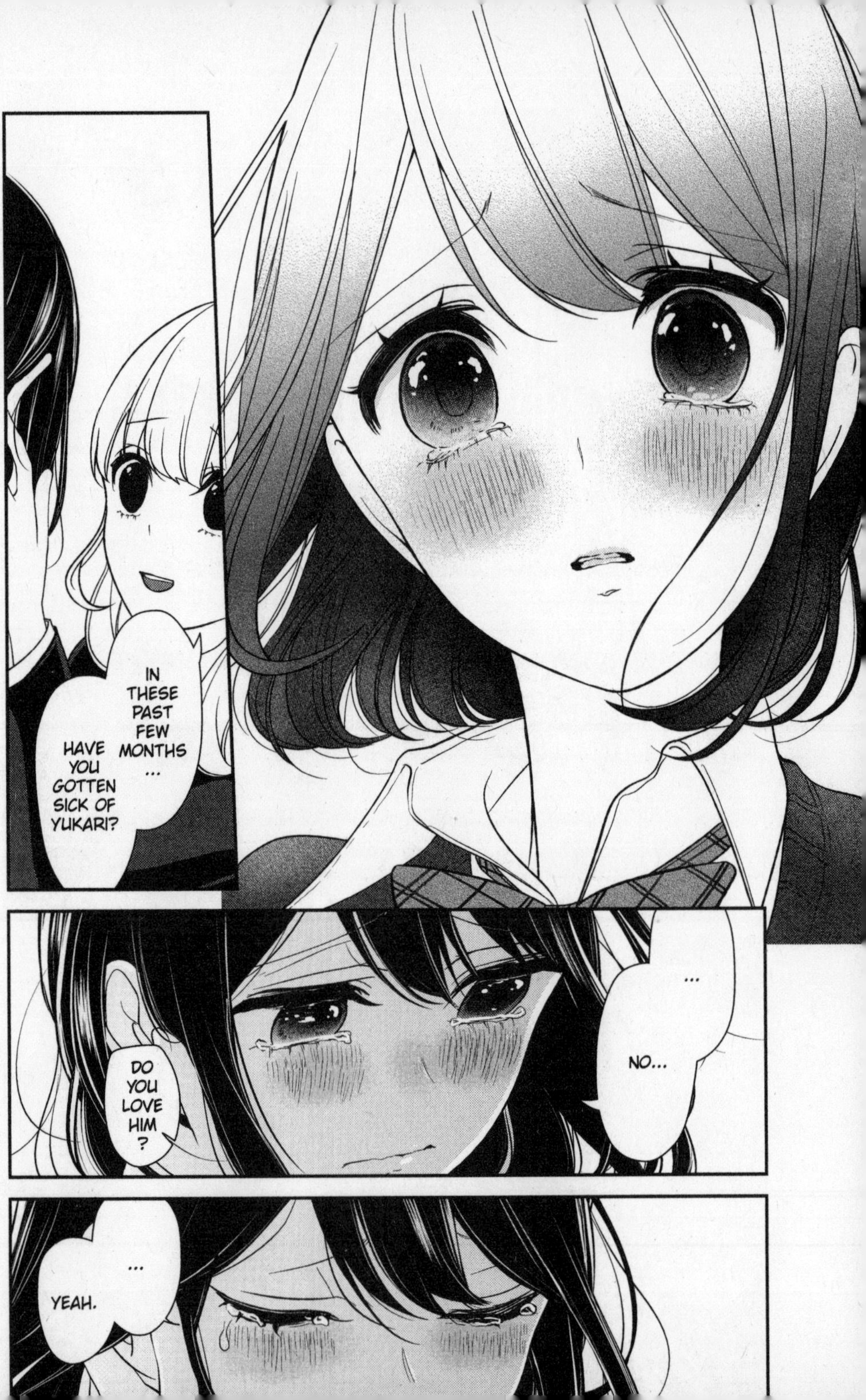
IN THESE PAST FEW MONTHS ...
HAVE YOU GOTTEN SICK OF YUKARI?
... NO...
DO YOU LOVE HIM?
... YEAH.

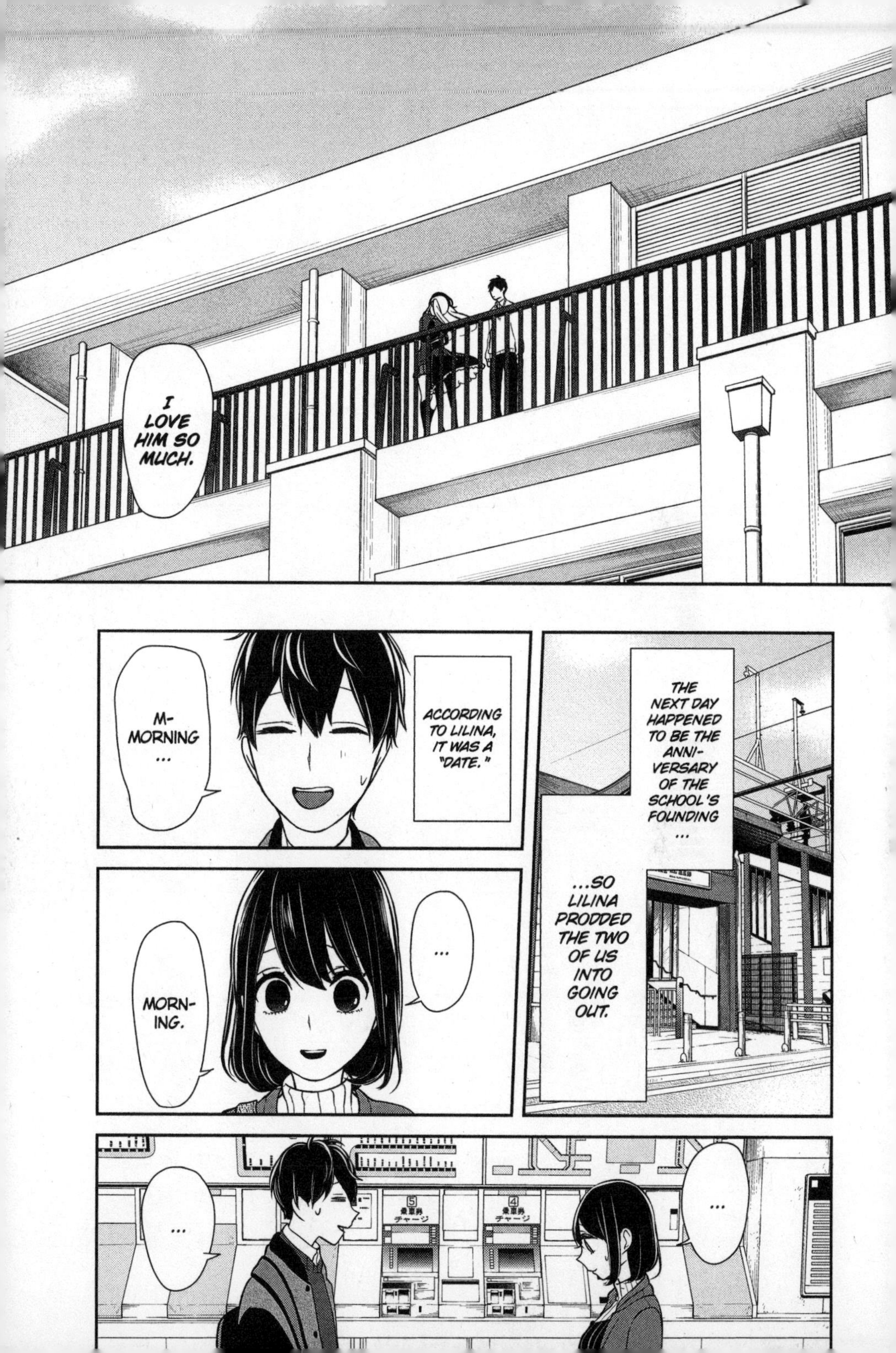
I LOVE HIM SO MUCH.
THE NEXT DAY HAPPENED TO BE THE ANNIVERSARY OF THE SCHOOL'S FOUNDING...
...SO LILINA PRODDED THE TWO OF US INTO GOING OUT.
ACCORDING TO LILINA, IT WAS A "DATE."
M-MORNING...
...
MORNING.
...
...

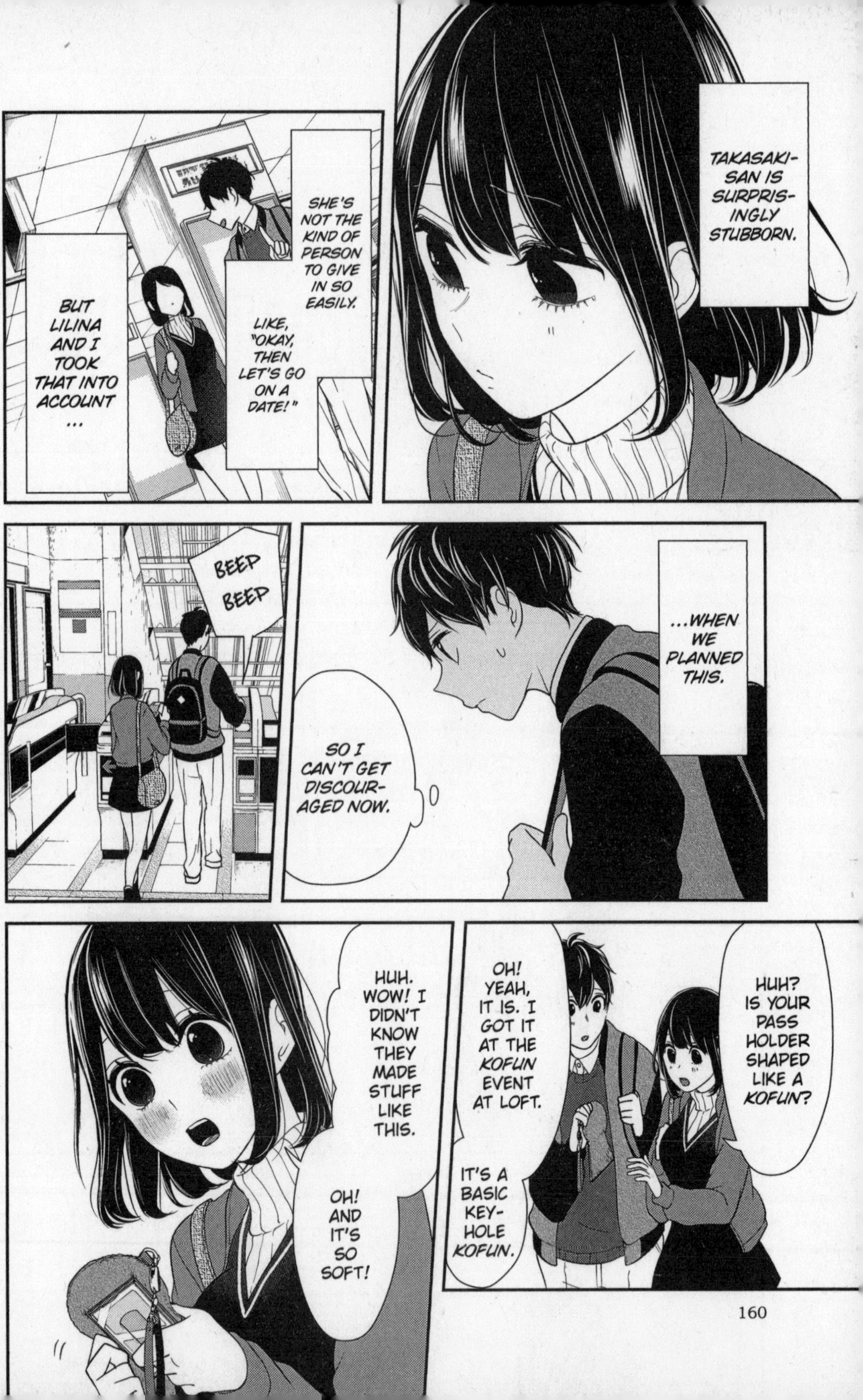
TAKASAKI-SAN IS SURPRISINGLY STUBBORN.
SHE'S NOT THE KIND OF PERSON TO GIVE IN SO EASILY.
LIKE, "OKAY, THEN LET'S GO ON A DATE!"
BUT LILINA AND I TOOK THAT INTO ACCOUNT...
...WHEN WE PLANNED THIS.
SO I CAN'T GET DISCOURAGED NOW.
BEEP BEEP
HUH? IS YOUR PASS HOLDER SHAPED LIKE A KOFUN?
OH! YEAH, IT IS. I GOT IT AT THE KOFUN EVENT AT LOFT.
IT'S A BASIC KEY-HOLE KOFUN.
HUH. WOW! I DIDN'T KNOW THEY MADE STUFF LIKE THIS.
OH! AND IT'S SO SOFT!

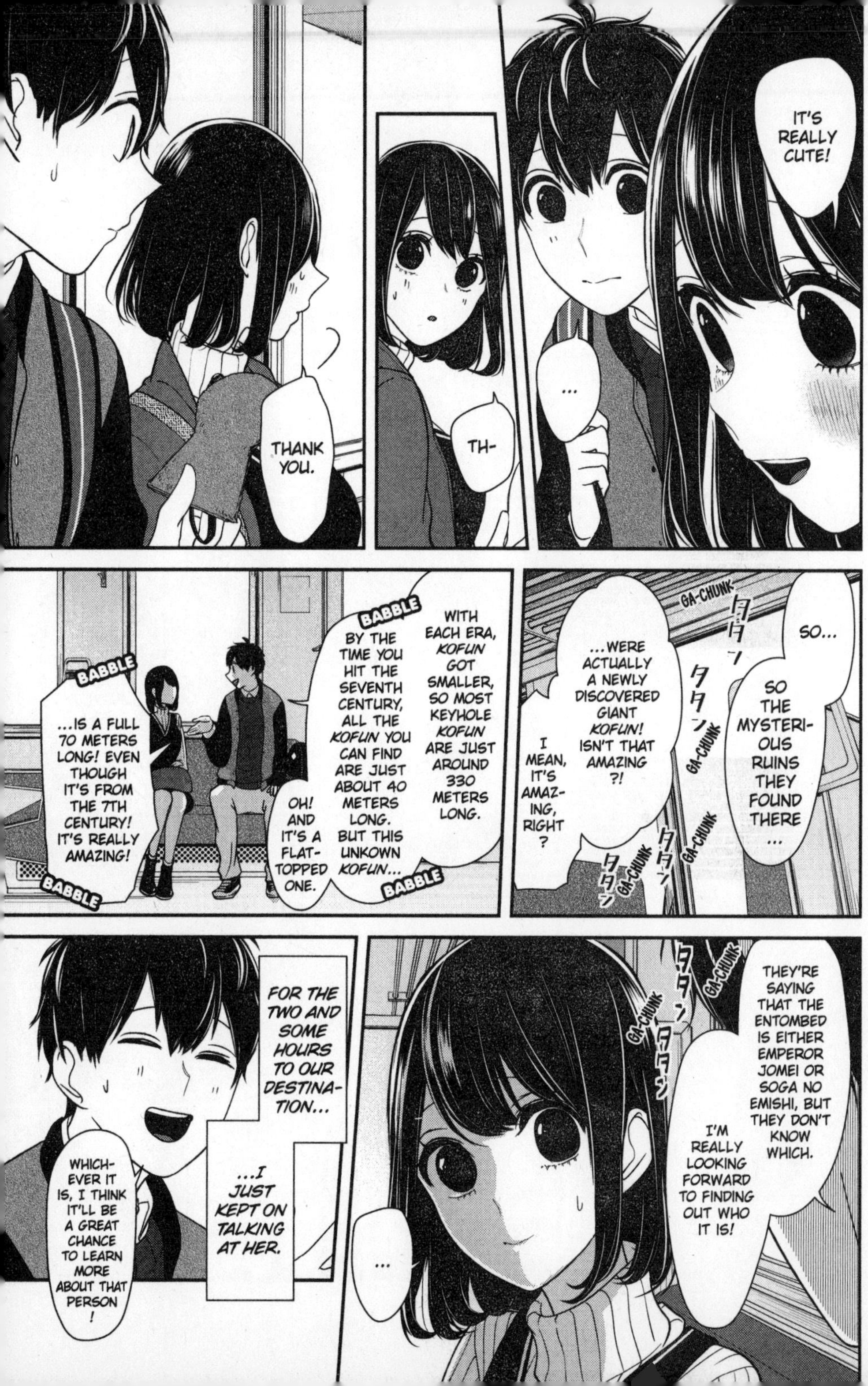
IT'S REALLY CUTE!
...
TH-
THANK YOU.
SO...
SO THE MYSTERIOUS RUINS THEY FOUND THERE...
...WERE ACTUALLY A NEWLY DISCOVERED GIANT KOFUN! ISN'T THAT AMAZING?!
I MEAN, IT'S AMAZING, RIGHT?
GA-CHUNK
タタン
GA-CHUNK
タタン
GA-CHUNK
タタン
GA-CHUNK
タタン
WITH EACH ERA, KOFUN GOT SMALLER, SO MOST KEYHOLE KOFUN ARE JUST AROUND 330 METERS LONG.
BABBLE
BY THE TIME YOU HIT THE SEVENTH CENTURY, ALL THE KOFUN YOU CAN FIND ARE JUST ABOUT 40 METERS LONG. BUT THIS UNKOWN KOFUN...
BABBLE
OH! AND IT'S A FLAT-TOPPED ONE.
BABBLE
...IS A FULL 70 METERS LONG! EVEN THOUGH IT'S FROM THE 7TH CENTURY! IT'S REALLY AMAZING!
BABBLE
GA-CHUNK
タタン
GA-CHUNK
タタン
THEY'RE SAYING THAT THE ENTOMBED IS EITHER EMPEROR JOMEI OR SOGA NO EMISHI, BUT THEY DON'T KNOW WHICH.
I'M REALLY LOOKING FORWARD TO FINDING OUT WHO IT IS!
...
FOR THE TWO AND SOME HOURS TO OUR DESTINATION...
WHICHEVER IT IS, I THINK IT'LL BE A GREAT CHANCE TO LEARN MORE ABOUT THAT PERSON!
...I JUST KEPT ON TALKING AT HER.

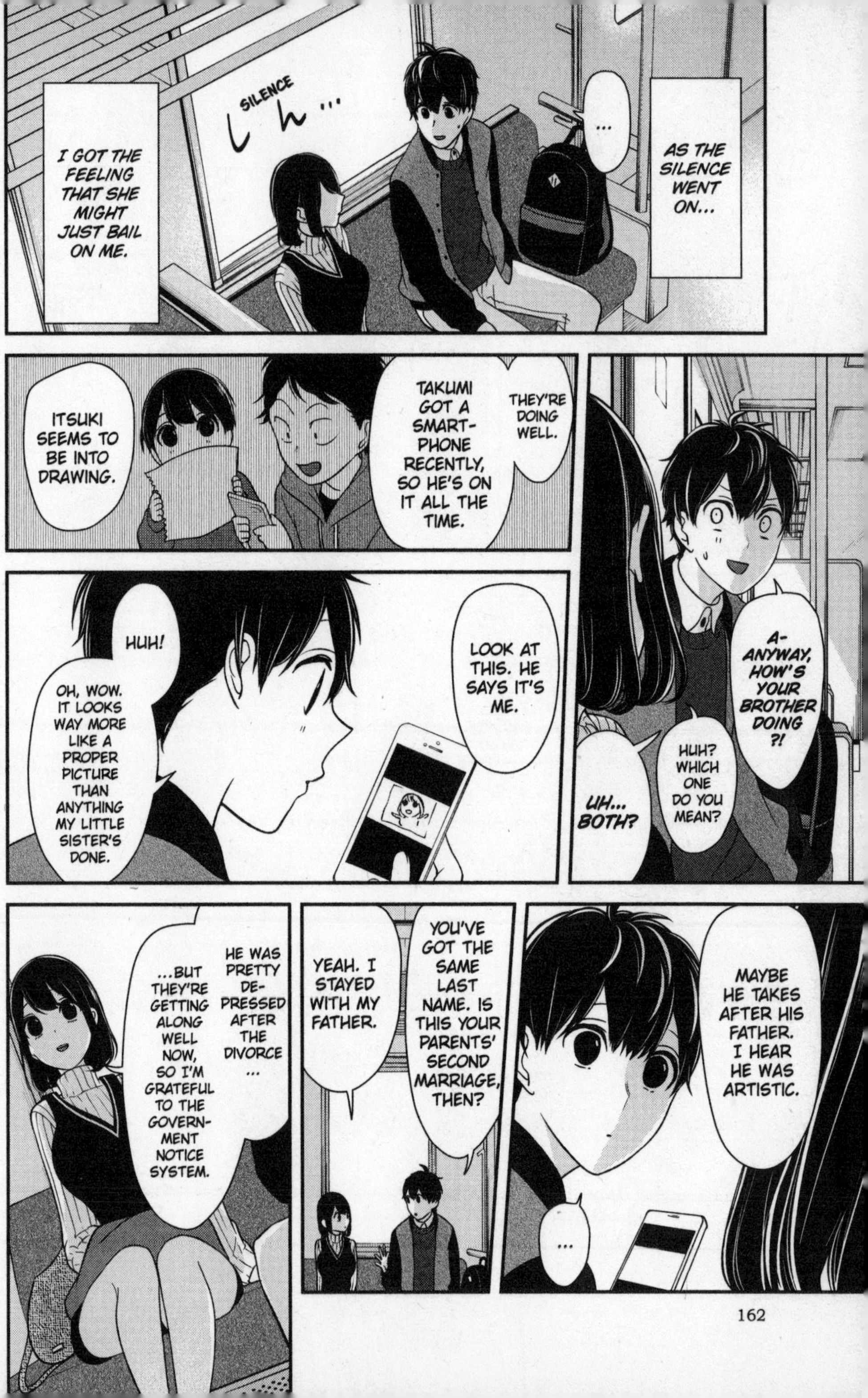
AS THE SILENCE WENT ON...
...
SILENCE
しん...
I GOT THE FEELING THAT SHE MIGHT JUST BAIL ON ME.
A-ANYWAY, HOW'S YOUR BROTHER DOING?!
HUH? WHICH ONE DO YOU MEAN?
UH... BOTH?
THEY'RE DOING WELL.
TAKUMI GOT A SMART-PHONE RECENTLY, SO HE'S ON IT ALL THE TIME.
ITSUKI SEEMS TO BE INTO DRAWING.
LOOK AT THIS. HE SAYS IT'S ME.
HUH!
OH, WOW. IT LOOKS WAY MORE LIKE A PROPER PICTURE THAN ANYTHING MY LITTLE SISTER'S DONE.
MAYBE HE TAKES AFTER HIS FATHER. I HEAR HE WAS ARTISTIC.
...
YOU'VE GOT THE SAME LAST NAME. IS THIS YOUR PARENTS' SECOND MARRIAGE, THEN?
YEAH. I STAYED WITH MY FATHER.
HE WAS PRETTY DE-PRESSED AFTER THE DIVORCE...
...BUT THEY'RE GETTING ALONG WELL NOW, SO I'M GRATEFUL TO THE GOVERN-MENT NOTICE SYSTEM.

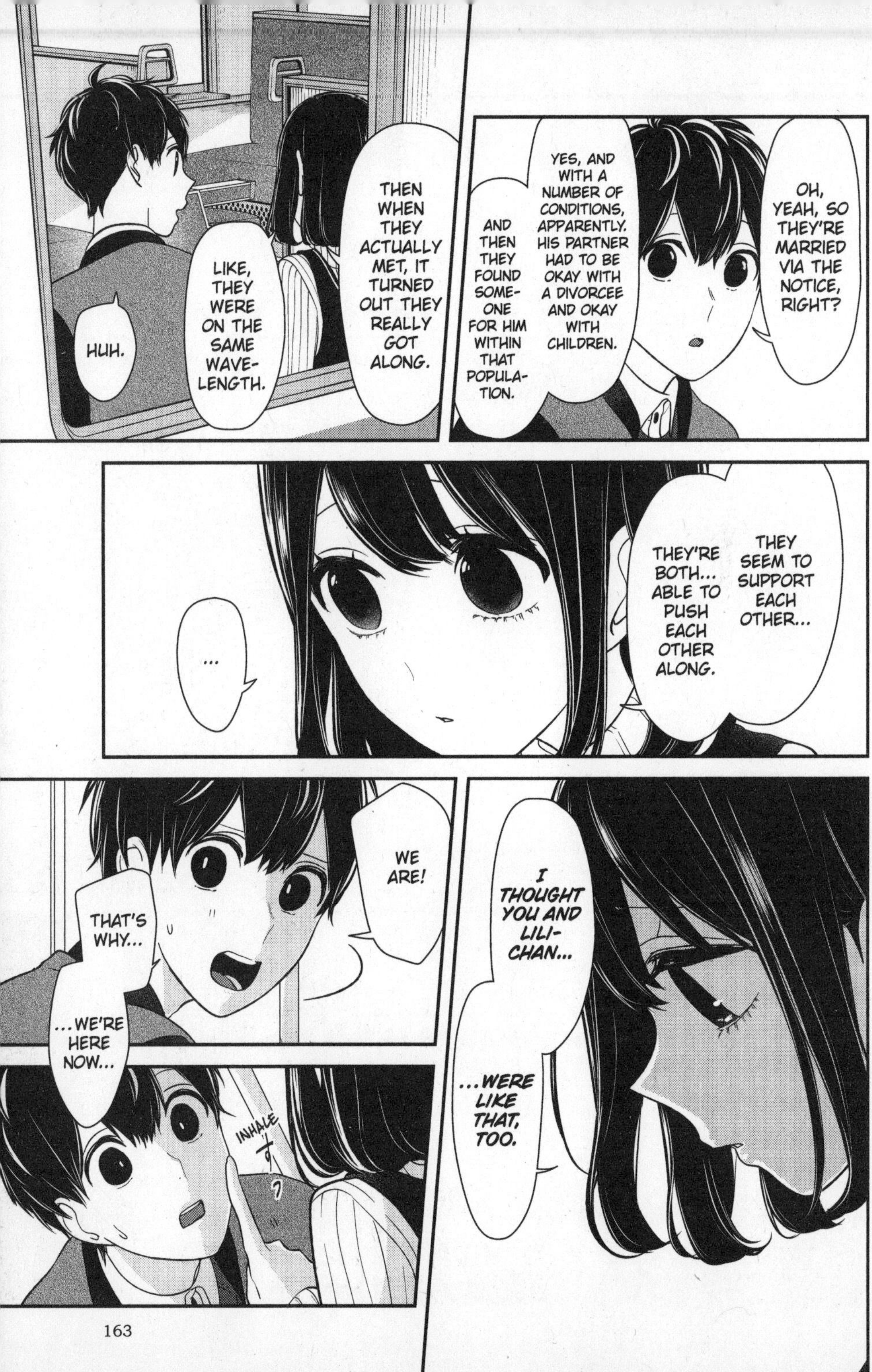
OH, YEAH, SO THEY'RE MARRIED VIA THE NOTICE, RIGHT?
YES, AND WITH A NUMBER OF CONDITIONS, APPARENTLY. HIS PARTNER HAD TO BE OKAY WITH A DIVORCEE AND OKAY WITH CHILDREN.
AND THEN THEY FOUND SOME-ONE FOR HIM WITHIN THAT POPULA-TION.
THEN WHEN THEY ACTUALLY MET, IT TURNED OUT THEY REALLY GOT ALONG.
LIKE, THEY WERE ON THE SAME WAVE-LENGTH.
HUH.
THEY SEEM TO SUPPORT EACH OTHER...
THEY'RE BOTH... ABLE TO PUSH EACH OTHER ALONG.
...
I THOUGHT YOU AND LILI-CHAN...
...WERE LIKE THAT, TOO.
WE ARE!
THAT'S WHY...
...WE'RE HERE NOW...
INHALE

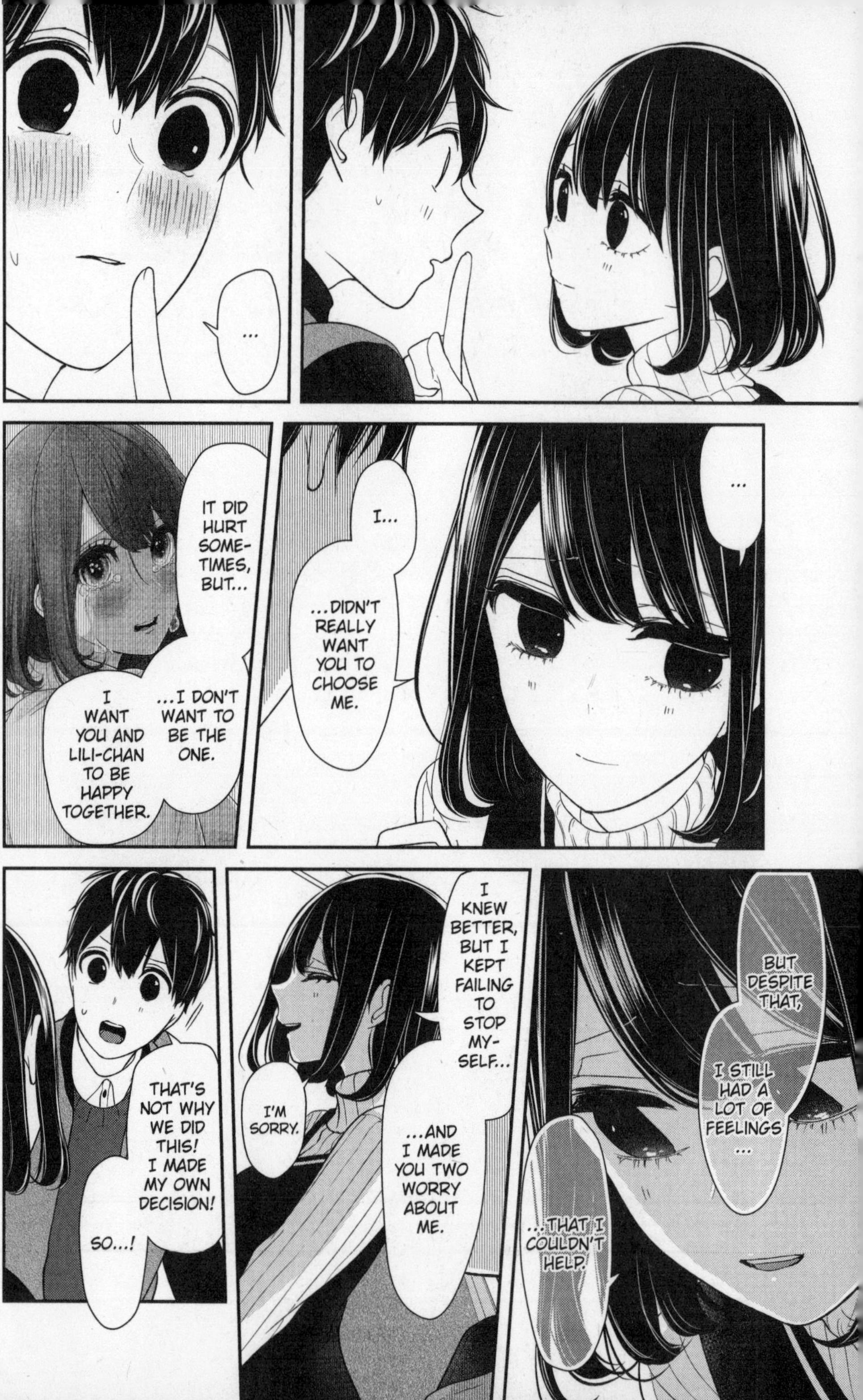
...
...
I...
...DIDN'T REALLY WANT YOU TO CHOOSE ME.
IT DID HURT SOME-TIMES, BUT...
...I DON'T WANT TO BE THE ONE.
I WANT YOU AND LILI-CHAN TO BE HAPPY TOGETHER.
BUT DESPITE THAT,
I STILL HAD A LOT OF FEELINGS...
...THAT I COULDN'T HELP.
I KNEW BETTER, BUT I KEPT FAILING TO STOP MY-SELF...
...AND I MADE YOU TWO WORRY ABOUT ME.
I'M SORRY.
THAT'S NOT WHY WE DID THIS! I MADE MY OWN DECISION!
SO...!

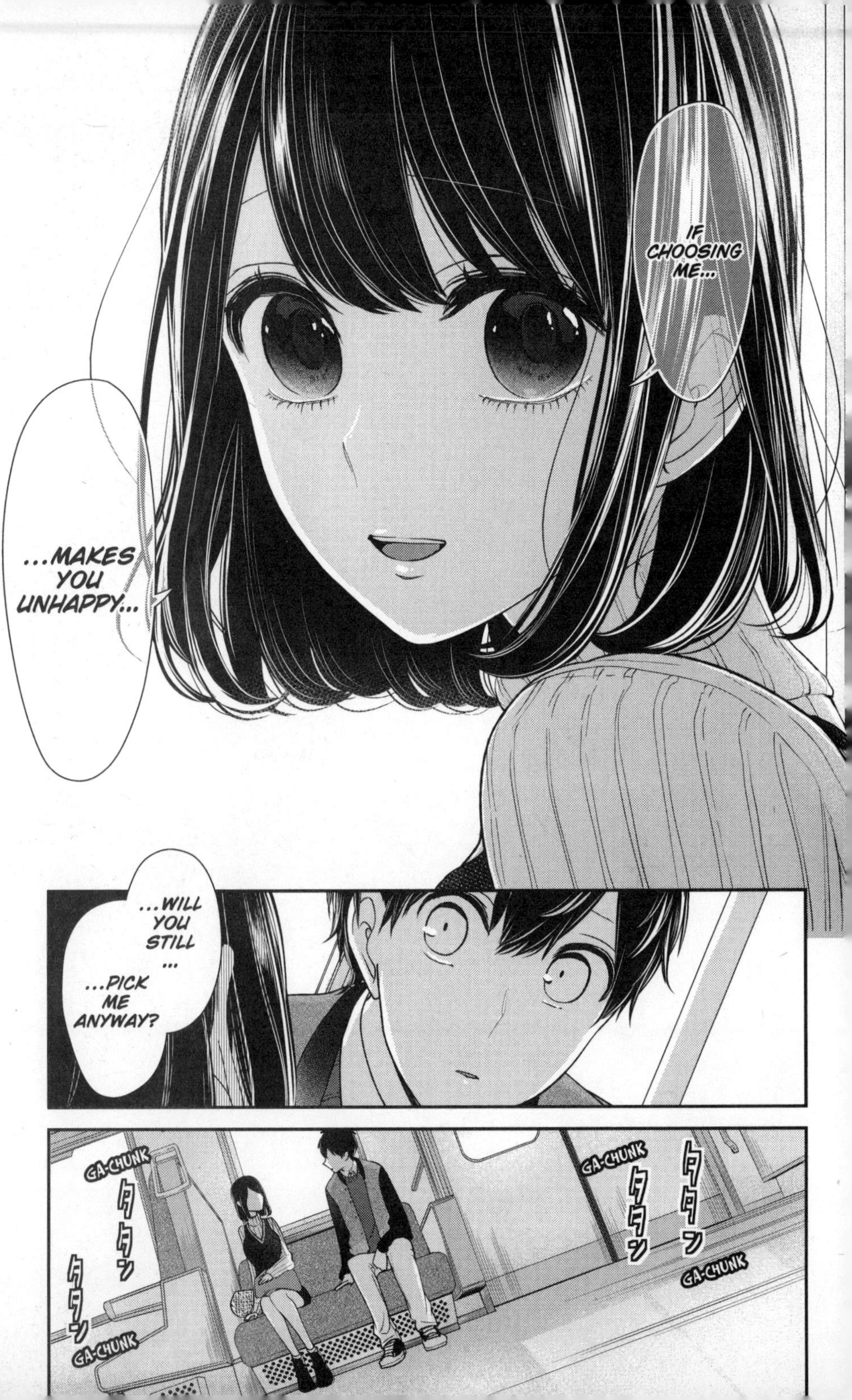

IF CHOOSING ME...
...MAKES YOU UNHAPPY...
...WILL YOU STILL ... ...PICK ME ANYWAY?
タタン
GA-CHUNK
タタン
GA-CHUNK
GA-CHUNK
タタン
タタン
GA-CHUNK

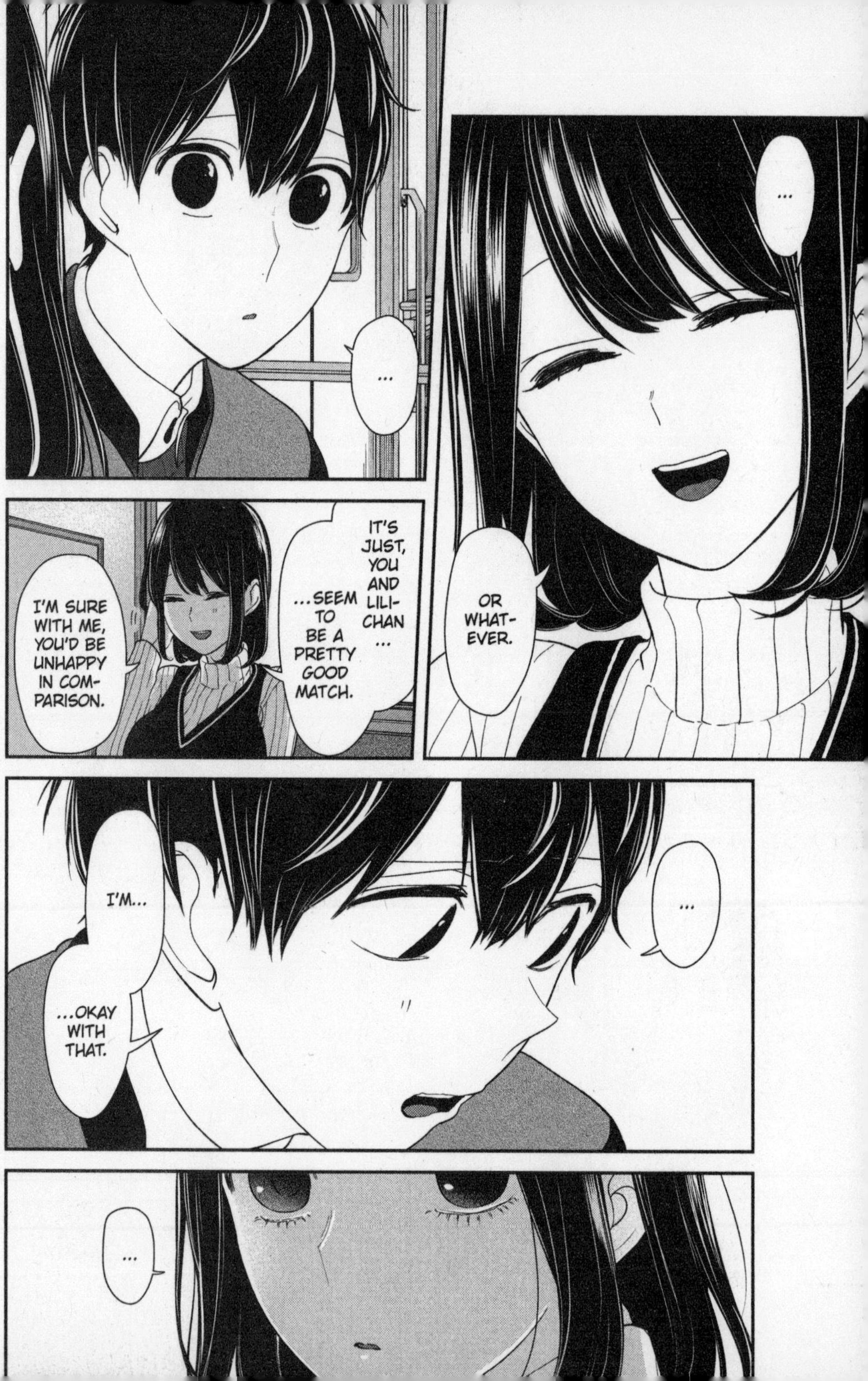
...
OR WHAT-EVER.
...
IT'S JUST, YOU AND LILI-CHAN ...
...SEEM TO BE A PRETTY GOOD MATCH.
I'M SURE WITH ME, YOU'D BE UNHAPPY IN COM-PARISON.
...
I'M...
...OKAY WITH THAT.
...

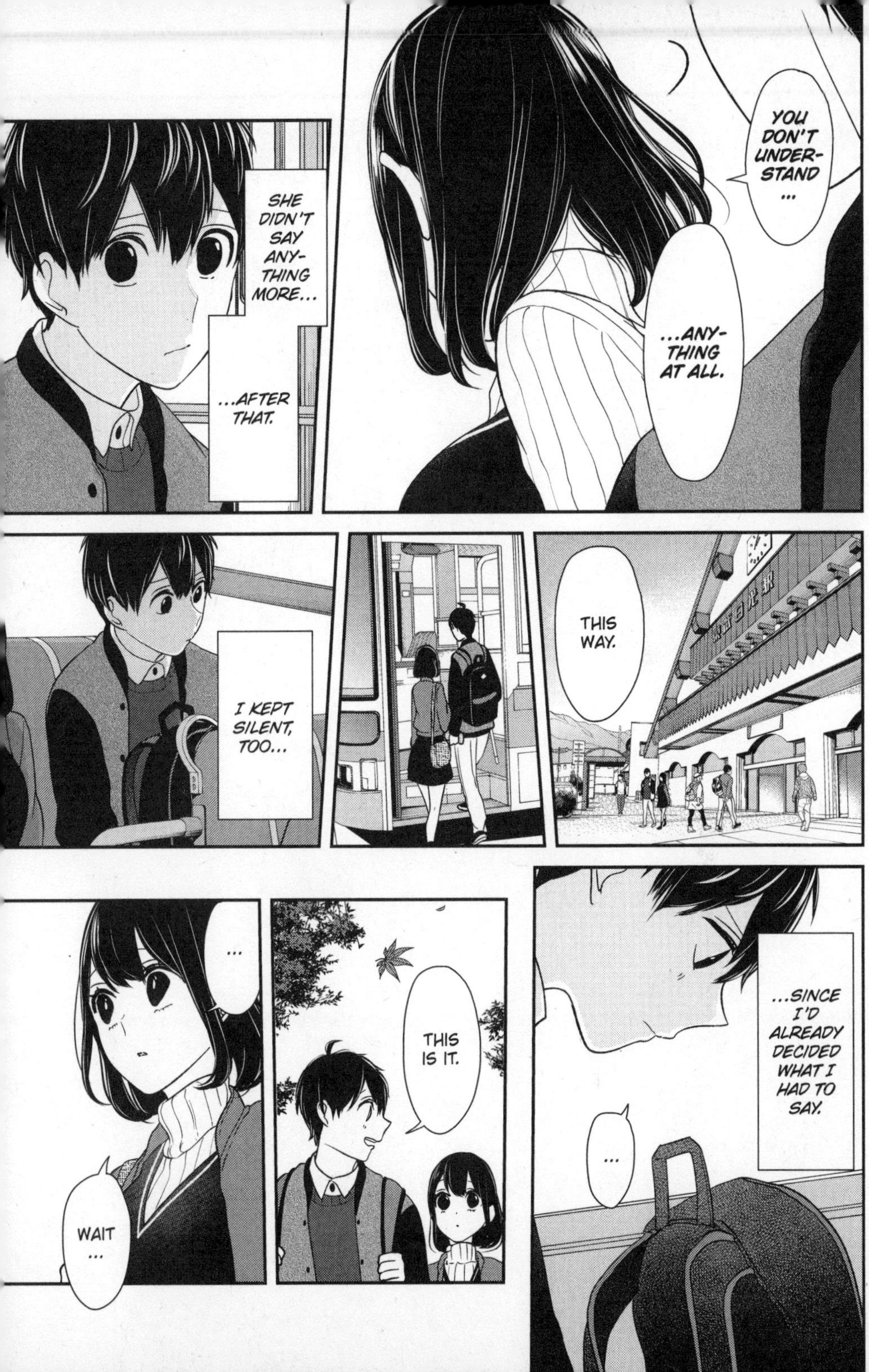
YOU DON'T UNDER-STAND...
...ANY-THING AT ALL.
SHE DIDN'T SAY ANY-THING MORE...
...AFTER THAT.
THIS WAY.
I KEPT SILENT, TOO...
...SINCE I'D ALREADY DECIDED WHAT I HAD TO SAY.
...
THIS IS IT.
...
WAIT...

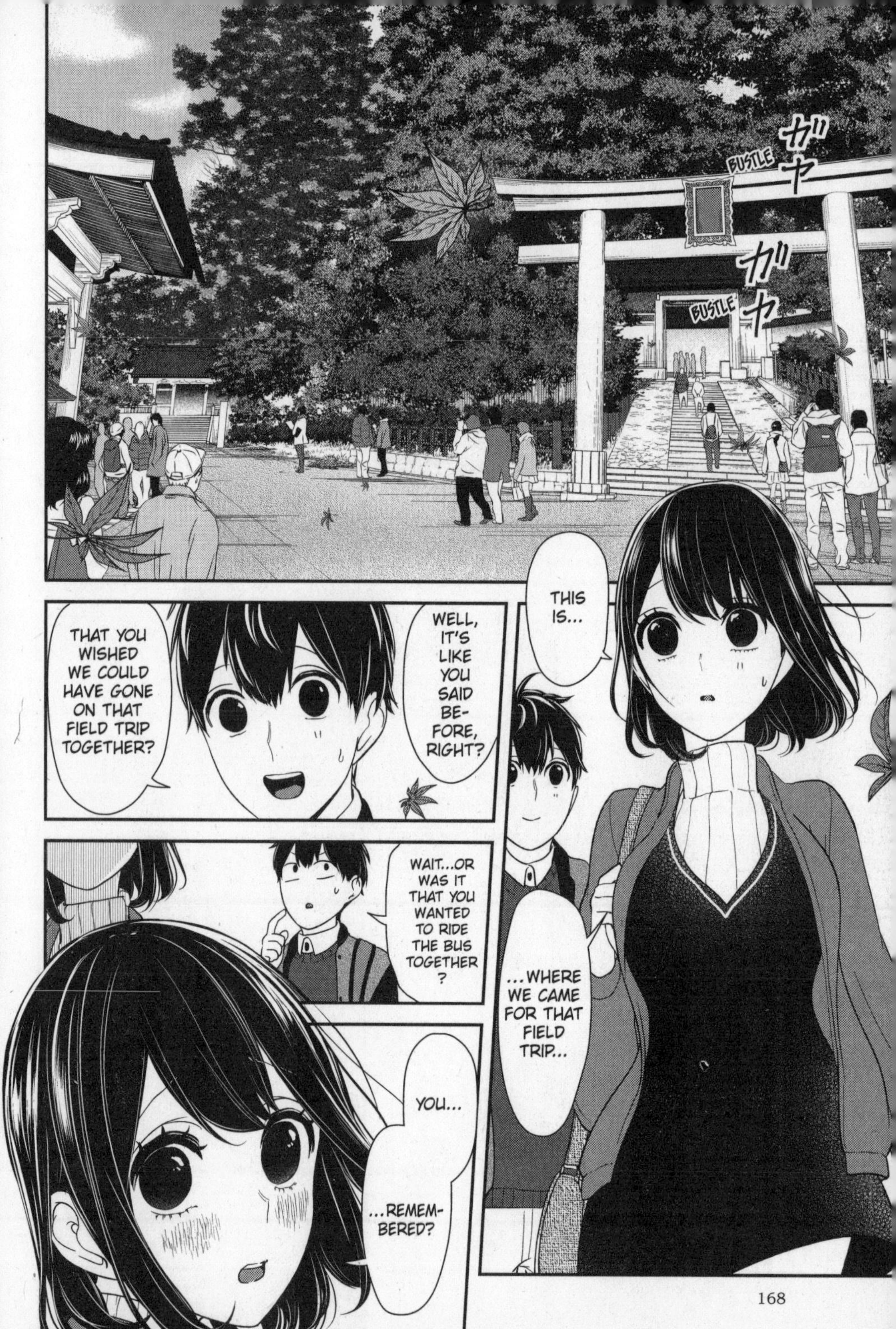
BUSTLE
ガヤ
BUSTLE
ガヤ
THIS IS...
...WHERE WE CAME FOR THAT FIELD TRIP...
WELL, IT'S LIKE YOU SAID BE-FORE, RIGHT?
THAT YOU WISHED WE COULD HAVE GONE ON THAT FIELD TRIP TOGETHER?
WAIT...OR WAS IT THAT YOU WANTED TO RIDE THE BUS TOGETHER?
YOU...
...REMEM-BERED?

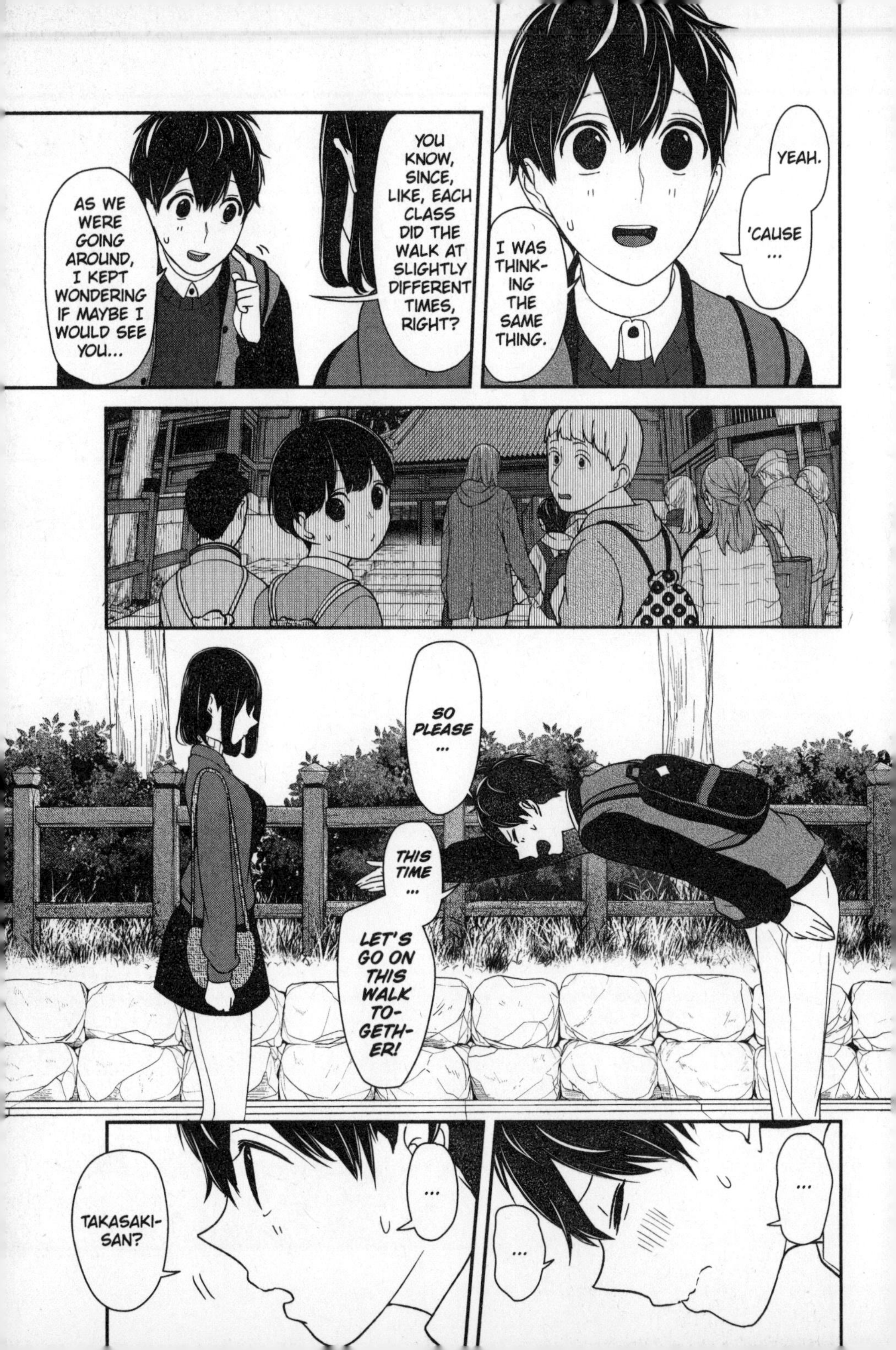
YEAH.
'CAUSE ...
I WAS THINKING THE SAME THING.
YOU KNOW, SINCE, LIKE, EACH CLASS DID THE WALK AT SLIGHTLY DIFFERENT TIMES, RIGHT?
AS WE WERE GOING AROUND, I KEPT WONDERING IF MAYBE I WOULD SEE YOU...
SO PLEASE ...
THIS TIME ...
LET'S GO ON THIS WALK TOGETHER!
...
...
...
TAKASAKI-SAN?

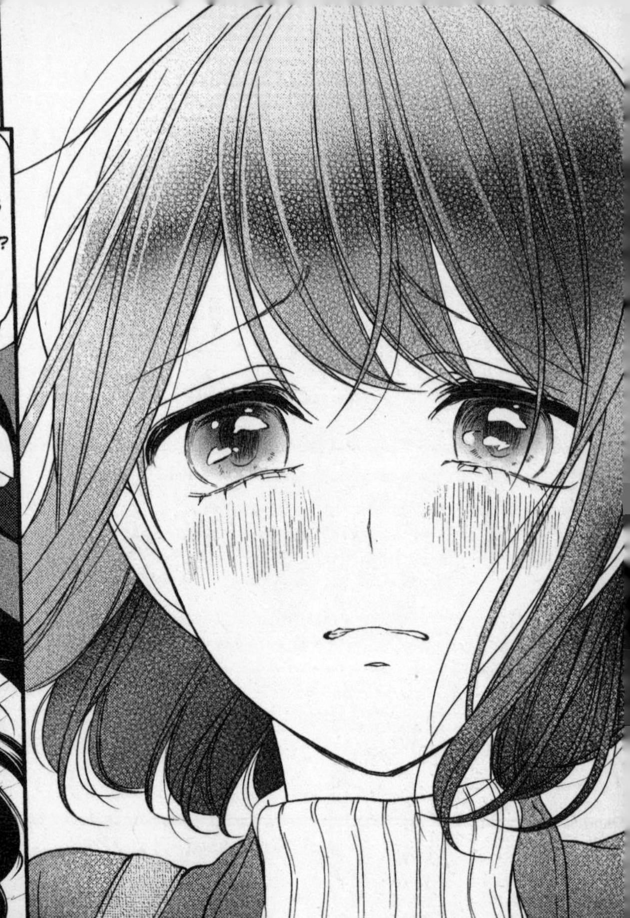

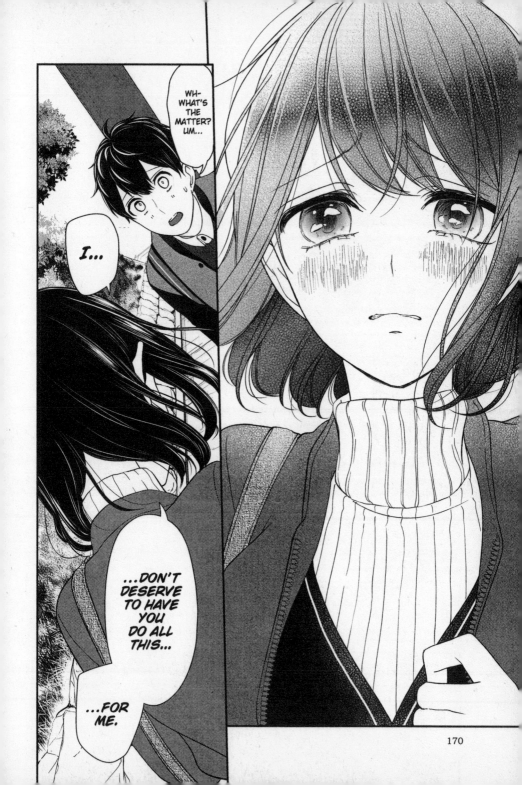

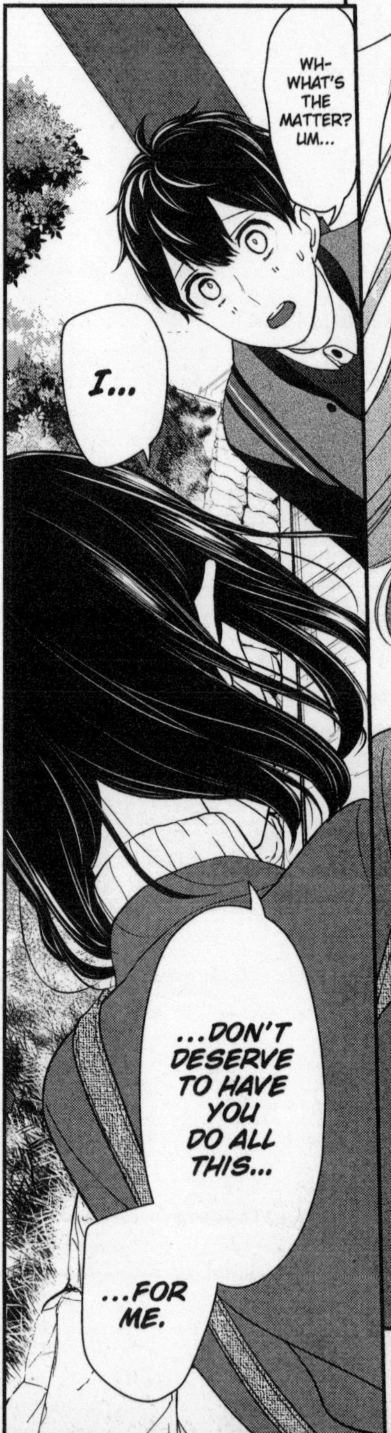
WH-WHAT'S THE MATTER? UM...
I...
...DON'T DESERVE TO HAVE YOU DO ALL THIS...
...FOR ME.

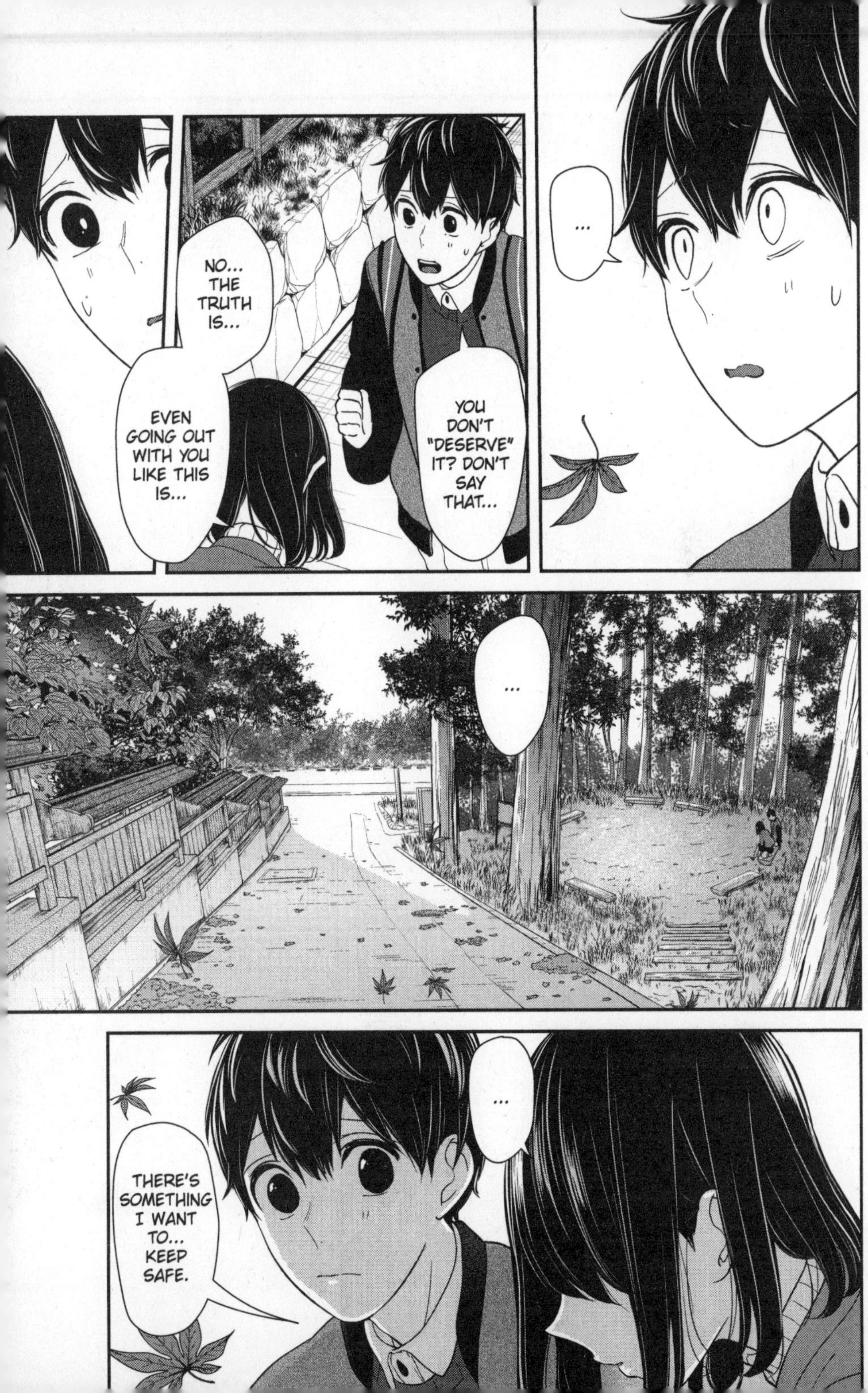
...
YOU DON'T "DESERVE" IT? DON'T SAY THAT...
NO... THE TRUTH IS...
EVEN GOING OUT WITH YOU LIKE THIS IS...
...
...
THERE'S SOMETHING I WANT TO... KEEP SAFE.

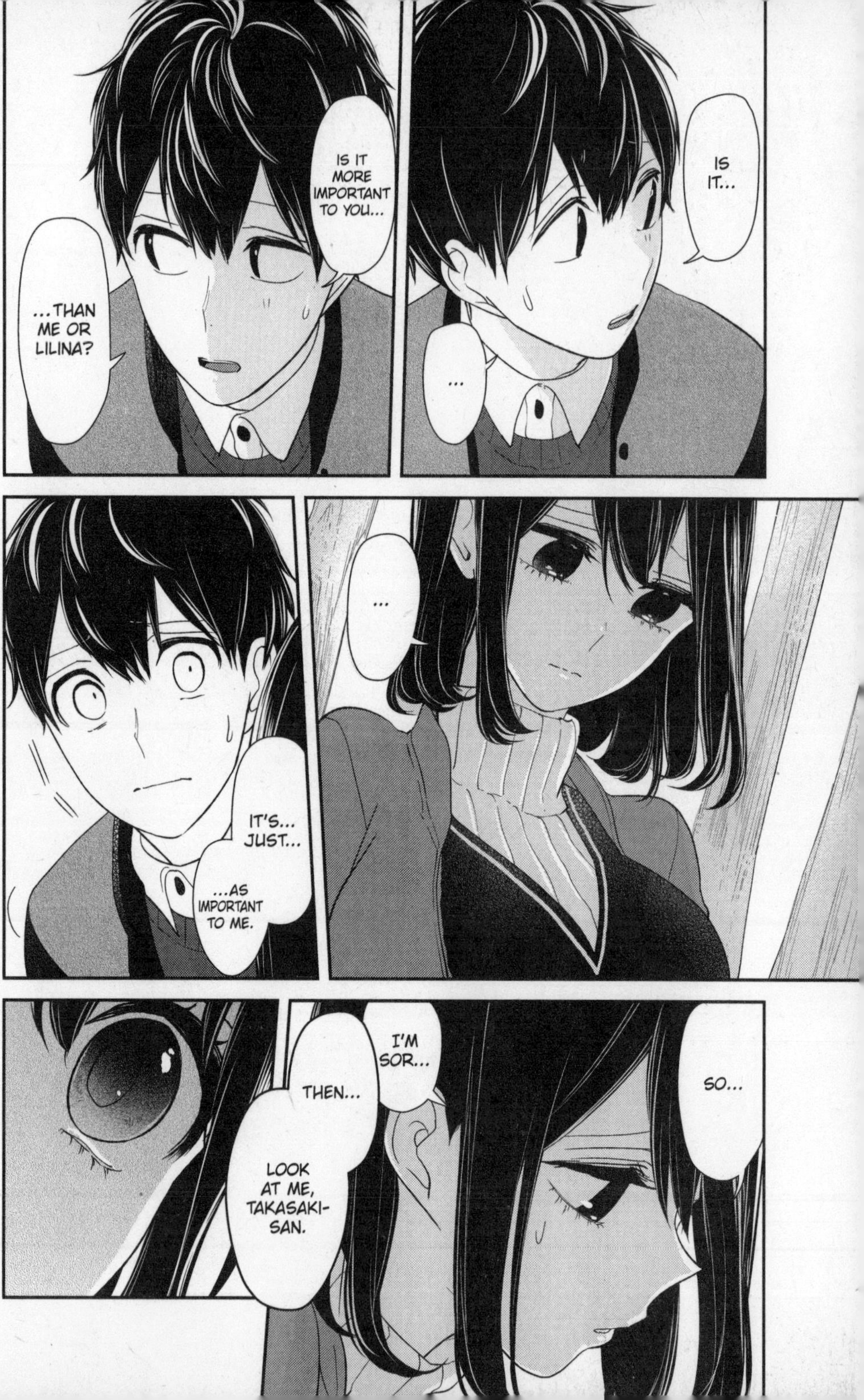
IS IT...
...
IS IT MORE IMPORTANT TO YOU...
...THAN ME OR LILINA?
...
IT'S... JUST...
...AS IMPORTANT TO ME.
SO...
I'M SOR...
THEN...
LOOK AT ME, TAKASAKI-SAN.

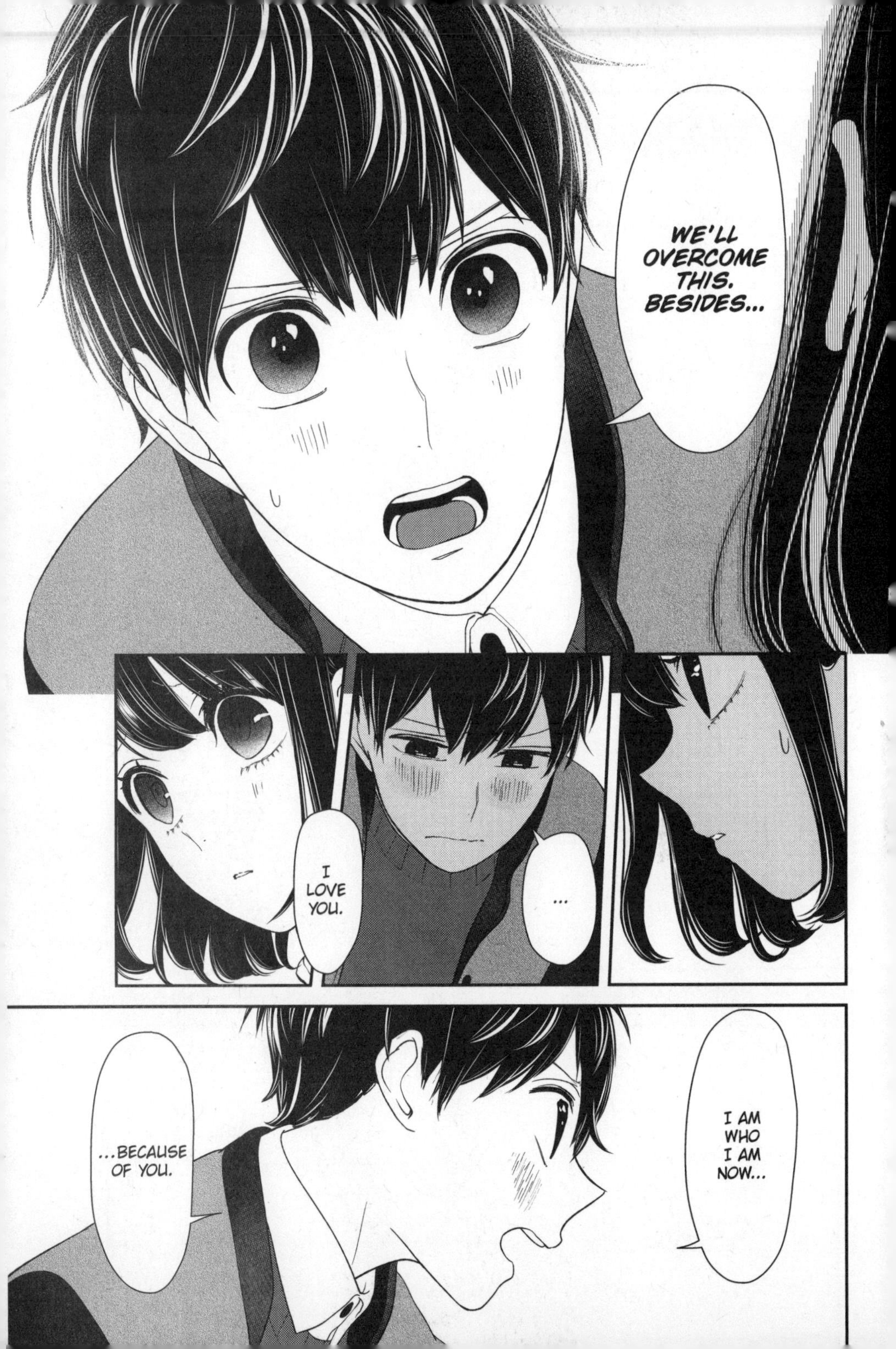
WE'LL OVERCOME THIS. BESIDES...
...
I LOVE YOU.
I AM WHO I AM NOW...
...BECAUSE OF YOU.

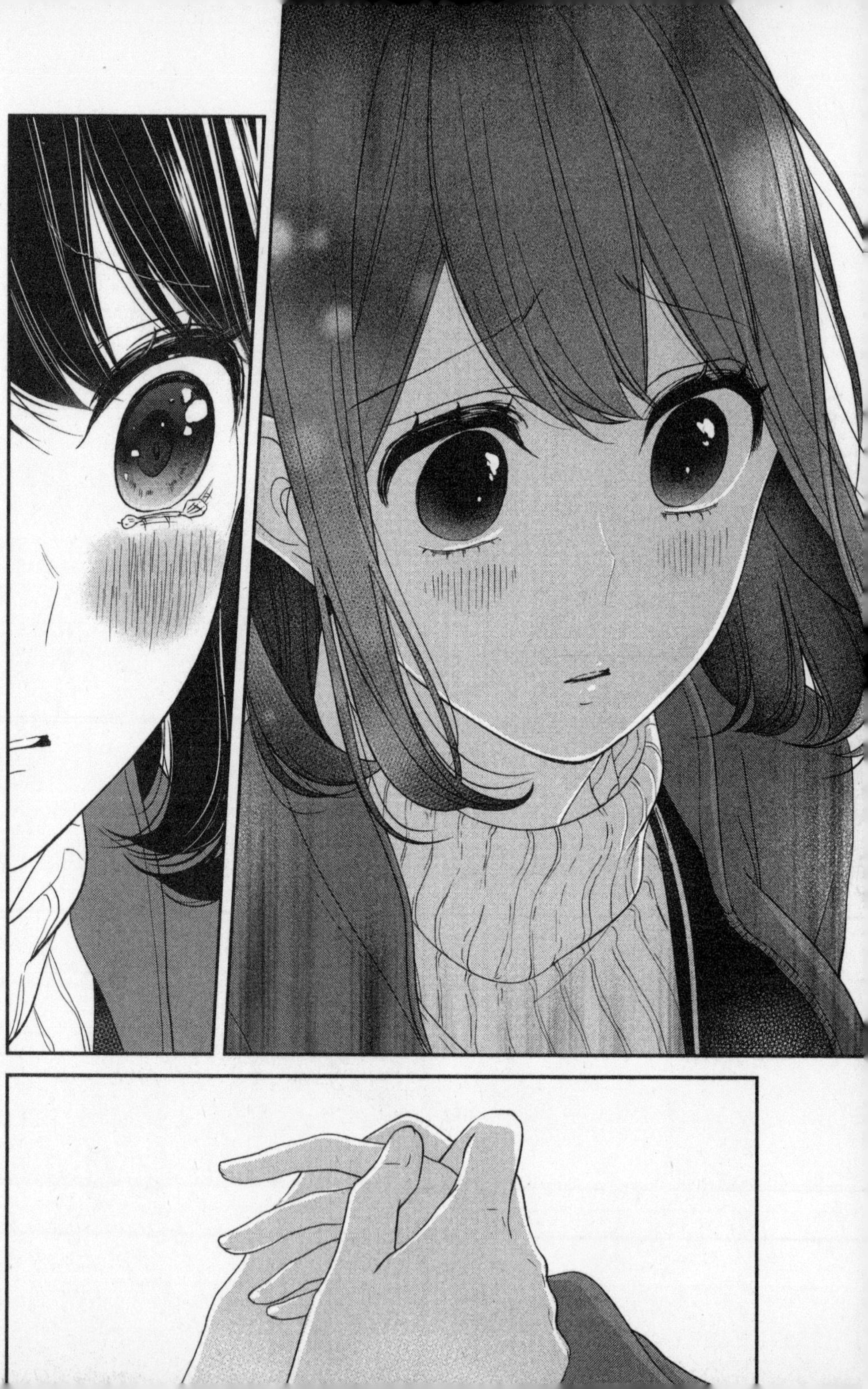

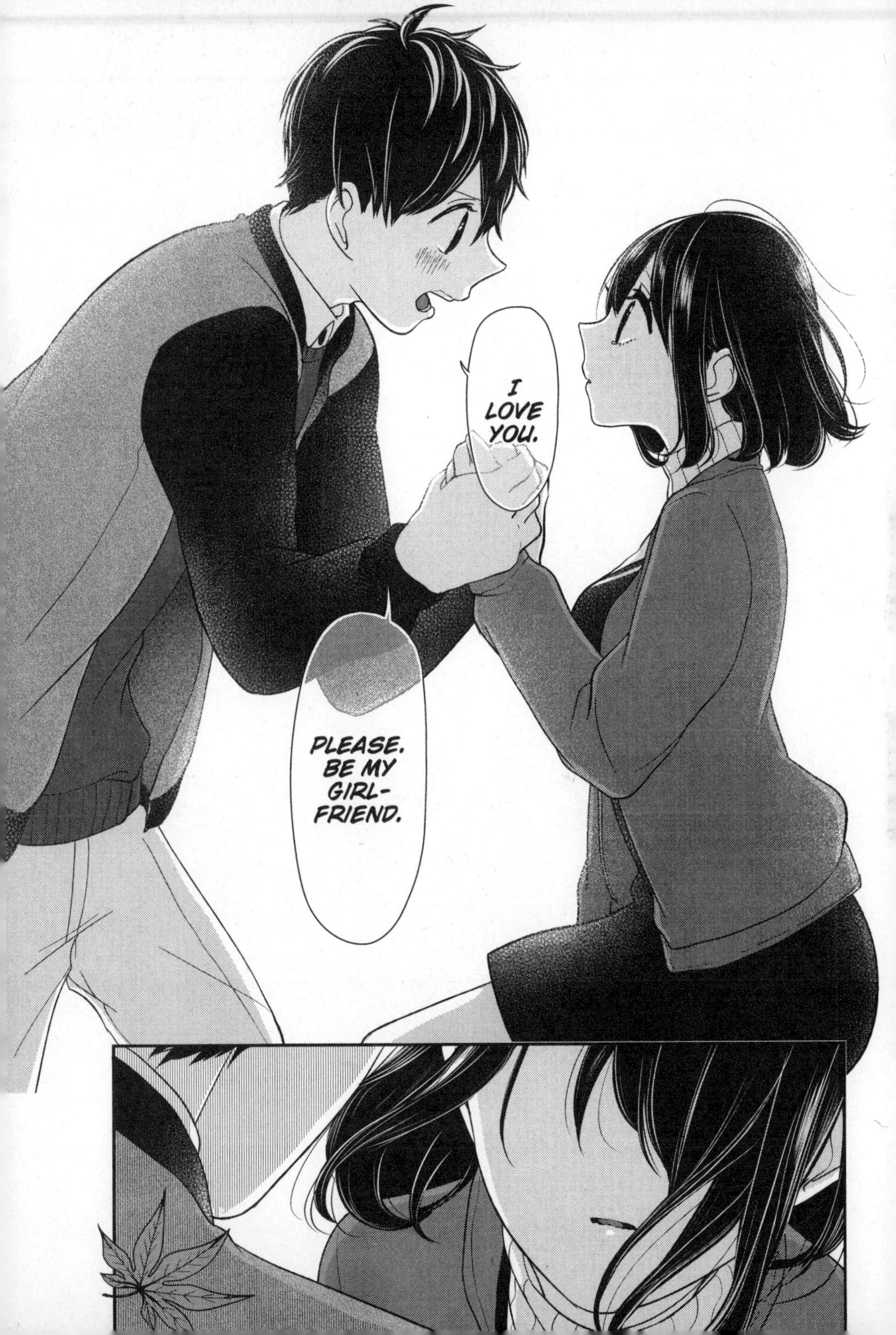
I LOVE YOU.
PLEASE. BE MY GIRL-FRIEND.

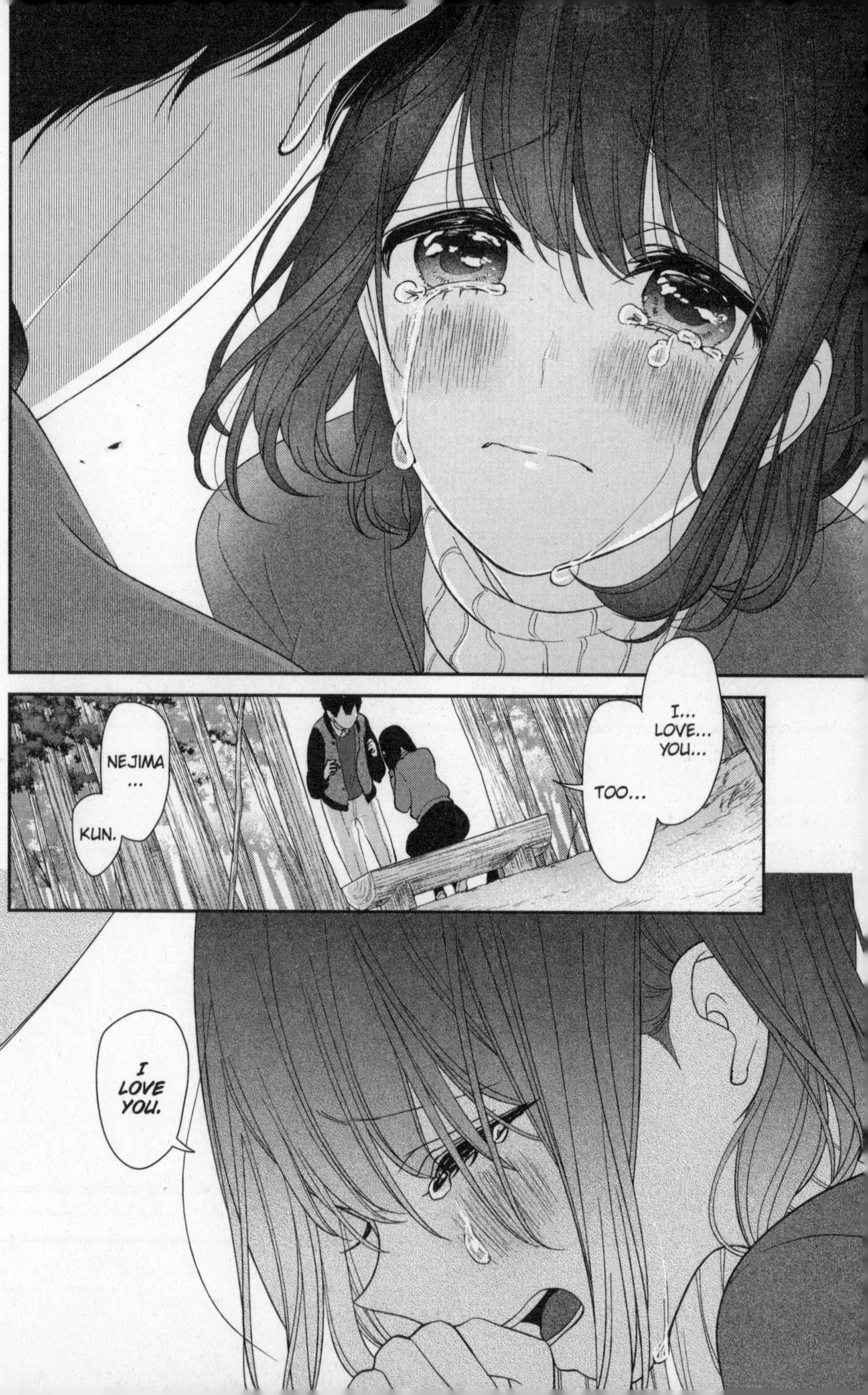
I... LOVE... YOU...
TOO...
NEJIMA ...
KUN.
I LOVE YOU.

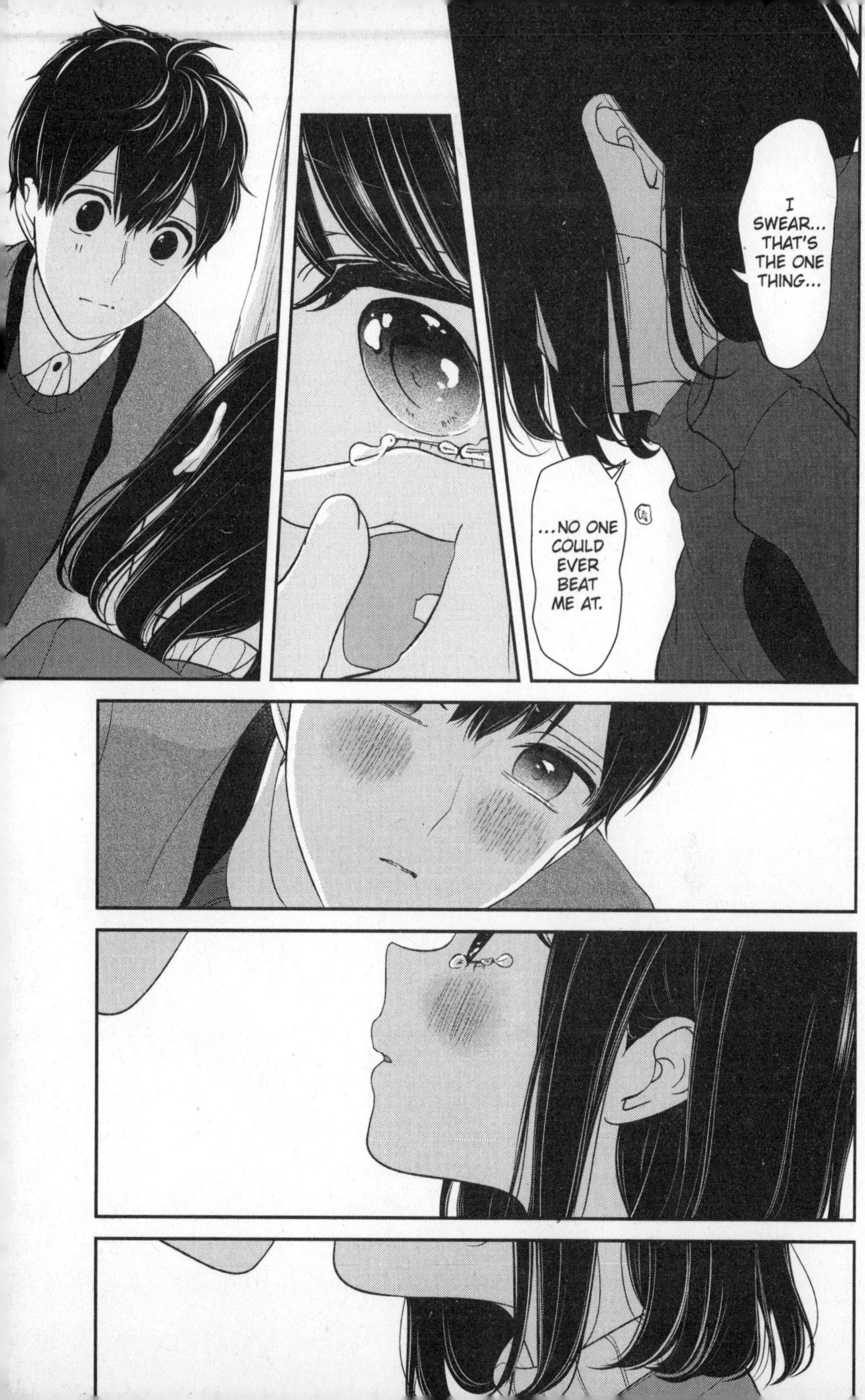
I SWEAR... THAT'S THE ONE THING...
...NO ONE COULD EVER BEAT ME AT.

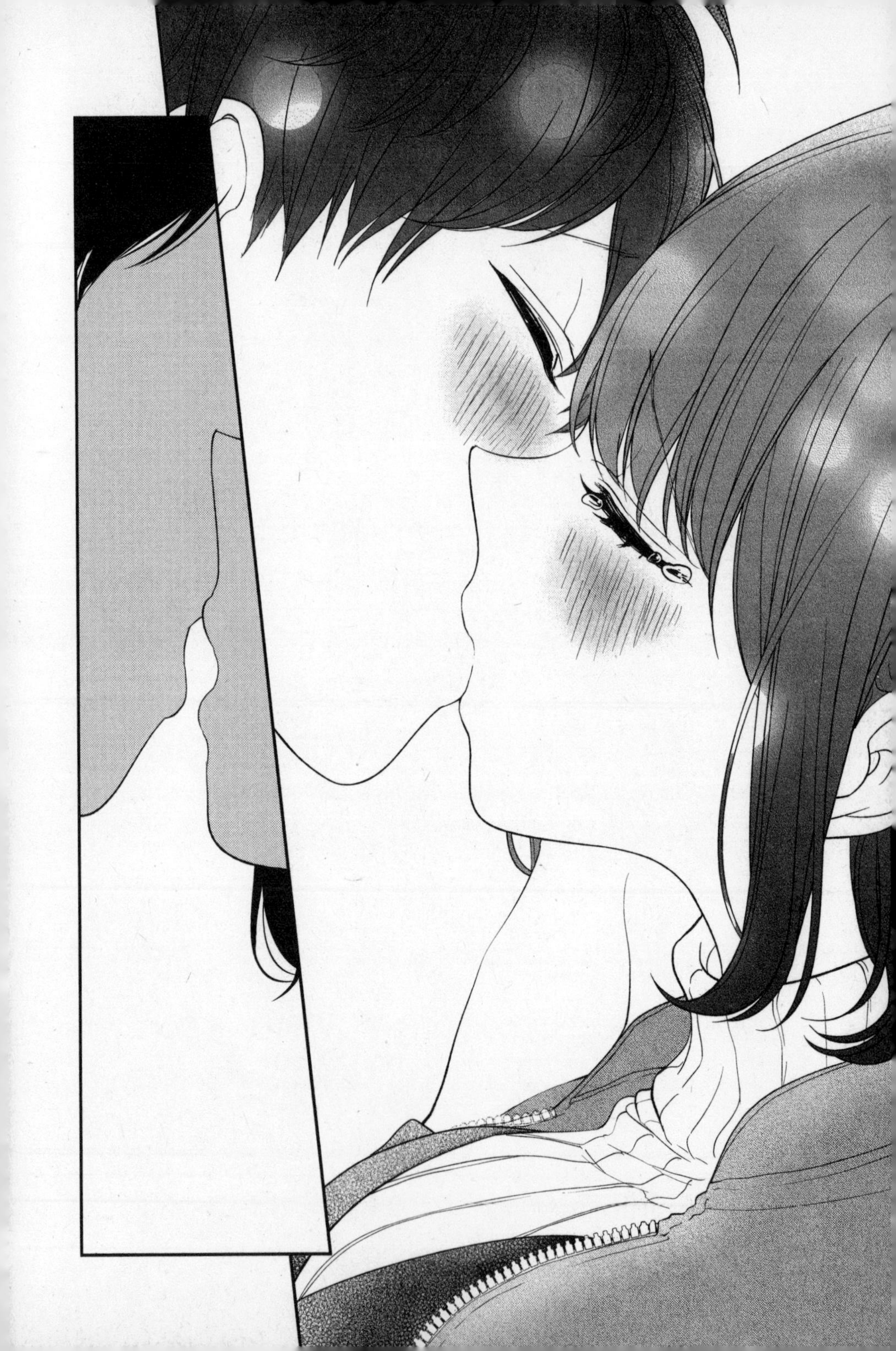

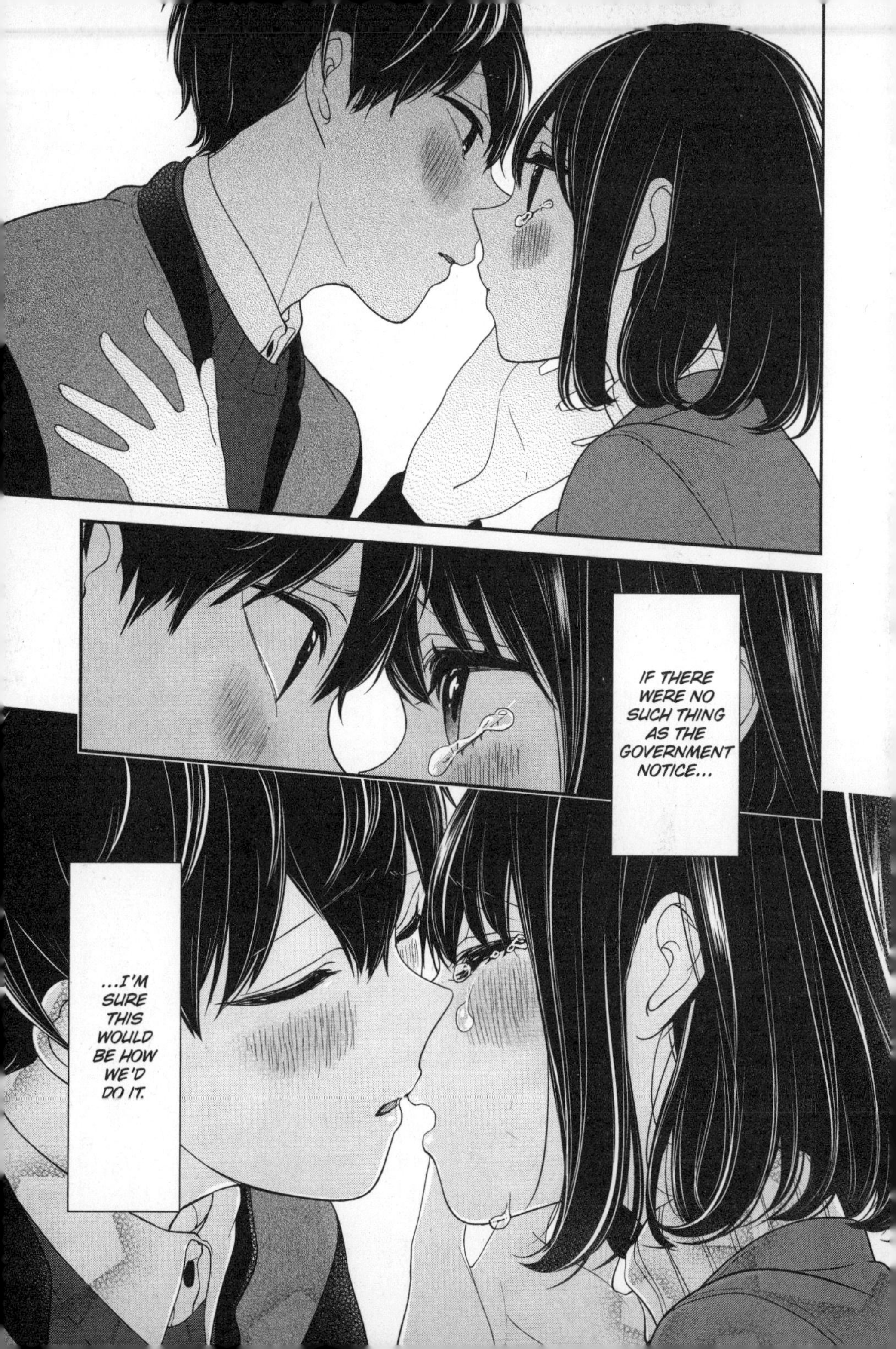
IF THERE WERE NO SUCH THING AS THE GOVERNMENT NOTICE...
...I'M SURE THIS WOULD BE HOW WE'D DO IT.

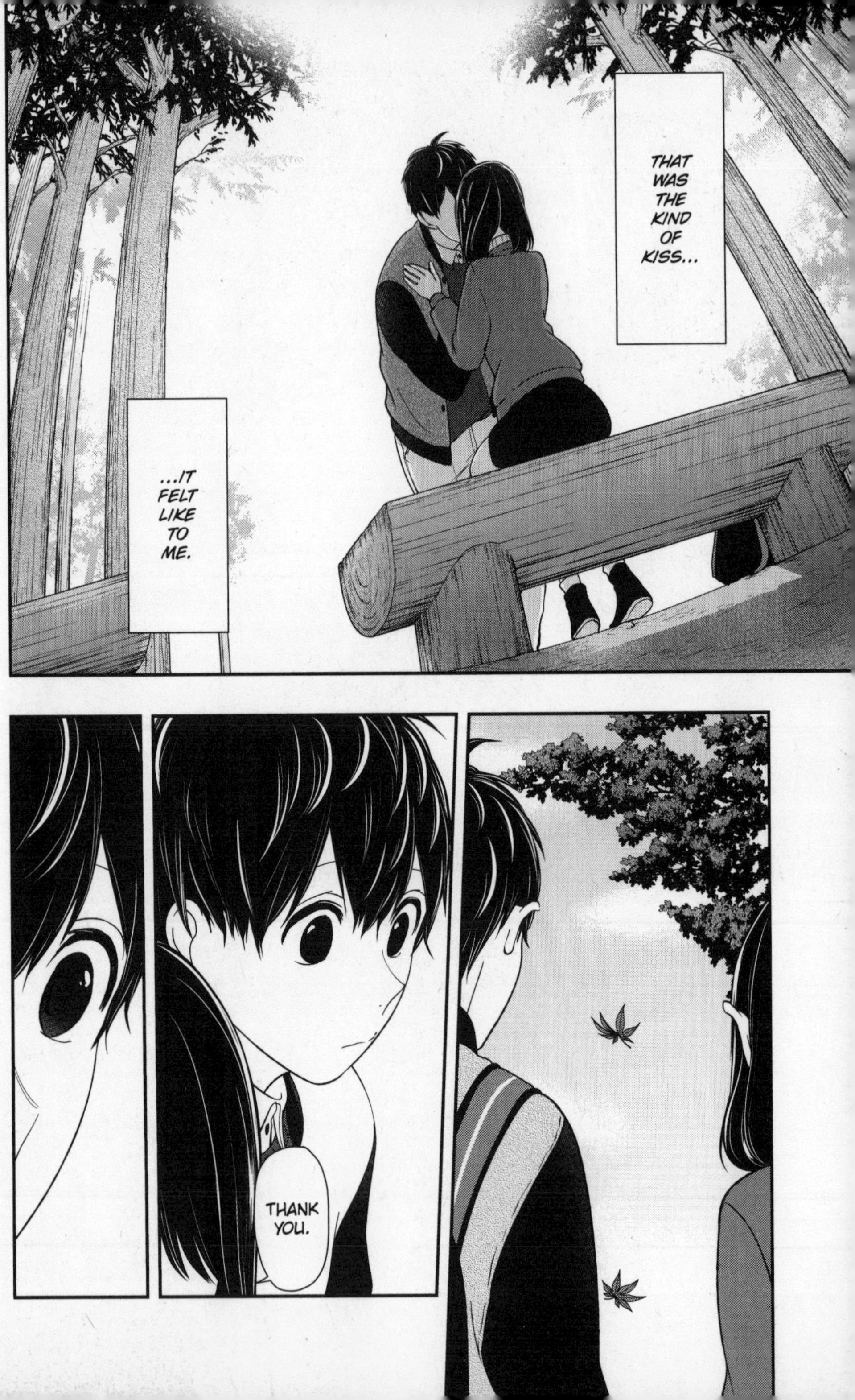
THAT WAS THE KIND OF KISS...
...IT FELT LIKE TO ME.
THANK YOU.

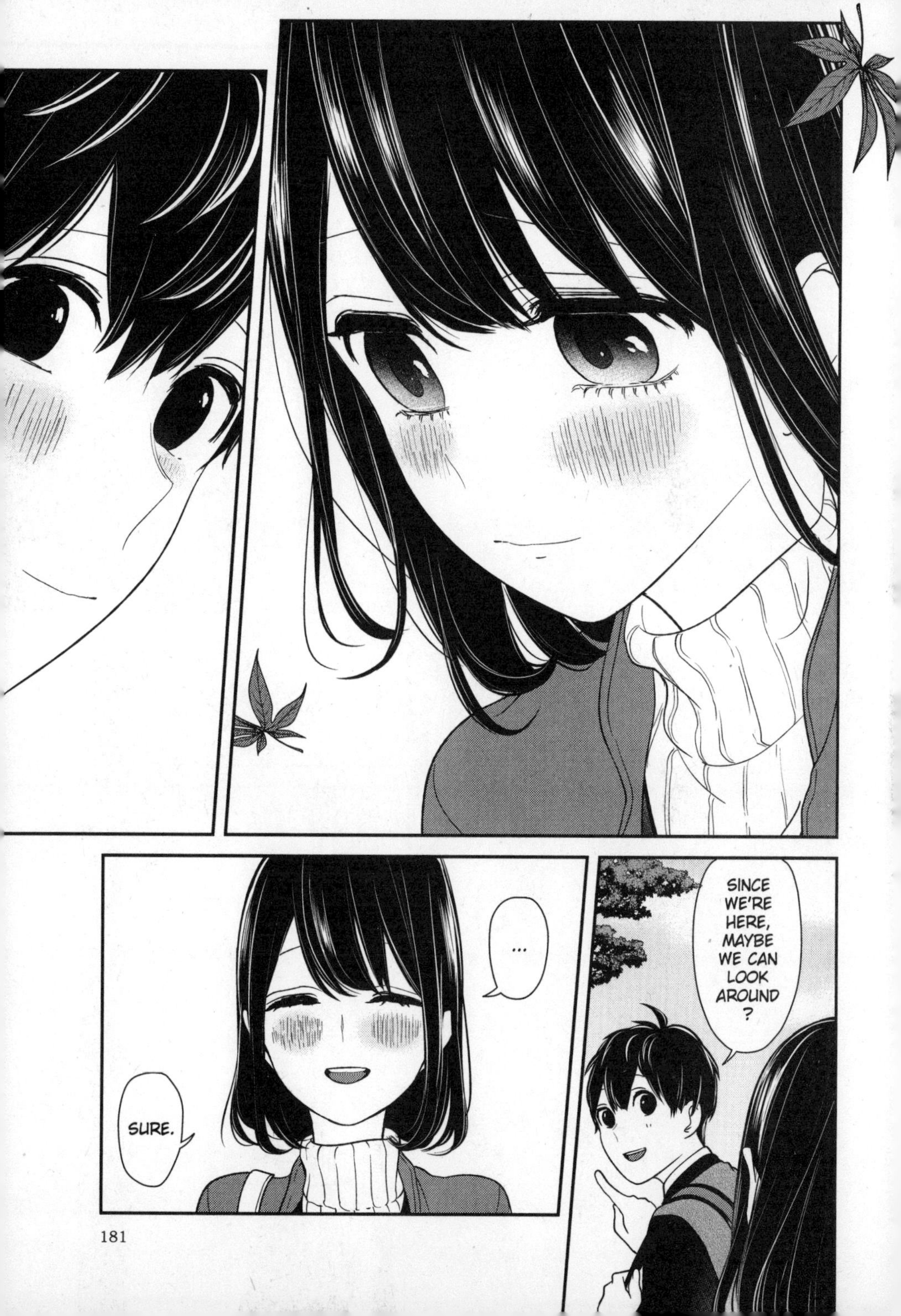
SINCE WE'RE HERE, MAYBE WE CAN LOOK AROUND?
...
SURE.

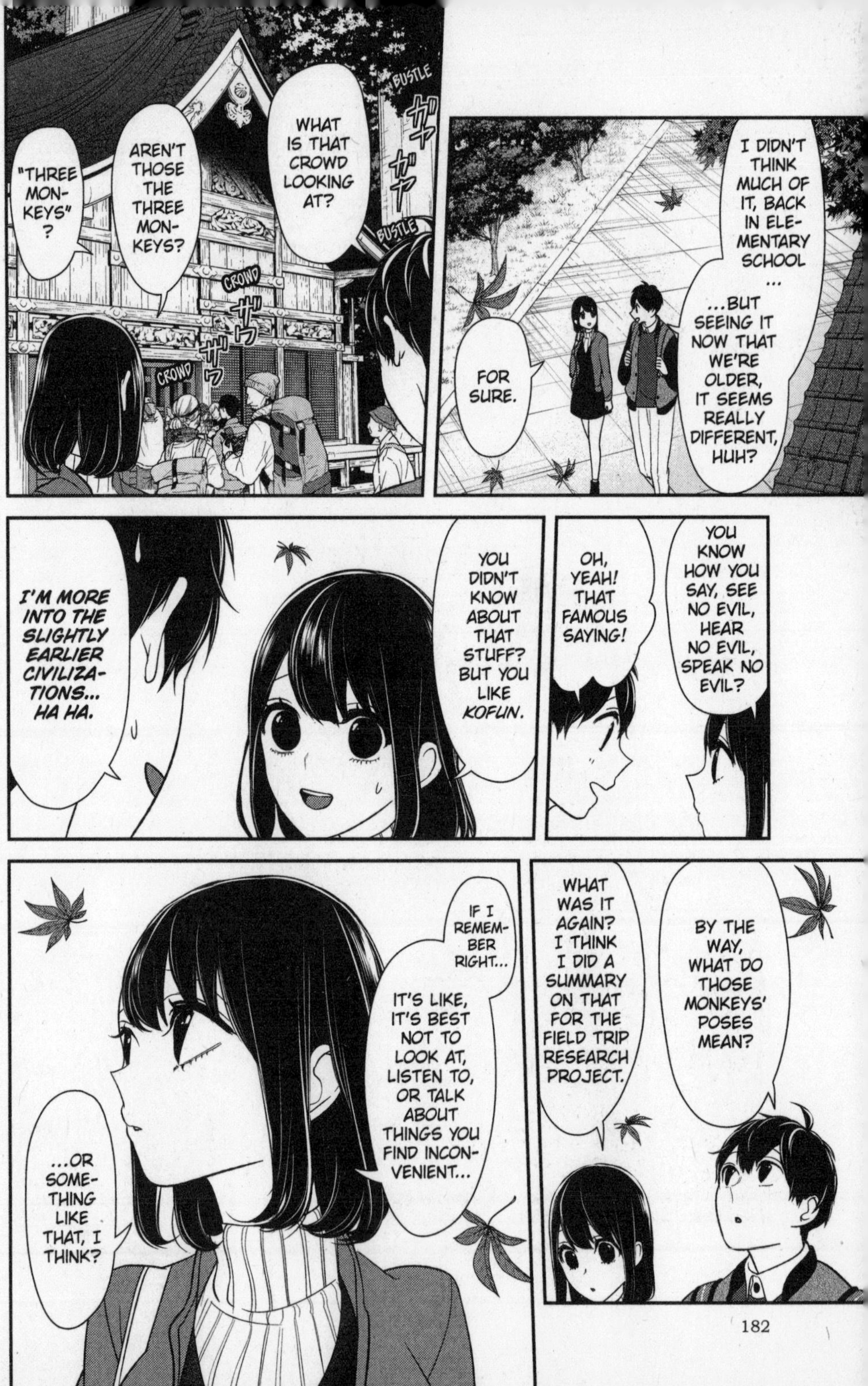
I DIDN'T THINK MUCH OF IT, BACK IN ELEMENTARY SCHOOL ...
...BUT SEEING IT NOW THAT WE'RE OLDER, IT SEEMS REALLY DIFFERENT, HUH?
FOR SURE.
BUSTLE
BUSTLE
WHAT IS THAT CROWD LOOKING AT?
AREN'T THOSE THE THREE MONKEYS?
"THREE MONKEYS"?
CROWD
CROWD
YOU KNOW HOW YOU SAY, SEE NO EVIL, HEAR NO EVIL, SPEAK NO EVIL?
OH, YEAH! THAT FAMOUS SAYING!
YOU DIDN'T KNOW ABOUT THAT STUFF? BUT YOU LIKE *KOFUN*.
*I'M MORE INTO THE SLIGHTLY EARLIER CIVILIZATIONS... HA HA.*
BY THE WAY, WHAT DO THOSE MONKEYS' POSES MEAN?
WHAT WAS IT AGAIN? I THINK I DID A SUMMARY ON THAT FOR THE FIELD TRIP RESEARCH PROJECT.
IF I REMEMBER RIGHT...
IT'S LIKE, IT'S BEST NOT TO LOOK AT, LISTEN TO, OR TALK ABOUT THINGS YOU FIND INCONVENIENT...
...OR SOMETHING LIKE THAT, I THINK?

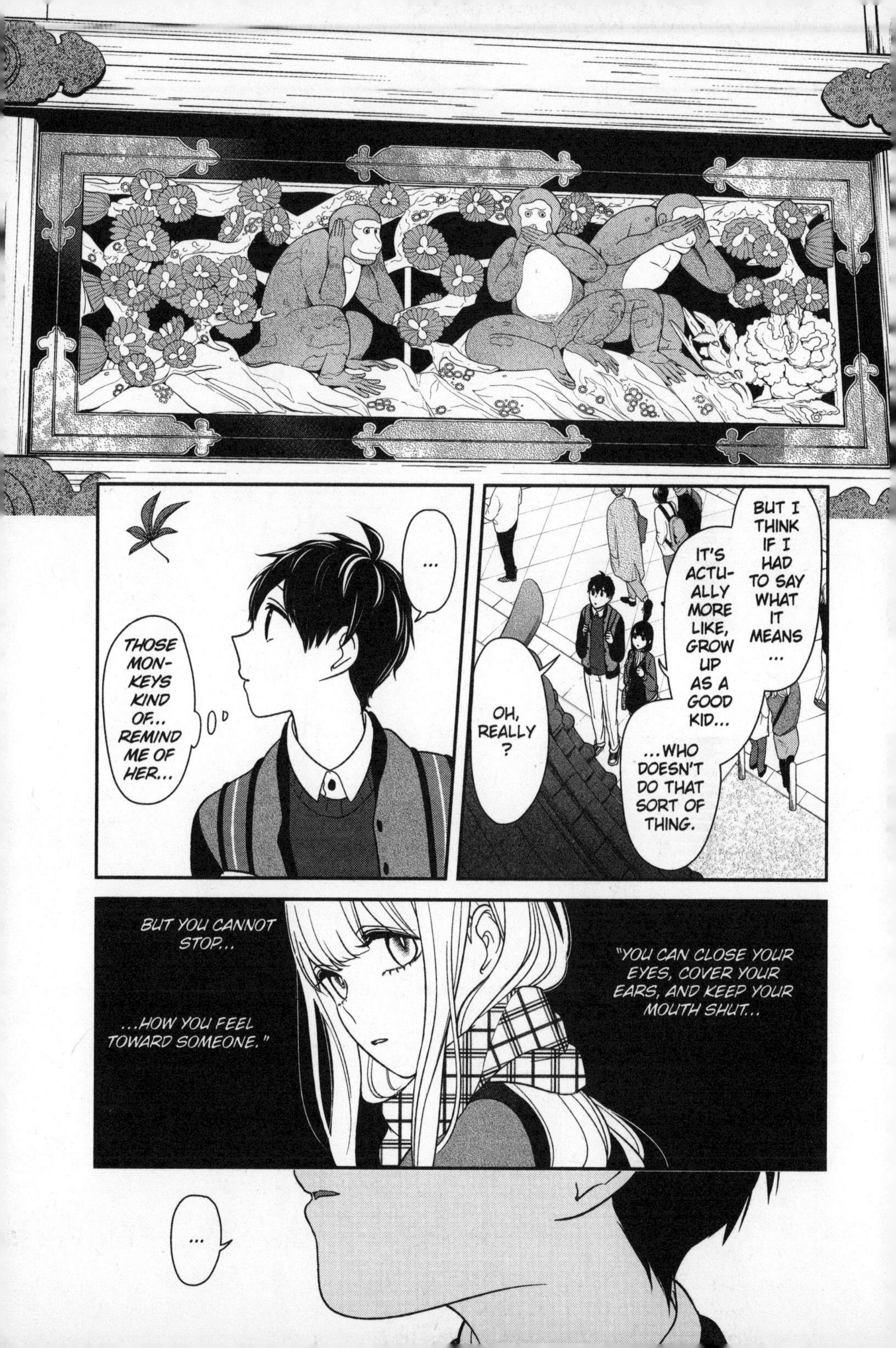
BUT I THINK IF I HAD TO SAY WHAT IT MEANS...
IT'S ACTU-ALLY MORE LIKE, GROW UP AS A GOOD KID...
...WHO DOESN'T DO THAT SORT OF THING.
OH, REALLY?
...
THOSE MON-KEYS KIND OF... REMIND ME OF HER...
"YOU CAN CLOSE YOUR EYES, COVER YOUR EARS, AND KEEP YOUR MOUTH SHUT...
BUT YOU CANNOT STOP...
...HOW YOU FEEL TOWARD SOMEONE."
...

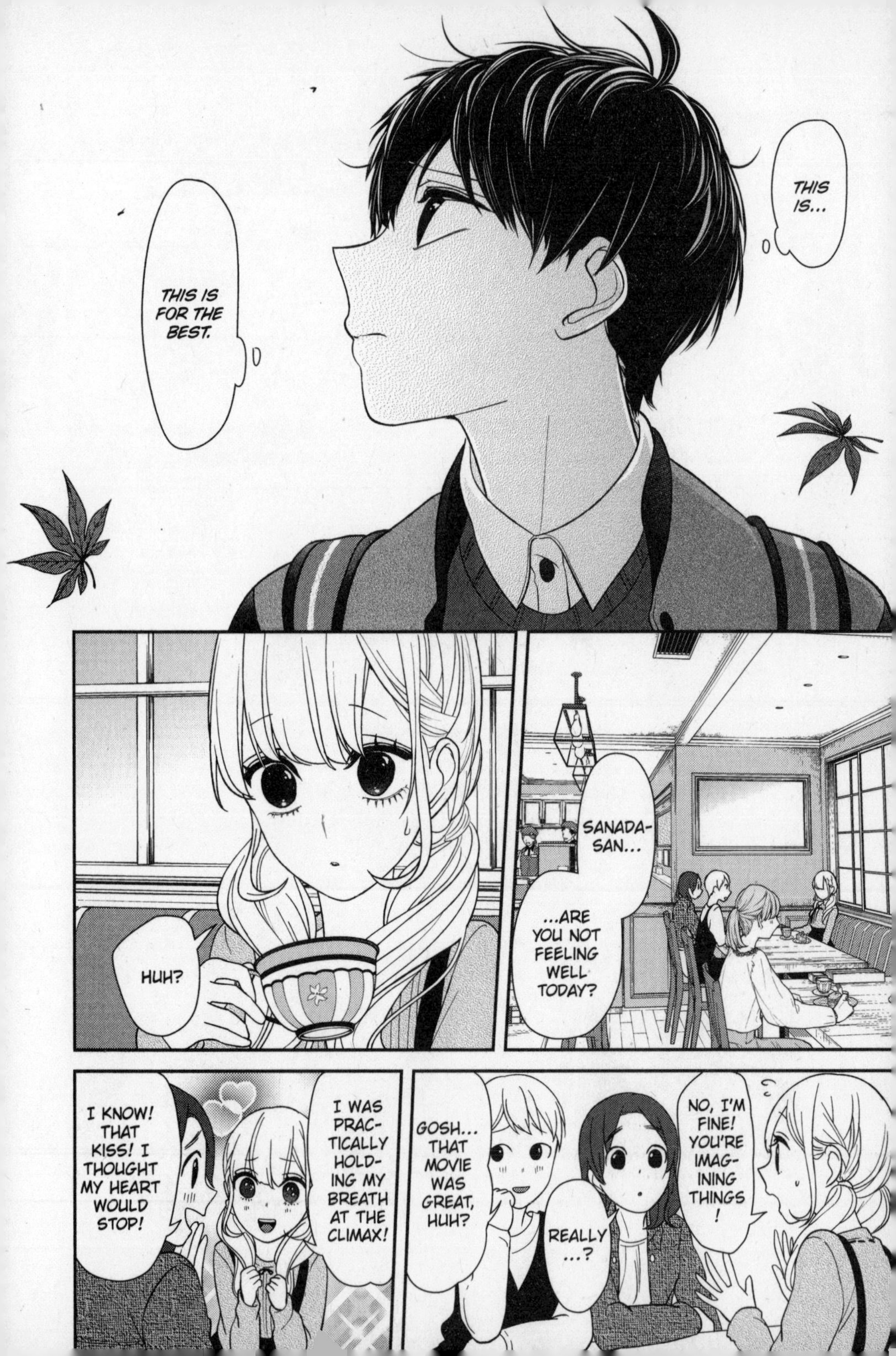
THIS IS...
THIS IS FOR THE BEST.
SANADA-SAN...
...ARE YOU NOT FEELING WELL TODAY?
HUH?
NO, I'M FINE! YOU'RE IMAGINING THINGS!
REALLY...?
GOSH... THAT MOVIE WAS GREAT, HUH?
I WAS PRACTICALLY HOLDING MY BREATH AT THE CLIMAX!
I KNOW! THAT KISS! I THOUGHT MY HEART WOULD STOP!

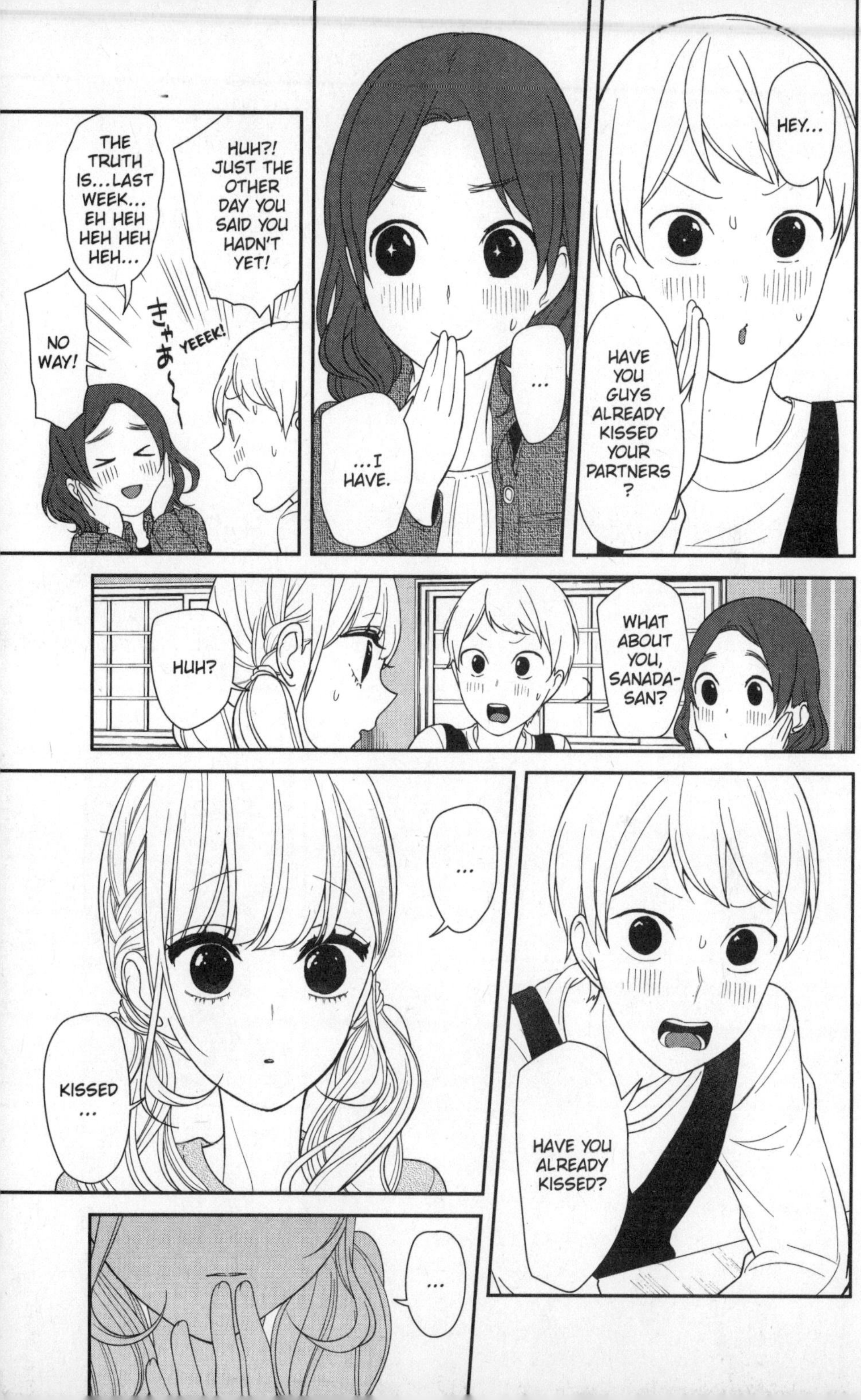
HEY...
HAVE YOU GUYS ALREADY KISSED YOUR PARTNERS?
...
...I HAVE.
HUH?! JUST THE OTHER DAY YOU SAID YOU HADN'T YET!
THE TRUTH IS...LAST WEEK... EH HEH HEH HEH HEH...
きゃあ~
YEEEK!
NO WAY!
WHAT ABOUT YOU, SANADA-SAN?
HUH?
HAVE YOU ALREADY KISSED?
...
KISSED...
...

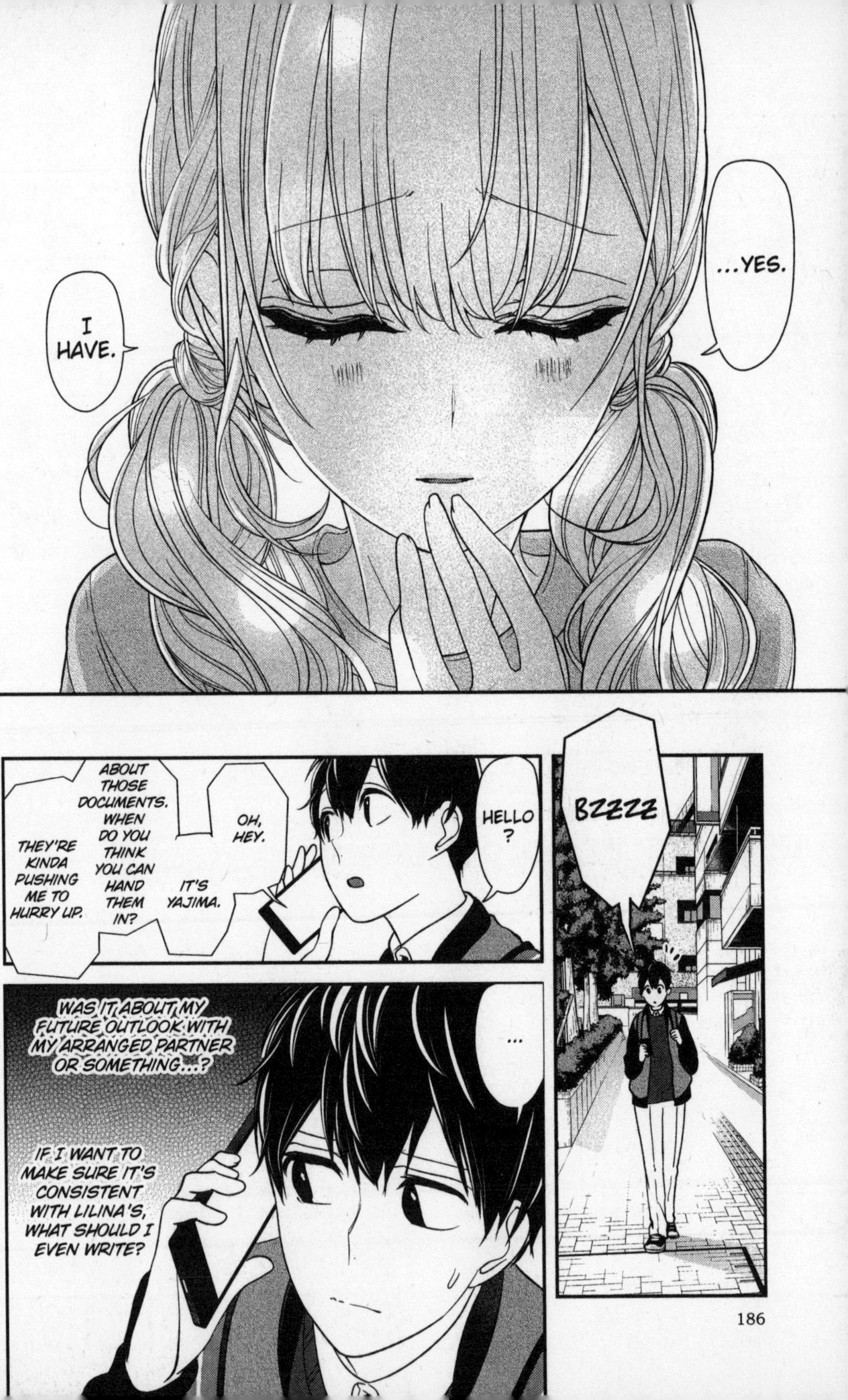

...YES.
I HAVE.
BZZZZ
HELLO?
OH, HEY. IT'S YAJIMA.
ABOUT THOSE DOCUMENTS. WHEN DO YOU THINK YOU CAN HAND THEM IN?
THEY'RE KINDA PUSHING ME TO HURRY UP.
...
WAS IT ABOUT MY FUTURE OUTLOOK WITH MY ARRANGED PARTNER OR SOMETHING...?
IF I WANT TO MAKE SURE IT'S CONSISTENT WITH LILINA'S, WHAT SHOULD I EVEN WRITE?

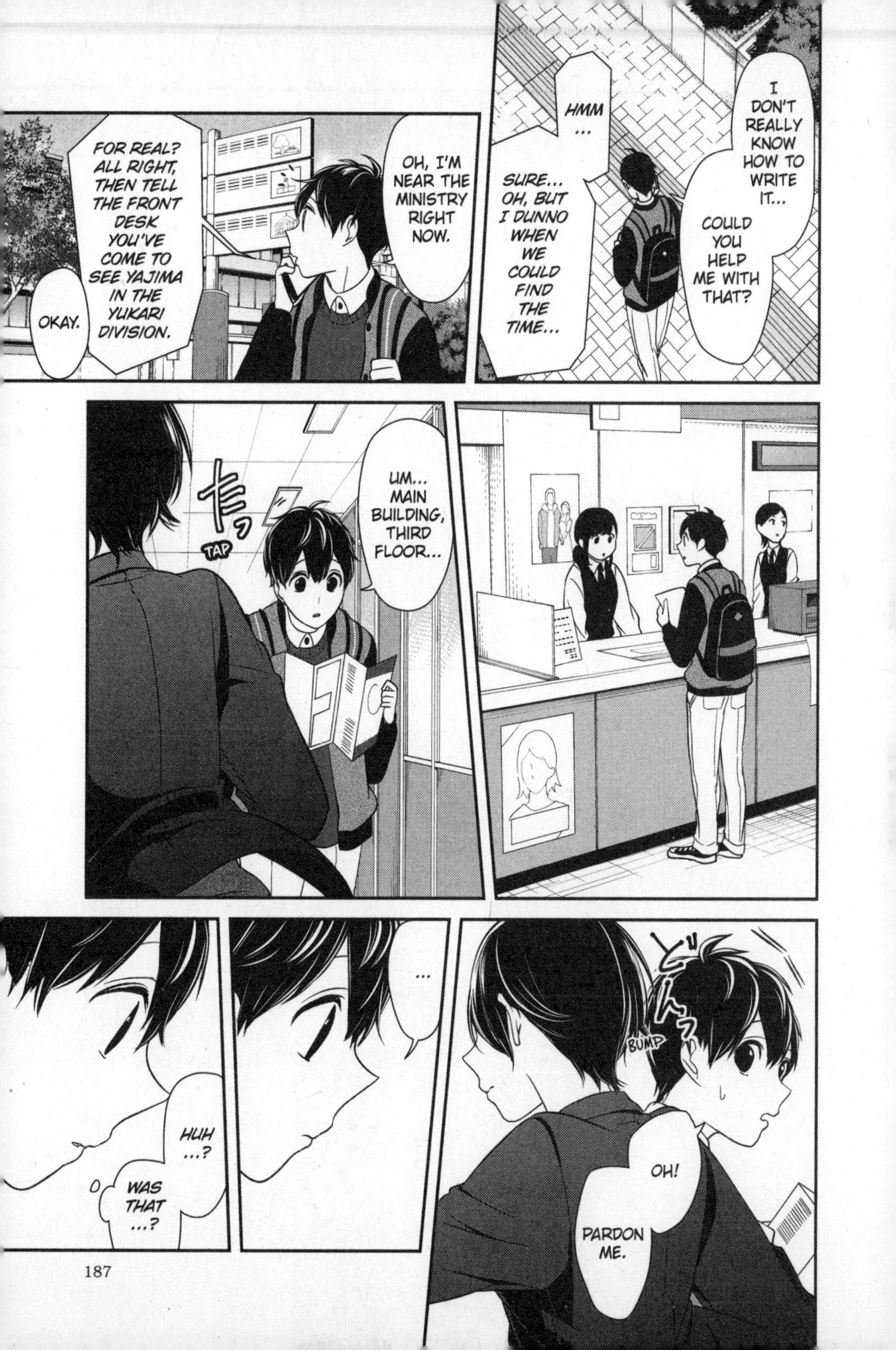
I DON'T REALLY KNOW HOW TO WRITE IT...
COULD YOU HELP ME WITH THAT?
HMM...
SURE... OH, BUT I DUNNO WHEN WE COULD FIND THE TIME...
OH, I'M NEAR THE MINISTRY RIGHT NOW.
FOR REAL? ALL RIGHT, THEN TELL THE FRONT DESK YOU'VE COME TO SEE YAJIMA IN THE YUKARI DIVISION.
OKAY.
UM... MAIN BUILDING, THIRD FLOOR...
TAP
BUMP
OH!
PARDON ME.
...
HUH...?
WAS THAT...?

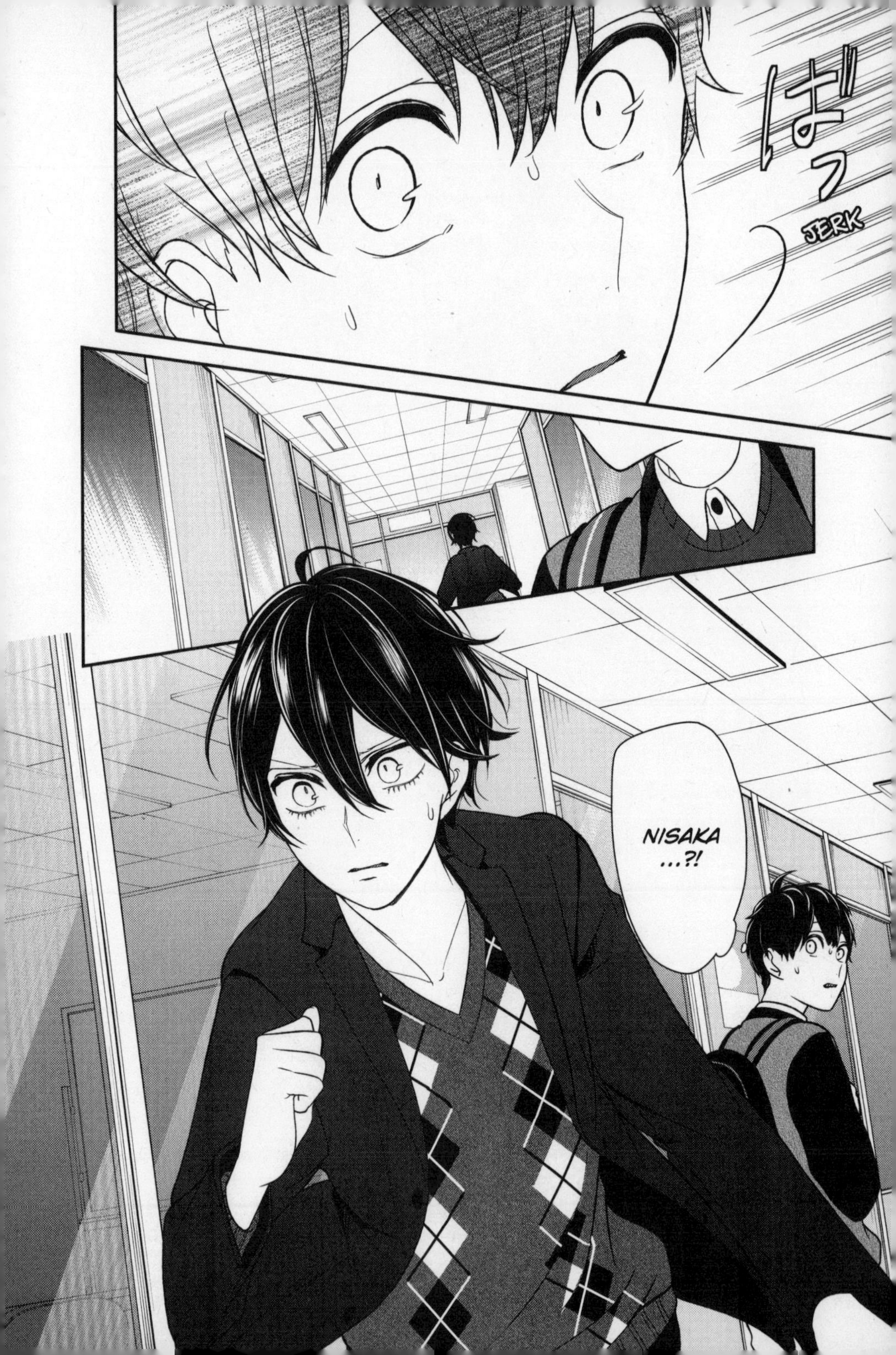
ばっ
JERK
NISAKA ...?!

Love & Lies

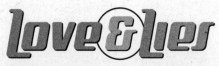

To be continued...

# NEXT VOLUME...

Neji chases down Nisaka to a room where  they find Nisaka's father, and the two finally confront one another...

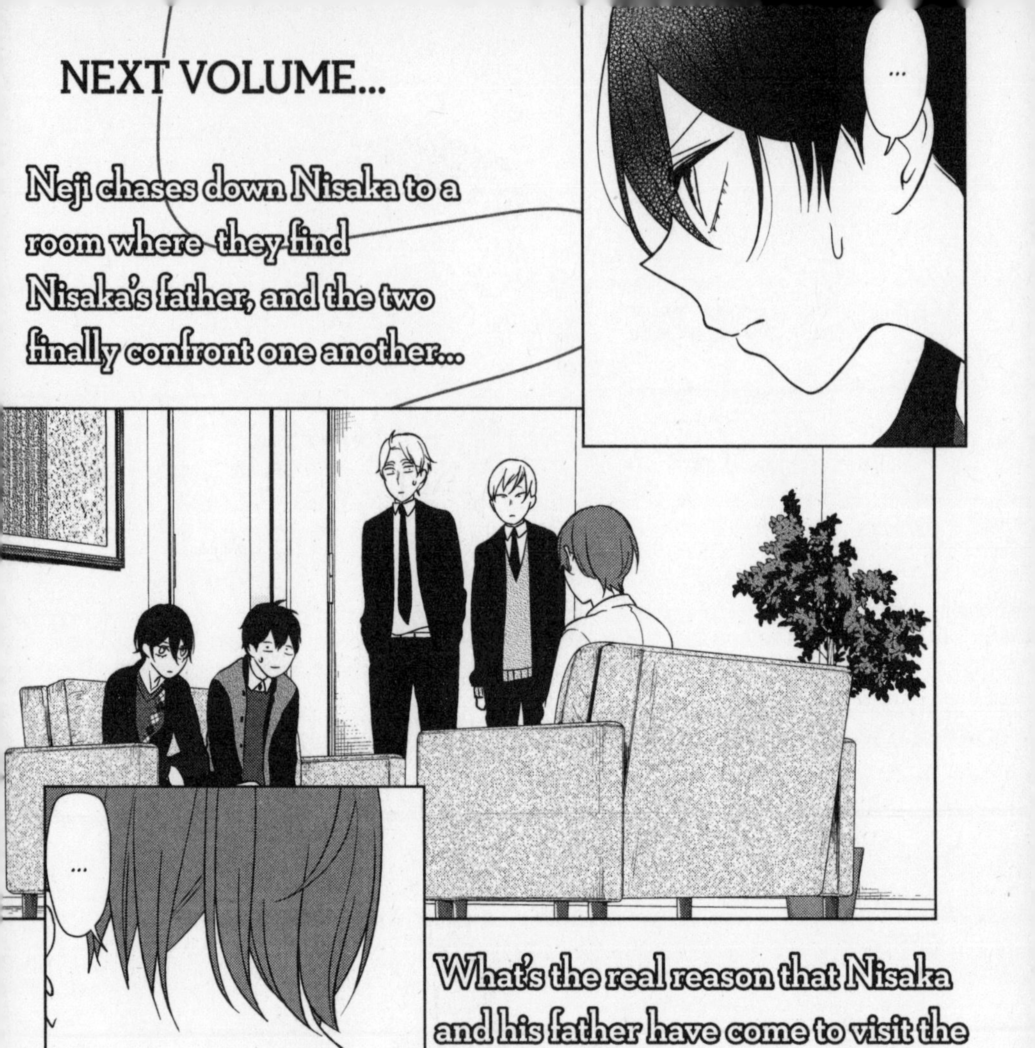

...
...


What's the real reason that Nisaka and his father have come to visit the Ministry of Health, Labour,j and Welfare?!

THINGS HELD CLOSE. THINGS HIDDEN.

BOTH HIS SECRETS AND HERS COME SLOWLY TO LIGHT IN THE TENSE SEVENTH VOLUME!

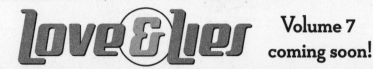

Love & Lies Volume 7 coming soon!

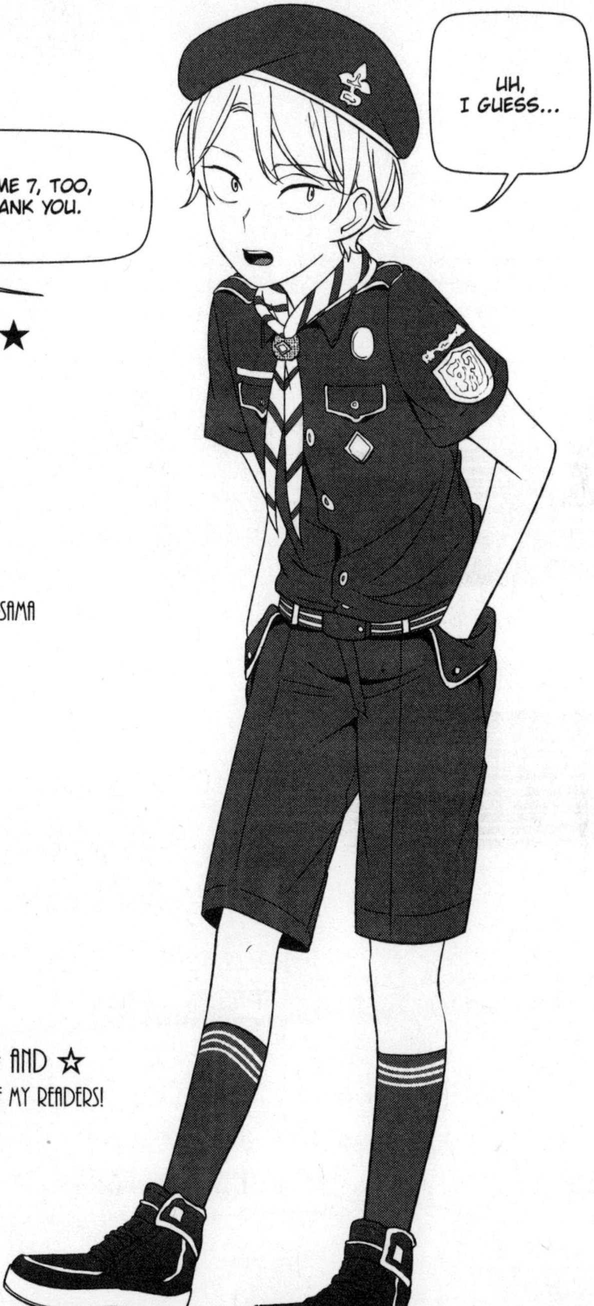
UH, I GUESS...
...PICK UP VOLUME 7, TOO, PLEASE AND THANK YOU.

★ SPECIAL THANKS ★

SHINOHARA-SAMA
YOSHIMURA-SAMA
KOU-SAMA
HANAWA-SAMA

EVERYONE AT PASS
MANARU AMAGAWA-SAMA
TOMOKO OROGUCHI-SAMA
KEI KOBAYASHI-SAMA
UTSUNOMIYA-SAMA
SAYU-SAMA

SUDOU-SAMA
FUKU-SAMA

EVERYONE IN
MY FAMILY

☆ AND ☆
ALL OF MY READERS!

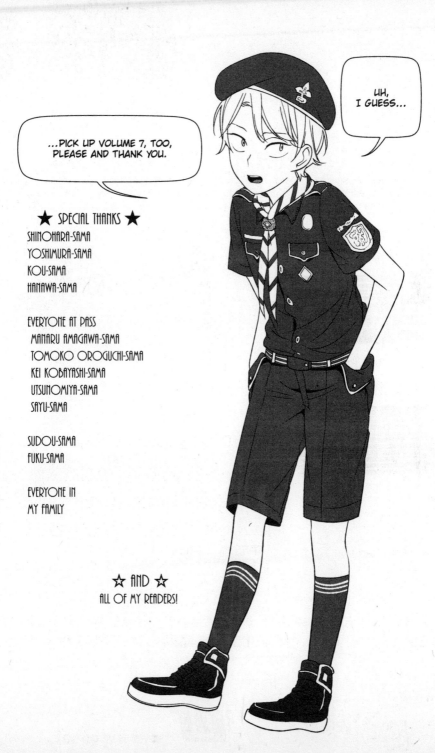

A Kodansha Comics Trade Paperback Original.

*Love and Lies* Volume 6 copyright © 2017 Musawo
English translation copyright © 2018 Musawo

Published in the United States by Kodansha Comics, an imprint of Kodansha USA Publishing, LLC, New York.

Publication rights for this English edition arranged through Kodansha Ltd., Tokyo.

First published in Japan in 2017 by Kodansha Ltd., Tokyo, as *Koi to Uso* Volume 6.

ISBN 978-1-63236-625-2

Printed in the United States of America.

www.kodanshacomics.com

9 8 7 6 5 4 3 2 1

Translator: Jennifer Ward
Lettering: Daniel CY
Editing: Paul Starr
Kodansha Comics edition cover design by Phil Balsman